THE BIBLE IN AMERICA

O God! beneath Thy guiding hand,
   Our exiled fathers crossed the sea;
And when they trod the wintry strand,
   With prayer and psalm they worshipped Thee.

Thou heard'st, well pleased, the song, the prayer—
   Thy blessing came; and still its power
Shall onward to all ages bear
   The memory of that holy hour.

What change! through pathless wilds no more
   The fierce and naked savage roams;
Sweet praise, along the cultured shore,
   Breaks from ten thousand happy homes.

Laws, freedom, truth, and faith in God
   Came with those exiles o'er the waves;
And where their pilgrim feet have trod,
   The God they trusted guards their graves.

And here Thy name, O God of love,
   Their children's children shall adore,
Till these eternal hills remove,
   And spring adorns the earth no more.[1]

[1] Taken from the front of Bacon's *Genesis of the New England Churches.*

THE PURITAN ELDER
(Statue by Saint-Gaudens)

The Bible in America

VERSIONS THAT HAVE PLAYED THEIR PART IN THE MAKING OF THE REPUBLIC

BY

REV. P. MARION SIMMS, PH.D.

AUTHOR OF

The Bible from the Beginning

ILLUSTRATED

NEW YORK

Wilson=Erickson

Incorporated

1936

DESIGNED BY GEO. E. NEUHEDEL

PRINTED IN THE UNITED STATES OF AMERICA
BY THE COLONIAL PRESS INC., CLINTON, MASS.

To

My Youngest Son

P. MARION SIMMS, JR.

A Candidate for the Ministry

Who for more than seven long and tedious years
has waged a heroic fight to regain his health,
against what seemed utterly impossible odds,
and who is still fighting, but now with every
encouragement and expectation of winning completely; at whose bedside, and with whose help,
the major part of this book has been written,
this volume is

AFFECTIONATELY DEDICATED

PUBLISHER'S NOTE

W HEN, three years ago, the writer resolved to include in his
publishing activities an authoritative account of the history of the
Bible in America and its part in the making of the republic, those
with whom he consulted agreed without dissent that the fit and
proper scholar to write such a book was Dr. P. Marion Simms.
The work now offered to the public amply justifies his selection.

In his opening chapters Dr. Simms relates the history of the
Bibles of the first colonists. In later chapters he deals with the first
translations of the Bible in America, including Eliot's Indian Bible;
the strange history of the clandestine Bibles now greatly prized
and vainly sought by collectors, and the first Bibles published openly
in America. And there is rare entertainment for the curious in his
account of the private translations by Americans—of the one
Thomas Jefferson prompted Charles Thomson to make; of how
Noah Webster turned aside for a time from dictionary-making to
edit the King James Version in order to remove from it what he
deemed "expressions repugnant to modern taste", and of the Bible
the learned Julia E. Smith of Glastonbury, Connecticut, labored
over in the middle years of the last century—the first translation
of the whole of the Bible into English or any other language ever
made by a woman.

Dr. Simms in his closing chapters deals with the varied and far-
reaching work of the American Bible Society, with representative
translations of the last hundred years, with modern speech translations, with translations of an unusual character or history, such as
the Bible of the Reorganized Church of Latter Day Saints, and
with the influence of the Bible upon the development of our social
and political institutions and the enrichment and uplifting of our
national life.

All in all, THE BIBLE IN AMERICA will be found to be a
narrative of rich and unfailing interest as well as a reference book
of the first class—an indispensable tool for the student, who will
quickly perceive that not the least of its excellencies is the tolerant
and forward-looking spirit in which it is written, the ripe fruit, be
it said, of the sure and mellow scholarship evident on every page.

RUFUS ROCKWELL WILSON

PREFACE

MORE books have been written concerning the Bible perhaps, in one form and another, than on any other subject in the world. Why another?

Many books tell about editions of the Bible; many others about its various translations and revisions; and still others have dealt with its influence on civilization. But no book has ever appeared dealing exclusively with the Bible in America; the various versions brought by the colonists; its translation into the numerous languages used among us; its more important editions; and its influence, both good and bad, on the institutions, laws and customs of our country. Such a book, it seems, would serve a valuable purpose.

This book was made possible by the researches of a busy pastor, covering a period of more than ten years, including over two years of quite intensive work. Generous assistance has been had from many sources. Some of the larger libraries have been visited. Books have been loaned freely by the Library of Congress; the library of the Presbyterian Theological Seminary of Chicago; the library of the University of Chicago; Princeton Theological Seminary library, and several others. Many of the books borrowed were from the Reference and Rare Book Rooms, not ordinarily loaned.

The writer desires to express his profound gratitude to the many who have so freely and generously aided in the work, without which his book could not have been written. The list of those to whom the writer is deeply indebted has grown so lengthy that he can name only those who have rendered the most valuable service.

First among this number comes our son, P. Marion Simms, Jr., Though seriously ill for more than seven years past, he has given more valuable aid than any other one person. He assisted in forming the outline, read the manuscript, making numerous and valuble suggestions from time to time, and finally wrote the section devoted to Christian Endeavor, because he was not quite satisfied with what we had written on the subject.

Among the individuals to whom we are greatly indebted may be mentioned Dr. Edgar J. Goodspeed, Dr. Ira M. Price and Dr. William W. Sweet, of the University of Chicago; Dr. G. MacLaren Brydon, Historiographer of the Diocese of Virginia, Richmond, Va.; Dr. Charles M. Andrews of Yale University; Dr. David M. Matteson of Harvard University; Dr. O. M. Norlie, Luther College, Decora. Iowa; Dr. Edward Mack, Union Theological Seminary, Richmon Va.; Dr. Harold McAfee Robinson, International Council of Rel gious Education, Chicago; Dr. Frank Gavin, General Theologic. Seminary, New York City; Dr. Norman B. Nash, Episcopal Th ological Seminary, Cambridge, Mass.; Rev. John Wargelin, presider Suomi College, Hancock, Mich.; Dr. S. M. Tenney, Historic. Foundation of the Presbyterian and Reformed Churches, Mo treat, N. C.; Professor Lansing B. Bloom, University of New Mexic at Albuquerque; William L. Worcester, New Church Theologic. School, Cambridge, Mass.; Dr. O. W. Hyman, University of Te nessee, Memphis; Dr. Peter Guilday, secretary Catholic Historic. Association, Washington, D. C.; Dr. Francis Borgia Steck, Catl olic University of America, Washington, D. C.; Dr. James A. Kleis S. J., St. Louis University; W. H. McClelland, S. J., Alma Colleg Alma, Calif.; Mrs. Mary Higgs, Oldham, England; Rev. Edgar I Pennington, Ocala, Fla.; Judge John H. DeWitt, Nashville, Tenn Dr. G. N. Swan, Sioux City, Iowa; Theodore G. Tappert, Philade phia; Very Rev. T. Albert Moore, D. D., secretary the Unite Church of Canada, Toronto; Sherman D. Wakefield, New York, Y.; and Rev. Thomas Sherrard, Bartlett, Tenn.

Many librarians and their assistants have rendered valuable pe sonal service. Among them may be mentioned the Rev. John I Lyons, Presbyterian Theological Seminary Library, Chicago; Kath erine M. Hall, University of Chicago Library; Dr. W. W. Rockwel Union Theological Seminary Library, New York City; W. B. Shed dan, Princeton Theological Seminary Library, Princeton, N. J. Randolph G. Adams, Director, William L. Clements Library, An Arbor, Mich.; Burton S. Easton, General Theological Seminar Library, New York City; C. N. Heller, Theological Seminary Li brary, Reformed Church in the United States, Lancaster, Pa. Henry Guppy, the John Rylands Library, Manchester, England Alexander Marx, Jewish Theological Seminary, New York City Thomas E. Keys, Library Mayo Clinic, Rochester, Minn.; Edwar S. Worcester, Sage Library, New Brunswick, N. J.; and Ruby C Wilder, University Library, Lincoln, Nebr.

In the New York Public Library, New York City, assistance ha been given by H. M. Lydenberg, Director, Victor H. Paltsits, Chie of the American History Division, and K. D. Metcalf, Chief of the Reference Department. Herman Putnam, Librarian, Library o

ongress and several assistants have given very valuable personal
rvice.

The story of the American Bible Society, the Bible among Amer-
an Indians and for the sightless, was made possible by the very
enerous cooperation of Dr. Eric M. North, General Secretary, and
ewis B. Chamberlain, the Recording Secretary. The British and
oreign Bible Society of London kindly provided information con-
erning Canada, as did the Canadian Bible Society, through its
eneral Secretary, the Rev. J. B. M. Armour, of Toronto. Albert
. Bates of the Connecticut Historical Society, Hartford, supplied
aluable information, as did the Pilgrim Society of Plymouth, Mass.

In addition to those mentioned many individuals rendered some
mportant service, the sum of total of which has been very consider-
ble.

References at the foot of the page to D. M. or Darlow and Moule,
re references to the *Historical Catalogue of Printed Bibles,* by Dar-
ow and Moule.

Jctober 2, 1936.   THE AUTHOR

ACKNOWLEDGEMENTS

THE writer desires to express his appreciation to the following authors and publishers for the privilege of quoting their copyrighted books:

Fleming H. Revell Company, *The Religious Foundations of America,* by C. L. Thompson.

Harcourt, Brace and Company, *Religion and the Rise of Capitalism,* by R. H. Tawney.

Augsburg Publishing House, *The Norwegian People of America,* by O. M. Norlie.

American Bible Society, *The Bible in the Life of the Indians of the United States,* by Thomas C. Moffett; and the *One Hundred and Nineteenth Annual Report, 1935.*

Henry Holt and Company, *Three Centuries of American Democracy,* by William McDonald, and *Republican Religion; the American Revolution and the Cult of Reason,* by G. Adolph Koch.

Methodist Book Concern, *Facing the Twentieth Century,* by M. King.

Longmans, Green and Company, *Christopher Columbus,* by M. Ayserling, translated by Charles Gross.

British and Foreign Bible Society, *Historical Catalogue of Printed Bibles,* by Darlow and Moule.

Louizeaux Brothers, *The Numerical Bible,* by F. W. Grant.

Charles Scribner's Sons, *The Supreme Book of Mankind,* by J. G. McClure, and *A History of American Christianity,* by L. W. Bacon.

The Colophon, New Series. Summer 1935. Vol. I, No. I. *America's First Bible,* by Randolph G. Adams.

The Catholic Encyclopedia, Inc., *The New Catholic Dictionary.*

Douglas Campbell, Jr., *The Puritans in Holland, England and America,* by Douglas Campbell.

D. Appleton-Century Company, *History of the United States,* by George Bancroft.

Yale University Press, *The Colonial Background of the American Revolution,* and *The Colonial Period of American History,* by C. M. Andrews.

American Magazine, July 1935, *30 Years as a City Editor,* by C. I. Blood.

Canadian Bible Society, *Story of the Earliest Scriptures in t Mohawk Tongue.*

Funk and Wagnalls Company, *Schaff-Herzog Encyclopedia Religious Knowledge.*

American Jewish Historical Society, *The Two Hundred and F tieth Anniversary of the Settlement of the Jews in the United Stat*

CONTENTS

xvii

LIST OF ILLUSTRATIONS

THE BIBLE IN AMERICA

𝕿𝖍𝖊 𝕭𝖎𝖇𝖑𝖊 𝖎𝖓 𝕬𝖒𝖊𝖗𝖎𝖈𝖆

———————•———————

INTRODUCTION

THE Bible as a book stands alone. The vast majority of all the books that has ever been published have been Bibles. It has been translated into more languages than any other book. In addition there have been countless thousands of books about the Bible, seeking either to explain and enforce it, or to discredit it. Men have thought to destroy the Bible, and thousands of copies have been burned. Men have been persecuted, even put to death, for translating it, for putting it within the reach of the common man; and multitudes have suffered even for reading it. But the Bible lives on.

It is a unique book. It has exercised a peculiar and powerfully beneficent influence on the world; over the best and most intelligent; over the worst and most ignorant. There is always a reason for everything; and all this could not have happened to an ordinary book. The explanation is to be found in the character and quality of the books that comprise it; in the service it renders to those who read it.

In the interest of a better understanding of the Bible and its influence on America, past, present and future, it is proposed in this introduction to discuss some matters of importance about which there is more or less ignorance or confusion.

THE CHIEF VALUE OF THE BIBLE

The chief value of the Bible is found in two things: It teaches individual men and women the way of life, and it provides the principles of the kingdom of God. It at once carries a message both individual and social. The men who wrote it, and those whose story it tells, had learned how to know God; how to have His help in their daily lives; how to be rid of their sense of guilt; how to endure sorrow and suffering with joy; how to live victoriously whatever

1

befel, and then meet death triumphantly. When Biblical writers talk on these subjects they speak infallibly, because they speak out of personal experience. And he who desires proof of Biblical truth, in such matters, may demonstrate its teachings by testing them out in his own life. And then, the Bible, and especially the Four Gospels, give us the great principles of the kingdom of God, which is destined, in the Providence of God, to rule the world. Jesus never made a move, taught a principle or preached a sermon, until He was certain that he had his Father's will in the matter; He, therefore, becomes the supreme authority in Christianity. We measure all others by Him, his spirit and his teachings. Teachings of the Bible that fall below the standard of his character, teaching and spirit, are freely considered to represent the passing and temporary, and not the permanent in Christianity.

Unfortunately the influence of the Bible has not always been good. A misconception of what the Bible is, and a misinterpretation and misapplication of parts of it, have sometimes resulted in evil. At the proper place this unfortunate influence will be discussed.

It is not claimed that the Bible and historic Christianity are the only influences for good in the world. The great religions of the world have not developed unwatched by Him; he has been with all nations, seeking to lead them into the truth. The Hebrews and Jews only proved better pupils, and so became the religious teachers of the world. As such they gave us the highest truths of God, the capstone of His revelation; that which is necessary for the highest spiritual development of mankind.

Such moralists as Socrates, Epictetus, Marcus Aurelius and others have greatly blessed the world by their courage, heroism and self-control. Lecky, in his *History of European Morals,* has shown that the notion of philanthropy, charity in the highest sense, and the recognition of the brotherhood of man, were not entirely wanting before Jesus Christ.[1] At its best, however, philosophy can do but little to save the world; it appeals only to the better element of society. If anything would save this world it must appeal both to the best and the worst; and that is exactly what Christianity does.

Nowhere have we seen the poverty of philosophy stated better than is done in *Ecce Homo,*[2] where it is said, "Philosophy is one thing, and Christianity is quite another. And the difference between

[1] Picton, *Man and the Bible,* p 219 note.
[2] *Ecce Homo,* pp 107-108 (Boston ed. 1867).

them lies here: that philosophy hopes to cure the vices of human nature by working upon the head, and Christianity by educating the heart . . . Both endeavor to lead, men to do what is right, but philosophy undertakes to explain what is right to do, while Christianity undertakes to make men disposed to do it." As *Ecce Homo* shows clearly, if men would do the right, they require a certain machinery which enables them to do it, and this is supplied in its most satisfactory form by Christianity alone.

Many influences, material, moral and intellectual, have had their effect on the slow advancement and development of the race. Part of the problem of this book is to estimate the influence of the Bible in this development. And it is not pretended that the judgment expressed is unbiased. Every man has a bias where religion is concerned. This is equally true of the anti-religious, as of the most devoted Christian. But an effort has been made to be fair and honest.

With all the facts considered, first place must be given Jesus Christ, among the influences that have blessed the world. It matters not that much that Jesus taught may be found in the teachings of others. His originality often consists in the new meanings which He puts into old words and sayings. God, man, love, lust and marriage, were words that others used, but He left them with meanings that were new and original. Jesus gave the world ideas of the fatherhood of God never before conceived; we seek in vain in literature for parallels to His doctrine. Nowhere else do we find such supreme value in man; by no other are children accorded the place Jesus gives them. His idea of the kingdom of God is not to be found elsewhere. "Thou shalt love thy neighbor as thyself," was a quotation from the Old Testament, and had been in use for centuries. The Jew had long debated the question as to who constituted his neighbor; and many considered only the desirable those who might give as well as receive benefit. They thus eliminated the undesirable, giving a selfish turn to the matter. Jesus' application of the words is wholly unselfish; with Him the question of importance is not, "Who is my neighbor?" but "To whom shall I be a neighbor?" When He had finished the parable of the Good Samaritan, the question of importance had become, "Which of these three, thinkest thou, proved neighbor to him that fell among the robbers?" [3]

That "proved neighbor" put an entirely new element into the

[3] Luke 10:36

question. In the new meaning put into this old commandment Jesus
is the first to suggest that the solution of our social problems is
found in terms of the other man.

The books that make up the Old and New Testaments were
selected and made a part of the Sacred Volume by a perfectly natural
process. That does not mean, however, that God had nothing to do
with it, since God works in natural ways. Stories of miraculous interference and help in determining the canon of the Bible are pure
fiction. The books of the Bible won their place on their own intrin-
sic merits. They carried their own attestation then, as now. Both
Testaments were selections from a larger literature that circulated
among the pious. But in some peculiar way the books of the Bible
ministered to, and satisfied man's religious needs, as no other books
did. Because of this fact they came in time to be considered sacred.
When such opinion became sufficiently unanimous, they were declared to be sacred, and placed among the Sacred Writings.

God gave no revelation concerning what books should comprise
the Bible; He inspired no individual to make such selection; and
Jesus left nothing from which an authoritative canon may be
determined. No ecclesiastical court, inspired or otherwise, had anything to do with it, except to register popular opinion. Many men,
however, have felt the need of some external authority to guarantee
their Bible for the purpose of confirming their own faith, and then
to judge their controversies. When men would urge their ideas upon
others, and become impatient at the slowness with which they are
accepted, they not unnaturally invent an external authority, which
they hope will compel conviction. All such are pure inventions,
unsupported by the slightest evidence. At bottom the want of such
authority is a want of faith in the power of truth over error,
and a distrust of spiritual experience. An external authority is
craved because it is easily applied, and is supposed to be irresistible.
But he who cannot accept the Bible on its own attestation, must
reject it, or suffer himself to be deluded.

Yet some still ask, "How can the Bible have authority, if the books
comprising it are only the selections of pious but fallible men?" And
this question might best be answered by asking, Is there no authority
in what the medical world has learned, because their work has all
been done by fallible men? Is there no authority in the discoveries

modern science, because fallible men made them? Most assuredly
ere is. Therefore, men's discoveries in religion may be trusted.

That the Bible does exercise authority cannot be denied; and it
as demonstrated it throughout its history, by its inherent power to
ip men's hearts, to convict of sin, to lead to repentance and re-
rmation, to comfort and guide. If one tests the teachings of the
ible and finds them true, what more does he want? Coleridge's
roof of the truth of the Bible cannot be improved upon: "Try it
ourself."

When men speak of the Bible they generally mean their own;
nd many people imagine the Bible is the same everywhere. But
ich is not the case. There is not now, and there never has been,
ich a thing as a Christian Bible of uniform content; one that all
hristians accepted. There are no less than eleven distinct Christian
ibles in use today,[4] all differing in the books which they contain.

This fact, however, need not disturb anyone. The usual Protes-
ant Bible contains thirty-nine books in its Old Testament, and
wenty-seven in the New Testament. These Old Testament books
re found in all Christian Bibles.[5] Some of these Bibles contain a
ranslation from the Septuagint, or Greek Old Testament, rather
han from the original Hebrew, with certain differences that have no
octrinal or moral significance. The twenty-seven books of the New
Testament are found in all Christian Bibles, except that of the
yrian Church,[5] which rejects five books: i.e. James, second and third
ohn, Jude and Revelation. Were those five books omitted from all
Bibles, those only who regard the book of Revelation as a divine
lan of the ages would lose anything of serious consequence. The
mportant truths contained in these books are found in the other
New Testament books. So that if we accept only the books of the
yrian Bible, we still have all that is vital and essential. That cer-
ain other churches regard several additional books as sacred is a
matter of no consequence.

Many charges of dishonesty in translating the Bible were hurled
 back and forth, especially in the early days of the Reformation.

[4] For a detailed description of the contents of ten of these Bibles, see *The Bible
from the Beginning*, Simms, pp. 128-48. The eleventh Bible is that of "The
New Church" (Swedenborgan), which accepts the usual Protestant Bible with
the following books omitted: Old Testament, Ruth, first and second Chronicles,
Ezra, Nehemiah, Esther, Job, Proverbs, Ecclesiastes and the Song of Songs: New
Testament, Acts and all the epistles.

[5] With the further exception of the "New Church" (Swedenborgan) as indicated in note 4 above.

Whatever may be true in other languages, it must be said that,
English translations, such charges are utterly without foundatio
No work of mankind was ever more faithfully and honestly don
Men have differed as to how certain words should be rendered,
course, but they were honest differences of opinion.

A misapplication of Scripture has doubtless had its influence
the matter. As it happened the book of Revelation was placed
the end of the New Testament.[6] This book closes with these word
"I testify unto every man that heareth the words of the prophecy
this book, If any man shall add unto them, God shall add unto hi
the plagues which are written in this book: and if any man sha
take away from the words of the book of His prophecy, God sha
take away his part from the tree of life, and out of the holy cit
which are written in this book." [7]

This saying, of course, applied to this book only; it came, how
ever, generally to be applied to the whole Bible, since it closed th
volume. Men have been afraid to tinker with the text. They hav
often proved that black is white with their pettifogging interpreta
tion, but translation has been honest. Some may have been onl
superstitiously honest, but we are not concerned with the motive
that moved them. In an early day, when the books were copied b
hand, and before the New Testament had come to be regarded a
fully sacred, certain changes were made in the interest of doctrine
but such alterations of the original can usually be corrected now.

The great differences today concerning the Bible are matters o
interpretation and not of translation. In translation there is ver
little difference between Jews, Roman Catholics and Protestant
The Roman Catholic Bible in English today is very close to th
King James Version, its chief differences being due to the fact that
is a translation from the Latin, rather than from the Hebrew and
Greek.

SOME CHANGING CONCEPTIONS

Men have believed through the ages that the Bible was inspire
by the Lord, word by word, and whatever it said was held to be in
fallibly true; every part of it the very Word of God. All reference
that might have a scientific bearing were supposed to contain exac

[6] For a fuller discussion of the order of the books of the New Testament, se
The Bible from the Beginning, Simms, pp. 114-17.
[7] Rev. 22:18-19.

cientific truth. Such ideas are now debatable. While the world as been learning about everything else, it has been learning about he Bible also. The Bible is a human book, written by men whose ndividuality is exhibited as in other books. It is not a book of eology, astronomy or other science. The Bible is a book of re-igion. Matters that might have a scientific bearing were spoken of in the language and according to the ideas of the day. Had its writers spoken in terms of modern science, they would not have been understood. The Bible is a historical record of a progressive ocial and spiritual revelation of what God is, and what He has lone for mankind.

Many things in the Old Testament, attributed to God, are morally objectionable. They have often been the chief stock in trade of un-believing writers and lecturers, who have dealt telling blows at such things as wars of extermination, that included women, children and cattle. Such Scriptures now take their natural and reasonable place in a book that gives a moving picture of the moral and spiritual development of the Hebrew and Jewish people. That primitive people thought God would do such objectionable things as are often attributed to Him, and said so freely, is no more than is to be expected of the early times.

Naturally when the new knowledge first challenged the old time conceptions of the Bible, it created a certain amount of confusion and uncertainty. Many good people felt that the very foundations were crumbling. But all such fears have been found to be entirely groundless; disturbed conditions were only temporary. Most of the leaders of the church have made the necessary readjust-ment in their thinking, and accept the modern conception of the Bible, with its historical approach. With time others will do so.

It is not intended by anything that has been said, or that may be said, to imply that God had nothing to do in writing the Bible. This whole volume, if it succeeds in any measure in what it is hoped to do, will bear testimony to the fact that the writer recognizes in the Bible an element of divinity found in no other book. It is that something which gives it its supreme value. Men usually speak of its writers as having been inspired; and there seems to be no better term to use.

Christianity is not the narrow thing sometimes imagined. It is not a system of doctrine, but a way of life. It is an embodiment of the spirit of Jesus Christ; and wherever we find men dominated by that spirit, we find Christians, regardless of the name by which they

may be known. The New Testament makes clear that there is n
salvation apart from Jesus Christ; for "in none other name is the
salvation: for neither is there any other name under heaven, that
given among men, wherein we must be saved." [8] But many peop
are Christian and do not know it. Jesus' parable of the Judgmen
involves that very idea. The human family is separated into tw
groups.[9] One of the most outstanding features of this parable is th
surprise expressed by both groups, at the grounds of their rewar
One group imagined that they had done many mighty works in th
Master's name; but what they valued most was found to be worth
less. They doubtless thought that Christianity consisted in a roun
of religious performances, or possibly a theological system. The othe
group did not know that they had rendered a really Christian ser
vice; they required to be told that the service they had showered
upon their fellowmen has been what the Master sought. They had
embodied the spirit of the Master in their lives. They were Chris
tians and did not know it.

This idea has a rather prominent place in the teachings of the
New Testament. Jesus said, "Other sheep I have, which are not of
this fold;" [10] and He rebuked his disciples for interfering with an
irregular and unorthodox outsider who was rendering a Christian
service, and assured them that "he that is not against you is for
you;" [11] and then He set his seal of approval on the unorthodox and
utterly impossible but Good Samaritan.[12] Paul shared the same opinion. He tells us that certain Gentiles who have not the law, "show
the work of the law written in their hearts, their conscience bearing
witness therewith" in the Judgment; [13] and that among the nations
God "left not himself without witness." [14] John taught the same
idea. He says, "There was the true light, even the light which
lighteth every man, coming into the world." [15] It was greatly to the
credit of John Wesley that, notwithstanding the narrowness of his
day, he was able to deny that God would finally condemn all who
had not heard of the historic Jesus Christ.

Many men not identified with historic Christianity and who were
more or less unorthodox, have rendered a valuable service to humanity, men whose personal lives have been entirely above reproach.
Measured by the spirit that moulded all their conduct, and the unselfish service they rendered humanity, they were Christian. We

[8] Acts 4:12
[9] Matt. 25:31-46   [10] John 10:16
[11] Luke 9:50   [12] Luke 10:30-37   [13] Rom. 2:14-16   [14] Acts 14:17   [15] John 1:9-10

have in mind such men as Abraham Lincoln and Thomas Jefferson.

Historic Christianity is loyalty to Jesus Christ. Loyalty to his spirit is loyalty to his person. To many He has been presented in such bungling fashion, that many good men have been betrayed into rejecting the caricature, thinking they were rejecting Him, when as a matter of fact they accepted his spirit, and embodied it in their lives—the only really essential thing. To think correctly is often as difficult as to act righteously; and God is as merciful to one failure as to the other. To know the historic Christ and accept Him for all that He is, is a great advantage; the doctrines of Christianity also have an important place. But they are not so important and essential as the spirit of Jesus Christ.

Religion is the deepest thing in man, being not the product of reason, but of an inner impulse. Man does not come to believe in God because he has found satisfactory evidence of his existence; he instinctively believes in God, and then seeks evidence and arguments to support his belief. Religion is woven inextricably into every fibre of his being, and is necessary to man if he is to live the most worthy and satisfying life.

The idea that the Bible has been outgrown in our modern world, or that there is the slightest danger that it ever will be, is utterly absurd. It is the Bible which satisfies man's religious needs as no other book in all the world; it is the Bible which makes known to man the power of transformation which he craves. Such a book can never be outgrown.

One travels toward the equator. He needs no thermometer to tell him so; the vegetation tells him. The closer one gets to the sun, the more vegetation and the more gorgeous it becomes. Every step of human progress has been, and will continue to be, toward the Sun of Righteousness.

The story of the Bible is not told by merely recounting the numerous translations that have been published. This is part of the story. But there has always been a power in the message of the old Book that profoundly influenced men and women, their customs, laws and institutions. It is the purpose of this volume to tell the story of both, as it relates to America. The treatment is not intended to be exhaustive. Only the more important matters can be mentioned.

CHAPTER I

THE SETTLEMENT OF AMERICA

1. THE FIRST COLONIZATION IN AMERICA A FAILURE

A. SPANISH SETTLEMENTS AND WORK EPHEMERAL

SHAKESPEARE echoed a profound Biblical truth, not recognize
today as it deserves to be, that

"There's a divinity that shapes our ends,
Rough-hew them how we will."

In the providence of God America was discovered at the righ
time, for the best interests of the kingdom of God. Had Americ
been discovered a hundred years, or several hundred years earlie
the Christianity transplanted to our shores would have been tha
of Europe when it had reached its lowest depths of degradation. A
it happened permanent colonization was delayed until God coul
prepare a people for the building of a new nation, that would mar
a decided advance on anything previously known.

The first colonization of America was entirely Spanish Catholic
But the missionaries who came first brought the Catholicism of th
sixteenth, and not that of the fifteenth century, because the Reforma
tion had reformed the Roman Catholic Church. It was in Spain tha
religion had sunk to its lowest depths; and it was there that Ximenes
confessor to the queen and Archbishop of Toledo, became the leade
of the reform in his own church. He sought to lift it and free i
from many corruptions, and succeeded in a large measure. But un
fortunately he favored the Inquisition. In the light of our day ther
is no condemnation too severe for the Inquisition; but he did no
have the light of our day. Therefore, the Christianity, first planted
in America, was that of Spain—the Spain of Ferdinand and Isabella
Ximenes, Loyola, Francis Xavier and Torquemada. The North Am
erican continent was held exclusively for more than a hundred
years after its discovery, by the Spanish.

From the very first voyage of Columbus, every expedition was
equipped with its contingent of the clergy, secular priests and friars,
all at the expense of the royal treasury. Columbus was both ex
plorer and missionary. His first act, on landing on San Salvador,
was the erection of the flag of his country, and the banner of the
Cross, side by side. Thereby, he dedicated the New World to the
spiritual dominion of the church. On his second voyage, he brought

welve Franciscan monks, whose purpose was to convert the natives.

Ponce de Leon, seeking the fabled Fountain of Youth, sailed for Florida, taking missionaries with his colonists and sailors. They demanded submission to the Catholic faith, and the king of Spain. The invasion was met, however, with effective resistance; and he was forced to withdraw to Cuba, where he died from his wounds. This was about 1521.

More than forty years later, September, 1565, the foundation of the oldest city of the United States was laid at St. Augustine, Florida. The colony seemed to give every hope of permanent success. Pastoral care was provided for the garrisons and settlements, and missionaries sent among the Indians. Before the end of seventy years, the Christian Indians were supposed to number twenty-five or thirty thousand, distributed among forty-four stations or missions. For one hundred and fifteen years Spain and her missionaries held Florida; and great results of a kind were accomplished. In 1680 the Spanish attacked a settlement of Scotch Presbyterians at Port Royal, South Carolina; and this proved the beginning of their end. A war of races and sects continued at intervals, until 1763, when the Treaty of Paris was signed. This treaty transferred the whole territory of Florida to the British Crown. The effort to Christianize by force *only in one instance.* tumbled into ruin.

Spanish explorers and adventurers, with their missionaries, passed on into New Mexico, where they planted a strong colony by 1598, and where they laid the foundations of Christian towns and churches. The stately walls of some of these ancient structures may be seen today. Marvelous progress of a kind was made; within ten years, eight thousand baptisms had been reported; the entire population were claimed as Christian. As many as sixty Franciscan friars served as pastors and missionaries. However, eighty years after beginning the work, there came an Indian uprising; and in a short time, no Spaniard was found north of El Paso. The value of enforced conversions was revealed. The cause of Catholic Christianity never recovered from that blow to this region, although twenty years later Spain sought to recover the country. Missionaries were sent back under the protection of soldiers; but little real progress was made.

Spanish missions in California did not begin until 1769. By this time the methods used in the conversion of the Indians had been changed; force was not used as formerly, but kindlier methods. At the end of sixty-five years, there were twenty-one stations, and a Christian population of more than thirty thousand. In eight years

more, the Catholic Indians had dwindled to less than five thousand
and most of the converts had lapsed back to paganism.

Spain finally extended her dominion over the present states o
Florida, Alabama, Texas, New Mexico and California. Through
all these years of Spanish rule, great missionary effort was put forth
The missionaries, Franciscan and Dominican monks, took long and
perilous journeys into the heart of hostile and cruel tribes; and their
reward was often death or worse. The missionary zeal of these monks
cannot be disputed; they were honest, sincere, self-sacrificing and
devoted men. But their whole policy, whether of force or kindness
was a failure. The work of the Spanish fathers left no permanent
results; and the history of their work has little relation to American
Christianity, and little influence on national life. It is to the great
advantage of the United States that it was not to be dominated and
Christianized by Spain.

Thomas O'Gorman, the Catholic historian, says of this work: "It
was a glorious work, and the recital of it impresses us by the vast-
ness and success of the toil. Yet, as we look around today, we can
find nothing of it that remains. Names of saints in melodious Spanish stand out from maps in all that section where the Spanish monk
trod, toiled and died. A few thousand Christian Indians, descendants of those they converted and civilized, still survive in New
Mexica and Arizona, and that is all." [1]

B. THE DREAM OF FRENCH EMPIRE BLASTED

It was not until 1608 that Champlain, a French Catholic, founded
Quebec. On the banks of the James River in Virginia an English
settlement had been founded in 1607; and an English colony was
planted at Plymouth, Massachusetts, a dozen years later.

Spanish colonization, in its methods, differed from that of the
English. Spain did not seek to plant groups of citizens in America.
To Spain American colonies, such as they were, meant rich revenue
with which to support dynasties at home. The native population
was virtually enslaved for the exploitation of the mines and native
products. France followed much the same plan; the French sought
chiefly profit in trade. No real effort was made to attract settlers to
come among them for the purpose of building a new nation. The
English method was entirely different; they planted colonies of men

[1] *The Roman Catholic Church in the United States,* (Vol. IX., American Church
History Series) p 112.

nd women with a view to permanent settlements and the building
of a new country.

The French methods of winning the Indians to Christianity were
different from those of the Spanish. They used kindness, as the
Spanish had done in California but in a very different way. The
Indians had been subsidized entirely too much in California. The
French sought to win the Indian as an ally, to make him a partner,
thereby giving him opportunities and responsibilities. They made
themselves brothers to those they would win, adapting their lives
to those about them. Missionaries followed the explorers and traders
wherever they went. For one hundred and fifty years the work went
forward, until Catholic France held undisputed sway over the basin
of the St. Lawrence and the Great Lakes, the basin of the Mississippi and the Gulf of Mexico. Throughout the very heart of America, along the Mississippi and its tributaries, there existed a cordon
of posts, military, commercial and religious, with outlying stations
in all directions. Dividing the continent into twenty-five equal parts,
according to Bancroft, the French held twenty parts, the Spanish
four parts, and the English only one.

Why this work failed so signally can not be easily explained.
After 150 years of colonization and missionary effort the French
Catholics left a thousand Catholic Indians in Maine, and a few
thousand elsewhere. Certainly from the first there was a powerful
religious motive, but circumstances finally forced the political to
the front. The mission work came finally under the almost exclusive
control of the Jesuits, and they lost favor.

The order of the Jesuits, founded by Ignatius Loyola, a Spanish
knight, spread in a few years everywhere, becoming the chief support of the Papacy, and did more to check the Reformation than
anything else by purifying the Catholic Church. Soon they exerted
a powerful influence all through Europe. In the missionary history
of the world nothing surpasses the heroic labors and unselfish devotion of this band of men. Their work greatly purified the Catholic Church. They cultivated literature and did a great work for
education, establishing free schools all over Catholic Europe. No
more honest, sincere, devoted Christian men ever served the cause.

But finally the Jesuits fell under suspicion of numerous and serious
crimes. This had its influence in America. Catholic authorities
finally brought such charges against them that the order was expelled from almost every nation of Catholic Europe, and was finally
suppressed by Pope Clement XIV, in 1773.

Part of the explanation of the failure was perhaps due to wha
they taught the Indian. It was too largely ceremonial and ritual
the observance of forms and feasts took too much the place of r
pentance and faith. Faith in a personal Saviour, perhaps, had littl
place in their teachings; they, therefore, offered little on which t
build character.

The Seven Years War broke out in Europe. By the treaty o
1763, which ended it, France transferred all her possessions in Amer
ica, from the Arctic to the Gulf of Mexico, to Great Britain. Th
dream of French empire in America was dead. America in th
providence of God, was not to be colonized and dominated by Frencl
Catholicism, "God having provided some better things concern
ing us."

That God providentially provided for the permanent Protestan
colonization of America is pointed out with no unkind feelings. In
the better understanding and growing toleration of our age, mer
with keen vision recognize clearly that every historic religion, Jew
ish, Roman Catholic and Protestant, had its place in God's manifold
wisdom. Only the blind are unable to see the virtues of all these
differing fraternities. Each has greatly ennobled the world with it
sacrificial service. And each has made its mistakes.

2. GENERAL CHARACTER OF THE FIRST PERMANENT COLONIST

The Protestant era of permanent colonization in America begar
with Jamestown in Virginia, in 1607, and was followed by the Pil
grims at Plymouth, Massachusetts, in 1620.

MEN WHO CARRIED THEIR BIBLES BOTH IN HEART AND HAND

From the landing of the Pilgrims America became the refuge for
the persecuted from all lands—Pilgrims, Puritans, Presbyterians
Quakers, Huguenots, Moravians, the Reformed, Mennonites, Roman
Catholics, Mystics, and Pietists; and they came from England, Scot
land, France, Germany and Austria. No nation in all history was
ever founded by people so dominated by the Bible as America. The
various charters and commissions, under which the colonies were
settled, placed religion in the forefront. The first permanent settle
ments of those in time destined to become the most influential,
were along the Atlantic seaboard; here were formed disconnected
colonies, of different languages and widely differing nationalities
and creeds.

The motives that brought colonists to America were mixed, of course. There were those who came to better their condition financially; but such motives are neither base nor ignoble. Doubtless many came from unworthy motives. However, the group that carried most weight among the early settlers came for religious reasons; some because of persecution, and others to find a home where they might worship God according to the dictates of their own conscience. The ideals of this better class of settlers were derived from the Bible. By providential direction these various colonies were finally drawn into confederation, and then into union, forming a new nation unlike anything that had existed before.

And this difference in our government had not been left to chance; God had prepared for just such a departure. America had been discovered at the right time, as has been said; and the men who founded the government had been hand-picked, trained and fitted for the work, by the discipline of the times. They even "builded better than they knew," because

"Behind the dim unknown,
Standeth God within the shadow, keeping watch above his own."

Only fifty years before America was discovered, printing had been invented. This had made possible such diffusion of knowledge as was necessary to a successful reformation of the church, and the development of democracy. The invention of printing had made a tremendous contribution to the Reformation, giving the people the Bible in their own vernacular, in such numbers as had never been dreamed before. And with an open Bible in their hands, the people soon came to see that it was their inherent right and privilege to find God, without the intervention of a priesthood.

The people were not satisfied with this discovery. They pressed on and soon came to see, not clearly, yet they saw, how Jesus had taught the supreme value of each soul, the equality of all men before God, and the universal brotherhood of man. These principles, even dimly perceived, are enough to remake the world. These colonists brought with them the spirit of the Reformation, and their love of the Bible, from which they drew the inspiration of their lives; and the principles which they learned from this old Book, they transmitted to us, in our national institutions and form of government.

The most desirable settlers in the early colonization of America came to our shores for conscience's sake, and they were earnest religious people who sought to make the Bible the guide of their lives. A very large part of the early colonists had suffered for their faith, and in suffering had grown strong. They constituted the very flower of Europe.

The early colonists were not ignorant men, taken as a whole, but well informed for their day. They were mostly of the middle class, noted for industry, temperance and frugality. Many had a good education; almost all could read. In all respects they were above the masses that did not come.

Religion was made their first business. The heroic determination, the steadfastness and virtue of the leading element of the colonies, were due to their faith in the Bible. Their ideas were often mixed with much that has been discarded, but there is something truly majestic about these early settlers. Their loyalty to ideals, and their appreciation of the supreme religious values, make them pioneers in the vanguard of the world's progress toward the kingdom of God.

None of the original colonies was wholly exempt from the faults and infirmities of their day; in certain respects they all failed now and then. It is not to their discredit. But their faces were to the future; they were conscious that God was using them in His purpose; and they were glad to be used by Him. Nourished by the Bible they grew and multiplied.

3. SETTLEMENTS ALONG THE ATLANTIC SEABOARD

A. COLONIES FOUNDED BY DISTINCT GROUPS

Jamestown, Virginia, as has been said, was the first permanent settlement. It was colonized by Englishmen of the established church, in 1607. While it must be admitted that many of the early Virginia settlers were undesirable citizens—perhaps a larger proportion of such were here than elsewhere—injustice has often been done this colony because of this fact, and the further fact that certain ministers of the colony proved unworthy. There was in the colony from the beginning, however, a genuinely religious element; and this element was the more influential.

The first charter of Virginia provided expressly for religious worship, and contemplated the propagation of the Gospel among the natives. The Rev. Robert Hunt was specially chosen to accompany the colonists, as spiritual adviser and pastor. A church was erected at once. "Wee did hang an awning (which is an old saile), to three or four trees to shaden us from the Sunne; our walles were rales of

wood; our seats were unhewed trees, till we cut plankes; our Pulpit,
a bar of wood, nailed to two neighboring trees . . . This was our
church till we built a homely thing, like a barne, set upon Cratchets,
covered with rafts, sedge and earth." [2]

This was the first Protestant church in America, and its first
communion was served June 21, 1607, only five weeks after landing.
Nothing could emphasize the dominant religious character of these
early colonists more than this first extemporized church. Interest
in religion continued unabated, and under the second charter Lord
Delaware made it among his first cares to provide the external
dignity of worship. The church building was put in order, and the
governor and his retinue regularly attended its services. "Every Sunday, when the Lord Governor went to church he was accompanied
with all the Councillors, Captains, other officers, and all the gentlemen, and with a guard of fifty Halberdiers in his Lordship's Livery,
fair red cloaks, on each side and behind him. The Lord Governor
sat in the choir, on which he knelt, and the Council, Captains, and
officers sat on each side of him." [3] They had a sermon every Thursday and two every Sunday.

What is termed the "first republic" in America grew out of the
charters of 1609 and 1612, which were drafted on the broad principles of Sir Edwin Sandys, whom King James regarded as his worst
enemy. These charters exercised considerable influence on the new
nation.

The Anglican Church had a very difficult time in its early history,
suffering numerous disadvantages during the colonial era. The British authorities aimed to have it established in America. Governor
Andros sought to establish it in New England, but this only injured
the church; and when Andros was overthrown, as was inevitable,
Anglicanism collapsed in New England. Efforts were made to establish this church in all the royal colonies, which finally became
numerous, but this provoked widespread resentment. The Anglican
Church was seriously handicapped by its alliance with the royal
government. Taxation to support it aroused bitter opposition. A
better day, however, dawned for this church in 1700. In that year
Dr. Bray, the founder of the Society for the Propagation of the
Gospel in Foreign Parts, began his work in America. For about
three-quarters of a century this society rendered a splendid service.
Among other things Dr. Bray founded many libraries. The An-

[2] Arber and Bidley, *Works of Captain John Smith*, Vol. II., pp 957-58
[3] Brown, *First Republic in America*, pp. 130

glican Church put forth a tremendous effort to build a large con
stituency, but it did not grow in like proportion.

The Cavaliers who were staunch churchmen, though not as pious
as some, came to Virginia in large numbers. They were courteous,
generous, honorable and high-spirited. Although originally royal
ists, under the influence of the new civilization, they and their
children were found in the forefront in the struggle for liberty
Virginia contributed her full share toward the shaping and build
ing of the nation.

The Pilgrims came next. For conscience's sake they had suffered
in England, and had been exiled in Holland for several years. They
might have remained there, because Holland granted religious toleration; but they came to America to plant a commonwealth in which
they could have freedom of worship, and where they could build
a church modeled, as they understood it, according to the New
Testament pattern. They hoped to provide a better future for their
children than Holland seemed to offer. Known as Separatists, they
were a group of Puritans who had lost all hope of reform in the
Church of England and now repudiated the foundation principle
of an established church. The New Testament knew no such. The
church, in their estimation, was a voluntary association, to be governed by the Scriptures. Many Separatists came finally to consider
the Church of England no church at all.

The Pilgrims landed at Plymouth, Massachusetts—previously
named by Capt. John Smith—on December 21, 1620, now celebrated as Forefathers' Day. They were brave men and women,
inured to hardship and disappointments. The sublimity of their
faith in the God of the Bible gave them a peculiar power of en-
durance; and they contributed greatly to the establishment of a
new order of civil and religious liberty.

John Robinson, their pastor in Leyden, did not come with them,
but continued to minister to that part of the congregation that
remained in Holland. The Plymouth church, however, deprived of
a pastor, continued rich in the faith, holding services regularly, and
William Brewster, an elder, preached for them, though he did not
administer the sacraments. Their first pastor, Rev. William Ralph,
arrived in 1629.

These Separatists represented the extreme radicals of their day,
but they were singularly free from the usual besetting sins of radi-
calism. They had been despised in England for their schismatic attitude; Puritans who remained loyal to the established church re-

ented their separation from the church, more especially since they felt the need of their presence in the church, to aid in securing its proper reformation. Animosity between the Puritans and the Separatists became quite bitter; but nothing of this bitterness was found in John Robinson, their pastor, before they sailed. Their want of bitterness toward their brethren was doubtless due in part to this fact, although the native nobleness of the Pilgrims probably had more to do with it. Little need be said about them, since their story has been told amply and repeated oftener than any other chapter of American history.

The Pilgrims were never a large colony, beginning with one hundred and two souls, and at the end of ten years, numbering only three hundred. Though handicapped by many ideas which were abandoned in time, their religious thinking was in advance of any religious body of their day. Under the influence of the Bible they were feeling their way, maturing definite and liberal views of church organization and government which profoundly influenced the American church and state. That the Pilgrims understood their Bible better than the New England Puritans is seen in several things; they gave a larger place to the teachings of the New Testament, and less to the Old; and their record with witchcraft, the Indians, the Quakers and Roger Williams was far in advance of these Puritans, and more distinctly Christian.

The Puritans began settlement in America at Salem, Massachusetts, in 1628, and soon spread over Massachusetts and Connecticut, having ten plantations or settlements in 1631, and no less than thirty-one in 1647. They differed from the Separatists in that they were loyal to the Church of England. They thought to remain in the church and reform it from the inside. They accepted a national church without question, but they demanded that the church return to something of its primitive simplicity and purity. While the Separatists had lost all hope of reforming the national church, had withdrawn to organize independent churches, and now repudiated the whole foundation upon which the national church rested, the Puritans still sought their rights inside the national church. Their differences were one of degree and not principle.

The early Puritan settlers in America came when Puritanism was at its best in England; at a time when they were suffering persecution, and had no camp-followers, such as became common when the Puritans came into power in England. New England received most of her settlers between 1630 and 1640. They were picked men intellectually, most of them could read and write, while the masses they left behind could not. Large numbers were college graduates; and morally they were the choice of the nation. By 1640 New England had some eighty ministers, college men who had been regularly ordained in the established church.

New England was settled not only by men exceptional in their morality and intellectuality, but also in their ability to accept new ideas. This may sound strange but it is true, nevertheless. This fact is seen in the very first settlement at Salem. These people had come to America with not the slightest thought of separation from the national church; instead they looked with grave suspicion upon those who had separated from it. But one of the very first questions that arose among them was as to what should constitute the new church in America. Should every citizen of Salem be included in the church of Salem? And if not, how should the matter be determined? The more they studied the New Testament, the more clearly it came to be seen that the primitive church was a voluntary institution. The outcome of their study of the matter was their decision that it was "necessary for those who intended to be of the church solemnly to enter into a covenant engagement one with another in the presence of God, to walk together before him according to his word." Thirty people, who made suitable public vows, were selected to constitute their first church.

Thus Puritanism in America at once became Separatist. This may have been made easier by the fact that Salem, in an epidemic, had been compelled to ask and accept the services of the physician of the Pilgrim colony of Separatists, only a few miles away. Governor Endicott appealed to Governor Bradford of the Plymouth colony, who generously sent Samuel Fuller, a deacon and a physician, to do what he could. This beginning of neighborly courtesy may have served to convince the Puritans that the Separatists were not altogether as bad as they had been pictured. In any event, the Salem church was organized on Separatist principles; and a delegation from Plymouth, headed by Governor Bradford, arrived after the organization had been completed, because of a belated ship, but in time to join the assembly, and add their approval of the day's doings.

They further indicated their departure from the established church by granting the new church the right to select its own pastor; and, declining to accept Episcopal ordination, proceeded to reordain the minister of their choice. The fact that these Puritans considered

heir church the national church of the new commonwealth they
had come to found does not militate against the fact that they proceeded on Separatist principles. They had yet much to learn, but
they were learning.

Dutch colonization in New York began in 1623. Peter Minuet,
n 1626, organized something like a civil government for all the
scattered Dutch inhabiting the region. He bought the island of
Manhattan from the Indians eighteen years before William Penn
was born. By this time the settlement on Manhattan had grown to
a village of thirty homes, and some two hundred souls. Two official
"sick-visitors" arrived, and began certain duties of pastors. Two
years later, in 1628, their first pastor came in the person of the Rev.
Jonas Michaelius, who organized about fifty of them into a church
after the Reformed discipline, and held his first communion service.
Their first services were held in a loft over a horse-mill. Michaelius
was a graduate of the University of Leyden, and brought with him
his frail, delicate, but heroic wife, who became the first "mistress of
the manse" in America. She soon died.

The church organized by Michaelius in 1628 is now known as the
Collegiate Reformed Dutch Church of New York City; and it is
the oldest church in America with a continuous history. The church
at Hampton, Virginia, founded by the English, is older, but it has
suffered greatly paralyzing periods without a minister of worship.
The Pilgrim church at Plymouth is also older, but it had no ordained pastor until 1629.

Although the Dutch colonization in New York was begun for
commercial purposes, there was among them a genuinely religious
element. While the church developed slowly, it continued to grow.
The Dutch settled not only in New York, but also in New Jersey,
Pennsylvania and Delaware. They were blessed with godly ministers.
Before the Revolution about one hundred Dutch and fifty German
churches were planted in America under the care of the Synods of
Holland. Dominie Megapolensis is said to deserve the high honor
of being the first Protestant missionary among the Indians.[4] Portions
of the Scriptures were translated into Mohawk.

In Holland the Dutch granted religious toleration, and the Dutch
West India Company, which founded the colony in America, ex-

[4] See Corwin, *History of the Reformed Dutch Church in America,* (in American Church History Series) p. 37. Compare the claim made for Whitaker,
"apostle to the Indians", Tiffany, *Protestant Episcopal Church,* p. 18; and the
work of Campanius in New Sweden, Jacobs, *The Lutherans,* p. 83. Bishop John
is said to have been the first to preach to the Indians in America. See p. 57.

pected toleration of religious opinions and worship in America; but it was not always practiced. Many sects came among the Dutch but no jealousies seem to have arisen until 1652, when the Dutch Lutherans, who had been worshipping with the Dutch Reformed, sought to have a church of their own. Opposition defeated their purpose for some time; and certain early Dutch pastors unfortunately insisted on various measures that handicapped other religious faiths. They even banished Quakers. But the West India Company finally put an end to religious intolerance among them.

Dutch rule ended in 1664 when the English conquered them. In 1696 the Dutch church, now known as the Collegiate Reformed Dutch Church, secured a special charter from William III (William and Mary) which guaranteed them complete religious liberty. This charter had a profound influence in the formation of the Constitution of New York, and the Constitution of the United States, in their provisions for religious liberty.

In 1634 Maryland was settled by adherents of the Roman Catholic Church, under a charter granted to Lord Baltimore. Many Protestants settled among them. The first Lord Baltimore died before he could take up the work, and his brother Cecilius Calvert, as the second Lord Baltimore, entered upon the task with great energy. This colony from its beginning granted religious liberty and equality before the law among all the Christian sects: this being the first example of religious liberty in America. It is not without interest that the first grant of religious liberty in America should be by a Roman Catholic. This, however, was not because Lord Baltimore accepted such ideas in principle, but rather as a business necessity. He was a man of practical common sense, engaged in an enormous land speculation; his whole fortune was tied up in it; and he was willing to be all things to all men, that he might profit by his investment. He thought he could succeed in no other way.

Roman Catholics had no organized existence during the colonial period, and were not numerous enough to affect seriously the early history of our country. "According to an official 'Relation on the State of Religion in the United States,' presented by the prefect apostolic in 1785, the total number of Catholics in the entire Union was 18,200, exclusive of an unascertainable number, destitute priests, in the Mississippi Valley. The entire number of the clergy was twenty-four, most of them former members of the Society of Jesuits, that had been suppressed in 1773." [5]

[5] Bacon, *History of American Christianity*, p. 214.

During the latter years of the effort at French empire in America, the English colonies suffered seriously, especially on their frontiers. French and Indian wars kept things stirred up and Catholic citizens were liable to be accused of sympathy with the French and Indian attacks. Jesuit priests had come generally to be regarded as political intriguers, falling finally, even in the Catholic Church, into such disfavor, that the order was suppressed by the Pope, to be reorganized forty years later. Under such circumstances Roman Catholics had little chance of success in the original colonies. These conditions, however, were all changed in 1763, when the dream of French empire was destroyed. This ending of French hopes prepared the way and made possible the great achievements of the Catholic Church in America since. It has rendered a splendid service, especially in the care of the great hordes of Catholic immigrants that have poured into America from Europe, and in the contribution it has made in their assimilation into the citizenship of the country.

When Roger Williams was banished from Massachusetts, he escaped to a place he named Providence, where in the same year, 1636, he planted a small colony. In 1638 another small colony was formed near by on Rhode Island, with the recognition of Jesus Christ as King of Kings and Lord of Lords. Williams, in 1643, secured a charter from England for his colony; and in 1647 Providence was united with the Rhode Island colony, taking the latter name, and under the liberal charter Williams had secured.

None of the colonies can boast a nobler name for its founder than that of Roger Williams, one of the most advanced Christians of his day. Moreover, Rhode Island was greatly in contrast to the exclusiveness of Massachusetts, and embodied the principles of "soul-liberty." No man was to be molested by the civil power for his religious beliefs; and this fact made this colony a refuge for those persecuted elsewhere in America. Many took advantage of the fact and moved to Rhode Island.

While "soul-liberty" was never seriously impaired in this colony, Roman Catholics were disfranchised in 1729, and Jews were not permitted to hold office. Roger Williams, however, believed in the right of every individual to take part in the government, but Rhode Island defined a freeman as a landowner.[6]

Roger Williams organized the first Baptist Church in America about 1639. Although the colony can hardly be called Baptist, "in

---

[6] Andrews, C. M.—*Our Earliest Colonial Settlements*, p. 110.

Rhode Island the Baptists may very well claim the honor of bein
probably the first group of Christian citizens to insist upon the com
plete separation of church and state and unlimited religious free
dom." [7] Whatever vagaries of opinion Roger Williams may hav
had, we should remember that he was the first American to stand
and suffer for the absolute separation of church and state, and the
supremacy of conscience in religion. The radical character of hi
opinions is seen in the bitterness against his revolutionary idea
which lasted for perhaps a century, and resulted in regarding Rhod
Island, which he founded, as a den of thieves and cutthroats. Bu
such is the usual treatment accorded those who first grasp any par
of the revolutionary principles involved in the teachings of Jesus
In speaking of him Bancroft says, "He was the first person in mod
ern Christendom to assert in its plentitude the doctrine of the lib
erty of conscience, the equality of opinions before the law." [8] I
was from the Bible that Williams drew his chief inspiration.

The Quakers first settled in America in 1656. Their most impor
tant settlement, however, was made in Pennsylvania, in what wa
called a "holy experiment for all mankind," which began in 1682
with the founding of Philadelphia by William Penn. His ideals were
high. He advocated equal toleration for all religious opinions, repu
diated all war, and declined to take oaths. His ideals were never
fully realized, however, for Jews and Catholics were, in spite of his
opinions, never permitted to vote, though the presence and wor
ship of both were permitted.

Quakerism grew out of the barrenness of Christianity at the time
of its origin. Religion consisted very largely in ritual performances;
and dead formalism was poor food for hungry souls. Many longed
for a spiritual experience, a conscious touch with God, which the
churches often did not supply; and out of this heart hunger grew
sects whose enthusiasm sometimes betrayed them into many vagaries
of thought and conduct. The Quakers were so afflicted in their early
history. Quakerism was also, in a measure, a protest against certain
features of Puritanism. Puritanism generally believed that God had
spoken once to men; and that they had a record of his Word in the
Bible. Having spoken once, He would never speak again. The Bible
and the Bible alone was their guide, in matters both civil and
religious. Therefore, they sought for proof texts from its pages for
all they did in both church and state.

---

[7] *An Outline of Christianity*, New York, 1926, Vol. III. p. 371.
[8] *History of the United States*, Vol. I, pp. 367-75. 7th ed.

The Quaker doctrine of the Holy Spirit, and that his "was the ue light, even the light which lighteth every man, coming into he world," was a welcome relief from much that had gone before. hey accepted the promise of Jesus that "when the spirit of truth come, he shall guide you into all the truth;" and they were the rst Christian sect to make a place for this promise, unless that onor belongs to the Schwenckfeldians. Quakers rendered a splenid service to Christianity by calling attention to the fact that God peaks to his children in every age.

The Quakers date back to George Fox, who began his work in ngland in 1647. He visited the colonies in 1671-73, and found dherents to his society in all the colonies from North Carolina orthward. They were the first to oppose slavery; and John Woolan in this was their leader. In 1758 he made a speech in the early Meeting in Philadelphia, resulting in a committee that was xpected to begin a campaign of active anti-slavery agitation at nce. They held advanced views on temperance and on all moral tandards; and their social service and community life were in adance of their day. They lived their Christianity. They had no reed-subscription and no liturgy, no priesthood and no sacraments; nd an equal place of responsibility was given both men and women. Their influence in all these things has been profound, especially heir opposition to slavery and war. They did much for religious iberty. Their principles and patriotism have been freely expressed y our chief lyric poet, John Greenleaf Whittier.

The colonization of Georgia, the last of the original thirteen, bean in 1733. No colony, among all the original group, was more listinctly Christian in origin. General James Oglethorpe, one of the nost interesting personalities of his period, was it founder. He was reatly interested in the unfortunate. Through his influence a comnittee investigated the condition of debtors' prisons in England; nd, as a result of their findings, he began a reformation there of the arbarous laws concerning imprisonment for debt. Primarily the olony of Georgia was founded for the debt ridden; but it was made n asylum for the oppressed of every kind. England made an apropriation of ten thousand pounds to aid the work, the only govrnment subsidy ever granted an American colony. Here flocked he persecuted from many quarters, and among them the Moravians. t was here that John Wesley came to labor; and it was here that he had an experience that led to a complete change in his character. At that time he was "an intensely narrow, ascetic, high-church sacra-

mentarian." The vessel on which he came to America brought
group of Moravian immigrants. A dreadful storm arose at sea. Wes
ley observed the terror of most of the passengers and felt great
alarmed for his own safety, while the Moravians were undisturbe
in their calm confidence in God. This set Wesley to thinking; an
later, as he observed their daily lives, he was further impressed wit
the fact that the Moravians had something which he did not have
After his departure from America, it was these same Christ-lik
people, first, in London and then, in Hernhutt, who taught Wesle
"the way of the Lord more perfectly."

Here is a glimpse of a Biblical influence that profoundly affecte
Wesley, and through him the development of the American com
monwealth. While the Methodist Church did not arrive in time t
exercise much influence in the colonial period, it has made a
enormous contribution to the religious and moral control of a chang
ing social order since the organization of the Republic.

B. NUMEROUS GROUPS FOUND IN OTHER COLONIES

The other colonies were mixed in their early settlements, and n
one dominated by any particular sect. Numerous denomination
were represented in these various colonies, and each made its con
tribution to the best in America.

A Swedish Lutheran colony was planted on the banks of the
Delaware in 1638. A fort was built where Wilmington now stands
and Christian worship begun by their first pastor, Torkillus. These
colonists brought with them all sorts of tools, as well as merchandise
to trade with the Indians. Through an interpreter, they soon ac
quired the title to a large tract of land, and named it New Sweden
Colonists continued to come until 1655, no less than seven hundred
all told, when the Dutch conquered them and annexed the colony
granting them religious liberty. Two venerable buildings remain
today as monuments to their history: the Gloria Dei Church o
Philadelphia and the Old Swedes Church of Wilmington.

They were supplied with ministers by the state church of Sweden
Torkillus died early, but his successor, Rev. John Campanius ren
dered a noble service, both to his own people and to the Indians
He translated Luther's Small Catechism into the Indian language
for missionary purposes, the first work ever translated by a Protes
tant into the Indian language. It was at least thirteen years
earlier than Eliot's New Testament.

French Huguenots were scattered in settlements from Maine to Florida. Many of them settled in New York, Massachusetts, Maryland, Virginia, Pennsylvania, and still larger numbers in North and South Carolina. After the Revocation of the Edict of Nantes, in 1685, thousands of them came, and were welcomed everywhere. They had been coming long before this, and were in Boston as early as 1662.

A Huguenot church was organized in Charleston, South Carolina, in 1686, with the Rev. Philip Troeillard as the first pastor. This church is still in existence and is the oldest Huguenot church in America.

These people have been called "the children of the Bible," a title rightly deserved. They were of fervent piety, and represented the very best in France, in moral vigor, intellectual culture and domestic virtue. The Huguenots were in contrast to many other colonists; they were not solemn and subdued, as were the Puritans of New England, but vivacious, buoyant and with a cheerfulness that was contagious. They loved beauty and enjoyed the world. They were reasonable and sensible in their judgments in non-essentials and social habits; and their love of life was accompanied with a love of liberty beyond their day. In their ranks were men skilled in almost every known field of useful labor.

Chauncey M. Depew, of Huguenot ancestry, has said, "Many streams have fertilized the soil of American liberty, but the three great sources of our institutions, and of their expansive, receptive and assimilating power, were the Puritans, the Dutch and the Huguenots." [9] They gave our country many of its best educators, financiers, statesmen and ministers.

The first German immigration of real importance began in 1682, when persecution sent them over by the thousands. For the most part they were deeply religious, and represented many varieties of faith. Large numbers settled in Pennsylvania; among them Mennonites, Tunkers or German Baptists, Schwenckfelders and Moravians. They were Lutherans in large numbers, but many belonged to the Reformed faith. The sects being so numerous were necessarily weak; but they gave us our first lesson in church federation, due to the broad principles of Count Zinzendorf. Little came of the effort, for the dream was too far ahead of their times. The chief home of the Lutherans was in Pennsylvania. Most of them were exiles, the victims of persecution. Their great leader, Henry Mel-

[9] King, *Facing the Twentieth Century*, p. 149

chior Muhlenberg, came in 1742, and began their organization; ꜩ
him Lutheranism in American probably owes more than to any
other one man. Germans came in large numbers for years; seve
thousand, mostly Lutherans, entering the port of Philadelphia alon
in 1749. German Lutherans in considerable numbers came to New
York, Maryland, Virginia and the Carolinas. Large numbers ᴏ
Germans were found among the colonists, and they were almost aﬂ
Protestants. Those from the Palitinate made the Reformed churches
of New York and Pennsylvania. No better material came to Amer
ica than its early German constituency, composed chiefly of farmer
and mechanics.

The Moravians trace their origin back to the Bohemian Brethren
who flourished in 1457 to 1627 in Bohemia and Moravia. In th
early part of the eighteenth century Herrnhut in Lusatia became
their headquarters, and Count Zinzendorf their leader.

They began their work in America in Georgia in 1735, but soon
relinquished that field, and in 1740 moved to Pennsylvania, wher
they built Bethlehem and other towns. Bethlehem remains to thi
day a powerful center of Moravian influence.

Count Zinzendorf came to America in 1741, and although hi
efforts in federating the numerous German sects failed, he left the
Moravian Church in a well organized condition, under the episco
pate of Bishop David Nitschmann. They then had nine congrega
tions in as many centers, and four schools. Moravian settlement
were made at various points in the colonies, north and south, anᴅ
their educational work grew. Their numbers have never been large
but their influence has been out of proportion to their numerica
strength. The work of the Moravians as missionaries among the
Indians was sufficient to put all other denominations to shame
They were the first Protestants to go among the heathen with nᴏ
other purpose than to save souls. The very soul of the Moravian
was on fire with the great commission; and they gave America much
of its missionary inspiration. Their example still knows no parallel
this side of the New Testament.

Many Scotch came to America. The Scotch Covenanters were bit
terly persecuted under James II, and this drove them to our shores
in large numbers. The Scotch-Irish came in much larger numbers;
and while they founded none of the original colonies, they were
absent from none. They were very numerous in New York, New
Jersey, and Pennsylvania, and the southern communities. At the
beginning of the Revolution there were more than five hundred

cotch-Irish settlements; and it has been estimated that they con-
ituted about one-third of the total population.

They came to America to escape persecution, and were the most
dventurous of the colonists, pioneers pushing on everywhere. The
econd tier of colonies was founded by them; and they did more to
xplore new regions than any others. Crossing the Alleghanies, they
ettled Kentucky and Tennessee.

Oppressive legislation in 1698 drove 20,000 from North Ireland
o America; but this was only the beginning of their exodus. In
704 the enforcement of the Test Act drove larger numbers across
ea; and this continued until 1782, when a Toleration Act for
reland was adopted.

These men were not undesirables, but the very best class of citi-
ens. Among them were wealthy yeomen, and the most intelligent
manufacturers of Ireland. They were above the average of their day
n education; in fact, no element of the colonial population were bet-
er educated. Certainly no others surpassed them in the love of lib-
rty, moral earnestness and the capacity for political achievement.
They were Presbyterians. Presbyterianism is a form of church government, and not a theological system. They believed, and they understood the New Testament to teach, the sovereign right of the people to conduct their affairs, through representatives of their own
choosing. Their influence did much to determine the forms of government in several states, and that of the nation; their contribution
o national independence was surpassed by no other denomination.
It was by them that American independence was first openly advocated. Theirs was a deep religious character, grounded on the Scriptures, with the family Bible the charter of their liberties.

The first Presbyterian Church organized in America was that of
the Reformed Dutch Church of New York, in 1628. The Reformed
churches are Presbyterian. This was, in fact, the first Protestant
church organized in the Western World. The church at Jamestown
was the English church transplanted; and the Pilgrims of Plymouth
had been organized in Holland. The first regular Presbyterian
Church, however, was organized at Snow Hill, Maryland, in 1684, by
Francis Makemie, an Irishman. An appeal from the Scotch-Irish of
Maryland to the Presbytery of Laggan in Ireland, had brought over
this fearless man of God. The Scotch-Irish played an important part
in every event of importance in the formative period of our history.

One of the first important accessions to Pennsylvania was a company of Mennonites, led by Pastorius, who founded Germantown, a

suburb of Philadelphia. Their outstanding principles were: volu
tary church membership of adults; the separation of church a
state; a refusal to bear arms or take oaths; and freedom of conscien
and toleration. So revolutionary were those ideas at the time th;
they were persecuted by both the state and the church. Menno Sir
ons, a native of Friesland, Germany, espoused the Anabaptist fait
and became their most influential leader. Because of his leadershij
they came to be called "Menists," and in America, "Mennonites.
They exercised a considerable influence.

Caspar von Schwenckfeld became the leader of a small group (
Christians. Occupying a position slightly different from other Pr
testants, he fathered a movement which came to be known as th
Reformation of the Middle Way. He laid great emphasis on the ir
fluence of the Holy Spirit, with a certain kinship to the Quaker pos
tion developed later, and insisted on freedom of conscience, th
separation of church and state, and other principles now generall
recognized. Under persecution some two hundred of his follower
fled from southern Germany to eastern Pennsylvania, in 1734.

The most important event of church history, in the closing perio
of the colonial era, was the planting of the Methodist Church, whicl
began in America too late, as has been said, to seriously affect th
early history of our country.

Methodism owes a great debt to America. It was in America tha
John Wesley, in 1736, had some experiences among the godly Mora
vians, to which reference has already been made, which led to a pro
found change in him, one that greatly enriched his movement
George Whitfield, an associate of Wesley, came to America, where h
rendered signal service to the Great Awakening; and it was Whitfield
on his return to England, who taught Wesley field-preaching, which
he used with great profit. And Edwards' "Narrative of Surprising
Conversions," written in America, had a peculiarly beneficent influence on Wesley's ideas.

It was in America that Methodism was destined, in the Providence of God, to render its most outstanding service; America, therefore, is under profound obligations to Methodism, and much of this
debt is due to Francis Asbury. He proved himself a genius. To
him Methodism in America owes probably more than to any one
man. For forty-five years he traveled on horseack, at the rate of five
thousand miles a year, preaching twice on week days, and three
times on Sundays. His salary was sixty-four dollars a year until 1800,
when it was increased to eighty dollars. He carried the church

hrough the perils of its infancy, and in his manifold wisdom adapt-
:d its machinery and practices to the requirements of a free people.
No other man contributed in fuller measure to the final success of
he work.

The beginning of the Methodist Church in America is traced to
Philip Embury, who had been a local preacher among the Metho-
lists in Ireland, and who, in 1766, began to preach in his own house
in New York. From Embury's house the growing congregation
moved into a sail-loft. Societies soon multiplied and spread. Board-
man and Pilmoor arrived in 1769, with a commission to organize an
American itinerancy. It was in 1771 that Francis Asbury came over,
and soon became director of the work; and in the following year he
was officially commissioned by Wesley.

4. THE IDEALS AND INSTITUTIONS OF THE COLONISTS

A. PERSECUTIONS

In the colonial life of America there were many dark spots; there
was much that does not approve itself to the modern world. But
that is exactly what we should expect. The early colonists made
many mistakes. But who does not? They should be measured by
the standards of their own times, and not by those of a later day, as
is often done. The dominant forces of the colonial era were deeply
religious. When God would use any people, He must take them as
they are; and He can use only the best that is in them, with the limitations of their times. God would found a new empire for His kingdom. To that end He selected souls great enough, under His influence, to outgrow the limitations imposed by the ignorance of the
past and to achieve what He set them to do. The colonists did just
that thing.

Laboring Under the Handicaps of Their Age

The Puritans of New England exercised a noteworthy influence
on our country. They were handicapped, as most of the colonists
were, by an impossible theology: that of Calvinism, with its celebrated five points, particular predestination, limited atonement,
natural inability or total depravity, irresistible grace and the perse-
verance of the saints. Such a doctrine should have paralyzed all
Christian effort; if God had foreordained and fixed the salvation or

damnation of every soul, and nobody could do anything to change it
why try? It did not destroy all effort, however, for two reasons
Calvinists, like most other people, were better than their theology
and those who accepted Calvinism believed that they had been elect
ed to salvation. It was always the other fellow whom the good Lord
had passed by.

The handicap of certain features of Calvinism, which makes little
appeal to the modern world, may be seen in the opposition to re
vivals of religion, so often consistently manifested by those who held
his system. It may best be seen perhaps in the contrasted growths of
the Presbyterian and Methodist churches, in the early years of the
republic. Presbyterians were in America a hundred years before
the Methodists, and had the advantage of being on the ground in
the beginning, the advantage of large numbers, education and influence; but they did not have the advantage of the "whosoever will
Gospel" which the Methodists carried everywhere. The Methodists
are many times stronger today. While the difference in theology is
not the only factor in the contrasted growths of these two denominations, it has been one of the most powerful factors.

John Calvin, however, taught many things, spiritual, ethical, social and political—more than the celebrated five points; and it is
these things not contained in his elaborate system that have so greatly blessed the world. Perhaps no modern man has more powerfully
influenced the world. Bancroft is correct when he says, "He who will
not honor the memory and respect the influence of Calvin knows
but little of the origin of American liberty." "The 'non-conformist
conscience' was born of Calvinism, and its contribution to the development of the social life of the entire English-speaking world is
beyond computation." [10]

In the Bible there is a doctrine of election to service, which Calvin
unfortunately conceived as an election to salvation. In his teachings
there is the idea that God calls men to do his work; that those who
are so called are co-workers with God in building His kingdom; and
that above the affairs of men is an all-powerful and overruling Providence. John Calvin, however, is not the only man who taught these
ideas. John Wesley believed in the infinite value of each soul, that
men were called of God and co-workers with Him, and that above all
was God's Providence. Such teachings gave an exalted sense of
human worth, equality and dignity to man. It gave real meaning to
life. Nothing is more valuable than such doctrines, and such ideas

[10] *An Outline of Christianity*, Vol. III. p. 84.

vere the keynote of Puritanism, which did so much in the building
f our nation. It was this same faith in an all-wise and overruling
Providence that formed the basis of Washington's hopes, and in-
pired the hearts of Lincoln and Grant.

Unfortunately the Puritans of New England made the mistake of
thinking they could destroy normal human instincts, which required
only to be regulated. Such repressions as they attempted produced
an unendurable dullness of life. They took themselves too seriously,
needing above all else a sense of humor. And yet they were slowly
outgrowing the delusions and superstitions of their times.

Witch Persecution Outgrown First in America

One of the serious blunders of the New England Puritans was
their persecution of witches. But this was no Puritan delusion.
Witch hunting went on all over Europe. It has been estimated that
Europe executed no less than 300,000 witches, many of them tortured and burned. The delusion began in England under Henry
VIII, before there were any Puritans anywhere, and it had existed
in Europe long before. The great English thinkers, such as Shakespeare, Bacon, Selden, Sir Walter Raleigh and Sir Thomas Browne
all believed in witches, but not one of them was a Puritan. Addison,
as late as 1711, defended the idea.[11] Puritanism in New England only
shared the common English and European opinion on the subject.
Yet the idea of witchcraft was denounced very early in New England.
From Holland came the first protests in 1563. This horrible idea
which had long held sway over all Europe found place only in New
England, where but twenty people were executed. None of them
was burned or tortured. In New England the delusion grew for a
short period, but was completely rooted out and destroyed in 1692,
long before England or Scotland took such a step.[12] This is the lesson of the Salem witchcraft; viewed properly it becomes a mark of
colonial progress.

Heresy Hunting Less Than Might Be Expected

The Puritans of Massachusetts adopted certain measures which
they doubtless felt necessary for self-protection in civil and religious

[11] Campbell, *The Puritans in Holland, England and America*, Vol. II, pp.
144-145.
[12] Campbell, *The Puritans in Holland, England and America*, Vol. II, p. 144.

matters. Roger Williams and Mrs. Ann Hutchinson were expelled
a few Quakers were banished, and when four of them returned the
were executed.

These acts have been both justified and condemned. Admittedl
the situation for the new colonists was difficult; and, after all, the
real surprise is that they made as few such mistakes as they did.

Roger Williams made himself a nuisance; there is no denying that
fact. He was a good man, but he had his faults. The colony bore
with him patiently. He was a very rabid Separatist, in a colony which
was attempting to maintain a state church, though organized on
Separatist principles. Williams' interference with civil matters, a
well as religious, led to his being expelled.

He had contracted a serious illness during his trial, from which he
had scarcely recovered, when he learned that it was the purpose of
the authorities to send him back to England to be dealt with by the
English, under the influence of the notorious Archbishop Laud. Wil
liams could well imagine what that would mean. He felt compelled
to plunge into the wilderness at once, in the dead of winter, regard
less of the state of his health, either accompanied or followed by a
few devoted associates, and make his way to his Indian friends.
Speaking of his experience, he says, "I was sorely tossed for one
fourteen weeks, in a bitter winter season, not knowing what bread
or bed did mean."

He had escaped in January and in June of that same year, 1636, he
reached a place of safety which he named "Providence," out of his
feeling that God had aided in his escape and final finding of a
home.

A better defense of the Puritans can perhaps be made for their
treatment of Williams than for the other cases of persecution; but
no defense seems entirely satisfactory. To have expelled him would
seem amply sufficient.

Mrs. Ann Hutchinson, a clever woman, but with an ugly censor-
iousness, involved the whole colony in an acrimonious quarrel.
Clearly something needed to be done; and they could have moved
against her on civil grounds; but they made the mistake of putting
her on trial for heresy. She was expelled.

Quakers came among them, some of the early and objectionable
variety, and did some outlandish things. Something required to be
done. They might have proceeded against them for several civil
offenses: disorderly behavior, public indecency, contempt of court or

ven sedition, but they were tried for heresy and banished. When ertain of them returned they were hung.

Bacon, in his *History of American Christianity*,[13] seems to think hat the treatment of Williams was satisfactory, but condemns the ther persecutions. Palfrey justifies the Puritans in their persecutions on the ground that religious intolerance "is simply self-defense whenever tolerance would be public ruin." [14] But if this principle is dmitted the floodgates are open, and all persecution can be justiied. That is the very ground on which it has been defended. It nust be admitted that freedom to think and to worship as one pleases involves certain perils; and those who believe in freedom nust accept those perils. Imagination has always conjured up far nore than really exists; but if liberty in religion cannot be maintained under any and all circumstances, then there is something wrong with the idea.

The most unpopular denominations in the colonial period were the Baptists, Quakers and Roman Catholics. They were often treated shamefully. Quakers would take no oaths of allegiance, which England demanded, and suffered more or less almost everywhere. The Baptists faced widespread persecution, one reason being that they suffered for the bad reputation of the Anabaptists in Germany, where they had engaged in certain revolutionary outbreaks. And then the Baptists denied the validity of infant baptism, which seemed to strike at the very foundation of the churches that practiced it, and tended to unchurch those who had been baptized in infancy. This fact was resented widely.

Laws against Roman Catholics were widespread in the colonial era. They were excluded from New England and New York, and their rights restricted in Virginia, and finally in Maryland. It was feared that Catholics might help the French against the English. Then, since the Pope had once exercised authority over rulers in Europe, it was feared that he would seek to do so in America, if he ever dared.

The colonies having the noblest record for religious tolerance were Rhode Island and Pennsylvania; these never had any established church.

[13] pp. 100-01.
[14] Thompson, *The Religious Foundations of America*, p. 140.

B. LAWS

In the laws framed by the New England Puritans the Bible was constantly appealed to, especially the Old Testament. All their problems were solved by the Bible. Rev. John Cotton published a set of proposed laws for New England in 1655, giving marginal references to the Bible for each law. While they were never adopted, he shows us how they went about such matters, making the Bible the ultimate standard both civil and religious.

Some attempts were made to found theocracies, to model their governments after the Old Testament. New Haven did this. When the people assembled to form the new colony, the first question proposed by John Davenport was: "Whether the Scriptures do hold forth a perfect rule for the direction and government of all men in all duties which they are to perform to God and men as well in the government of families and commonwealth as in matters of the church." They all answered in the affirmative. For every procedure, rule or law they found a Scripture.

Contrasted With Others With Favorable Results

Much has been said concerning the severity of the Puritanical laws of Massachusetts; and they were severe, as compared with the colonies of New York and Pennsylvania. But in many respects the laws of Virginia, enacted earlier, were worse. They were first established by Sir Thomas Gates, and enlarged by Sir Thomas Dale. Dale's code was published in 1612.[15] This code prescribed death for blaspheming the trinity or the king; for the third conviction for profane swearing; and for the third offense in not attending church. For the first offense in not attending church, the loss of a week's provisions was assessed, and for the second, they provided a whipping.

In speaking of these laws Alexander Brown says: "They seem terrible to us now; but really they were not much, if any, more severe than the Draconian Code, which then obtained in England, in which nearly three hundred crimes, varying from murder to keeping company with a gypsy were punishable by death." [16]

The penal afflictions of the colonies are often considered terrible; and they were when measured by the standards of today, which is altogether unfair. Those of Virginia and New England both should

---

[15] Neil, *Colonization in the Seventeenth Century*, p. 49.
[16] *Genesis of the United States*, Vol. II, p. 529.

e judged by their own times; and so judged America was in advance of the rest of the Christian world.[17] By 1650 the death penalty in England was inflicted for no less than 223 crimes, of which 176 were without benefit of clergy. In the New England colonies no code recognized more than fifteen capital crimes.[18] In public affairs among the New England Puritans the Old Testament rather than the New exercised the dominant influence; the code of Moses was their model. But in the recognition of human rights the colonies everywhere were far ahead of England and Europe.

The Connecticut blue laws, about which so much has been said, like Washington's famous cherry tree, exist only in fiction. The Rev. Samuel A. Peters, a disgruntled Tory minister, who was forced to flee to England, wrote a history of Connecticut out of revenge for his treatment, inventing the blue laws, which had no existence outside his fertile brain.

Sabbath Laws Resulted in Great Good

American workmen especially owe an enormous debt of gratitude to the New England Puritans and the Presbyterians, for they gave America Sunday as a legal rest day. Sunday was observed as a day of rest generally in all the colonies, but the regulations of New England were the most rigid. However, men were indicted in Virginia for hunting, and playing cards and checkers on Sunday.

In the Church of Rome, Sunday had always been kept as a festival commemorating the resurrection of Jesus Christ. Religious services were enjoined in the morning, but innocent amusements were permitted in the afternoon. The Reformation sought no change in this regard. The fourth commandment, "Remember the Sabbath day to keep it holy," was not considered binding on Christians by the Reformers; an enlightened Christian conscience was supposed to indicate how the day should be observed. Luther enjoyed good music on Sunday afternoons, while Calvin permitted his young men to drill on Sunday afternoons, and the old men to play games.

England, in the sixteenth century, had very little innocent amusements. Theaters were schools of immorality, and Sunday was the favorite day for their performances. Moreover, the day was given over largely to the most brutalizing sports—bull-baiting, bear-baiting

---

[17] Chitwood, *A History of Colonial America*, p. 191, says that American laws were milder than those of England.
[18] Dorchester, *Christianity in the United States*, p. 122.

and drunkenness. Sunday became a day of terrible debauchery. May-Day in England and other festivals were given over to the grossest dissipation; people often forgot all decency. It is no wonder that the Puritans were driven to the extreme of trying to abolish all pleasures, for about the only ones they knew were very wicked and demoralizing. Things were bad enough in Elizabeth's day and later, but when the Stuarts were restored, there came such scenes of immorality as the modern world has rarely known.

The Puritans protested and rightly so. They went to the Bible for the solution of this problem, as they went to it for the solution of every other, feeling in this case the special need of a "Thus saith the Lord," that applied directly. Dr. Nicholas Bound, an English minister, found it for them. He preached a sermon in 1575, in which he insisted that the fourth commandment was binding on all Christians. The Sabbath law was moral and perpetual; Sunday had been divinely substituted for the Jewish Sabbath, and man must go to the Old Testament to learn how it should be kept. Yet for the first five centuries of the Christian era the Sabbath and the Lord's Day were never confounded, but were carefully distinguished. After the fifth century there began a tendency to confound them.

Bound had not been the first to suggest this idea; but he was the first to publish it successfully. His sermon was printed and circulated widely, though efforts were made to suppress it. Moreover, it soon became very popular. At once men began to apply the word "Sabbath" to Sunday; and Puritans everywhere became distinguished for their regard for the day. The Westminster Confession of Faith, in use among Presbyterians everywhere, is committed to this idea that Sunday was divinely substituted for the old Jewish Sabbath. And the New England Puritans and Presbyterians brought the idea to America; and chiefly through their influence Sunday was made a legal rest day.

The Puritan was narrowminded. To have been otherwise would have been the outstanding miracle of the ages. In the Providence of God, it was best that he should be, for no other could have done God's work so well in that day. It was a deep sense of duty that alone sustained him in his work, and the world may well be thankful for what he did.

Many Puritan ideas, however, were terrible. To understand this, one needs but to read Edwards' sermon, "Sinners in the Hands of an Angry God." Nothing more horrible can well be imagined than a statement found in another of his sermons, "The sight of hell tor-

ents will exalt the happiness of the saints forever." Notwithstand-
ng all their good, it must be admitted that, by such things as these,
ttimes the Puritans pretty nearly proved their doctrine of total
epravity, which was an essential element of their creed.

C. STATE AND INDEPENDENT CHURCHES

he course of history, both in Europe and America, led gradually to
he mutual toleration of religious bodies. The Peace of Westphalia
1 Europe, an epoch-making event, compelled mutual toleration be-
ween the states of different religions, as a practical necessity, the
dea growing naturally out of the requirements of the times. By
uch natural means does the Lord often teach and lead His children.

Toleration and Religious Liberty of Slow Growth

The spirit of religious liberty began to make itself felt among the
arly Waldenses, and the Bohemian Brethren in the Middle Ages;
hen among the Anabaptists and Quakers, in more recent times.
These people lived close to their Bibles, drawing their chief inspira-
ion from the New Testament, rather than the Old. The Mennonites
n the Netherlands made considerable contribution to the idea.
When the old evangelical type of New Testament Christianity, as
epresented by these people, blended with Puritanism, it began
o influence the Christian world powerfully in favor of liberty of con-
cience. Robert Browne, a clergyman, was the first Englishman to
dvocate the idea. The Baptists are the first body of English Chris-
ians to formulate and enforce a doctrine of religious liberty. Their
parent church at Amsterdam, in 1611, put forth a declaration of faith
which said: "The magistrate is not to meddle with religion or matters of conscience, nor compel men to this or that form of religion;
because Christ is King and Law-giver of the church and conscience."[19]
Others had taught the idea before this, but it had not been form-
ulated.

The earliest colonial churches, however, made no provision for
toleration or liberty. In Massachusetts and Connecticut the Calvinistic theocratic idea prevailed in church government, and conformity was required. The English Church which had control in Virginia,
the southern colonies, and New York, after the Dutch were conquered, required conformity. The Dutch, during their few years of

[19] Campbell, *The Puritans, etc.,* Vol. II., p. 202.

rule, had practiced a certain amount of toleration; Rhode Island ha
granted religious liberty; and Pennsylvania had practiced toleration
But among the original colonies Virginia and New York alone guar
anteed religious liberty in their constitutions. These were adopte
late, that of New York in 1777, and Virginia in 1785. The othe
colonies made religious discriminations of some kind, Pennsylvani
even denying a vote to the Jews and Catholics.

America, however, had been, from its earliest history, a refuge fo
nonconformists and Separatists. Groups of state churches had com
to America also; such as the Dutch Reformed, the German Reforme
and the Episcopal. They owe their separation from the state to thei
colonial environment.

Certain sects came to America already committed to the idea o
religious liberty; and the idea constantly grew. South Carolina re
ceived many dissenters; among them were some of the earliest Amer
ican Baptists, who believed in religious liberty. Baptists also cam
from New England, where they were not quite comfortable. Man
Dutch who were generally tolerant, being displeased with Eng
lish domination, came from New York. Large numbers of Frenc
Huguenots settled here, as did also many Scotch-Irish, all making
contribution to toleration and liberty of conscience, as did colonist
more or less everywhere.

The Great Awakening Promoted a Sense of National Unity

While the Bible powerfully affected the social and political de
velopment of the colonies, it also greatly influenced their inner lif
and character. The Great Awakening (1640-1660) can certainly b
attributed to the Bible. It spread throughout the colonies, to in
fluence the whole population in a remarkable manner. It gave a new
impetus to higher education, resulting in the establishment of at leas
four colleges, Princeton (Presbyterian), Dartmouth (Congregational), Brown (Baptist), and Rutgers (Dutch Reformed). It greatl
fostered the tendency toward democracy; being somewhat in revol
against the established order, it gave the common man a greate
influence in religious affairs, and this naturally led to a greater influence politically. Furthermore, it advanced religious liberty
Whitfield, one of the most powerful preachers of the day, was quite
tolerant. It stimulated humanitarianism. Whitfield established an
orphan asylum in Georgia, and did much for its support. Other
charity schools were established, and such work bred sympathy for

ιe unfortunate. Moreover, it lifted the general moral tone of the
εople, gave a decided stimulus to evangelistic and missionary effort,
ιd helped to build the churches.

At the time of the revival there was in effect in New England what
known as the "Half-Way Covenant", which provided a form of
ιurch membership for worthy people, who had not been converted,
r at least had not enjoyed the standard and more explosive type of
ϵligious experience, which had formerly been required universally.
·oubtless many of them had not been converted. The total con-
ϵrts of this revival, including large numbers already in the church,
ιas been estimated at about fifty thousand, in a total population of
ξ0,000 people. The additions to the churches amounted to no less
ιan twenty-five thousand; the Baptists and Presbyterians were
ϵeatly strengthened, and one hundred and fifty new Congregational
ιhurches arose as a result. Other denominations profited by it. It
ιade a very great contribution to practical religion, and had also a
rofound political significance in promoting a sense of national
ιnity. Such revivals are of inestimable value to any country.

D.   SCHOOLS AND COLLEGES

Ιo one familiar with the early history of the educational system of
·ur country can question the fact that the Bible was the dominant
ιnfluence in its origin. The early settlers of New England gave great
ιttention to the instruction of their children, first in the home, in
ιhe ministers' houses, and then in the public schools.

Schools Were Christian in Origin

As early as 1642 schools were established by law in Massachu-
etts. In 1647 it was provided by law that every town or district,
ιaving as many as fifty householders, should have a common school;
ιnd towns and districts of a hundred families, a grammar school that
vould prepare for college. Connecticut provided for schools in 1650.
Νew Hampshire was originally a part of Massachusetts, but when it
ιeparated in 1680, it adopted practically the Massachusetts law. The
ιrst "Latin School" in America was established at Boston in 1635.
Τhe tercentenary of this beginning of secondary education was cele-
ɔrated in the United States in 1935. The inspiration of all these
ιtate schools was the Bible.

Outside of New England schools were generally provided by the

church, or were private institutions, except more or less general
there was a certain provision for the education of orphans, and th
children of the poor. The Dutch of New York established school
importing their teachers from Holland. These were a combinatio
public and parochial school, provided by public authorities, whic
were a mixture of church and state. After the Dutch were conquere
by the English, the church provided schools. Parochial schools wer
common among the numerous sects. The Quakers were enthusia
tic about education, and provided numerous parochial schools, a
did also the Moravians, Mennonites, German Lutherans, Germa
Reformed and Catholics.

In Virginia and the South schools developed more slowly, becaus
of the large plantations which scattered the population, and mad
schools difficult. Then the Virginia colonists maintained the Eng
lish attitude toward education, considering it a matter of private o
church interest, and not the state. This same attitude was held i
Rhode Island, New York, Delaware and the Carolinas, where privat
or parochial schools were to be found. New Jersey had many paro
chial schools, but finally adopted a public school system.

The most influential elements of the colonists everywhere wer
choice spirits of the countries from which they came, men and wom
en of the Bible. Practically all of them were intelligent, and man
were highly educated. It was the intelligent alone that could appre
ciate the blessings for which they came to America; and they believe
in education. Schools were established wherever it was found pos
sible. No class of settlers contributed more in this direction than th
Scotch-Irish Presbyterians, who planted both schools and college
wherever they went.

Colleges Were Christian in Origin

The early colonists felt the need of colleges as well as schools
they were jealous for the promotion of religious faith, and an edu
cated ministry was felt to be necessary.

The first college among the settlements was founded by the Eng
lish Episcopalians at Henricopolis, where is now Dutch Gap, Vir
ginia, but it was wiped out by an Indian massacre in 1622, fourtee
years before the next college was established. Harvard was founde
in 1636, and thus appeared the first college that continued to live
Before 1776, when the Revolution began, there had been organized a
total of ten colleges that continue to this day. They were Harvar

n Massachusetts, 1636; William and Mary in Virginia, 1693; Yale in Connecticut, 1701; Pennsylvania in Pennsylvania, 1740; Princeton in New Jersey, 1746; Washington and Lee in Virginia, 1749; Columbia in New York, 1754; Brown in Rhode Island, 1765; Rutgers in New Jersey, 1766; Dartmouth in New Hampshire, 1769. However, some of these began under other names.[20]

Of these ten colleges nine were founded by religious denominations—Congregational, Episcopal, Presbyterian, Baptist, Dutch Reformed. The University of Pennsylvania alone was without ecclesiastical connection, but grew out of a charity school of George Whitfield, one of the world's greatest Bible evangelists. On its campus stands a magnificent statue of Whitfield, with an appropriate inscription acknowledging its origin and bearing eloquent tribute to him. These colleges began as Bible institutions, making the Bible the standard of wisdom. The teachers were theological professors whose main purpose was to train ministers of the Gospel.

The whole purpose of education, as conceived by the early colonists, may be seen in the Massachusetts Order of 1647, and that of the Connecticut Code of 1650, establishing schools. Both begin with these words: "It being one chief project of that old deluder Satan to keep men from the knowledge of the Scriptures." A New Haven ordinance directs that endeavor be made "that all their children and apprentices, as they grow capable, may through God's blessing, attain at least so much as to be able to read the Scriptures." [21]

The *New England Primer* indicates that the purpose of the colonists in education was primarily to teach the Bible, it being a Bible Primer. By this book they taught the alphabet, how to spell and read, as well as an immense amount of distinctly religious matter. Under the letter A we read:

> "In Adam's fall
> We sinned all."

Other lines of theological or Biblical teachings, felt to be appropriate, were used for each letter of the alphabet. For the letter Z we read:

> "Zacchaeus he
> Did climb the tree
> Our Lord to see."

[20] Princeton was known as the College of New Jersey; the University of Pennsylvania, as the Academy; Columbia University, as King's College; and Rutgers, as Queen's College.
[21] *American Catholic Quarterly Review*, Vol. III., p. 139.

Here, too, we find:

> "Hush my dear, lie still and slumber,
> Holy angels guard thy bed."

And in this Primer is found the prayer taught more people than any
other in all the world, unless it be the Lord's Prayer:

> "Now I lay me down to sleep,
> I pray the Lord my soul to keep,
> If I should die before I wake,
> Pray the Lord, my soul to take." [22]

Only a short time before he died, the venerable John Quincy Adams
said that, on retiring at night, he had never failed to say this prayer
as his mother had taught it to him in his childhood.

For a hundred years this Primer was the schoolbook of the
overwhelming masses of the people of America; and was often reprinted for another hundred years. It is estimated that during this
period of one hundred and fifty years, no less than 3,000,000 copies
were sold and used. This fact is all the more significant when it is
realized that the population during this period was sparse. It was
popular in all the colonies until after the Revolution, when it was
supplanted by Webster's blue-back speller, and was long known as
"the little Bible of New England."

E. THE GROWTH OF DEMOCRACY

Democracy existed in ancient times quite different in form from
that of today, attaining its highest and best development in the
Athens of Pericles. Through the ages since there have been more or
less ideas of democracy advanced and practiced; but the first effort at
democracy in state and church is found in the Bible. The first demo-
crat of all history was Korah of Biblical fame. Gathering about him
two hundred and fifty princes of the congregation, "men of renown,"
he led a movement in the interest of his ideas, registering a vigorous protest against both Moses and Aaron. Korah makes clear that
his demand is simply that the people shall have a voice in the management of both church and state. "Ye take too much upon you, seeing all the congregation are holy, every one of them, and Jehovah is
among them; wherefore then lift ye up yourselves above the assem-

[22] This is the form of the prayer in the editions of 1773, 1780 and 1785.

MARTIN LUTHER

ly of Jehovah?" [23] Moses was a dictator, supported by Aaron; orah demanded that the people be permitted to play a part in the management of affairs. Korah and his followers seem to have lost their lives in some calamity which, in that day, was interpreted as a punishment for their presumption. His real sin, if any, was in demanding that the people be permitted to rule before the world was ready for it; and he deserves a much higher place in public estimation than is usually accorded him. His difficulty was that he was born several thousand years too soon.

The Inevitable Outgrowth of Christian Principles

Democracy grew among the early settlers everywhere throughout the colonial era; and many influences contributed to this development. "The foundation of democracy is the sense of spiritual independence which nerves the individual to stand alone against the powers of the world." [24] It owed something to the doctrines of the rights of man, as popularized by such men as Voltaire, Rousseau, Thomas Jefferson and Thomas Paine. The same God who taught the Christian has not left himself without witness among other men; and that others not identified with historic Christianity should have some truth is not surprising, when he seeks to give to all alike. But Christianity, with its emphasis upon man's supreme value, and the brotherhood of man, has been the chief influence; and it is certain that it could not have been established when it was without Christianity. In fact, democracy is a natural and inevitable outgrowth of an advanced development of Christianity.

Bryce gives four outstanding contributions of the Gospel to democracy: "These are that the Creator has given each individual a special divine worth; that in the Creator's sight all souls are equal; that the inner life of the kingdom of heaven within the individual is supreme; and that it is the duty of God's creatures to love one another." [25]

Puritanism from its first breath meant democracy. In all the colonies the government was substantially the same, founded everywhere on charters granted by the English king, providing always for a governor and some sort of elective assembly. By the beginning of the eighteenth century every colony had a representative assembly.

[23] Numbers 16:3.
[24] Tawney, *Religion and the Rise of Capitalism,* p. 271.
[25] *An Outline of Christianity,* Vol. IV, p. 240.

England and America are the two most democratic nations on earth and that fact is due to Puritanism. Democracy has religion at it heart. "For I say at the core of democracy, finally is the religiou element." [26]

Democracy is our highest ideal of government. It may not be th most efficient or the most economical; but more than any other form of government it guarantees all the people a fair and just considera tion in their common interests. The underlying philosophy of dem ocracy recognizes the fact that it is better for a people to govern themselves badly, and learn from their mistakes, than to be bette governed by an educated minority. It is that form of governmen which permits participation by all the people, and thereby guaran tees to them personally a higher development. Professor John Dewe says: "Democracy has many meanings; but if it has any moral mean ing, it is found in resolving that the supreme test of all political in stitutions and industrial arrangements shall be the contribution the make to all-around growth of every member of society." [27]

F. SOURCES OF COLONIAL INSTITUTIONS

Hannis Taylor [28] has sought to show that the germs of all our free institutions existed among the Anglo-Saxons, and were developed somewhat by their Norman conquerors. It should be remembered in this connection, that St. Augustine, "the apostle of the English," landed in England in 597 A.D. and began at once to convert the people to Christianity, reaching King Ethelbert the same year. The English soon became strong supporters of Christianity. Moreover after the wreck of the Roman Empire, England was the first west ern nation to achieve a measure of self-government, and this wa because Christianity had a more advanced development in England than elsewhere. It is not, therefore, difficult to determine from whence came the principal seeds of progress.

Neither England Nor Holland, But Cosmopolitan

It has often been supposed that the thirteen original colonies were simply a transplanted England; that all of our institutions were de rived from England; but such is far from the truth. Douglas Camp

---

[26] Walt Whitman, *Democratic Vistas.*
[27] *An Outline of Christianity*, Vol. IV, p. 233.
[28] *The Origin and Growth of the English Constitution.*

bell, in his two very readable volumes [29] takes great pains to show that almost everyhing worth while in America, in its early history, was derived directly or indirectly from Holland.

Our debt to Holland is great beyond all doubt; we also owe much to England; but the origin of the ideals and institutions of the colonial period, as well as since, have been cosmopolitan. At the beginning of the Revolution Englishmen were even in the minority in several of the colonies; and scattered through the colonies everywhere were many nationalities. Each made its contribution. This fact can be illustrated no better than by a quotation from Campbell: "Nine men prominent in the early history of New York and of the Union represent the same number of nationalities. Schuyler was of Holland, Herkimer of German, Jay of French, Livingston of Scotch, Clinton of Irish, Morris of Welsh and Hoffman of Swedish descent. Hamilton was born in one of the English West India Islands and Baron Steuben, who became a citizen of New York after the Revolutionary War, was a Prussian." [30] The chief influences that built our institutions, like our citizenship, were Bible-inspired men from everywhere. "At no time were American colonies a reproduction even on a lessened scale of the mother country. English political institutions were from the outset freely adapted to American needs." [31]

Puritanism the Dominant Force in Colonial Life

Puritanism was the most powerful influence in the colonial era. In the thinking of most people perhaps the term Puritan is applied to New England alone, but this grows out of a misconception. "Puritanism was the reawakened temper of early Christianity," [32] a spiritual movement, belonging to no single group, but which covered the colonies like a blanket; the Scotch, the Scotch-Irish, the Dutch, the Huguenots and many others were Puritans. Puritanism was a product of the Bible, an effort to get back to it more closely; it increased its demands directly in proportion as it understood the Bible better.

Historians have often made entirely too sharp a distinction between Puritans and Presbyterians. In doctrines they were agreed in all the essentials; it was in political aims that they differed. Their

---

[29] *The Puritans in Holland, England and America*, New York, 1892.
[30] *The Puritans, etc.*, Vol. I., p. 7.
[31] William MacDonald, *Three Centuries of American Democracy*, p. 284.
[32] Andrews, *The Colonial Period of American History*, Vol. I, p. 462.

spirit was the same. The movement led by John Wesley was Puritan distinctly so, and nobody had a better claim to the title than the Quakers. Puritan churchmen, Presbyterians, Independents, Baptists, Quakers, the Dutch, the Huguenots, and others, however much they differed about many things, possessed a common soul.

The early church retained its apostolic simplicity during the first three centuries but after its adoption by Constantine, its character was changed, soon becoming loaded with ecclesiastical power, taking on in a short time a heterogeneous admixture of extraneous rites and pagan superstitions.

The Reformation sought to rescue the church from the dark system of priestcraft which had been developed, but the thoroughness of the work in England was hindered by its temporal rulers. Henry VIII remained a Catholic and made himself pope, and Elizabeth did the same. But as the Bible, in the vernacular, circulated more and more, many men became determined to see the Reformation complete its work.

Puritanism began in England as a protest against certain vestments and ceremonies, required by law in public worship. By the Act of Uniformity, in the first year of Elizabeth's reign, the Book of Common Prayer was established as the only form of worship for any religious assembly. Some of its requirements were regarded by certain people as symbols of superstition; and the rigid enforcement of this act served to kindle the fires of opposition, which led many to seek still further reforms, and Puritans soon demanded a complete revision of the whole ecclesiastical establishment. Later they were led to demand moral reforms; and then the movement finally became an effort to restore primitive Christianity.

Many Puritans finally lost all hope of any successful reformation of the Church of England, and began the formation of independent churches. The Pilgrims were such a group, the Presbyterians another. They did not cease to be Puritans when they left the established church; their Puritanism had only worked itself out further toward its logical and inevitable end. Puritanism was not confined to the English alone. The Dutch were Puritans, because they stood for the essential elements of the movement, as did the Huguenots, Quakers and others. Puritanism, as a matter of fact, was a ripening of religious thought over areas widespread, and came, as progress often comes, revealing itself about the same time in unconnected areas.

Much has been attributed to Puritanism which is no part of it.

Puritanism was not a rigid observance of Sunday, as the Christian Sabbath. Many Puritans did so observe the day, but not all of them. It had happened that certain English Puritans had been driven to such position by the debaucheries of Sunday; but the Dutch were Puritans, and they did not so observe the day. It was not Puritanism that persecuted witches. The New England Puritans did so; but no others in America did it; and the New England people did so, not because they were Puritans, but because they were Englishmen, who still shared the universal English opinion on the subject. Nor do we see it in the stringency of their laws. As we have already seen, those of New England were no worse than those of Virginia, and neither so terrible as those of England at the time. Puritanism was not responsible for long faces; the Puritans of Holland wore no such faces. Their religion was not joyless, nor were they enemies of art. The Huguenots were Puritans, but they lent a much needed cheerfulness to America. Doubtless the New England Puritans had many defects, but they were the defects of their times in England. Their opposition to all pleasure was but a quite natural reaction of good men from the debauching sports of their day, and not a product of essential Puritanism.

Some Essential Elements of Puritanism

Puritans generally accepted the teachings of Calvin which had in them an exalted sense of human worth. There were no Puritans who did not share this conviction. It played an important part in the formation of the laws and institutions of the colonies, and stimulated their passion for liberty and their hatred of all oppression and wrong.

The Puritans insisted upon an evangelical Christianity in which men must be born again. Perhaps they erred in demanding one type of religious experience to the exclusion of all others, but they were right in insisting that men must be converted. They believed in conscious touch with God, and insisted upon a mystical Christianity, rather than sacramental. To them the sacraments of the church were simply symbols; and in this they rendered an outstanding service.

An essential mark of the Puritan was his insistence that morals and religion be wedded. The history of Europe, in the fifteenth and sixteenth centuries, cannot be understood without knowing that in these times, in many countries, there was very little connection between morals and religion. To the larger class religion was an intellectual affair, having little or nothing to do with daily life. This

fact needs to be known to appreciate fully the contribution Puritanism made, for among other things, it was a fight for higher moral
standards.

In the fifteenth and sixteenth centuries many devout Catholics
would steal and murder; and they were not hypocrites, but thoroughly sincere men; their religion simply did not interfere. The Roman
Catholic Church was no worse in this respect proportionally than the
Protestant; Catholics were more numerous than the Protestants,
therefore, there were more of them to do such things. Large numbers of Protestants, devoutly religious, utterly disregarded any moral
code. Many of the leading men who built the English Church
were devotedly religious, though thoroughly immoral. Of course,
there were many men among both Catholics and Protestants, who
were both religious and moral.

Moral conditions of the times may be better understood when it
is remembered that the word of the good Queen Bess was utterly
worthless; she had no conception of good faith. She swore like a
trooper, although she was devout. To Cox, a high dignitary in the
church, she wrote: "Proud prelate! You know what you were before
I made you what you are; if you do not immediately comply with my
request, by God, I will unfrock you. Elizabeth." [33]

It was in the latter years of the reign of Elizabeth that the Puritans began to give attention to moral, as distinguished from ceremonial and theological questions. It was this movement for better
morals that gave the world what is known as the "Christian Sabbath."

Puritanism had its face set to the future; it was ready to learn.
There was in it the spirit of progress. "There was in Puritanism an
element which was conservative and traditionalist, and an element
which was revolutionary . . . a divine recklessness which would
make all things new." [34]

The Puritans, especially those of New England, have been called
narrow-minded. Measured by the standards of our day they were,
but measured by the standards of their own times the matter appears
in a somewhat different light. Much has been said about the narrow-
mindedness of the ministers among them; but a very high place must
be assigned their ministers. For the most part they were men of the
highest education, having nobility of character, courage and lofty
faith. Their faith in an overruling Providence had a powerful in-

[33] Campbell, *The Puritans*, etc., Vol. I, p. 356.
[34] Tawney, *Religion and the Rise of Capitalism*, p. 212.

luence on colonial life, and even much later bore precious fruit.
Among them was a new spirit of independence. Great progress was
made throughout the colonial era, and the ministers were the leaders
in this progress.

The Massachusetts Puritans were the narrowest of the lot; Puritanism here went to seed as nowhere else in America. Politically and
socially Massachusetts contributed to American laws and institutions probably less than has sometimes been suggested. Her leaders
certainly had little sympathy with the American idea of church and
state, religious liberty or popular government. It is a good thing, in
the Providence of God, that the colonial charter of Massachusetts
was annulled in 1684. Whether this was done illegally or not need
not trouble us; we are concerned only with results. This overthrow
proved a good thing for the cause of progress,[35] depriving the minority of the power to dictate in matters religious; and the various experiences through which the colony passed, as a result, served in the
end to give a larger measure political liberty.

But even Massachusetts made progress. Leaving England with no
thought of separation from the established church, her colonists
soon found it profitable to organize their churches on Separatist
principles, and did not hesitate to do so. They discarded witch hunting early, even before their brethren in England did so. The *New
England Primer*, the greatest school book of the day, was issued by
them; and its earlier editions contained much matter that was pronouncedly anti-Catholic. The Great Awakening came and an edition was put out very soon afterward, in 1768, and this feature of
the book was eliminated.[36] They were making splendid progress.

By the beginning of the eighteenth century there had developed in
New England, even in staid old Massachusetts, a tendency toward
liberalism in theology. The liberals were beginning to reject the Calvinism which denied every man a chance of salvation. There began
to grow up the idea that every man could repent and have salvation,
if he wanted it.

Perhaps no one event of the colonial period better illustrates the
progressive character of Puritanism than the reception it gave in
America to *"The Psalms of David Imitated in the Language of the
New Testament,"* by Isaac Watts. Previously only the Psalms, literally translated, had been used in public worship. To use Watts'

---

[35] For a fuller discussion, see *Our Earliest Colonial Settlements*, by C. M. Andrews, pp. 81-86.
[36] Dorchester, *Christianity in the United States*, p. 170.

Psalms was quite revolutionary, for it involved and violated a long settled principle by which they had been governed—their opposition to the use of "human compositions" in public worship. These Psalms appeared to be and were an infringement on the exclusive authority and sufficiency of the Scriptures.

Watts' Psalms were "human compositions" beyond a doubt. He freely rewrote them, putting into them a New Testament meaning. The Gospel was everywhere substituted for the law; the sacrifice of bullocks and oxen were always made into the sacrifice of Christ; where the Psalmist speaks of fear, Watts knows only faith and love. However, they came into America "like a glow of sunlight breaking in upon a gray and cloudy day." At the same time Watts introduced hymns also; and there is not today a hymn book published by any denomination that does not contain some of his work. The introduction of these Psalms and hymns provoked considerable controversy, but they were soon in general use everywhere. Thus progress had won, and divine worship was greatly enriched.

The Revolution was not simply the result of a struggle against unsatisfactory regulations of the colonies, on the part of England, as so often has been supposed. This helped to be sure, and provided the occasion or excuse for a break of relations; but to attribute it to this alone, or chiefly, is to make it a surface affair. The real causes lay much deeper. "The impulses behind the movement did not originate in the question of parliamentary right." [37] It should be remembered that "those most affected by the Navigation Acts and other constraining measures were the merchants and men of business, and not the agricultural population; yet it was the 'embattled farmer,' and not the 'embattled merchant,' whose shot was heard round the world." [38]

While doubtless a majority of the colonists were English, they were far ahead of their brethren across the Atlantic, morally, socially and politically; and the Revolution was at heart a Puritan movement, an inevitable outgrowth of the spirit of progress, and a part of a world movement of the times.[39]

Thomas Paine made a tremendous contribution to the spirit of independence and revolt in America. His *Common Sense,* and similar publications, were powerful because they made articulate the

[37] Andrews, *The Colonial Background of the American Revolution*, pp. 63-4, 181.
[38] Andrews, *The Colonial Background, etc.*, p. 47.
[39] Andrews, *The Colonial Background, etc.*, p. 181.

secret and subconscious yearnings of the masses. He did not win the masses to his way of thinking so much as he interpreted for the common man what he already felt, brought to the surface his deep inner sense of his own right to manage his own affairs in his own way, thereby greatly hastening the ripening of ideas that had long been germinating.

The idea of freedom of conscience was gaining ground; democracy was growing everywhere; the church and religion had advanced far beyond the conditions found in England; and a sense of liberty and providential destiny had created a widespread feeling of independence. New England made its contribution, and the Puritanism of the middle and southern colonies made a powerful contribution. The colonists did not fight the Revolution simply to escape a few insignificant taxes, but for something infinitely deeper; it was a part of their inevitable onward march. And it was the Puritanism of the Scotch-Irish settlers of Mecklenburg, North Carolina, on May 2, 1775, which first asserted that Americans were "a free and independent people." With all its faults Puritanism was the best thing in colonial life; it was in the very van of human progress; and the Bible was the chief inspiration of Puritanism.

Sometimes advocating the absurd and ridiculous, Puritanism, in its essential elements, has been unaffected by the changes of time, and while it has shed much of the passing and temporal, it has kept its soul, and is today the mightiest force making for righteousness in both England and America. Sunday schools, popular hymns, temperance societies, open air preaching and missions, both home and foreign, are all Puritan in origin. It was the Puritan who led the way in almost every advance. Puritanism has been the guardian of freedom and the champion of righteousness.[40] America today is a vast empire of many peoples, many faiths, but its language, laws, civilization and even religion itself have been and still are profoundly influenced by Puritanism.

[40] For a splendid discussion of the influence of Puritanism, past and present, see *The Influence of Puritanism*, by J. S. Flynn, London, 1920.

CHAPTER II

PRINCIPAL BIBLES BROUGHT TO AMERICA BY THE COLONISTS

No previous writer, so far as we have learned, has made any effort to determine the various translations of the Bible brought to America by the colonists. To do so, and provide proof of every statement, would probably require a research out of all proportion to the value of the information, if, indeed, the matter could be determined in all its details. The more important translations, however, may be identified without undue labor; and where the matter cannot be settled with absolute certainty, it is easily possible to point out what translations were available and most likely in use.

It seems reasonable to assume, necessary in fact, that any considerable group of men so devotedly Christian that they came to America to escape persecution, because of their religion, and to found a Christian state, where they might have religious liberty, would bring their Bibles with them. It is known that practically every nationality coming to settle in America, in the colonial era, had access to Bibles or New Testaments in their own tongue, which they could have brought.

In the numerous libraries of America today are many Bibles in the various languages used during the colonial era; but less can be learned from these volumes than might be supposed. Many of these copies came to America quite recently and were never used here; others that were used during the colonial period often contain little or nothing to indicate the use they may have had, or what use the version they represent had in America. The history of most of the copies of such Bibles in the libraries of America is unknown.

The order in which the various translations of the Bible came to America has been given extended research, but without the results anticipated; and the order we give is admittedly conjectural, and, because of that fact, we submit the reasons on which our conclusions are based.

The following would seem to be the most probable order and the dates, when the principal Bibles reached colonial America: First, the Latin Vulgate, possibly as early as 1000 A. D., but certainly before any other; second, and third, the French and German, together at Beaufort, in 1562; fourth, the English, possibly as early as 1579, and certainly by 1585; fifth, the Dutch, between September, 1609, when Henry Hudson arrived, and September 6, 1619; sixth, the Danish on September 7, 1619; seventh and eighth, the Swedish and Finnish, together, probably as early as 1638, but certainly very soon after. Moreover, it is entirely possible that Old Norse translations were brought to America soon after 1220.

1. LATIN PROBABLY THE FIRST LANGUAGE TO FURNISH A BIBLE

The first Bible brought to America was most probably the Latin Vulgate, and while such conclusion is only an inference, it cannot well be doubted. This is the Bible used by Roman Catholics universally since the very early centuries. Roman Catholics came first to America, and after its discovery by Columbus, it was held exclusively by Catholics for centuries, during which they did extensive missionary work. The Latin Bible must have been used during that time.

A. NORSEMEN PROBABLY BROUGHT LATIN BIBLES TO AMERICA

The American continent was discovered by Norsemen about 500 years before Columbus landed on San Salvador.[1] Vinland was an old Norse colony somewhere on the American continent, which some would locate within the boundaries of Rhode Island and Massachusetts;[2] while others locate it elsewhere. There was widespread knowledge of the existence of Vinland for centuries. The Claudius Clavus map of Greenland and Vinland was published in 1427, eight years before Columbus was born. Gudrid, the wife of Thorfinn Karlsefne, made two trips to Vinland, lived there three years, gave birth to a child there, later went to Rome, finally becoming a Catholic nun in her native land. The popes knew about Vinland, which was of such importance that they appointed bishops for Greenland and Vinland for more than 300 years. The probabilities are that the settlement of America by the Norsemen influenced Columbus in making his voyage.[3] He was in close touch with the Pope who

[1] For a more extended account of the Norsemen and their settlement of America, see *History of the Norwegian People in America*, by O. M. Norlie, 1925. This book is authority for much of what is said here on the subject.

[2] Jackman, *History of the American Nation*, Vol. I, pp. 9-10.

[3] There is documentary evidence, as well as circumstantial, to prove that in 1476, or shortly before, an expedition was sent by King Christian I of Denmark-Norway to America, at the suggestion of the Portuguese government, to rediscover the "Cod Fish Country" of Labrador and Newfoundland. Two Portuguese noblemen, Cortereal and Homen, went along as representatives of Portugal.

knew about Vinland. "Columbus was familiar not only with the work of Portuguese navigators, but not impossibly with Vinland voyages of Northmen also."[4]

Greenland was discovered as early as 876 A. D. In 999 Leif Erikson made a trip to Norway where he accepted Christianity. King Olaf Trygvasson commissioned him to Christianize Greenland, where he spent his life, excepting the one voyage in which he discovered the mainland of America. "King Olaf sent also Leif Erikson that same spring (1000 A. D.) to Greenland to proclaim Christianity there, and he departed that summer to Greenland. He rescued in the ocean a ship's crew, who then were lying helpless on a wreck; later he found Vinland the Good, and came that summer to Greenland, and had along with him a priest and teachers, and made his home at Brattalid with his father Erik."[5]

On his voyage to America he landed at least three times. The first point was named Helluland, meaning stoneland; the second, Markland, meaning woodland; and the third, Vinland, which is Norwegian for Wine Land. This latter name was due to the fact that a man named Tyrker had found some grapes, which so excited him that he began to talk in German. He was, therefore, the first German on the continent. Leif Erikson "was the first Christian missionary to America. He was the first to set out to find America, and one of the first to set foot on the American continent."[6]

From 986 A. D. to 1409 A. D. there was uninterrupted communication between Greenland, Norway, Iceland and the American continent, a period of 400 years. "The Norwegians have been in America since 876 A. D. (Greenland is a part of America) . . . They explored America from Greenland as far south as Florida, and as far west as Minnesota. They made settlements in Greenland, New England (Vinland), the Chesapeake country (Great Ireland), and possibly in other localities . . . It was the intention of the Norsemen to

Cordeyro, therefore, credits these men with the discovery of the "Codfish Country," and the king of Portugal gave them lands and official appointments in the Azores, in recognition of their services. It is interesting, in this connection, to know that Columbus, who was a map maker and geographer, lived in Portugal at that time, and that he, as shown by a letter written to his son from Bristol, England, in 1477, was then making a trip to Iceland. See *The Discovery of America Twenty Years Before Columbus*, by Sofus Larsen, Archivist-in-Chief of the University of Copenhagen, Copenhagen, 1925.

[4] Andrews, *The Colonial Period of American History*, p. 10.

[5] Translated by Dr. O. M. Norlie, Luther College, Decorah, Iowa, from the history, *Kongesagaer*, by the great Icelandic historian, Snorre.

[6] Norlie, *History of the Norwegian People in America*, p. 57.

ettle these lands and live there. Therefore Erik the Red called his and Greenland, hoping, as he said, to attract settlers. Therefore Leif would not sell the huts he had built in Vinland, but was willing o lend them . . . It is said of Thorfinn Karlsefne that he brought with him (to Vinland) a company of 160, besides 'all kinds of cattle, or it was their intention to settle there, if they could' . . . The Pope kept on appointing bishops of Greenland and Vinland from 1112 o 1482." [7]

In 1008 A. D. Snorri Thorfinson was born to Thorfin Karlsefne and his wife, Gudrid, in Vinland, and he was, therefore, the first white child born on the American continent, of which we have any record.[8] From him descended Bertel Thorvaldsen, the great sculptor. Virginia Dare, born at Roanoke on August 18, 1587, was only the first Anglo-American born in America.

There is evidence in America today that the Norsemen were once on the continent. "There have been rumors of blond and blue-eyed Indians . . . G. B. Joergenson, Stanwood, Washington, set out to investigate this question. He has found considerable concrete evidence of the intermixture of Norse and the Indian races. He has listed a thousand or more words in the Indian languages of Washington and Western Canada, derived from the Old Norse . . . He has also discovered a number of Indian traditions about the coming of the Norsemen, their intermarriage with the Indians, and the warfare between the white Indians and the Red Men." [9]

The evidence of the presence, in an early day, of many Norsemen on the continent of America would seem to be overwhelming, and it is entirely possible, and we believe probable, that these Norsemen brought the Latin Vulgate to America. They were Roman Catholics. Bishop John, who preached in Iceland four years, joined the colony in Vinland, where he preached to the Norsemen and the Indians, some of whom were converted. He was the first to preach to the Indians in America, of whom we have any record.[10] Possibly the Latin Bible came to Vinland as early as 1000 A. D., when Leif Erikson made his discovery, since he had a priest and teachers with him. In any event Bishop John would probably have a Latin Bible. It is also entirely possible that these Norsemen brought at

[7] Norlie, *History of the Norwegian People in America*, pp. 69-70.
[8] *America. Great Crises in our History, Told by its Makers. A Library of Original Sources*, pp. 48-58.
[9] Norlie, *History of the Norwegian People*, etc., p. 64.
[10] Norlie, *History of the Norwegian People*, etc., p. 58.

least a part of the Bible to America in Old Norse, as well as in Latin.

The oldest translation of the Bible in Old Norse (the language of Norway and her colonies in Iceland, Greenland and Vinland) was made in 1220 A. D. under Hakon IV. A second was made under Hakon V, in 1310, and a free translation or paraphrase was made at the command of Hakon V during his reign, 1299-1319. Very considerable portions of these translations still exist. The literature of Iceland from 1100 to 1500 contains many references to these translations, and they are quoted very freely.[11]

B. THE SPANISH FATHERS DOUBTLESS BROUGHT LATIN BIBLES

It is not all impossible that Columbus brought Bibles on his first voyage. On his second, he brought missionaries who would probably have Bibles with them. Missionaries accompanied the various expeditions following the discovery of America, and they always conducted divine worship. The first congregation of Roman Catholics, in what is now the United States, was formed at St. Augustine, Florida, in 1565, but they had held services long before. Missionaries accompanied Coronado's expedition or exploration in 1540, reaching into New Mexico. The Spanish fathers, of course, brought and used Latin Bibles during their work in Florida, New Mexico and elsewhere; all their services were read from it.

Whether the early fathers brought to America translations of any part of the Bible in Spanish is not known. They could have done so. As early as 1490, Liturgical Gospels were translated into Spanish by Juan Lopez, a Dominican, and published at Zamora.[12] Ambrosio de Montisino, a Franciscan preacher at the court of Ferdinand and Isabella, translated and published a Harmony of the Gospels in 1502, which was frequently reprinted, even as late as 1615.[13] He published also at Toledo, in 1512, Liturgical Epistles and Gospels,[14] which were repeatedly reprinted. Some time before 1586 this was revised, and published as late as 1614-15; but was finally prohibited by the Spanish Inquisition. Other portions of the Bible in Spanish were in use among Catholics. The Spanish Fathers might have used any of these in America, but more likely those of Ambrosio de Montisino. Some Catholic authorities think they probably did.

[11] For an account of the translations of the Bible into Norwegian, see *The Translated Bible*, O. M. Norlie, pp. 142-157.

[12] Darlow and Moule, 8462.   [13] Darlow and Moule, 8463.   [14] Darlow and Moule, 8464.

It is now known that certain parts of the Bible were translated by the Spanish fathers into the languages of the natives of the New World in Mexico and Peru. This fact indicates an attitude toward vernacular translations, among these early missionaries, that was entirely favorable, and may have extended to those who worked within the confines of the United States. No evidence, however, is known to exist.

History of the Latin Vulgate

Just when the Bible was first translated into Latin is unknown. Some have thought it the first version of Christian times; the Syriac, however, is generally considered entitled to this honor. But it is generally supposed that the Bible was translated into Latin before the end of the second century A. D. Only certain parts or fragments, however, of the Bible in Latin from this early version have come down to us, known as the Old Latin.

Toward the end of the fourth century there had come to be felt the need of a revision of the existing Latin Bible, by this time considerably corrupted from frequent copying; and Damasus, the Pope of Rome, commissioned Jerome, the greatest Biblical scholar of the day, to undertake the task. Jerome's work covered a period of twenty-two years (383-405 A. D.), giving to the world the Bible that is known as the Latin Vulgate. The various parts of this version, however, are by no means of equal worth, because it is made up of elements of varying value.

Jerome began with the idea of revising the Old Latin only. The Old Testament of this version had been made from the Septuagint, a Greek translation from the Hebrew, which had been completed about 100 B. C. This Greek translation was quite different[15] in many respects from the Hebrew, and not nearly so valuable as the original. Fully realising this fact, Jerome finally translated from the original Hebrew what Protestants call the canonical books of the Old Testament, those books which they consider properly to belong to it. This new translation is by far the most valuable part of the Latin Vulgate in Protestant estimation.

For this monumental work Jerome was bitterly criticised, even by his best friends, the chief criticism being that he had translated from the Hebrew rather than from the Septuagint. At that time the

---

[15] For the principal differences between the Hebrew and Greek Old Testaments, see *The Bible from the Beginning*, Simms, pp. 42-7, 84-8.

Greek Old Testament was widely used and considered superior to the original Hebrew, and itself inspired. There was current a legend of the miraculous origin of the Greek Old Testament—later exploded—that had put about it a halo of sanctity, something like the superstitious reverence many people once had for the King James Version, and which is not entirely dead yet. In time, however, Jerome's version won its way into general use, because of its unquestioned superiority over the Old Latin.

The Middle Ages may be said roughly to extend from 500 to 1500 A. D. Throughout this period the history of Western Europe is the history of the Latin Vulgate. In the East the Bible circulated in various other languages, but in the West Latin was everywhere the language of literature. The Roman legionaries carried Latin into Africa, Gaul, Spain, Britain, and into parts of Germany. Moreover, the various nations communicated with one another in Latin, and it was the language of the monasteries. It may be said that for a thousand years the Latin Vulgate reigned supreme, as the one and only Bible of the Western Church. All the early translations of the Bible into English were made from it, as was the case in all the earlier Catholic translations into various European languages. Of course, later Catholic translations have been from it, because they rarely translate anything else.

This Bible rendered a noble service throughout the Middle Ages. "It did its appointed work, and brought peace and strength to many hearts, opening up to them a glimpse of the glorified One above and beyond the crucifix, creating a fulness of trust that felt no need of saintly mediation, nursing a loyalty to Him so intense and absorbing that it looked down upon the keys of St. Peter as a paltry symbol, while it sustained a confidence in Him that hard dogma could not deaden, and an adoration of Him which a complicated and inflexible ritual could not petrify. The religious community, whose book it was, kept the Roman Empire from falling into barbarism at its dissolution . . . the Latin Bible which preserved for centuries the knowledge of the Gospel, and gave their first inspiration to the Reformers." [16]

The very extensive use of the Latin Vulgate by Roman Catholics would be sufficient, in itself, to give unusual importance to this version; but it also is highly important for other reasons. No Bible has influenced the whole world more. It is in no sense a peculiar

[16] Eadie, *The English Bible,* Vol. II, pp. 110-11.

went out of the caue, and cryed after Saul, saying, My lord the king. And when Saul looked behinde him, Dauid stouped with his face to the earth, and bowed himselfe.

9 ¶ And Dauid said to Saul, wherefore hearest thou mens words, saying, Behold, Dauid seeketh thy hurt?

10 Behold, this day thine eyes haue seene, how that the LORD had deliuered thee to day into mine hand in the caue: and some bade me kill thee, but mine eye spared thee, and I said, I will not put foorth mine hand against my lord, for hee is the LORDS Anointed.

11 Moreouer my father, See, yea see the skirt of thy robe in my hand: for in that I cut off the skirt of thy robe, and killed thee not, know thou and see, that there is neither euill nor transgression in mine hand, and I haue not sinned against thee: yet thou huntest my soule, to take it.

12 The LORD iudge betweene me and thee, and the LORD auenge me of thee: but mine hand shall not be vpon thee.

13 As saith the prouerbe of the ancients, wickednesse proceedeth from the wicked: but mine hand shall not be vpon thee.

14 After whom is the king of Israel come out? after whom doest thou pursue? After a dead dogge, after a flea.

15 The LORD therefore be Iudge, and iudge betweene me and thee, and † see, and plead my cause, and † deliuer me out of thine hand.

16 ¶ And it came to passe when Dauid had made an end of speaking these words vnto Saul, that Saul said, Is this thy voice, my sonne Dauid? And Saul lift vp his voice, and wept.

17 And he said to Dauid, Thou art more righteous then I: for thou hast rewarded mee good, whereas I haue rewarded thee euill.

18 And thou hast shewed this day how that thou hast dealt well with me: forasmuch as when the LORD had † deliuered me into thine hand, thou killedst me not.

19 For if a man finde his enemie, will hee let him goe well away? wherefore the LORD reward thee good, for that thou hast done vnto me this day.

20 And now behold, I know well that thou shalt surely be King, and that

† Heb. iudge

† Heb. shut vp.

the kingdome of Israel shall be established in thine hand.

21 Sweare now therefore vnto me by the LORD, that thou wilt not cut off my seede after mee, and that thou wilt not destroy my name out of my fathers house.

22 And Dauid sware vnto Saul, and Saul went home: but Dauid and his men gate them vp vnto the holde.

CHAP. XXV.

1 Samuel dieth. 2 Dauid in Paran sendeth to Nabal. 10 Prouoked by Nabals churlishnesse, hee mindeth to destroy him. 14 Abigail vnderstanding thereof, 18 taketh a present, 23 and by her wisedome 32 pacifieth Dauid. 36 Nabal hearing thereof, dieth. 39 Dauid taketh Abigail and Ahinoam to be his wiues. 44 Michal is giuen to Phalti.

AND * Samuel died, and all the Israelites were gathered together, and lamented him, and buried him in his house at Ramah. And Dauid arose, & went downe to the wildernesse of Paran.

2 And there was a man in Maon, whose ‖ possessions were in Carmel, and the man was very great, and hee had three thousand sheepe, and a thousand goates: and he was shearing his sheepe in Carmel.

3 Now the name of the man was Nabal, and the name of his wife, Abigail: and shee was a woman of good vnderstanding, and of a beautifull countenance: but the man was churlish and euill in his doings, and hee was of the house of Caleb.

4 ¶ And Dauid heard in the wildernesse, that Nabal did sheare his sheepe.

5 And Dauid sent out ten yong men, and Dauid said vnto the young men, Get you vp to Carmel, and goe to Nabal, and † greete him in my name;

6 And thus shall ye say to him that liueth in prosperitie, Peace be both to thee, and peace be to thine house, and peace be vnto all that thou hast.

7 And now, I haue heard that thou hast shearers: now thy shepheards which were with vs, wee † hurt them not, neither was there ought missing vnto them, all the while they were in Carmel.

8 Aske thy yong men, and they will shew thee: wherefore let the yong men finde

*Chap. 28.
2. ecclus.
46. 13, 20.*

‖ Or, busines.

*† Heb. aske
him in my
name, of
peace.*

† Heb. shamed.

reasure of the Roman Catholic Church, as many seem to suppose, but belongs rather to the whole Christian world; and while it lives inside the Roman Church, it continues to live outside as well.

"The Old Latin Bible or Vulgate still lives in the midst of us, or we owe to it all our Christian terms ending in 'ation,' and nearly all the distinctive words of our theological vocabulary—as person, essence, scripture, lecture, sermon, text, grace, adoption, repentance, spirit, glory, satisfaction, conversion, sacrament, regeneration, justification, santification, redemption, privilege, election, eternity, predestination, communion, congregation, discipline, missionary." [17] This list may be greatly increased with terms freely used by our churches, such as moderator, minister, manse, elements, offering, censure, ordination, suspension, deposition and many more.

Copied by hand, as it necessarily was for centuries, the Vulgate became corrupted, and was often revised, in an effort to restore Jerome's text. The Council of Trent, in 1546, set forth a list of books considered as properly belonging to the Bible, but there existed, at that time, no officially recognized and authoritative text of these various books. The preparation of an official text for Roman Catholics, therefore, engaged the attention of several popes. Under Pius IV and Pius V the oldest and best manuscripts were collected, and a committee named to carry forward the work. Sextus V displayed great zeal in the matter, appointing a committee of cardinals and scholars, under the presidency of Cardinal Caraffa, setting them to the task, while he himself gave much time to the work. The result of this revision was published in 1590, and declared to be the official Bible of the Roman Catholic Church.

Clement VIII, in 1592, called in all the copies of this edition that were in reach, to replace it with a further revision, which was prepared under the direction of Cardinal Colonna, and published in 1592. Whatever the reasons for recalling the edition of Sextus V, the Clementine edition, as it is commonly known, is generally regarded as an improvement; and yet scholarship recognizes the fact that it is far from satisfactory.

In 1907, Pius X began the first recent steps looking toward a very thorough revision of the text of the Latin Vulgate, the idea being to restore Jerome's original text as nearly as possible. Some day this revision will be completed, and the world will then probably have the best text modern scholarship can provide.

[17] Eadie, *The English Bible,* Vol. II, pp. 154-5.

The Official Bible of the Roman Catholic Church

The Clementine edition of the Latin Vulgate is the official Bibl
of the Roman Catholic Church, used all over the world, and con
sidered superior to the original Hebrew and Greek. This church ha
never authorized anybody to translate it into any vernacular, bu
such translations are now permitted when properly authorized b
church dignitaries.

The liturgy of the Roman Church is in Latin; all its service
including all its Bible readings, are everywhere in this language.
This seems rather strange to Protestants, who universally use ve
nacular translations which the people can understand. But Roma
Catholics have reasons for so doing that are entirely satisfactor
to themselves, which ought to be sufficient. Some of the more im
portant reasons assigned for this practice by Catholic authorities are

"The formulae used are most ancient and are approved expression
of Catholic Faith; Latin, being a dead language, is not subject t
change as are modern tongues; the beauty and harmony of liturgica
compositions would be lost if translated; a change of language woul
destroy the sacred music which was written for Latin meter an
cadence . . . it provides an atmosphere of home for the travele
in every land."[19]

The liturgical tongue of the Roman Church was first Greek, bu
in the third century Latin became the language of the Christians i
Rome, resulting, in time, in a Latin liturgy. Once adopted it ha
never been changed.

There are probably reasons for this continued practice far deepe
than those usually given. It should be remembered that, at the tim
of the Reformation, the Latin Vulgate had been for nearly
thousand years the exclusive Bible of the Roman Church; its liturg
had been in Latin throughout this time, during which there ha
been small reason for change, because there was very little use fo
vernacular translations in the West. Outside the monasteries fe
people could read, and manuscripts were too expensive to circulat
extensively. Besides, the great majority of the people of that da
did not feel the need for them; they preferred a religion externalize
in an institution. A few spirits of higher order were to be found, c

---

[18] The only exception to the universal use of Latin in Roman Catholic servic
is that Slavonic has been used since the eleventh century in churches along th
eastern coast of the Adriatic, and on certain occasions Mass is said in Greek i
Rome. See, *The New Catholic Dictionary*, p. 542.

[19] *The New Catholic Dictionary*, p. 542.

course. It was not an age of reflection, but of obedience, finding satisfaction generally in the guidance of the visible church.

We may well be thankful that, in the Providence of God, the Roman Church took the course it did through the early years. "For when the old world fell to pieces, the Church was the one and only institution which survived the general wreck. Unless this Church had thrown a halo of sanctity over the Latin tongue by retaining it as the language of her Bible and of her worship, as well as the channel of her diplomatic intercourse, her ecclesiastical administration and her religious study, the fate of classical learning must inevitably have been sealed." [20] Not only that, but it was the Roman Church, with its Latin Bible and liturgy, that preserved the spiritual, as well as the intellectual inheritance of Christianity from the blind deluge of northern barbarism.

The Roman Church dreamed of one Empire, and one Church, with its one Bible, the Latin; a beautiful dream, and the most deep-seated conviction of the times. It is not at all surprising that many Catholics opposed vernacular translations; they must have seemed to dethrone the one church Bible. The Latin had been so hallowed by time, in both the Bible and liturgy, that doubtless it seemed well-nigh sacrilegious to propose any change. It would be perfectly natural for Catholics to oppose vernacular translations, or any change in the liturgy, for exactly the same reasons, and with far better excuse, than many Protestants have today for preferring the King James Version. The English and Episcopal churches even today refuse to accept any revision of the Psalms of the Prayer Book, though they are thoroughly antiquated.

It is foolish for anybody in modern times to deny that Roman Catholics at one time opposed vernacular translations. Such opposition was not due to a want of proper reverence for the Bible, but was the outgrowth of an excessive reverence, a sort of fetishistic superstition that the Bible was too sacred for unconsecrated hands. This excessive awe was reinforced by the fear of heresy, and by certain Scriptures which spoke of things hard to be understood in the Bible, and which some people wrested to their own destruction.

Most Important Difference Between Catholic and Protestant Bibles

The Roman Catholic Bible differs from that of the Protestant in one important respect that requires explanation. The Catholic

[20] Hoare, *Our English Bible*, p. 15.

Bible contains, as a vital part of it, in the Old Testament, seven books, Wisdom, Ecclesiasticus, first and second Maccabees, Baruch, Judith and Tobit, and additions to the books of Daniel and Esther, which are not considered inspired by Protestants.[21] They are known among the Protestants as the apocrypha.[22] These books, once printed in all Protestant Bibles, but separate and apart from the other books, were finally omitted entirely from most Protestant Bibles through the influence of the Puritans. The first Bible to omit the apocrypha was the Geneva under date of 1599.

When the Old Testament was translated into the Greek, from 250 to 100 B. C., certain books were included, in addition to those found in the Hebrew, and among them the books now called apocrypha. This Greek Old Testament was certainly in use in Palestine in the days of the apostles, because most of the quotations from the Old Testament found in the New, were taken from the Greek rather than the Hebrew. The early Christian Church, for several centuries, was Greek, and used this Greek Old Testament containing these books. The Old Latin which Jerome revised had been made originally, in its Old Testament, from the Greek, and very naturally these books found a place in the Latin Vulgate. In this way they became a part of the Roman Catholic Bible, where they are considered equally inspired and authoritative with the other books.

But the fact that the Old Testament used by the Christian Church in apostolic times, and for centuries afterward, was the Greek Old Testament containing the apocryphal books, is not proof that these books were regarded as of equal value with the other books. It is a fact that the early Christian fathers quote the books of the apocrypha freely as "Scripture"; but Origen, who does so freely, very definitely recognized the books of the Old Testament as accepted by the Palestinian Jews, as quite superior. Others may have made the same distinction earlier. In the fourth century certain men of importance questioned the inspiration of the apocrypha, Jerome among them; but these books remained a part of the Bible until the Reformation.

In the Protestant Church Carlstadt, in 1520, was the first to reject

---

[21] The apocrypha is found in the Bible of the English and Episcopal churches, and five books are found in Luther's Bible, but they are not considered inspired, only worthy of being read.

[22] For the character and influence of the apocrypha, and their use in various Bibles, see *The Bible from the Beginning*, Simms, pp. 95-106, 128-148, 197-99.

hese books as inspired, giving them an inferior position in the Bible. In the Roman Catholic Bible these books are distributed hrough the Old Testament; but Luther, assigning them an inferior place, put them in a separate section, as an appendix to the Old Testament. Protestant Bibles, following Luther, always gave them a separate place.

Since the Christian Church received the Old Testament from the Jews, Protestants have always insisted that only such books should be considered inspired as the Jews of Palestine, the leaders of the nation, accepted. They did not accept the books of the apocrypha, and they were never a part of the Hebrew Old Testament; therefore, Protestants have either rejected these books outright, or assigned them an inferior place.

There is no doubt that the apocrypha fills an important gap in the literature and history of the Jews, between the times of the Old and New Testaments; but it contains also much that Protestants consider unreliable.

2. FRENCH BIBLE BROUGHT TO AMERICA

The Bible in both French and German probably came to America at the same time. The Huguenots at Beaufort, in 1562, would certainly have French Bibles with them. Moreover, in this colony were some Germans[23], and they would probably have Bibles in German.

A. THE HUGUENOTS AT BEAUFORT PROBABLY HAD FRENCH BIBLES

The Huguenot effort at Beaufort, on Port Royal Harbor, in 1562, under the auspices of Coligny, was the first attempt at Protestant colonization in America, soon ending disastrously. These Huguenots were Christians who fled persecution on account of their religion, and came to America to found a Christian state. They landed and "kneeling on the ground, they gave thanks to God, who had guided their voyage to an issue full of promise."[24] They undoubtedly brought Bibles in their native tongue. Such conclusion is only an inference from the facts in the case, but it seems a necessary one. The Huguenot colonists at Fort Caroline, Florida, in 1564, doubtless had Bibles in French also.

They might have brought Olivetian's translation of 1535,[25] the most popular Protestant version, or more probably some revision of

---

[23] The presence of Germans in the Huguenot colony will be discussed in connection with the German Bible, in Section 3 following.

[24] Francis Parkman, *Pioneers of France in the New World,* part I, p. 36.

[25] D. M. 3710.

it. The one put out by the ministers of Geneva, in 1560, appeared in time for their use.

Whether the Jesuit priests used translations in French, in their work in America (1608-1763) is unknown. They may have done so. They had access to the Louvain revision of Le Fevre's version,[26] and the popular Mons, or De Sacy New Testament of 1667.[27] Other versions were accessible, among which was a New Testament by Dominque Bonhours, a Jesuit, which was published in 1696,[28] and again in 1711 with the Latin Vulgate. This was revised by others and published in 1713, 1748, and even after the middle of the nineteenth century. These by no means exhaust the list of possibilities. It is not at all impossible that Jesuits in America used translations made by Jesuits in France. No matter how much opposition to the use of vernacular translations existed, among certain authorities of the Catholic Church, these translations had a wide use among Catholics at that time. Catholics of various nationalities were determined to have vernacular translations, and many were provided. They became a source of great trouble to Catholic authorities.

Roman Catholic Translations in French

The beginning of a French Bible may be traced to the early twelfth century. Various parts were translated from time to time. An edition completed by different hands was issued by the order of Charles VIII, about 1498, edited by the king's confessor, Jean De Rely, published in Paris, and known as *La Grande Bible* to distinguish it from an inferior work,[29] being a revision of one published about 1474.

A complete Bible by the well-known humanist, Jacques Le Fevre d'Eaples, appeared in 1530, but it was put on the papal Index in 1546, because its notes were supposed to favor Protestantism. It was extensively used, however; came to be known as the Bible of Antwerp and was approved by the doctors of the Louvain.[30]

In 1550, at Louvain, a revision of Le Fevre's Bible by members of the faculty of Louvain was issued with their authority, remaining a Catholic standard for more than a century.[31] It is estimated that no less than two hundred editions were finally published.

[26] D. M. 3717. [27] D. M. 3756. [28] D. M. 3774. [29] 3703 D. M. [30] D. M. 3708. [31] D. M. 3717.

There was printed at Mons, in 1667, a New Testament known as he Port Royal version, De Sacy's version, or the Mons New Testament. This translation was begun by Antoine le Maistre and revised and completed by his brother, Louis Isaac le Maistre, better known by his assumed name De Sacy.[32] The whole was partially revised by others. It is regarded as one of the best translations ever made in French, and had a very wide circulation. While the hostility of the Sorbonne forced its publication outside of France, it carried the privilege of Charles II of Spain, and was warmly welcomed in France. These translations were all made from the Latin.

Roman Catholics were not numerous in America in colonial days, so that any use they may have made of translations in French, in that early period, is a matter of small importance. However, the Catholics published at Boston, in 1810, an edition of De Sacy's New Testament, which was their first printing of French Scriptures in America.

Protestant Translations in French

The first French Protestant Bible, a translation based on the original Hebrew and Greek, was made by Pierre Robert Olivetian, and published at the expense of the Waldensians, 1535. He was related to John Calvin, who wrote a Latin preface for this version, which was based on Le Fevre's Bible.[33] To Olivetian is due the introduction of the French term *L'Eternel*, still in use in French Bibles, as an equivalent of the Ineffable Name. Dr. James Moffatt adopted this term in his translation of the Old Testament.[34]

In 1560, a fresh revision of this version was prepared under the direction of the ministers of Geneva, known later as the "French Geneva Version".[35] It was often reprinted. Again, in 1588, a fresh revision of this version was published at Geneva, under the editorial direction of C. B. Bertram.[36] The work was done by a "venerable company" of the pastors of Geneva. This came to be regarded as the standard text, and during the seventeenth century was known as "the Geneva Bible." One of the very successful revisions of this Bible was made, in 1724, by Frederic Ostervald, who was a Swiss theologian and a man of great influence. This was published at Amsterdam and Rotterdam,[37] and his final revision was made in 1744.

---

[32] D. M. 3756. [33] D. M. 3710. [34] The only other English Bible to use this term, so far as we know, is that of J. M. Ray, published London or Glasgow 1799. [35] D. M. 3722. [36] D. M. 3736. [37] D. M. 3793.

Jean Diodati, the author of a well-known Italian translation of 1641, published at Geneva, in 1644, a French version, which found favor among the Huguenots, and was used freely in America. Most of these Protestant translations and revisions were used in America in the colonial era and later. Many copies of these Bibles are preserved in the libraries of the country, yet it is difficult to determine with any measure of accuracy the use they had in America.

In 1562, the French Protestant hymn book was completed, containing 49 Psalms in metre by Clement Marot, and 101 Psalms rendered into metre by Theodore Beza. From 1562 to 1565, no less than 62 editions of this book were published, its popularity resulting finally in its translation into 22 languages. The Psalms appeared also in many editions of the Bible, and were freely used in America.

3. GERMAN BIBLES BROUGHT TO AMERICA

GERMANS PROBABLY HAD VERNACULAR BIBLES AT BEAUFORT

The German Bible, as has been said, was probably brought to America first by the Germans who came with the Huguenots to Beaufort, on Port Royal Harbor, in 1562. Among these Huguenots were some Germans. Henbuch, in his *Handbuch des Deutschtums in Auslande,* mentions Germans in this colony. Faust says,[38] "At Port Royal, in South Carolina, which was settled in 1562, by a band of Huguenots under Jean Ribault, there seem to have been some Alsatian and Hessian Protestants at the very beginning," and he refers in a footnote to German authorities. This colony was planted for the express purpose of establishing a Christian state, where men could worship God according to the dictates of their own consciences, and by men who were escaping persecution on account of their religion. Only Germans who would bring Bibles would be likely to join such a colony. Naturally they would have Luther's translation.

History of Luther's Bible

In the early history of the Christian church, for several centuries, the Bible was translated as soon as possible into every language where Christianity was introduced, on the supposition that this was

[38] *German Element in America,* Vol. I, p. 7.

the best means of propagating the Gospel. The Roman Catholic Church, however, changed this policy, and came to deny vernacular translations to the people, as far as it could. The official attitude of this church has so far been changed that vernacular translations are now permitted freely.

The Bible, in whole or in part, had been translated into some 25 languages before the invention of printing from movable type, about 1450. The whole Bible had been printed in 19 languages and dialects, and parts of it in three other languages [39] before Luther published his New Testament.

While this was done before Protestants divided the church, the Roman Catholic Church can hardly claim credit for it, since some of these translations were made while the Greek Church was dominant; and the Roman Church did not foster such work at any time, but for long would have prevented it, if it had been possible. Notwithstanding Catholic opposition, and all efforts at their suppression, there was a stream of such translations throughout the Middle Ages and the period of the Reformation, made by Roman Catholics who evidently did not share the common church or official position on the subject.

No less than 18 complete Bibles in German, 22 editions of the Psalms, and a dozen other parts of the Bible were printed in German between 1466 and 1521—this before Luther published his New Testament, all being translated from the Latin. Of the 18 complete Bibles, 14 were in High German. These editions, however, were small. It is estimated that these High German Bibles did not exceed a total of 15,000 copies.[40] The Bible, therefore, was in no sense the book of the people before Luther's translation.

Few men have influenced history as did Martin Luther. He made an enormous contribution to human welfare and the forces of change in his time, by his new interpretation of Christianity, which was derived from the Bible itself. Paul's doctrine of justification by faith had been degraded into a doctrine of salvation by theological opinion, which strangely some modern fundamentalists seem still to hold. Luther repudiated such ideas. His Bible moulded the German language: "It is unquestionably due to Luther's Bible that the Germans have now one language for all literary purposes".[41]

Luther made the first Protestant translation into any language,

---

[39] Norlie, *The Bible in a Thousand Tongues*, pp. 6-8.
[40] Norlie, *The Translated Bible*, p. 80.
[41] Von Dobschutz, *Influence of the Bible on Civilization*, p. 129.

inspiring a like effort wherever Protestant influence reached. Most translations followed his model; the Dutch, Danish, Swedish, Finnish and Lettish and the Lithuanian Bibles were largely influenced by Luther's Bible, or based on it. Even Tyndale, in his English translation, was considerably influenced by Luther. In fact, Luther launched the greatest era of Biblical translation in the world's history, a translation from the original languages rather than from the Latin.

Luther began his New Testament in December 1521, the first draft being finished in three months, then corrected and published September 25, 1522.[42] It was issued without date, printer's name or publisher. However, the place of printing, Wittenberg, was given. Only about 40 copies of the original are known to exist. This translation was based on Erasmus' Greek Testament, the second edition of 1519.

Luther began to translate the Old Testament before the New had been published, using the Hebrew Old Testament published at Brescia, in 1499. He consulted the Septuagint, the Greek Old Testament, and the Vulgate. The Old Testament was published in sections, beginning 1523, and the completed Bible, in 1534.[43]

A special committee was appointed by Luther to assist in revising his work, which also aided in the original translation. This commission consisted of Melanchton, Bugenhagen, Cruciger and Aurogallus. Sometimes others attended. The first results of their work of revision appeared in 1541,[44] and the final revision, in 1545.[45] But whatever help Luther may have had, he was the dominating personality, the ultimate authority; and the final result is correctly called Luther's Bible. He placed the apocrypha, for the first time, in a separate section, other Protestants doing likewise. Luther's Bible at once became the standard, and soon was the most widely read book in Germany.

Luther's Bible was often revised more or less, but it is with his Bible that we are chiefly concerned, because his is the chief German version brought to America by the colonists, and it has held first place among German Bibles throughout our national history.

In 1863 a committee was appointed by the Eisenach Conference in Germany to undertake a revision of Luther's Bible. The New Testament appeared in 1867, and the whole Bible in 1883, the revision, however, not being finally completed until 1890, and published at Halle, in 1892. Most parts of Germany adopted it at once.

[42] D. M. 4188. [43] D. M. 4199. [44] D. M. 4204. [45] D. M. 4205.

Other German Translations

Many other German Bibles were published in an early day, both by Roman Catholics and by Protestants.

Roman Catholics made several translations of the German Bible. In 1534, John Deitenburg, a Dominican, made a translation which was published at Mainz. It was revised often and reprinted, becoming the chief Catholic Bible in German during the sixteenth century.[46] Johann Eck, a bitter opponent of Luther, published, in 1537, a Bible in German, using the pre-Lutheran versions represented by the Augsburg Bibles of 1477 and 1507, revised and partly conformed to the Vulgate. In the New Testament he retains Emser's version, with certain changes.[47] There are copies of this Bible in America, indicating that it had a small use here.

Count Zinzendorf and the ministers of the Moravian Brethren community, which he had established at Herrnhutt, prepared and issued an edition of Luther's Bible, in 1727, which was used among the German Moravians.[48] Its comments are in his spirit. Zinzendorf also published the New Testament translated from the Greek, which was published in 1739 and in 1774-76.[49] His work in America would naturally encourage the use of his translations here.

The ministers of Zurich published a complete Swiss-German Bible at Zurich, in 1527-29, in six parts,[50] the whole Bible printed first in 1530.[51] This is one of several "combined Bibles" that appeared at this period, using Luther's translation as far as available, adding other parts from other sources. It was often reprinted. This was the Bible of the Reformed Church of Switzerland.[52]

In 1742 there appeared a German revision that came to be known as the Berleburg Bible, from the place of its publication. It was a vigorous revision of Luther's Bible, based on the originals, with reference to the Zurich Bible, and was edited by J. F. Haug and other scholars with mystical sympathies. It appeared in eight volumes, in 1726-42, never being reprinted.[53] This Bible contained a commentary, and those who made it considered that the Scriptures have three meanings, a literal, a moral and a secret or prophetic; to interpret the latter these commentators profess superior qualifications. Curiously enough it contains numerous apocryphal books,

---

[46] D. M. 4200. [47] D. M. 4203. [48] D. M. 4229 note. [49] D. M. 4235 note. [50] D. M. 4196. [51] D. M. 4195.
[52] Four copies of the Zurich Bible are in the Lancaster, Pa., Seminary library, the oldest published in 1531.
[53] Darlow and Moule, 4239.

not found in other Bibles, both in the Old and New Testaments. This Bible was used in America.

The Zurich Bible was altered somewhat and published by P. Schoeffer at Worms, in 1529, the edition coming to be known as the Worms or Baptist Bible, and was the earliest Protestant Bible to bear the general title of *Biblia*. It was reprinted in 1534,[54] and was extensively used among the Reformed sections of Germany. The Reformed Germans of America would naturally use this Bible. Moravians used Luther's Bible of 1740.

4. ENGLISH PROBABLY THE FOURTH LANGUAGE TO FURNISH A BIBLE

The fourth language to furnish a Bible in America was probably the English. Four different versions in English were in use in colonial times; but the exact order in which they came to America is unknown. The order we give is conjectural. There would seem to be little room to doubt that the Bishops' Bible was brought over first, and that the Rheims-Douai came last. We know when certain copies of the Geneva Bible and the King James Version arrived in an early day; but we do not know that other copies may not have come over sooner and in reverse order. From our information on the subject we are inclined to think that probably the Geneva Bible was the second English Bible, and was brought to Virginia first probably in 1607, but certainly by 1611; and that the King James Version was the third, probably brought to Virginia before a copy reached New England. But we have no proof of this.

A.   FIRST ENGLISH BIBLE PROBABLY THE BISHOPS'

It is our deliberate judgment that the Bishops' Bible was the first in English brought to America, having been used probably in several different places. Such conclusions are only inferences, but seem well justified.

Sporadic Uses of the Bishops' Bible

"The first services of the Anglican Church on this continent appear to have been those held by Sir Francis Drake's chaplain in California in 1579"[55]. This chaplain would certainly have his Bible with him. Since there was no element of the Puritan, about Drake,

---

[54] Darlow and Moule, 4194 note.   [55] *An Outline of Christianity*, Vol. III., p. 260.

e may suppose that he would choose a chaplain free from such aint. The chaplain must have had the Great Bible or the Bishops' which had been in use eleven years at that time. The conclusion hat he used the Bishops' seems to be reasonable.

Sir Humphrey Gilbert, a half-brother of Sir Walter Raleigh and Christian man of distinction, obtained a commission to plant a olony in Newfoundland, where he landed at St. Johns, taking ormal possession in the name of his sovereign. In further explora-ion, he lost his largest vessel with all on board. This forced him to eturn to England at once. He had only two vessels left, one the *quirrel*, was a boat of only ten tons, brought over for exploration n shallow water. He refused to permit the humblest of his men to ake a risk that he did not himself take; therefore, he chose to sail n the small boat, which was too heavily loaded for ocean travel.

A terrific storm arose, but he sat calmly reading a book, as was observed by those on the larger vessel. This book was unquestion-bly the Bible, since Christian men do not read any other book mid such dangers as surrounded him at that time. He sought to encourage his men who were panic-stricken, and was heard to cry o them, "We are as near heaven on sea as on land." That night, September 9, 1583,[56] those on the larger boat saw the light of the *Squirrel* suddenly disappear, never to be seen again. There is every probability that Sir Humphrey Gilbert was reading the Bishops' Bible, since it had been in use fifteen years, and he had no taint of Puritanism about him.

Sir Walter Raleigh made a disastrous experiment in an attempt to plant a colony in North Carolina, and we know that this colony had a Bible. This fact is recorded by Captain John Smith,[57] and by Bancroft, and is the first reference we have been able to find in his-tory, stating definitely that a Bible was used in the colonies. Neither tells what version was used, but with all the facts, the conclusion that it was a copy of the Bishops' Bible seems inescapable. We think it may be set down as a fact that the first Bible brought to America in any language, mentioned in history, was the Bishops'; and that it was the first Bible in English used in the colonies.

Some colonists led by Ralph Lane, in 1585, settled at Roanoke Island. With them was one Thomas Hariot, an eminent mathe-matician, and a devout Christian, carrying numerous mathematical instruments, burning glasses, sea-compasses, guns, clocks and books.

---

[56] Strachey, *Historie of Travaile into Virginia Britannia*, p. 8.
[57] *General History of Virginia, New England*, etc., Glasgow edition 1907, p. 23.

These greatly impressed the natives and inclined them to believe
what he said about God. Hariot used the opportunity to teach them
Christianity. Speaking of the matter, Bancroft says, "In every town
which Hariot entered he displayed and explained the Bible; the
Indians revered the volume rather than its doctrines; with a fond
superstition, they embraced the book, kissed it, and held it to their
breasts and heads, as an amulet." [58]

John Gilmary Shea states the case quite satisfactorily, when he
says, "What was the English Bible thus primarily used on our shores
by the Oxford bred mathematician? . . . It was not the King James
Version, then unwrit. His college life, his acquaintance with Raleigh
and Northumberland, and association with the court circles, all
lead to the inference that Hariot's Bible was that officially recognized at the time by the Church of England and the crown, that
commonly known now as the Bishops' Bible." [59] This must have
been the Great Bible or the Bishops', which then had been in
use seventeen years. This conclusion is further strengthened by the
utter absence in the colony of any Puritan influence which might
have preferred the Geneva Bible.

George Popham attempted an English settlement in Maine at the
mouth of the Kennebec River, in 1607. "They all went ashoare where
they had made choise of their plantation and where they had a
sermon delivered unto them by their preacher (Richard Seymer);
and after the sermon, the president's commission was read, with the
lawes to be observed and kept." [60] This preacher would certainly
have his Bible with him. Shea says this colony used the Bishops'
Bible.[61] While this is probably unsupported by documentary evidence, it seems a highly probable inference, especially since there was
no Puritan influence in this colony. This colony was abandoned
after one winter.

Use of the Bishops' Bible in Virginia

There seems to be a widespread opinion that the Bishops' Bible
was used freely, if not exclusively, in the Virginia colony in an early
day. Shea says, "Virginia was the home of the Bishops' Bible until
the gradual popularity of the King James Version replaced it." [62]

---

[58] *History of the United States,* Vol. I., p. 73 (ed. 1891).
[59] *American Catholic Quarterly Review,* Vol. III, pp. 133-34 (1878).
[60] Strachey, *Historie of Travaile into Virginia Britannia,* p. 172.
[61] *American Catholic Quarterly Review,* Vol. III., p. 135 (1878).
[62] *American Catholic Quarterly Review,* Vol. III, p. 135.

But he offers no proof. His conclusion is evidently an inference from the fact that the colony was composed of Englishmen, loyal to the established church; but he probably overlooked entirely the fact that the Puritans, who dominated this colony in its early history,[63] while loyal to the established church, generally preferred the Geneva Bible.

The Virginia Company, which founded this colony, certainly contained a strong Puritan influence, and it has been called a Puritan company.[64] Among its corporators were the brothers Sandys, sons of the Puritan Archbishop of York, one of whom held the manor at Scrooby, a hot-bed of Puritanism; others were William Brewster of Scrooby and his son Edward. Sir Edwin Sandys, one of the corporators, considered by King James as his worst enemy, wrote two of the charters of this colony. In the fleet of Sir Thomas Gates, in May 1609, were noted Puritans, one being Stephen Hopkins, who was clerk to the Rev. Richard Buck. It was said of the Rev. Mr. Buck that he was "not strict conformist", which probably means that he was a Puritan.[65] This company had frequent dealings with leading Puritans, and was willing to receive the Puritan Pilgrims of Leyden into the colony, which would probably have been impossible had it not been a Puritan company. This company was very careful of its choice of chaplains for the colony, requiring them to preach trial sermons before being chosen,[66] which was not the practice of the ritualists. The Puritanism of this company is the explanation of the administration of Sir Thomas Dale, who was selected for the task, and who imposed a code of laws abundantly supplied with Puritan teeth.[67]

Considerable literature was put out and numerous sermons were preached in London, in the interest of the colony in Virginia, and much of this, at least—practically all, in fact, that we have been able to examine—was provided by men, who used the Geneva Bible, presumably Puritans. The *Good Speed to Virginia,* written by Robert Gray, in the interest of the enterprise, was published in Lon-

[63] C. M. Andrews, in *The Colonial Period of American History,* p. 228, says there were no Puritans in Virginia until 1642. This statement, he says in a letter, will be corrected in forthcoming issues. He thinks, however, that Bacon, in his *History of American Christianity* is mistaken in saying that the Virginia Company was a Puritan corporation.

[64] Bacon, *History of American Christianity,* p. 44. For further proof of the Puritan influence in Virginia see Neil's *Hours at Home,* Vol. VI., pp. 22, 201.

[65] Any man who named his children Marah, Peleg, Gershom, and Benoni, as he did, must have been Puritan.

[66] and [67] Bacon, *History of American Christianity,* p. 45 and note.

don, in 1609, and he quotes from the Geneva Bible.[68] Several ser
mons were preached before the Virginia Company in London, fo
which service they chose freely, if not uniformly, Puritans. Perhap
the first such sermon was delivered at White Chapel on April 25,
1609, by the Rev. William Symonds, the minister of Saint Saviour
in Southwark. He used the Geneva Bible, as his Scripture quota
tions prove.[69] While they are not all exact quotations, he certainl
does not quote from the Bishops' Bible. The pulpit was again in
voked and Daniel Price "preached a sermon at Paule Cross upon ;
Rogation Sunday, being the 28 of May, 1609." He used the Genev;
Bible.[70] The Rev. William Crashaw, preacher at the Temple ir
London, later to become a member of the Virginia Company, de
livered a sermon, on February 21, 1610, before Lord Delaware anc
other important members of the company, in view of Delaware':
contemplated departure for Virginia. While some of his Scripture
quotations are inaccurate, there can be no doubt that he used the
Geneva Bible.[71]

The prosperity of the colony of Virginia was such that the Vir
ginia Company ordered a thanksgiving sermon to be preached at
Bow Church in London, and the Rev. Copland, a Puritan, was
chosen to deliver it. This famous sermon bore the title, "Virginia's
God Be Thanked," and was preached on April 18, 1622. The text
was read from the Geneva Bible, and other quotations were from
the same source.[72] Copland must have been a favorite with the
Virginia Company, since they chose him to be the chaplain of the
new college founded at Henrico. An Indian massacre, in 1622,
wiped out the college and all prospects for one, and he did not come
to Virginia, going rather to the Bermudas, where he labored many
years. He went thence to the Bahamas, his Puritanism being so
strong that he finally became a Separatist, and founded an independent church.

William Strachey was the secretary of the Virginia Company
under Lord Delaware, coming over at the time of the second charter,
and remaining a few years. He wrote an account of the colony in
which his Scripture quotations are from the Geneva Bible.[73] He
uses one expression found only, so far as we can learn, in Whittingham's New Testament of 1557.

[68] and [69] Brown, *Genesis of the United States*, Vol. I, pp. 294-300, 283-91.
[70] Brown, *Genesis of the United States*, Vol. I., pp. 312-16.
[71] Brown, *Genesis of the United States*, Vol. I., pp. 360-75.
[72] Neil, *English Colonization of America in the 17th Century*, p. 180.
[73] *Historie of Travaile into Virginia Britannia*, pp. 20-22.

Rev. Alexander Whitaker, "the apostle of Virginia", and the most noted among the ministers of the colony, who came over with Dale and was associated with him, used the Geneva Bible. In his "Good Newes from Virginia" is a sermon from a Genevan text.[74] Whitaker was the son of the author of the Calvinistic Lambeth Articles, and had a brother who was an independent or Separatist minister in London. "What was his position in relation to church parties is shown by his letter to his cousin, the arch-Puritan, William Gouge, written after three years' residence in Virginia, urging that non-conformist clergymen should come over to Virginia, where no questions would be raised on the subject of subscription or the surplice." [75]

While Whitaker regularly used the Geneva Bible, he had some familiarity with the Bishops'. In "Good Newes from Virginia" he uses this expression, "That . . . he would thrust forth his laborers into the harvest".[76] "Thrust forth" came from the Bishops' Bible, because every other version in use at that time used "send". So he probably had a copy of the Bishops' Bible.

Nansemond, settled near Norfolk, in 1619, was Puritan.[77] In 1642 its founders sent a letter to Boston asking for three good ministers, who came bearing letters from Governor Winthrop, but Virginia was then a royal colony with Berkeley in charge, and he forbade their preaching. Lawn Creek in Isle of Wight County, settled in 1621, was Puritan, and its first minister was Rev. William Bennett.[78]

Bermuda was a colony of Virginia, and very intimately associated with it, and Bermuda was a veritable Puritan stronghold. Several ministers were finally banished from this colony because of their Puritanism.[79]

George Abbott, the Puritan Bishop of London, was a member of the Virginia Company, and it was through him that the Rev. Richard Buck was chosen to succeed the Rev. Robert Hunt, as chaplain in the colony. He would probably choose a Puritan.

---

[74] Brown, *Genesis of the United States*, Vol. II., p. 579.

[75] Bacon, *History of American Christianity*, p. 46. The fact that this letter is given one ending by Purchase and another by Hamer does not affect the matter. That Whitaker was a Puritan and used the Geneva Bible is supported by proof abundant without this letter.

[76] "Thrust forth" is used in the text of Matt. 9:38, and in the margin of Luke 10:2. See Brown, *Genesis of the United States,* Vol. II, p. 588.

[77] Bacon, *History of Christianity in America*, pp. 48-9.

[78] Neil, *The London Company*, p. 194 note.

[79] Andrews, *The Colonial Period of American History*, pp. 228, 231-33.

While we have found abundant evidence from Scripture quota
tions, in sermons and elsewhere, that the Geneva Bible was use
freely in the Virginia colony, we have found no evidence that a
minister there used the Bishops' Bible, except the single expressio
referred to above, found in the writings of Rev. Alexander Whi
aker. Our study of the matter leads us to think that probably t
Geneva Bible was used exclusively there by the ministers in its earl
history, Puritan influence preferring it. After Virginia was made
royal colony in 1624, Berkeley came over and made it very difficu
for the Puritan element, and when many refused to conform to th
Church of England, they were driven out of the colony, findir
refuge in Maryland.[80] Those of the royal colony who did not prefe
the Geneva Bible, would most probably use the King James Versio
rather than the Bishops', which was not printed later than 1606.

We found one Bible, however, in the hands of laymen of th
Virginia colony that we believe to have been the Bishops'. Ther
may have been other such, of course. Captain Samuel Argoll trade
with the Indians, among them one Jopassus, a king of some sma
place. He recovered a boy, Henry Spilman, who had been hel
captive among the Indians a whole year, and until he had despaire
of ever seeing his own people again. Strachey reports the use of
Bible in one of Captain Argoll's expeditions:

"The last yeare 1610, about Christmas, when Captain Argoll wa
there (on the Potomac) trading with Jopassus the great king's bro
ther, after many daies of acquaintance with him, as the pynnac
road before the town Matchopongo, Jopassus comying abourd an
sitting (the weather being very cold) by the fier, upon a hearth i
the hold, with the Captaine, one of our men was reading of a Bibl
to which the Indian gave a very attent care, and looked with a ver
wisht eye upon him, as if he desired to understand what he read
whereupon the Captayne tooke the booke, and turned to the pictur
of the Creation of the World, in the begynning of the booke, an
caused the boy, one Spilman, who had lyved a whole yere with thi
Indian Kinge, and spoke his language, to shewe yt unto him, an
to interprete yt in his language, which the boy did".[81]

This Bible was probably the Bishops'. It could not have been th
King James Version, since that had not appeared. It must hav
been the Geneva or the Bishops', since they were the only ones i

[80] Thompson, *The Religious Foundations of America*, p. 93.
[81] Strachey, *Historie of Travaile into Virginia Britannia*, p. 98.

use at that time. The story informs us that "the Captayne tooke the booke, and turned to the picture of the Creation of the World, in the begynning of the booke." The Bishops' Bible had such a wood-cut in its front,[82] but if any edition of the Geneva Bible ever had such picture it its front part, or elsewhere, we have not learned about it. From this fact we conclude that this was probably a copy of the Bishops' Bible.

History of the Bishops' Bible

The Bishops' Bible was the fourth in regular succession of transla-tions in English. The publication of the Geneva Bible, in 1660, had produced an awkward situation in the English Church. It was a Puritan Bible, made so especially by its numerous notes, and could not, therefore, very well be made the Bible of the whole church, since a large part of the church were in no sense Puritan. The of-ficial Bible of the church, at this time, was the Great Bible, but the very superior scholarship of the Geneva successfully discredited the church Bible.

Matthew Parker, the Archbishop of Canterbury, therefore, launched a movement for a fresh revision, appointing fifteen men who were to do the work under his direction and editorship. Each man worked separate and alone, with the result that its parts vary considerably in quality. It is now impossible to determine exactly who did the work of revision, since the initials appended to the different parts do not quite correspond with the list of translators given. Most of them, however, are known, and were bishops—hence its name.

The work of translation began not later than 1564, and was com-pleted and published in 1568. Parker sought to have Queen Eliza-beth license and declare this the official Bible, but in this he failed; it was not even licensed. The Convocation, however, on April 3, 1571, ordered its use. Every archbishop and bishop was directed to provide it and place it where it might be useful for servants and strangers. Every cathedral was to have a copy, and every church, "as far as it could be conveniently done."

The Bishops' Bible was the most sumptious of all the early Bibles,

[82] The first edition of 1568, and the second edition of 1569, contained wood-cuts of Creation at the beginning of Genesis. See Dore, *Old Bibles*, pp. 241, 244. The third edition of 1572 had a woodcut of the same place, but what it was is not told by Dore, in *Old Bibles*, p. 251.

but was never very popular, having little but ecclesiastical use. No means were spared, however, to insure it a wide circulation, but all such efforts failed. The best scholarship in England had not been used in its production; no Puritan served on its committee. Some of its illustrations helped to bring it into disrepute. The Psalter was very unsatisfactory, and the third edition of 1572, to meet this criticism, contained the Psalms of the Great Bible, in parallel columns with those of the Bishops'. The ninth edition of 1579 contained only the Psalms of the Great Bible. After this date the Psalms of the Bishops' Bible were rarely printed in this Bible.

In the third edition of the Bishops' Bible published in 1572, the New Testament was considerably revised and improved; and from this edition the King James Version was made.[83] This edition became known as the Leda Bible, because several initial letters used in the New Testament had been prepared to illustrate an edition of Ovid's *Metamorphoses*. The initial at the Epistle to the Hebrews was a representation of Jupiter appearing to Leda under the form of a swan. No other edition ever used these objectionable illustrations.

One feature of this Bible deserves mention. It was the Bishops' Bible that first translated the Greek word *ecclesia* practically uniformly with the word "church." Tyndale had uniformly rendered this word "congregation." This he considered of primary importance among Protestants at that time, and as necessary in safe-guarding a community of equals, such as an assembly of the New Testament worshippers must have been. In fact, Tyndale had dealt a severe blow to the doctrines and practices of the Church of Rome by his rejection of several ecclesiastical terms, on which this church relied rather heavily, such as "priest", which he rendered "elder", and "penance", which he translated "repentance", etc. This was one reason why Tyndale's New Testament provoked so much opposition. Coverdale had been a bit more conciliatory than Tyndale, and, in his Bible of 1535, had restored certain of these terms, using them interchangably with those of Tyndale's renderings. But nowhere did he translate *ecclesia* by the word "church." Neither was this word rendered "church" in Matthew's Bible, nor in the Great Bible, both using "congregation" uniformly.[84]

---

[83] Dore, *Old Bibles*, p. 272, says the King James Version was based on an edition of 1602.

[84] The word "church" occurs but once in the Great Bible as a translation of a word meaning "temple" or "sacred edifice." See Acts 19:37.

It may seem a bit singular that the Geneva Bible, at this time of bitter controversy, should have used the word "church" and "congregation" interchangably—one about as often as the other. This may have been due, in part, to the state-church element of Presbyterians, but no matter why, by using the terms interchangably, the word "congregation" naturally defined and explained the word "church."

The Bishops' Bible, except in two instances [85] renders *ecclesia* by the word "church". The reason is probably not far to seek. The word "church", in Catholic usage, had come to signify an organized and authoritative institution, governed by ecclesiastics. Parker probably meant, as far as possible, to repudiate the original democratic constitution of the early Christian assemblies, and thereby help to pave the way for ecclesiastical domination and uniformity in the English Church.

King James I gave, as one of the rules that should govern his translators, that they should use the old ecclesiastical term "church" uniformly, which they did. He was determined to maintain the ecclesiastical authority of the Church of England, and sought to have Biblical authority to bolster his right to dominate. Such is the history of how the word "church" became the commonly accepted translation of the Greek word *ecclesia*. "Thus the word for which Tyndale had so earnestly contended, the word which had stood on the sacred page as an incorruptible witness against priestly usurpation, was thenceforward blotted from the English Scriptures".[86]

It is not without interest to Americans that a note in the Bishops' Bible, on Psalm 45:9 reads, "Ophir is thought to be the Ilande in the vvest coast, of late founde by Christopher Columbo, from whence at this day is brought most fine golde." The reference, of course, is to America.

Two other notes in this Bible are interesting. At Psalm 103:5 it is said, "An Egle of all birdes liueth a long tyme without all kind of feebleness: dying never of age, but of famine."

In Psalm 104 is found the word "Leviathan", which is explained to be "a whale of a ballan, a beast that is King of the sea, for his

---

[85] Matt. 16:18 and Heb. 12:23. The word "congregation" was used in both these passages. The troublesome use of the first by Roman Catholics was probably the explanation here. The second passage refers to the hereafter, and Parker probably had no concern for the word that designated the redeemed in the world to come.

[86] Conant, *The English Bible*, pp. 400-01.

greatness and strength: he appeareth aboue the top of the sea a
bigge as a Ilande, or a greate huge mountayne."

The Bishops' Bible bequeathed to us a few quaint and beautiful
expressions, such as "Rend your hearts and not your garments";[87]
"the middle wall of partition"; [88] "less than the least of all the
saints"; [89] "now we call the proud happy"; [90] and "he that hath
a bountiful eye shall be blessed".[91]

This Bible had a reign of forty-three years, and the highest honor
it ever received was its use as the basis of the King James Version.

The Bible in English

The Bible in English differs from all other vernacular translations
in two important respects. Most other versions, both ancient and
modern, were produced by individuals, sometimes rather hurriedly,
and, for the most part, have remained much as they were from their
first appearance; while the Bible in English today is the work of a
succession of scholars, sometimes large committees, and covering a
period of 400 years. Only by slow degrees has it been brought
to its present high degree of perfection. On no other translation in
all the world has so much scholarly work been done. Moreover, it
is the most widely circulated book in the world today.

The first translation of the whole Bible into English, made from
the Latin, is generally known as Wyclif's Bible, published in 1382.
John Wyclif was educated at Oxford, became deeply interested in
the great ecclesiastical controversies of the times, and has been
called "the morning star of the Reformation." He sought to purge
the church of his day, and his purity of character, deep spirituality
and utter unselfishness, gave him great power. He felt that the
translation of the Bible into English for the use of the common man
the surest method of defeating the purposes of the Roman Church
at that time.

When Wyclif began the work of translation is not known; and
how much of the work was done by Wyclif himself cannot now be
determined. That he had assistance is certain. Nicholas Hereford
undoubtedly translated much of the Old Testament. There is a
break in the middle of Baruch, which is supposed to mark the end
of his work, and which is supposed to have occurred when Hereford
was summoned to Rome to answer the charge of heresy. Wyclif

[87] Joel 2:13.   [88] Eph. 2:14.   [89] Eph. 3:8.   [90] Mal. 3:15.   [91] Prov. 22:9.

.imself may have finished the work from this point, publishing the
New Testament in 1380 and the whole Bible in 1382.

When this Bible had been completed Wyclif organized a kind of
religious order of poor preachers, though not mendicants, whose
chief work was to teach the Bible to the common people. His Bible,
having to be copied by hand, was expensive and few could afford to
own a copy. Wyclif's followers came to be called Lollards, and
they soon spread over the whole country. He died in 1384.

Wyclif's Bible was revised in 1388, and while it is not known for
certain who did this work, it is generally attributed to John Purvey,
his former curate at Lutterworth. These two Bibles, but Purvey's
revision chiefly, served the English-speaking world nearly 150 years.

Wyclif's Bible was proscribed in 1408, when it was made a penal
offense to read any of his writings or translations in the province of
Canterbury. In 1414 a much more vigorous law was enacted, providing that anybody who read the Bible in English should "forfeit
land, catel, lif, and goods from their heyers for ever." In 1415
Wyclif's bones were removed from the churchyard where he had
been buried, and then in 1428, his bones were dug up, burned and
the ashes scattered on the stream that flows by Lutterworth.

This Bible was kept in manuscript for about 500 years. Only
170 manuscripts of these two Bibles are known to exist today,
some thirty of which contain the text of Wyclif's Bible. Both texts
were published in four volumes in 1850 by Foreshall and Madden.

Great intellectual, literary and material advance marked the
latter years of the fifteenth and the first years of the sixteenth century. Among the mighty influences of that day, destined to revolutionize the whole world, was the invention of printing in Germany
about 1450. Caxton had introduced the printing press into England
by 1470. Progress in other lines inspired the religious forces. Into
this fast changing world William Tyndale was born in 1484. He
studied at Oxford and Cambridge. Early it became his conviction
that it was his mission to provide the common man with the Bible
in his native tongue, and to that work he dedicated his life, becoming
the first to translate into the English from the original Greek and
Hebrew.

Tyndale sought to do his work in England, but soon found this
impossible. In his own words, "I vnderstode at the laste, not only
that there was no rowme in my lorde of londons palace to translate
the new testamente, but also that there was no place to do it in all
englonde." Therefore, in 1524, he went to the free city of Hamburg,

and may have visited Luther at Wittenberg. In 1525 he began the printing of the New Testament at Cologne. Cochlaeus, a bitter enemy of all reform, learned what Tyndale was doing, and set the authorities to work to suppress the publication. By good fortune Tyndale, with his amanuensis, Roye, escaped to Worms with the printed sheets.

At Cologne Tyndale had begun the printing of a quarto edition of the New Testament with notes, but since Cochlaeus had sent to England a description of the publication, Tyndale laid this aside and printed an edition of 3000 copies of an octavo edition without notes, and, following this, he finished the edition begun at Cologne. Both were smuggled into England, hidden in cases of merchandise. On reaching England the copies were sold rapidly among the common people. The ecclesiastical authorities pounced upon them at once, and sought to destroy both editions. The books were bought up and burned in London, Oxford and Antwerp. But all such efforts failed to stop the work.

The enemies of vernacular translations, however, succeeding in destroying many copies. Of the quarto edition, begun at Cologne and finished at Worms, there is known today but one small fragment, which is now in the Grenville Collection in the British Museum.[92] Of the octavo edition there is one copy, perfect except the want of a title page, which is now in the Baptist College at Bristol, England, and a very imperfect copy in the library of St. Paul's, London.[93]

Tyndale revised his New Testament three times. He published the Pentateuch in 1530 and the book of Jonah in 1531, leaving other portions of the Old Testament in manuscript, which later were used by John Rogers. It is calculated that ninety per cent of the words of the New Testament today are from Tyndale's translation.

For this work of translation he was strangled and burned at the stake in 1536, his last words being, "Lord, open the king of England's eyes." Tyndale, however, had won his fight for the right of the common man to have the Scriptures in his own vernacular; for, although he did not live to provide it, he had created conditions that insured that others would do it. To Tyndale more than to any other man the English-speaking world is indebted for the English Bible of today; he set the standard and determined the style.

[92] Published in facsimile with valuable introduction by Edward Arber in 1871.
[93] The perfect copy was reproduced in facsimile in 1862 by F. Fry, reprinted by G. Offer in 1936, and reprinted in America by J. P. Dabney in 1837.

To Myles Coverdale, however, belongs the honor of the first whole Bible printed in English,[94] the 400th anniversary of which was celebrated by the English-speaking world quite universally and appropriately in 1935.

Coverdale was born in 1488, studied at Cambridge, where, in 1531, he received the degree of Doctor of Canon Law. He was made a priest in 1514, soon becoming a Protestant. Early he formed a deep friendship with Thomas Cromwell, with whom he was in intimate association as early as 1527; and it was under his patronage that Coverdale made his translations. Cromwell was King Henry's chief officer, under various titles, exercising a profound influence. There exists an undated letter to Cromwell in which Coverdale solicits his assistance: "For now I begyne to taste of Holy Schryptures: now (honor be to God) I am sett to the most swete smell of holy lettyres, with the godly savour of holy and awncyent Doctoures, unto whose knowledge I cannot attayne, without dyversyte of bookys, as is not unknown to your most excellent wysdome. Nothying in the world I desyre but books as concerning my lernynge. They once had, I do not dowte but Allmyghty God schall perfourme that in me, whych He, of Hys most plentyfull favour and grace, haith begone".[95] There is no doubt that Cromwell encouraged and assisted him all he could.

It should be interesting to know that the first whole Bible printed in English was born in exile. England finally distinguished herself for her zeal in printing and circulating the Scriptures, but she was late in getting started in such work. Germany had a vernacular Bible as early as 1465, Italy in 1471, France in 1474 and Bohemia in 1488, but no Bibles were printed in England until 1537.

So Coverdale's Bible was put out, not in England, but on the continent somewhere, and the imprint states that the book was "Prynted in the yere of our Lord 1535, and fynished the fourth daye of October." Where this Bible was printed has never been determined, except that it was abroad, and who the printers were is unknown. It is known that Froschover of Zurich printed an edition of this Bible in 1550, and this fact, with other things, has led some authorities to think that he put out the original edition. But the authorities are not agreed. It seems that the work was done by Froschover of Zurich, or by Jacob van Meteren of Antwerp.

The first edition appeared with a dedication to Henry VIII, signed

---

[94] A reprint of this edition was issued by Baster in 1838.
[95] Eadie, *The English Bible*, Vol. I., p. 258.

by Myles Coverdale, and without so much as the king's license, but it was not suppressed. Coverdale did not pretend that his Bible was a translation from the original languages. The first edition indicated that it had been translated "out of Douche (German) and Latyn." This expression in the title page was eliminated in the second edition, but authorities are not agreed as to the reason. Coverdale made clear that he translated from "fyue sundry interpreters." Scholars are generally agreed that these five sources are: (1) the German-Swiss version of Zwingli and Leo Juda, published in 1524-29; (2) the Latin version of Pagninus, published in 1528; (3) the German version of Luther, published 1522-34; (4) the Latin Vulgate; and (5) Tyndale's translations, the New Testament, published 1525 and later, and the Pentateuch, published 1529-30. Tyndale's work was used with considerable revision. Because this Bible was so largely a translation from a translation, it does not rank as the primary version of the English Bible, that honor being given to what is known as Matthew's Bible.

While Coverdale was a devoted Protestant, he was more conciliatory than Tyndale, and was, therefore, willing to make haste more slowly; and his Bible, with certain ecclesiastical terms restored, or at least used interchangeably with the terms used by Tyndale, so far met the requirements of all parties that his Bible became popular, for only a year after Tyndale's death, 1537, two editions of Coverdale's Bible appeared, bearing the statement, "set forth with the Kynges most gracious licence." These were a folio and a quarto edition, the folio being the first Bible printed in England.

Tyndale had been forced to print his New Testament abroad and smuggle it into England the best way he could, and thousands of copies had been burned in an effort to destroy it. He died at last praying the Lord to open the eyes of the king of England, and so twelve years after the printing of his New Testament and one year after his death, the whole Bible in English was printed and distributed in England with the king's approval.

Thomas Cromwell was executed in 1540, and Coverdale found it convenient to leave England, shortly afterward marrying Elizabeth Mucheson, a sister-in-law of Dr. Joannes Macchabaeus MacAlpinus, who had assisted in translating the Danish Bible. While in exile he assumed the name of Michael Anglus. He returned to England in 1548 and was made a bishop in 1551, but under Mary he was deprived of his see, and found himself in trouble. Through the influence of Christian III, king of Denmark, he was permitted to

ave England, Coverdale's brother-in-law MacAlpinus having in-
erceded with the king to use his influence in Coverdale's behalf. He
ied at the age of 81.

While the world owes more to Tyndale for the English Bible of
oday than to any other man, the next greatest debt is due Myles
Coverdale. These two men seem to have been a sort of complement
f each other; and because of their work the whole Bible in English
vas given to the world in such form and character as to win
vorld-wide acceptance. Coverdale's contribution consisted chiefly in
peautiful language, felicitious turns of expression, his work being
preeminent in beauty and melody. One grave injustice is done
Coverdale. He is often said to have used Tyndale's translations with
ery slight revision; but this is hardly true. He revised it rather
reely and his revisions are generally improvements, showing his
peculiar gift in smoother sentences and beautiful phrasing. Much
of the beauty of the King James Version came from him. Among
he renderings owed to him are: "Seek the Lord while he may be
ound, call upon him while he is nigh." [96] "My flesh and my heart
aileth, but God is the strength of my heart and my portion forever." [97] "Thou, Lord, in the beginning hast laid the foundations
of the earth, and the heavens are the work of thy hands. They shall
perish but thou shalt endure: they all shall wax old, as doth a gar-
ment, and as a vesture shalt thou change them, and they shall be
changed. But thou art the same, and thy years shall not fail." [98]

Moreover, Coverdale deserves great credit for giving the world its
first printed Bible in English. He was an honest and good man, and
remarkably popular as a preacher.

The second Bible printed in English was prepared by John Rogers,
a graduate of Oxford, who became chaplain to the "English
House" in Antwerp, where Tyndale was living. He and Tyndale
became warm friends, and before his death Tyndale turned over to
him his unpublished translations, consisting of Joshua to Second
Chronicles inclusive.

Rogers prepared a revision of the whole Bible which was published
in 1537, probably in Antwerp, bearing the king's license; and this
has been said to be the first Bible licensed by Henry VIII. This
Bible consisted of Tyndale's Old Testament from Genesis to second
Chronicles inclusive—using Tyndale's unpublished manuscript—and
the rest of the Old Testament, including the apocrypha, was taken

[96] Isa. 55:6. [97] Psa. 73:26. [98] Psa. 102:25-27.

from Coverdale's Bible; the New Testament was Tyndale's last revision of 1535. The whole was slightly revised, and provided with introductions and notes, some controversial.

This Bible was published under the name of Thomas Matthew, but just why scholars have not agreed. Some think Matthew the name of some man who aided in the enterprise, while others think Thomas Matthew was simply a pseudonym used for Rogers. Since there is evidence that Rogers used such pseudonym, this is probably the explanation. In any event, it would not have been wise to publish it under the name of Tyndale, whose it was chiefly. This is recognized as the primary English version of the Bible; from it has descended the regular line of revisions since. John Rogers became the first martyr under "bloody Mary."

In the regular line of succession, the Great Bible, so called from its size, was the second, although it was the third English Bible printed. Coverdale retained a close connection with Thomas Cromwell as long as Cromwell lived; and it was he who engaged Coverdale for the preparation of the Great Bible, which was published in 1539, being a revision of Matthew's Bible, rather than of Coverdale's Bible of 1535.

Henry VIII had proscribed Tyndale's New Testament in 1525, and within a year after his martyrdom, which the king, at least, made no effort to prevent, he had authorized the sale of two Bibles containing Tyndale's work. It would be interesting to know just how much of these facts were in the king's possession. It is interesting to speculate on the chief motive of Cromwell in his effort to provide another revision of the Bible. Was he inspired mainly with the hope of a better translation, or chiefly did he seek to turn the king's mind in a direction that would make it less likely that he would discover that he had authorized Tyndale's work under other names?

Coverdale seems to have been deficient in Hebrew and Greek scholarship, and the title page of the Great Bible informs us that experts in these languages aided in its preparation. The work, however, is mainly a revision of Matthew's Bible; the Old Testament, on the basis of Sebastian Munster's Latin translation of 1535, and the New Testament, by the use of the Latin version of Erasmus and the Latin Vulgate.

Printing of this Bible was begun in Paris by Francis Regnault, because, at that time, there was no press in England fitted to do such work. Cromwell obtained a license from the king of France, authorizing Coverdale and Richard Grafton, the London printer, to print and transmit this Bible to England. They arranged with Regnault to do the work. The undertaking went forward for seven or eight months unmolested, when the Inquisition interfered, seizing many of the printed sheets, a part of which was recovered later. Cromwell then brought over to England types and presses, and the work was finished in London by Richard Grafton and Edward Whitechurch.

Henry VIII ordered the Great Bible to be placed in all the churches, and this is the only "authorized version" in English ever issued in England. The King James Version never had any claim to such title, and the Bishops' Bible was authorized only by the Convocation, and not by the queen. The Great Bible was published in numerous editions, and underwent more or less revision from time to time, enjoying a reign of thirty-eight years. The usual order of the books of the Bible in English is that of the Latin Vulgate; but the first Bible in English to follow that order completely was the Great Bible of 1539.

Several beautiful expressions and phrases have come to us from this Bible, such as "through the valley of the shadow," and "I will dwell in the house," [99], "born from above," [100], and "scapegoat".[101]

This Bible, as a whole, was probably never used in America; but parts of it have had extensive use here. The Book of Common Prayer in the English Church, prepared in 1549, took its Gospels and Epistles, and also its Psalms from this Bible; and thousands of copies of the English Prayer Book were brought to America. In 1662 the Gospels and Epistles of the Prayer Book were conformed to the King James Version; but the Psalms of the Great Bible are still in use. The Prayer Book of the Episcopal Church of America also uses these Psalms. Several efforts have been made to revise them, but no proposed changes have been accepted, either in England or in America.

B.   SECOND ENGLISH BIBLE PROBABLY THE GENEVA

It is our opinion that the Geneva was the second Bible in English brought to America, and that it probably came to Jamestown in 1607, but there is no proof. Just when the first copy came over is a matter of conjecture. There seems little room to doubt that the first ministers of Virginia were Puritans, and we would expect them to bring this Bible. Strachey who came to Virginia in 1609 used the Geneva Bible in writing his history of Virginia, and probably

[99] Psalm 23.   [100] John 3:3.   [101] Lev. 16:8.

brought this Bible with him. Alexander Whitaker, who came over in 1611, and who became the most powerful minister of this early colony, used the Geneva Bible, and doubtless brought a copy with him. It is a well known fact that the Pilgrims brought copies of the Geneva Bible to Plymouth in 1620, it having been the Bible used by Pastor Robinson in Leyden.[102]

Use of the Geneva Bible in America

Being a Puritan Bible, the Geneva would be used throughout the early colonies wherever English-speaking Puritans were found. New England used it extensively and the Plymouth colony used it exclusively. These facts are proved by the writings and sermons of the times.[103] Governor Bradford's history quotes the Geneva. Certain Puritans, however, used the King James Version in New England as early as 1630. Sermons and other writings prove that the Geneva Bible was used in Virginia at an early day. How long it continued to be used is difficult to say. The last edition seems to have been published in 1644, though it was used long after this; but, of course, when it could no longer be had, its use became restricted. Wright mentions numerous Geneva Bibles in use in the colonial era, among which are two copies that were brought over on the Mayflower.[104] The Pilgrim Society of Plymouth, Massachusetts, has three copies, the best known being the one which belonged to Governor Bradford, and was printed in London in 1592. John Cotton had a copy of the Geneva Bible.[105]

History of the Geneva Bible

When Mary Tudor became queen of England, in 1553, no less than 800 people escaped to the continent before the storm broke. Among their number were five bishops, five deans, and fifty eminent divines, many of the most prominent and best citizens of England. Out of Mary's persecution issued the Geneva Bible, which, in a few years, became the household book of England and Scotland. To understand the popularity of this Bible, it is necessary to know

[102] Bacon, *Genesis of the Church*, pp. 284-85 and note 1.
[103] Shea in *American Catholic Quarterly Review*, Vol. III, pp. 136-38.
[104] *Historic Bibles*, p. 65-7.
[105] *Massachusetts Historical Proceedings, 18, 363, 41, 167.*

something of the veneration in which Geneva, where it was translated and published, was held in the Protestant world. Geneva early became a free city, and then it became Protestant. Her destiny was entrusted to John Calvin, who soon brought it to rank with Wittenberg, home of Luther. From Italy, France, England and Germany, students flocked to her schools. Refugees from everywhere found asylum here. It was not only the home of John Calvin, but Theodore Beza, recognized as the most prominent Biblical scholar of his day, lived here also.

A New Testament was published at Geneva, in 1557, and though it appeared anonymously, it was translated by William Whittingham, who had distinguished himself at Oxford. He succeeded John Knox as pastor of the English Church at Geneva, and later was made dean of Durham, though a layman who had never been ordained.

The Geneva Bible was published at Geneva in 1560, being the third in regular line of revision. It is a pity that so little seems to be known concerning exactly who were the men engaged in this work. It has been credited to no less than nine different men, but it is impossible that all the nine mentioned had any part in it. William Whittingham was undoubtedly the chief translator. Probably he had associated with him only two other men who rendered any extensive service [106]: Thomas Sampson, who was also an Oxford man, and Anthony Gilbey, a Cambridge man. They tell us that they worked "two years and more, day and night." The necessary expenses were borne by the Geneva congregation, "such as were of most ability."

This Bible, in its Old Testament, was a revision of the Great Bible; the New Testament a revision of that published in 1557, which had been a revision of Tyndale's New Testament, as found in Matthew's Bible. The Geneva Bible was unquestionably the most satisfactory and scholarly translation produced up to its time.

The Geneva Bible was the first in English to use verse numbers, italics for words not found in the originals, and the first printed in Roman type, these features being copied from the New Testament of 1557. The division of the Bible into chapters and verses is no part of the originals, and no one thing has been more unfortunate in connection with the Bible than its arrangement into verses, and its printing as if every verse was a separate paragraph. Nothing else contributed so much to the conception of the Bible as being a col-

[106] Anderson, *The Annals of the English Bible,* pp. 455-6.

lection of texts for doctrinal purposes. Its only advantage is that it makes reference easy.

It is often called the Breeches Bible because of its translation of Genesis 3:7, which reads: "They sewed figge tree leaues together, and made themselues breeches." This translation, however, is not peculiar to this Bible; Wiclif's Bible uses the word "breeches". Other translations use "aprons."

The explanatory notes of this Bible were Calvinistic, and a Calvinistic catechism was added after the edition of 1579. Its usefulness was further enhanced by maps, tables, woodcuts, and an appendix of metrical Psalms. Being published in small sizes and at moderate prices, it was easily accessible to the common people.

The Geneva Bible soon became the family Bible of England and Scotland, being the first Bible ever printed in Scotland. While it was frowned on by the ecclesiastical authorities, it won its way into the hearts of the people for three quarters of a century, and against two powerful competitors, backed by ecclesiastical authority—the Bishops' Bible and the King James Version. It was also the Bible of the Puritan ministers. No less than 160 editions were published. The long popularity of the Geneva Bible was something quite remarkable in that day, finding parallels only in Wyclif's manuscript Bible, and in Tyndale's New Testament. Wyclif's Bible was used from 1380 to 1525, and Tyndale's New Testament from 1525 to 1605, the date of the last edition as noted by Cotton.

Among the beautiful expressions inherited from the Geneva Bible are, "At the name of Jesus Christ every knee shall bow," [107] and "Remember now thy Creator in the days of thy youth." [108]

One thing marred this version. Its translators had not learned to respect the rights of conscience; they knew no such thing as religious liberty, or even toleration. The book was dedicated to Queen Elizabeth, and exhorted her to show no mercy to Roman Catholics. It is perhaps too much to expect men to be ahead of their times.

The Geneva Bible was never revised, but a fresh revision of the New Testament by Laurence Tomson, published in 1576, at once became very popular, being reprinted twelve times in less than a dozen years; and in 1587 it supplanted the regular Geneva New Testament, in an edition of the Geneva Bible. Hereafter most editions of the Geneva Bible contained Tomson's New Testament.

Tomson was of Magdalen College, Oxford, a professor of Hebrew in Geneva and familiar with a dozen languages. Theodore Beza ex-

[107] Phil. 2:10.   [108] Eccl. 12:1.

CHARLES THOMSON

ercised a profound influence at Geneva at this time, and Tomson's revision represents in fullest measure Beza's influence.

In 1643 there was published in England "The Soldier's Pocket Bible". This contained texts of Scripture "which doe shew the qualifications of his inner man, that is a fit Souldier to fight the Lord's Battels." Nearly all the passages were taken from the Geneva Bible, and published in pamphlet form for the use of Cromwell's troops. This publication is of special interest to Americans, because about 50,000 copies—five distinct editions—a reprint of this Bible, were published in America and distributed among the Federal troops during the Civil War.[109]

C. THIRD ENGLISH BIBLE PROBABLY THE KING JAMES VERSION

The third Bible in English brought to America was probably the King James Version; but when the first copy came over can only be conjectured. It seems reasonable to suppose that it began to be used in America soon after its appearance in 1611. Virginia, it would seem, might have had copies first; but if it was used there early we have no proof.

Use of the King James Version in America

The first copy of the King James Version to come to America, of which we have any knowledge, was one brought by John Winthrop in 1630, it being the edition of 1614.[110] Henry Dunster, the president of Harvard College, also had a copy of the King James Version.[111] Probably there were many copies of this version throughout New England in an early day, and elsewhere.

Virginia was made a royal colony in 1624, and, although the Puritan influence remained quite strong, it is more than likely that from this date, at least, the King James Version was used quite extensively there. This version won its way against the Geneva slowly in England, and probably did the same in America. In time, however, it came into universal use among English-speaking Protestants; and then it reigned without a rival for more than 200 years.

---

[109] *Historical Catalogue,* Darlow and Moule, pp. 198—D. M. 447.

[110] *Massachusetts Historical Society Proceedings,* I, 277n., 54. 1.

[111] Dunster's copy of the King James Version is now in the Harvard College Library.

History of the King James Version

The King James Version resulted from the Hampton Court Conference. When James I became king of England there were two parties in the English Church, the Ritualists and the Puritans. The latter, not satisfied with certain requirements to which they were subjected, petitioned the new king for relief. The Hampton Court Conference was set for January 14, 16 and 18, 1604, to consider the matter. It soon became evident that the king would grant no favors to the Puritans. Dr. Reynolds, a distinguished professor at Oxford and a Puritan, suggested a new revision of the Bible. The king agreed. Just why he accepted a suggestion from such a source is difficult to determine; but, before the end of June following, a list of suitable translators was selected, suggested probably by the Universities, totaling 54 names, only 47 of whom seem to have taken part in the work. Preparations seem to have been completed by the end of the year 1604; the work, however, was not formally begun until 1607. Certain men may have begun their work before that time. According to the translators "about two years and three-quarters" were spent in the revision.

The committee was undoubtedly composed of men representing the best scholarship of the age. A singular broadmindedness governed the selection of this committee. All classes of the ministry of the church were represented; even Puritan scholarship was asked to make its contribution. All the most learned men of England were asked to make suggestions and criticisms for use in the work, thereby enlisting the universal interest of the scholarly.

This Bible is generally known as the "Authorized Version," which seems to be a misnomer. The title page was evidently modelled after previous Biblical titles, and, therefore, the legend "appointed to be read in churches", was used. While this legend is almost always used in this version today, and appeared in the original edition, it was often omitted from early issues.[112] No evidence has ever been found to indicate that this version was ever authorized by the king, the state or any ecclesiastical court. King James appointed a committee to make the translation, giving certain rules to govern in the work, and that seems to be all.

[112] This legend was not used even in the folio edition of the New Testament in 1611, and was omitted from the first octavo Bible, the second quarto, the folio of 1616 in Roman letters, the quarto of 1613-12, the octavos of 1615, 1617, 1621 and others. See Dore, *Old Bibles* p. 326.

Several things contributed to the long and universal popularity of this version. In the first place, it was unquestionably a decided improvement over any previous version. The men who made it had a higher grade of Hebrew and Greek scholarship than any previous translators; it was made by a large committee, representing all shades of opinion in the English Church; and it was made at a time when the sense of literary style and literary taste were much more developed than at any previous time. It deserved to displace all others.

In the second place, it contained no notes or comments, but consisted of the bare text, with such additional marginal renderings as were felt necessary to throw additional light on certain Hebrew and Greek words. Bibles previously had generally contained numerous notes and comments, which had often rendered them obnoxious to certain people. Especially was this true of the Geneva Bible, the one then in most general use among the Puritans. King James hated the Geneva Bible because of its notes, some of which were not in keeping with his ideas of the divine right of kings. For that reason he directed as one rule, governing the translators, that no notes or comments should be used. His reasons were doubtless purely political; he did not propose to take the risk of having any notes appended which might question his authority; but it served a splendid purpose in providing the public with a Bible containing nothing to which anybody could object. The Geneva version lost its influence sooner than it otherwise would because of its notes.

In the third place, after the restoration of the Stuarts in 1660, moral conditions in England became so terrible that interest in Biblical revision was practically lost. Fashionable society had grown weary of Puritan restraints and fairly reveled in the new freedom. The Puritans were persecuted and their principles of morality and religion trampled under foot. While this was true of royalty and its chief supporters, there remained an undercurrent of deep Christian principles, but it was so far crushed that no authoritative revision of the Bible could have been undertaken. This left the King James Version to come into world-wide use among English-speaking Christians.

While there is no doubt that this version might have been improved in the century in which it was made, there had not been accumulated at that time sufficient materials to have made a really worth while revision; and it is fortunate that this version, like the Geneva which it displaced, became finally the Bible of the common people. It would be difficult to overestimate the influence of this version on literature and religion. For centuries every English author, whether of prose or poetry, bears marks of its influence. Newspapers and books, everywhere, even today, are literally full of phrases borrowed from it. "Salt of the earth," "labor of love," "handwriting on the wall," "the widow's mite," "the apple of his eye," "the powers that be," "a mess of pottage," "all things to all men," "the fat of the land," "the laborer is worthy of his hire," "whited sepulchers," "vanity of vanities," "as a lamb to the slaughter," "weighed in the balances," "the wings of the wind," "blind guides," "pearls before swine," "filthy lucre," and "we are the people" are only a few of the expressions of common everyday life that came from this Bible. Its influence on religion was even greater. It has been "universally accepted as a literary masterpiece and most beautiful book in the world".[113]

Unfortunately the King James Version came finally to be considered as itself divinely inspired, and the idea is not entirely gone even today. In fact, many people, who ought to be more intelligent, seem to think that the King James Version is the original Bible which God handed down out of heaven, all done up in English by the Lord himself. Very naturally those who so regard this version feel that there is a peculiar sacredness about it, which is well-nigh sacrilegious to change. The amount of such ignorance among people who are supposed to be intelligent is astounding.

Yet the King James Version is the tenth revision of the whole Bible in English,[114] the seventh Protestant revision in English, and the fifth in the regular line of revisions, and has no more sacredness than the others.

People who so venerate the King James Version imagine that what they have today is an exact duplicate of that which appeared originally, but such is not the case. In fact, two separate editions were put out in 1611, and even they differed. The most famous difference between these two issues is found in Ruth 3:15, where we read in one: "he went into the city", and in the other, "she went into the city." Because of this fact these two editions are known as the "He" Bible and the "She" Bible.

[113] Hoare, *Our English Bible,* p. 241.

[114] The regular line of revisions in English are: Matthew's Bible, 1537; the Great Bible, 1539; the Geneva Bible, 1560; the Bishops' Bible, 1568; the King James Version, 1611. Two Protestants had made translations not in the regular line: Coverdale, 1535, and Taverner in 1539. Three Catholic translations in English had been made: Wyclif's, 1382, Purvey's, 1388, and the Rheims-Douai, in 1582-1610.

This version has been revised several times, three of which occurred within 37 years after it first appeared, in 1615, 1629, and 1638. Then Dr. Paris revised it for Cambridge in 1762 and Dr. Blayney revised it for Oxford in 1768.

Very many changes from the original have been made, and they may be illustrated in the use of italics. In the Gospel of Matthew, in the original edition of 1611, there were 43 italicised words and phrases; but these were gradually increased in number until, in the Cambridge Paragraph Bible of 1870, there were a total of 583.[115]

Besides all this, silently through the years innumerable changes have been introduced, many of them being real improvements. The spelling has been modernized. The average man would have difficulty in reading an original copy. He would find numerous unfamiliar words, such as "creeple," "ayre," "middes," "thorow," "murther," "fornace," "ancres," "damosel," "moe," "fet," "Moyses," "Hierusalem," and "Gethsemani." Numerous misprints have crept into the text. The most famous misprint of all history is found in this Bible. Matthew 23:24 reads, "strain at a gnat," when it should read "strain out a gnat."

Finally the King James Version, when it was first published, contained the apocrypha, which continued to be printed with it for more than 200 years; and it was considered of such vital importance, when the version was made, that Archbishop Abbott, one of its translators, issued an order in 1615, forbidding the sale of Bibles without the apocrypha, on pain of imprisonment for a year. If people would have the King James Version as it appeared originally, they must have a copy containing the apocrypha.

While the King James Version was unquestionably the best translation of the Bible in English in its day, it is now thoroughly antiquated and even misleading. Biblical scholarship since 1611 has made great advance; Hebrew and Greek are much better understood now. The discovery of thousands of manuscripts, many very ancient, and other sources of information, unknown in King James' day, now make it possible to provide a text of the Hebrew and Greek much nearer the originals. Moreover, the King James Version contains more than 200 words now completely obsolete, or so changed in meaning that the average man is misled when he reads them. Who knows what is meant when he reads such words as "habergeon", "wimples", "cracknel", "besom", "leasing", "botch", "neesing"?

[115] Dore, *Old Bibles*, p. 340.

In the King James Version the Hebrew word *Sheol* is translated "pit" three times, "grave" 31 times, and "hell" 31 times, and all are mistranslations. The Christian "hell" was entirely unknown to Old Testament writers, and the average man is misled. The Greek word *hades* in the New Testament is translated "hell" ten times, but this word never means "hell" anywhere, and the average man is misled again. The average man reads in the King James Version such words as "damned", "damnation," and he knows what the words mean today, but he has no idea what they meant when used in the King James Version. He reads such words as "prevent", "conversation," "carriages," "let", "mortify," "thought," and "usury," and knows their meaning today, but he has no idea of their meaning in King James' day, and he is misled again. He reads about "witches", and the fabled "unicorn," but such things do not even exist.

The King James Version when first published contained a rather lengthy preface, very valuable, but which has regularly been omitted for centuries, so that the average man never saw it and has no idea of its existence. Much of the ignorance concerning this version is due to this omission. Dr. Edgar J. Goodspeed considers the matter of such importance that he has recently published this preface, properly edited, for the public benefit. If the general public would only read this preface extensive ignorance concerning this version would be avoided.

Thousands of people who pride themselves on having the latest and best of everything else, when they buy a Bible, insist on having the most antiquated, out of date and misleading Protestant translation in English in print today.

D.   FOURTH ENGLISH BIBLE PROBABLY THE RHEIMS-DOUAI

Brought by Roman Catholics to Maryland

Roman Catholics settled Maryland in 1634, under Cecelius Calvert, the second Lord Baltimore. Shea says the priests under him brought the Rheims-Douai Bible to America with them.[116] Whether Shea had documentary evidence to support his statement, or simply surmised it, makes no difference. Catholics brought this Bible over then or later and, in any event, it became the fourth Bible in English in America. This colony contained many Protestants, and there

---

[116] *American Catholic Quarterly Review*, Vol. III, p. 136.

s as much probability, perhaps, that the King James Version came
over in 1634 as there is that the Rheims-Douai came at that time.

History of the Rheims-Douai Bible

Like the Geneva Bible, the Rheims-Douai was translated by men
who were in exile for their religion. When Mary Tudor came to
the throne England became Catholic again, and the fires of Smith-
field were soon kindled. Protestants fled to the continent and made
the Geneva Bible, and when Elizabeth became queen, Catholics
fled to the continent and produced the Rheims-Douai.

Many English Catholics settled at Douai in Flanders, in 1568, establishing a seminary for the training of priests. Because of political disturbances, the seminary was removed to Rheims in France,
returning to Douai in 1593.

The work of translation was done at Rheims and the New Testament published there, in 1582, while the Old Testament was published almost thirty years later, in 1609-10, at Douai—hence the
name Rheims-Douai.

A very important point to be observed in connection with this
Bible is that it was a translation of the Latin Vulgate, and not from
the Hebrew and Greek originals, from which all Protestant translations were made. Catholics preferred the Latin Vulgate because it
had been the Bible of their church for a thousand years. Although
itself a translation, it was considered superior to the originals,
which it was charged had been corrupted.

The moving spirit of the work was William Allen, who had been
a fellow of Oriole College, Oxford, and the canon of York under
Mary Tudor. His untiring zeal for Catholicism was rewarded with
a cardinal's hat in 1587. The translation was made under the direction of Gregory Martin, who received his master's degree from
Oxford. He became divinity reader at Rheims. His death is said to
have been greatly hastened by the long, hard task of this translation.
Richard Barstow was another of the company. He was of Christ
Church, Oxford, and then fellow of Exeter College, becoming divinity reader at Douai, and afterward at Rheims, where he prepared the
notes for the New Testament.

Thomas Worthington prepared the notes for the Old Testament.
He studied at Oxford, joining the party at Douai, and later becoming president of the college at Rheims.

Among all the English versions of the Bible ever made no other has been so unintelligible, being greatly marred by Latinisms. Numerous terms, impossible of understanding by the common man, are used, such as "pasche", "bread of proposition", "depositum", "parasceue", "prepuce", "tentation", "perigrination", "preoccupated" and "coinquinations". A few examples of the text will be of interest:

"Before your thornes did vnderstand the old bryar: as liuing so in wrath he swalloweth them." [117]

"Thou hast fatted my head with oyle; and my chalice inebriating how goodly it is!" [118]

"The Syrach owls shall answer there in the house thereof, and mermaids in the temples of pleasure".[119]

"Give vs to day our supersubstantial bread".[120]

"And Ioseph bying sindon, and taking him downe, wrapped him in the sindon, and laid him in a monument." [121]

"Vntil the day wherein giuing commaundement by the Holy Ghost to the Apostles whom he chose, he was assumpted: to whom he shewed also him self aliue after his passion in many arguments." [122]

"Purge the old leauen, that you may be a new paste, as you are azymes".[123]

"Let vs cleanse our selues from al inquinatio of the flesh and spirit." [124]

"And contristrate not the holy Spirit of God".[125]

"But he exiniated him self, taking the forme of a seruant".[126]

"And beneficence and communication do not forget, for with such hostes God is promerited." [127]

"Euery spirit that dissolueth Iesus is not of God".[128]

While this translation abounded in such renderings as these, there were many splendid translations, and the Rheims New Testament influenced to a considerable extent the King James Version.[129]

This version used the verse numbers which first appeared in English in the Geneva, but it does not make of each verse a paragraph, as had been done in both the Geneva and the Bishops' Bible, and as later was done in the King James Version. The verse numbers were placed in the margins, an arrangement decidedly preferable.

[117] Psa. 58:10. [118] Psa. 22:5—(Prot. Psa. 23:5). [119] Isa. 13:22. [120] Matt. 6:11. [121] Mark 15:46. [122] Acts 1:2-3. [123] I Cor. 5:7. [124] II Cor. 7:1. [125] Eph. 4:30. [126] Phil. 2:7. [127] Heb. 13:16. [128] I John 4:3. [129] Carleton, *The Part of the Rheims in Making the English Bible,* 1902.

Certain of the notes accompanying this version, especially those of the New Testament, were very bitter; but it should be remembered that it was made in the days of angry controversy, and its translators, like those of the Geneva version, had not learned religious liberty or even toleration.

This translation was not made because those engaged in the work were anxious to provide the common man with the Scriptures in his vernacular. They did not believe it wise for the common man to read the Scriptures, and would have prevented it, had it been possible. They were honest, but mistaken in such opinion. Protestants were freely providing vernacular translations in spite of all opposition, and the people were reading them freely. The growing demand for such among Catholics finally forced them to provide an English translation. But when it was published no Catholic was permitted to read it until he had obtained a special license from the proper authorities. This enabled them to withhold it from such as they desired.

The second edition of the New Testament was published in 1600, the third in 1621 and the fourth in 1633. The Douai Old Testament appeared in a second edition in 1635, and was not again issued for 115 years.

Ignorance, superstition and a want of toleration were not all on one side. The Rheims New Testament and its notes provoked bitter opposition in England, and many copies were seized and confiscated by Elizabeth's searchers. Priests were imprisoned, if found with a copy; even torture was used on those who would circulate it.

William Fulke, master of Pembroke Hall, was appointed to prepare a suitable Protestant reply to its notes. His refutation was published in London, in 1589, containing the entire Rheims New Testament, and the New Testament of the Bishops' Bible, edition 1572, in parallel columns, to which were added the annotations of the Rheims version and Fulke's refutation of them. This book passed through four editions, and by such means this New Testament was widely circulated among Protestants.

The Rheims-Douai Bible has been revised several times, the most important perhaps being that of Richard Challoner, in 1749-50. His revision has been the one most used by English speaking Catholics, though there are several other versions that have been used. It was his revision that was first published in America in 1790. This Bible is still known as the Rheims-Douai, although the versions in use differ very widely from the original issue, both in text and notes. Cardinal Wiseman said, "To call it any longer the Doway or Rhemish version is an abuse of terms. It has been altered and modified till scarce any verse remains as it was originally published." [130]

This Bible has been used widely in America among Roman Catholics. The revision of Challoner, bearing the imprimatur of His Eminence Cardinal Gibbons, is the most commonly used.

5. DUTCH PROBABLY THE FIFTH LANGUAGE TO FURNISH A BIBLE

DUTCH TRADERS NO DOUBT HAD DUTCH BIBLES

The opinion expressed concerning the first appearance of the Dutch Bible in America is purely conjectural; but we feel that there is a high degree of probability that Dutch was the fifth language to furnish a Bible in America.

Henry Hudson, an Englishman, in the *Halfmoon,* a ship belonging to the Dutch East India Company, sailed up the Hudson River in September 1609, looking for the northwest passage to China. Thus began the Dutch occupancy of America. Trading posts were soon established at the head of navigation on the Hudson, on Manhattan Island and on the Delaware River. Real Dutch colonization did not begin, however, until 1623, when the Dutch West India Company had secured its monopoly of trade and perfected its organization. But these numerous early trading posts, and the prompt reaching out everywhere of the Dutch to capture the lucrative fur trade brought many Dutch to America. It seems reasonable to conclude that some of these numerous Dutch traders, coming to America between September 1609 and September 6, 1619 —a period of ten years—would bring their Bibles with them. They were a Christian people. If the Dutch Bible was brought within this time, it becomes the fifth language to provide a Bible in America.

The first minister of the Dutch Reformed Church, the Rev. Jonas Michaelus, arrived in 1628, organizing a church immediately with fifty members. For some years before he arrived the Dutch had been holding services where the Bible was read. Many Dutch settled in America, and Dutch Bibles were used quite extensively in an early day.

---

[130] O'Callaghan, *List of Bibles,* p. lii.

History of the Dutch Translations

The first Dutch Bible printed, not quite complete, however, was made by an unknown translator, and has been ascribed to the fourteenth century, being published in Delft in 1477.[131] Various translations of parts of the Bible followed this version.

The first complete Bible in Dutch was a translation from the German, mostly Luther's Bible, and was printed at Antwerp, in 1526, by Jacob Liesvelt. This was corrected and reprinted several times until 1546, when Charles V prohibited the edition. The version was finally based wholly on Luther's Bible.[132]

Dutch Protestantism early developed into various parties, the Reformed, the Lutherans and the Mennonites, resulting in the production of various versions of the Dutch Bible.

The Reformed Church used first a Bible published in 1556 at Emden, it being based partly on Liesvelt's Bible of 1542, but more largely on the Zurich Bible of 1548-49, and edited by Jan Gheylliaert.[133]

In 1562 there was published at Emden a Bible prepared especially for the Dutch Reformed Church, by G. van Wingen, made in part from Luther's Bible. The New Testament had been published in 1559. From 1562 to 1737 this was the accepted version of the Reformed Dutch Church.[134]

However, in 1571-72 Jan Canin published a new edition of van Wingen's Bible, and this edition is the first Bible, the sale of which was authorized by the United Provinces of the Netherlands.[135] It was often reprinted.

In time, however, the questions raised by an advancing scholarship created a demand for a new revision, and the Synod of Dort, which is said to have "made hell tremble", meeting in 1618-19, ordered such translation made. In the meantime, while this authorized version was in preparation, there was published, in 1631, at Amsterdam, a temporary and intermediate edition, intended to provide as correct a text as possible, until the new edition should be ready.[136]

As has been said, the Synod of Dort ordered that a new Dutch translation be made, and directed its preparation. This work was to be done from the originals of Hebrew and Greek, and six translators, qualified for the task, were named. But such action required

[131] D. M. 3271. [132] D. M. 3280. [133] D. M. 3289. [134] D. M. 3293. [135] D. M. 3298.
[136] D. M. 3305.

the approval of the States General, which would be expected to provide the funds, and release the translators from their usual duties. The Old Testament committee began its work in 1628 and the New Testament committee in 1630, finishing the first draft in 1632 and the final revision in 1635. While the printing was completed in 1636, it was not published until 1637, the date of its license. In this Bible the apocrypha was placed at the end of the volume.[137] In an edition published at Amsterdam, in 1657, numerous printer's errors were corrected, and the text adopted as a standard.[138] This Bible was authorized by the States General and became the standard for the Dutch Reformed Church, where it occupied the same position that Luther's Bible did among Lutherans, and the King James Version among English-speaking Protestants.

The Dutch brought to New York certain editions of the van Wingen Bible, and also the temporary edition of 1631. Copies are to be found in the libraries of the country. When the regularly authorized version appeared in 1637 they began its use in America also.

This Bible has been revised within recent times. The New Testament of a revised edition, made by the theological faculty of Leyden, was finished in 1866; the first part of the Old Testament (Gen-Esther) appeared in 1900, and the second part (Job-Malachi) in 1901.

The Dutch Lutherans used at first a Bible published at Emden in 1558.[139] It was based on the Low German Bible printed at Magdeburg, in 1554, which had been a translation from Luther's Bible. This Bible served the Dutch Lutherans until 1648. In this year a Bible was published at Amsterdam that was a revision of Bietskin's Bible,[140] having been prepared by Adolph Visscher of the Lutheran Church of Amsterdam. It became the standard Bible for Dutch Lutherans. However, they used also the Bible of van Wingen, prepared for the Reformed Church, published first in 1561-62. An edition of their standard Bible was published at Amsterdam, in 1734. These are the Dutch Bibles Lutherans brought to America.

The Dutch Mennonites used a different revision. In 1554 a New Testament appeared, probably at Amsterdam, which was a new translation, influenced somewhat by the Latin version of Erasmus, published especially for the use of the Dutch Mennonites. Another edition, with certain corrections, appeared in 1558, being several times reprinted.

[137] D. M. 3307.   [138] D. M. 3315.   [139] D. M. 3291 note.   [140] D. M. 3311.

A Bible had been published at Emden, in 1558, based on the Low German Bible printed at Magdeburg, in 1554, and which had been a translation from Luther's Bible of 1545.[141] This Bible of 1558 was reprinted at Emden, in 1560, slightly modified, omitting Luther's preface, and it became the Bible of the Dutch Mennonites. This was the first Dutch Bible with verse numbers. Doubtless some of these Bibles were brought to America.

5. DANISH PROBABLY THE SIXTH LANGUAGE TO FURNISH A BIBLE

BROUGHT BY THE FIRST LUTHERAN PASTOR

While the Danes comprise but a small part of the population of our country, they began to come early. King Christian IV sent two ships headed by a Norwegian captain, Jens Munk, and a crew of Norwegians and Danes, sixty-six men in all, to discover the northwest passage to Asia, and they rediscovered Hudson's Bay only eight years after Hudson had discovered it; landing at Churchill River September 7, 1619, they took charge of Northern Canada, calling it New Denmark. They had brought along a Lutheran pastor, the Rev. Rasmus Jensen Aarhus, he being the first Lutheran pastor in America. Munk's diary at Copenhagen records the Christian services which they held during their ice-bound winter stay. This record gives a detailed account of the Christmas service. "The Holy Christmas Day was celebrated by us all (as behooves Christians). There was preaching and mass (chanting), and after the sermon we offered gifts to the pastor according to the old custom (still in force), everyone according to his ability, even though money was not plentiful among the men, yet they gave of what they had. Some gave fox skins so that the pastor got enough to line his coat." [142]

In 1892 the United States wanted Munk's Diary for the World's Fair, offering to send a war ship to bring it over, but, being very precious in Denmark, it was not loaned lest some mishap might befall it.

Aarhus had his Bible, of course; therefore, the Danish Bible came to America first, September 7, 1619. There was in use at this time in the Danish Church, a Bible that had been prepared by a committee appointed by Christian III, and this is doubtless the ver-

---

[141] D. M. 3291.

[142] On authority of a letter from Dr. O. M. Norlie, Luther College, Decorah, Iowa.

sion first brought to America. Copies of this Bible may be found in the Morgan Library, New York City, the library of the University of Chicago, and the library of Luther College at Decorah, Iowa.

Henry Hudson, who discovered Hudson's Bay may have been a Dane, but whether he was or not, he had Danes with him. There were many Danes in the colony of New Netherlands (New York), the most noted perhaps being Jonas Bronch, whose name lives in Bronx Borough, New York, Bronx Park and Bronxville. He came to New York in 1639. Washington had Danes in his army. No better people have come to America than the Danes. Danish farmers built the first creameries, organized the first cow-testing association and the first co-operative dairy-farming on a large scale in the United States.

History of the Danish Translations

Bishop Henrik Stangeberg, who died in 1465, admonished the priests of his diocese to read the Epistle and Gospel Lessons in Danish, as a part of the regular church service, and from this fact we know that at least parts of the Bible had been translated into Danish at this early day, but all such translations have been lost.

Hans Mikkleson and Dr. Kristian Winther translated the New Testament from the Latin and Luther's version, and published it at Leipzig, in 1524, and though a poor piece of work, it had considerable use.

Christian Pederson, a distinguished scholar, translated the New Testament into Danish and published it at Antwerp, in 1529. Pederson is the father of modern Danish literature, creating a Danish literary language, as Luther created modern German. He had finished a translation of the whole Bible by 1543, and the Danish king, Christian III, appointed a committee of distinguished scholars to collaborate with him in a translation for general church use. The greater part of the work was done by Pederson. The revision occupied five years. No printer in Denmark could undertake to print it, and Ludwig Dietz was engaged for the purpose. He came to Copenhagen in 1548, and the Bible was published in 1550. Every parish church in Denmark and Norway was supplied with this Bible, and it served Denmark for centuries. All Danish Bibles up to this time had been translations from the Latin of Erasmus, or Luther's German, this last being made from Luther.

Hans Paul Resen translated the Bible for the first time into Danish from the original languages, which he published in 1607, but his work proved unsuited to church use, and a revised edition was published in 1633. Then Bishop Hans Svane revised Resen's Bible again, publishing it in 1717. A new revision of this Bible was published in 1819, and this version has been in general use among the Danes up to the present time.

In 1881 Professor Axel Sorensen made a modern speech translation of the New Testament in Danish. A new translation of the whole Bible was made by a royal commission and published in 1931, and this version is now the authorized Bible of the Danish Church.

7. THE SWEDISH BIBLE BROUGHT TO AMERICA

FIRST SWEDISH COLONISTS HAD BIBLES

A Swedish colony was planted on the Delaware River in 1638, and there seems little reason to doubt that they brought the Scriptures in their native tongue with them. One important reason for founding the colony was that they might Christianize the Indians, and people who came with such purpose would have Bibles. However, previous to 1640-41 they could have only the New Testament in Swedish, and certain parts of the Old.

History of Swedish Translations

Portions of the Bible were translated into Swedish in the fourteenth century, but the first complete New Testament was published at Stockholm in 1526, based chiefly on Luther's New Testament.[143]

Under the supervision of Laurentius Petri, Archbishop of Sweden, the Bible was translated into the Swedish language and published at Stockholm in 1540-41.[144] This was based on Luther's Bible, but other authorities were consulted. This remained the standard church Bible of Sweden for almost 400 years, or until 1917. In honor of the reigning king it was called the Gustavus Vasa Bible, a copy being provided for every church in the country.

Improvements were constantly made in the matter of helps in succeeding editions. An edition considerably improved, but with the same text, was published in 1618, and is known as the Gustavus Adolphus Bible.[145]

[143] D. M. 8806.   [144] D. M. 8808.   [145] D. M. 8810.

With practically no change in the text, but with other improvements, an edition was published in 1702-03, and is known as
Charles XII's Bible.[146] This edition being well supplied with
helps became the standard for general use, remaining so until very
recently, occupying the place in Sweden that the King James Version
occupied among English-speaking Protestants.

The advancement of scholarship in time created a demand for
a Bible with a text as required by modern discoveries and knowledge.
Commissions were appointed to prepare it. As early as 1773 a
new revision was finished, but the church rejected it. The commission was continued and other revisions were offered, only to
be turned down. Finally, a revision was accepted in 1917, after
several commissions had served over a period of 140 years. The
new revision has been authorized by the king.

The state church of Sweden is Lutheran, and colonists were
supplied with ministers from the state church. Colonists began to
come to America in 1638 and continued to arrive until 1655, a total
of twelve expeditions. It is a matter of record that between 1696
and 1750, there were sent to America for use of Swedish colonists,
at the expense of the king of Sweden, no less than 58 Bibles, editions
of 1688, 1703, 1713 and 1745. The text was the same in all these
Bibles. Through Bishop Svedberg's influence a special edition of
the Swedish Bible was printed at Skara in Sweden, in 1727-28, at
the expense of Sebastian Tham, to be given to the colonists on the
Delaware.[147]

8. THE FINNISH BIBLE BROUGHT TO AMERICA

FIRST FINNISH COLONISTS HAD BIBLES

Many Finns came to America along with the Swedes, dating back
to 1638.[148] They were originally a Mongolian race, but extensive
intermixture with the Swedes, Norwegians and Russians has given
them the appearance of the Caucasian. They are about one-fourth
Scandinavian, and are located chiefly in Minnesota and Michigan,

[146] D. M. 8817.

[147] G. N. Swan, in his *Gamala Svenske Biblar Amerike*, tells of numerous
Swedish Bibles in America, printed from 1526 on through the colonial era,
but none of those he has located seems to have belonged to the colony on the
Delaware.

[148] See E. A. Louhi's, *The Delaware Finns, or, The First Permanent Settlements
in Pennsylvania, Delaware, New Jersey and the Eastern Part of Maryland.*

NOAH WEBSTER

but scattered over the whole country there are more than 300,000 Finns in America.

Since the Finns had the New Testament in their vernacular for nearly a hundred years before they came to America, and some part of the Old Testament a shorter time, there seems little reason to doubt that they brought at least the New Testament with them, probably as early as 1638. They had the first whole Bible in their tongue in 1642.

History of Finnish Translations

Mickael Agricola, who became acquainted with Luther in Wittenberg, made a translation of the New Testament into Finnish, which was published in Stockholm, in 1543, translating later certain books of the Old Testament. In 1642 the first whole Bible in Finnish was published in Stockholm, having been prepared by a committee of prominent Biblical scholars, and made directly from the originals, but compared with Luther's Bible.

The second edition of the Finnish Bible was published in 1685, being a revision of the Bible of 1642, made by Rector Henrik Florinus. A further revision was made by Rector Anders Lizelius, assisted by others, and published in 1758. Lizelius was again appointed to prepare another edition which was published in 1776, it being a revision of the previous edition. This fourth edition became the official Bible of Finland and remained such until 1933. Other Finnish editions that were not official have been published.

Several different committees were appointed to revise the church Bible, but their work failed to secure official recognition. The change of language and the advancement of scholarship finally made revision necessary. The New Testament was finished in 1912, and the Old Testament in 1932, whereupon the Church Convention of 1933 approved this translation, and it is now the official Finnish Bible. It was made from the original texts. The Finns in America, however, use the King James Version quite extensively.

CHAPTER III

EARLY BIBLES OR PARTS IN THE COLONIAL ERA

1. EFFORTS AT PUBLICATION DEFEATED

THREE rather important efforts to publish Bibles in the colonial period failed for the want of sufficient encouragement. The first proposal to print a Bible in America was made by William Bradford of Philadelphia, who, in 1688, announced his purpose as follows:

"These are to give Notice, that it is proposed for a large house-Bible to be Printed by way of Subcriptions, (a method usual in England for the Printing of large Volumns, because Printing is very chargeable) therefore to all that are willing to forward so good (and great) a Work, as the Printing of the holy Bible, are offered these Proposals, viz.: 1. That It shall be printed in a fair Character, on good Paper and well bound. 2. That it shall contain the Old and New Testaments, with the Apocraphy, and all to have useful Marginal Notes. 3. That it shall be allowed (to them that subscribe) for Twenty Shillings *per Bible*. (A Price which one of the same volume in *England* would cost.) 4. That the pay shall be half Silver Money, and half Country Produce at Money price. One half down now, and the other half on the delivery of the Bibles . . . Also, this may further give notice that *Samuell Richardson* and *Samuell Carpenter* of *Philadelphia,* are appointed to take care and be assistant in the laying out of the Subscription Money, and to see that it be employ'd to the use intended, and consequently that the whole Work be expedited. Which is promised by William Bradford." [1]

The offer failed, however, and he removed to New York in 1693. The first portion of Scripture printed in that city came from his press in 1715, being a selection of certain parts of both the Old and New Testaments, attached to the Book of Common Prayer, printed in the Mohawk language. Furthermore, Bradford became the best printer of the entire colonial era, and a far better one than Benjamin Franklin. Authorities on early printing in America recognize the superiority of his publications. He is said to have introduced printing into the Middle Colonies, and into New York; and to have

---

[1] Wright, *Early Bibles of America*, p. 322.

published the first Book of Common Prayer[2], the one referred to above, and the first drama in America; and the first poem in New York and the first newspaper.

The most pretentious effort of the period, however, was made by Rev. Cotton Mather. Somewhere about 1695, he began the preparation of what he called *Biblia Americana*, spending fifteen years in compiling and writing notes and comments on the text. The completion of the work was announced in 1710, with the hope "that the Glorious Head of the church will stir up some generous minds to forward an undertaking so confessedly worthy to be prosecuted." No printer in the colonies, however would take the hazard involved.

Mather made a second effort to find a publisher in 1713, publishing his appeal in London, addressed mainly to London printers, but nobody there would undertake the work. He died in 1728 and, in that same year, after his death, his friends made a third attempt to find a publisher, but it also proved unsuccessful. The manuscript, in six folio volumes, now sleeps forgotten and almost unknown among the collections of the Massachusetts Historical Society.

John Fleming of Boston made still another effort that failed. Undated, but according to O'Callaghan in 1770, he published a portion of Genesis, with detached sentences from the New Testament, accompanied with his proposal to publish the Rev. Samuel Clark's edition of the Bible, announcing it as "the first undertaking of the kind ever attempted in America." It failed for the want of three hundred advance subscribers.

2. EARLY EFFORTS AT REVISION

A. THE BAY PSALM BOOK

The first book printed in America was what is commonly known as "The Bay Psalm Book" published in 1640. Its title reads: "THE WHOLE BOOKE OF PSALMES Faithfully TRANSLATED into ENGLISH Metre. Whereunto is prefixed a difcourfe declaring not only the lawfullness, but alfo the neceffity of the heavenly Ordinance of finging Scripture Pfalmes in the Churches of God . . . Imprinted 1640." The book contained no name, place or printer, but it is known to have been printed by Stephen Daye at Cambridge,

[2] The New York Public Library paid $1,300 in 1904 for a copy of this publication.

Massachusetts. The work was done on a press, the gift of friend in Holland, and was the first printing done on it. Later editions o this book came to be called, "The New England Version of th Psalms."

The work of rendering these Psalms into metre was done chiefl by Rev. Thomas Welde, Rev. John Eliot and Rev. Richard Mather who wrote the preface. Only eleven copies of the original editior are said to be known.[3]

This is a very crude specimen of English, but that is not surprising In order properly to understand and appreciate this old book, it is necessary to know that the early New England colonists were a singing people, who used music in all their social gatherings. In their religious services they also sang freely, but the Book of Psalms was given first place in musical expression in church services. They considered nothing but Scripture suitable for singing in religious worship, and, therefore, permitted no human compositions.

Those who made this book were handicapped by certain very definite restrictions. In the first place, the Hebrew Psalms must be translated or paraphrased in the metre of only a few familiar tunes. In the second place, the translation must give a faithful account of every letter and accent of the Hebrew.

The following specimen will illustrate the character of the work:

> "The earth Jehova's is
> and the fulness of it:
> The habitable world and they
> that thereupon doe sit."

This is certainly not literature, but it can be sung smoothly to some grand old short-metre tunes; and it is a splendid literal rendering of the Hebrew, which was all the makers of the book hoped to accomplish.

This book has often been pointed out "as a pitiful indication of the literary poverty of the days and the land in which it was popular."[4]

Such criticisms betray a monumental ignorance, and do a grave injustice to the makers of this translation. They had no thought of making poetry, which they tell us frankly in their preface. Their

---

[3] A reprint of 71 copies of the original edition was issued at Cambridge, Massachusetts, in 1862.

[4] See Richardson, *American Literature*, II, 3-4, 6-7.

ranslation, however, met the conditions imposed, and served the purpose intended, and that ought to be sufficient.

Moreover, putting the Psalms into English poetry is a very difficult task, and few men have made any measure of success, though hundreds have tried it. Bacon, a man of literary renown, failed wretchedly, when he tried it. The colonists essayed a new metrical version of the Psalms only because English poets, men of literary ability, had failed to produce a satisfactory one.

This book was used extensively and for many years in New England, passing through several revisions. The first edition contained nothing but the Psalms. A second edition appeared in 1647, containing a few spiritual songs, which were other portions of Scripture. The Rev. Henry Dunster, president of Harvard College, and Mr. Richard Lyon, were appointed a committee to revise and further improve it, and their edition, the third, appeared in 1650. Rev. Thomas Prince revised the book again, publishing, in Boston in 1768, an edition of 30,000 copies, containing large numbers of scriptural songs and hymns, written by Mr. Lyon. "This revised version went through numerous editions in New England: it was reprinted in England and Scotland; and was used in many English dissenting congregations, as well as in a number of the churches in Scotland. It was added to several English and Scotch editions of the Bible; and went through fifty editions, including those published in Europe."[5]

The Library of Congress owns a Gutenburg Bible, the first book printed from movable type. It is in Latin. Furthermore, the government paid about $400,000 for it, and had a bargain at the price. But this Library does not own a copy of "The Bay Psalm Book," the Gutenberg Bible of America. While only eleven copies of the original edition are known to exist, our government has had ample opportunities to buy, but a niggardly policy in such matters has prevailed. By all means the Library of Congress should own this book.

B. THE MASSACHUSETTS PSALTER

This is an edition of the Psalms in prose, prepared by the Rev. Experience Mayhew, employed for the purpose by the Commissioners of the Society for the Propagation of the Gospel among the Indians, and published at Boston in 1709. While it was based on

[5] Thomas, *History of Printing in America*, Vol. I, p. 233.

Eliot's Indian Bible, it is a revision in almost every line. This book, published in the interest of the Indians, is now very rare. It bore the title, "The Massachusetts Psalter: or, Psalms of David with the Gospel according to John, in columns of Indian and English."

C. PSALTERIUM AMERICANUM

The Rev. Cotton Mather, in 1718, published at Boston the "Psalterium Americanum: the Book of Psalms, in a Translation exactly conformed unto the Original: But all in Blank Verse, Fitted unto the Tunes commonly used in our Churches," etc. An appendix contained other portions of the Old Testament and several of the New. This was never used extensively and was published anonymously.

A specimen of this translation should be of interest:

Psalm LVIII

3. The wicked are estranged from God, || ev'n from the very womb; || they go astray as soon as born, || the speakers of a lie. ||

4. Their poison's like the poison which, || a serpent has in it; || like that of the deaf adder which || does obdurate the ear. ||

5. She will not hearken to the Voice || of any Charming one; || No, though the Charmer should be one || never so skill'd in Charms. ||

This is so arranged as to look exactly like prose, and may be read as such, and yet it is so modulated that it may be sung as lyric verse.

The most curious book perhaps ever published by Cotton Mather was one entitled "The Wonders of the Invisible World", in which he defends the reality of witchcraft.

D. THE LORD'S PRAYER

THE first translation of any part of the New Testament from the Greek into English in America was made by Rev. Samuel Mather, and printed in Boston, in 1766, by Kneeland and Adams for Wharton and Bowes. The title was "THE LORD'S PRAYER or, A New Attempt to recover the right Verfion, and genuine Meaning of that Prayer." It contained a translation of this prayer only, in the following language:

"Our Father, *who* art *in the Heavens; sanctified* be thy Name;

Thy Kingdom come; Thy Will be, done, *as in Heaven, so upon the Earth;* Give us to *Day* that our Bread, *the supersubstantial;* and forgive us *our Debts,* as we forgive *them who are our Debtors;* And *introduce us not into afflictive Trial;* but deliver us *from the wicked One: Because* thine is the Kingdom and the Power and the Glory *for the Ages:* Amen" The italics are the authors.

3. CLANDESTINE PUBLICATIONS

Isaiah Thomas, one of the most prominent citizens of his day, and a great publisher of Bibles, was honored by Dartmouth College with the master's degree, and by Alleghany College with the degree of LL.D., in recognition of his standing and service to the country. After extensive research, he wrote *The History of Printing in America,* which was published in 1810, and this book is still regarded as one of the best authorities on the subject.

A. THE ROGERS AND FOWLE NEW TESTAMENT

Thomas, in his history, tells us that, "During the partnership of Rogers and Fowle they printed an edition of about 2000 copies of the New Testament, 12mo., for D. Henchman and two or three other principal booksellers, as has been already observed. This impression of the New Testament, the first in the English language printed in this country, was, as I have been informed, completed at the press before Kneeland and Green began the edition of the Bible which has been mentioned. Zechariah Fowle, with whom I served my apprenticeship, as well as several others, repeatedly mentioned to me this edition of the Testament. He was, at the time, a journeyman with Rogers and Fowle, and worked at the press. He informed me, that on account of the weakness of his constitution, he greatly injured his health by the performance. Privacy in the business was necessary; and, as few hands were intrusted with the secret, the press work was, as he thought, very laborious. I mention these minute circumstances in proof that an edition of the Testament did issue from the office of Rogers and Fowle, because I have heard that the fact has been disputed." [6]

This New Testament was published with a London imprint because American printers could not obtain the right to print Bibles, and that fact explains the secrecy required in the work. Had they

[6] Thomas, *History of Printing,* Vol. I., p. 123, (ed. 1874).

been caught the penalty would have been severe. The books were
such close imitations of the London editions that nobody suspected
their source. All we know about this New Testament is what Isaiah
Thomas tells us; no copies of it have ever been identified. Many
have even questioned that such was ever published.

B. THE KNEELAND AND GREEN BIBLE

Isaiah Thomas says further, "The booksellers of this town were enterprising. Kneeland and Green printed principally for Daniel
Henchman, an edition of the Bible in small quarto. This was the
first Bible printed in America in the English language. It was carried through the press as privately as possible, and had the London
imprint from the copy from which it was reprinted, viz.: 'London:
printed by Mark Baskett, Printer to the King's Most Excellent Majesty,' in order to prevent a prosecution from those in England and
Scotland, who published the Bible by a patent from the Crown;
or, *Cum privilegio,* as did the Universities of Oxford and Cambridge.
When I was an apprentice (1756-1765), I often heard those who had
assisted at the case and press in printing this Bible, make mention
of the fact. The late Governor Hancock was related to Henchman
and knew of the particulars of the transaction. He possessed a copy
of this impression. As it has a London imprint at this day it can be
distinguished from an English edition, of the same date, only by
those who are acquainted with the niceties of typography. This
Bible issued from the press about the time that the partnership of
Kneeland and Green expired (1752). The edition was not large; I
have been informed that it did not exceed seven or eight hundred
copies. An edition of the New Testament, in duo-decimo, was printed by Rogers and Fowle not long before this impression of the Bible
came from the press, for those at whose expense it was issued. Both
the Bible and the Testament were well executed." [7]

Search as they would no expert, in our early history, was able to
locate a copy of this Bible, and, because of this fact, it became very
common, especially among the best authorities, to consider that
Thomas had simply been mistaken on this point, and that no such
Bible had ever been printed. George Bancroft rejected the whole
story of a clandestine publication, saying that, "to print the Bible
in British America would have been piracy and the Bible, though
printed in German and in a native dialect, was never printed there

[7] Thomas, *History of Printing,* Vol. I., p. 107 (ed. 1874).

till the land was free."[8] He refused to believe the story until a copy could be produced. Since that time it has been the almost universal opinion, both in England and America, that no such Bible was ever printed.

E. B. O'Callaghan, in his *List of Editions* [9] declines to accept Thomas' story; Wright, in his *Early Bibles in America,* rejects the story, and quotes, as contradicting it, from the back of the title page of a presentation copy of the Aitken Bible in 1782, now in the British Museum: "This first copy of the first edition of the Bible ever printed in America in the English language, is presented to Ebenezer Hazard, Esq., by the Editor," [10] which, of course, proves nothing, except that Mr. Aitken thought his Bible was the first in English in America.

In 1895 John Anderson, Jr., a prominent auctioneer of New York City, announced a Kneeland and Green Bible, dated 1761, bearing the autograph of Philip Livingston, one of the signers of the Declaration of Independence. He regarded this as a copy of a second edition of the book. The critics, however, declined to be impressed. Wright, in his *Historic Bibles,*[11] however, accepts Livingston's Bible as a genuine Kneeland and Green Bible, and includes a description of it, which he attributes to George L. Sullivan, but which was prepared by Mr. Anderson himself for the Boston *Globe.*[12]

Again in 1902, John Anderson, Jr., advertised a copy of a Kneeland and Green Bible, original edition, this time, from the library of Thomas J. McKee of New York. "We are ignorant of the claims made for the book when it was sold to Thomas Jefferson McKee. In fact, until the description of the book appears in the catalog of the McKee sale of 1902, it is not on the records. The auctioneer of the McKee sale was the distinguished John Anderson, Jr., who, if we may infer from the description in the McKee catalogue, certainly was sure that Mr. McKee had the real thing. At the McKee sale the book was bought by George C. Thomas of Philadelphia,[13] and it next appears in his sale of 1907 . . . Bought by George H. Richmond, the book reappears in Richmond's catalogue No. 120 (1910) . . . The book was then purchased by Dr. A. S. W. Rosenbach, and

[8] *History of the United States,* 11th ed. 1874, Vol. V, p. 266.
[9] pp. XIII-XVII.
[10] pp. 60-63.
[11] pp. 71-2.
[12] The writer had this information from Mr. Anderson himself.
[13] Barker, in *English Bible Versions,* p. 253, says this Bible was sold at the sale to George D. Smith, who resold it to George C. Thomas of Philadelphia.

appears in his catalogues No. 17 (1913) and No. 19 (1917) . . The end of the book's career may be found recorded in the Bulletin of the New York Public Library (XXXVI D. 308, 1932) which states that 'After holding it for some time, Dr. Rosenbach came to agree with other scholars in questioning the accuracy of the imprint, and rather than offer it for sale with this doubt attached he gave it to the (New York Public) Library as an addition to its collection of Bibles in English."

"The late learned Dr. Charles L. Nichols examined the book with great care when it was in George H. Richmond's possession. Then he wrote two articles, one in 1919 (Transactions of the Colonial Society of Massachusetts, XXI, p. 285) and the other in 1927 (Proceedings of the American Antiquarian Society, XXXVII, p. 24), in which he completely blasted the book's reputation, and proved that it was a volume actually printed in London, probably in 1763, with the date altered to read 1752." [14]

Then came the claims of Rev. Acton Griscom of New York City, who was convinced that he had solved the problem, and located genuine copies.[15] He offers an easy solution of the long difficulty in identifying this Bible. According to him, the experts had used for comparison a genuine Kneeland and Green Bible, supposing it to be a genuine London edition, and by comparison with other Kneeland and Green Bibles, found them all identical, concluding, therefore, that all were London Bibles, whereas all copies used had been the long sought edition.

In proof of his claims, he exhibits photographs of the title pages of two Bibles, both dated 1767, and both containing the London imprint of Mark Baskett. In these titles a number of differences appear. In the one he considers a genuine London edition, "Original Greek" is composed of capitals and lower case letters, while, in the other it consists of capitals only. In the genuine edition "Most excellent" is found on one line, but in the other these words are on two lines. There can be no doubt that one of the title-pages referred to by Dr. Griscom was set up in imitation of the other; but Mark Baskett might have imitated his own title-page when the type of the original became pied.

---

[14] Adams, Randolph G., in *The Colophon* New Series, Summer 1935. Vol. I New Series Number I., pp. 15-17.

[15] Myer, John Nichols, *Colonists' Bible a "Bootleg" Book,* in New York *Times,* Sunday, November 7, 1926.

Kneeland and Green are supposed to have published their Bible not later than 1752, while this Bible is dated 1767. This difference of dates, however, is explained by Mr. Griscom as due to the practice, sometimes followed by publishers, of dating the books when sold and not when printed. If Mr. Griscom be correct, there is a copy of the Kneeland and Green Bible in the Harvard Library, one in the library of the American Antiquarian Society of Worcester, Massachusetts, and several copies in the New York Public Library, besides four copies owned privately.

The critics, however, remain unconvinced as to the identity of a genuine copy of this Bible, but one of the best American authorities, and one who gave very considerable attention to this particular matter, has made a notable concession. Dr. C. L. Nichols of the American Antiquarian Society, widely recognized as an authority, read a paper before the Society in 1927, in which he conceded the publication of both the Rogers and Fowle New Testament and the Kneeland and Green Bible.[16] Dr. Nichols visited Dr. Griscom and discussed with him his claims, but was convinced that Dr. Griscom's discoveries were of absolutely no value whatever. As matters now stand, the Kneeland and Green Bible is as much of a mystery as it has ever been. With Dr. Nichols, the writer believes that such a Bible was published, and he hopes that a copy may some day be identified.

[16] Nichols, *The Boston Edition of the Baskett Bible,* 1927.

CHAPTER IV

SOME IMPORTANT BIBLES PUBLISHED IN THE EARLY REPUBLIC

1. THE SAUR GERMAN BIBLE

THE first Bible printed in America was the Eliot Indian Bible in 1663; and the second published was in German, printed by Christopher Saur [1] at Germantown, a suburb of Philadelphia, in 1743, this being the first Bible in America in any European language. Both Indian and German Bibles were published in America before the first in English, the clandestine publication of Kneeland and Green of Boston, not later than 1752, and which bore a London imprint.

Christopher Saur was born and reared in Germany, where he secured what little education he had. With his wife, he came to America in 1724, and settled in Germantown, which he left for a few years, returning in 1731. He was a deeply religious man, quite pronounced in his views, yet singularly charitable for his day. There seems to be no proof that he was ever a member of the German Baptist Church,[2] though he was undoubtedly in sympathy with it. His son Christopher, however, was a leading member of the Dunker Church of Germantown.

Numerous Germans had settled in Pennsylvania, and he sought to serve them in every possible way. They had little reading matter, and he imported books and Bibles freely for their use; but this was found quite difficult, and often very expensive. Moreover, he even induced Germans of the Fatherland to donate Bibles for the poor, which he gladly distributed.

The Germans were broken up into numerous sects. Lutherans and the Reformed groups preferred Luther's Bible; while the Ephrata Mystics, the Dunkers and Mennonites preferred the Berleberg Bible. Saur imported and sold many Berleberg Bibles along with Luther's translation, in his efforts to serve all parties.

The Berleberg Bible was in four volumes and very expensive, out of reach of the poor, in fact. Moreover, many of Luther's Bibles

[1] When writing in English Mr. Saur changed the spelling of his name to Sower, which his descendants use. The German way of spelling is used in this volume because of the spelling used in the title of his Bible.

[2] Sachse, *The German Sectarians of Pennsylvania*, Vol. II., pp. 22-3.

were in quite small type, and old people could not read them, because of failing eyesight, since glasses were almost unknown among the poor Germans. These conditions, with the difficulty and expense of importation, led Saur early to advocate the printing of Bibles in America, and in type large enough for the old to read them.

The Tunkers or Baptists of Germany raised a sum of money for the purpose of providing religious books for their friends in America, and also a printing press, with which they might print their own books. Accordingly, a quantity of books and a press were shipped to Pennsylvania, to be managed by a German named Jacob Gaus,[3] who proved incompetent for such an undertaking; and, finding nobody else capable, the business was suspended. Mr. Saur then secured the press with its equipment and began a publishing business, which he followed the rest of his life. It has been said that he imported printers from Germany.

In 1738 he printed the first German almanac in America, which was furnished the people for no less than forty years. The Germans consulted this almanac religiously for its weather predictions. A good farmer, desiring to make a trip and finding that the almanac promised "fair" weather, not doubting the prediction, made it in an open wagon and received a thorough drenching in a heavy rain. He felt that he had been imposed upon and in anger demanded an explanation of Mr. Saur, who quietly replied, "My friend, I made the almanac, but the Almighty made the weather."

Mr. Saur also began the publication of a German newspaper, using both his almanac and his newspaper to urge the publication of a German Bible, and to plead for assistance in the undertaking. His first proposal to print the Bible appeared in 1740. He appealed even to Germany for aid. Dr. H. E. Luther, a man highly educated, and a prominent type-founder of Frankfort-on-the-Main, presented him with a font of type suitable for Bible printing, asking only to receive a copy of the book when finished.

The work began as soon as the type was received, although he could print but four pages at a time; but the last sheets of an edition of 1,200 copies went to press in August, 1743.

Mr. Saur deserves very great credit for his publication of this Bible.[4] He had neither the training, experience nor financial ability for such an undertaking, and met numerous obstacles, in so doing,

---

[3] Thomas, *History of Printing in America*, Vol. I, p. 271.
[4] Wright, *Early Bibles*, pp. 380-83 lists owners of 12 copies of the Saur Bible in Europe, and 119 copies in the United States.

that could not have been surmounted by one of less resourcefulness and determination. Nobody in the colonies had any right to print Bibles, and he laid himself liable to prosecution on that account; but feeling the need keenly, as he did, he dared the risk. Few men would have done so. The character of the man may be seen in the motto which adorned the walls of his shop, printed in the boldest type in his possession, and which, in English, read: "To the Glory of God and the Good of Mankind." [5]

Saur met the bitterest opposition in his effort. In fact, no man ever encountered so much difficulty in printing a Bible in America. The Rev. Henry Melchior Muhlenberg, of the German Lutheran Church, arrived while the book was in the press, and did everything in his power to embarrass the work. The Rev. Casper Schnoor, of the German Reformed Church at Lancaster, did the same. Even Schwenkfelders preached against his Bible. Doubtless they were conscientious in their opposition, knowing that Saur was poorly equipped for such work, and fearing numerous typographical errors. The chief difficulty, however, was found in the fact that religious controversy was bitter at the time, and Saur was classed as an "arch Separatist"; and, such being the case, nothing he could do would please the more orthodox.

It was Saur's hope to print a Bible that all parties could use, and he was quite generous about it, announcing his purpose to reprint the 34th edition of Luther's Bible, published at Halle, and which contained only that part of the apocrypha which Luther used. To appease the Sectarians, who would have much preferred the Berleberg Bible, he proposed to add an appendix to the apocrypha from the Berleberg Bible, consisting of III and IV Esdras [6] and III Maccabees, books in considerable favor among them. He then most generously offered to bind the Bible with or without the appendix, according to the wish of the purchaser. This, it was thought, would please everybody.

When Saur's Bible appeared, however, a storm of criticism was raised. The title page was revised and reprinted at once, and very few of his Bibles exist with the original title page. There was some ground for criticism here, because the title page was not an accurate description of the book. Then, his Bible was criticised because it contained, in Job,[7] a section of double text, that of the Berleberg

[5] Sachse, *The German Sectarians of Pennsylvania*, Vol. II, p. 18.
[6] Generally known among Protestants as I and II Esdras.
[7] Job 19:25-27.

Bible and that of Luther's for comparison. Finally, fault was found with it because of a "Brief Compend," an appendix to the New Testament, consisting of matter prepared by Saur himself.

The principal, if not the exclusive, sale of his Bible was confined to the German Sectarians, the Ephrata Mystics, Dunkers, Mennonites, and those who had renounced the Lutheran and Reformed churches; and it required almost twenty years to dispose of the first edition.

One feature of the appendix to the apocrypha in this Bible is quite interesting. Fourth (second) Esdras originally contained a section of seventy verses, following verse 35 of chaper 7, which became lost. It has now been determined that this lost section once belonged to Codex Sangermanensis, a Latin manuscript from which all manuscripts omitting it have been derived. The lost section is known to have been deliberately cut out, most probably for dogmatic reasons, because it contained an emphatic denial of the value of prayers for the dead.[8] This lost section, however, existed in certain other languages, but because no Latin manuscript contained it, scholars declined to accept it as a part of the original. They regarded these extra verses of certain other languages as an interpolation.

R. L. Benson, librarian of Cambridge University, however, discovered in 1874, a Latin manuscript of the ninth century, containing these lost verses. Other such Latin manuscripts have been found since. With this discovery scholarship no longer doubted that this lost section properly belonged to this book. Accordingly, when the apocrypha was revised in England, in 1895, it was restored to its rightful place.

These lost verses, however, restored from the Arabic to the Berleberg Bible in 1726-42, were copied from the Berleberg Bible into Saur's Bible. Saur's Bible, therefore, contained this section of Fourth (second) Esdras 150 years before the Protestant world recognized its right to a place in the apocrypha.

Mr. Saur was versatile, it having been said that he was familiar with sixteen different trades. He is credited with originating the business of making cast iron stoves. Just before his Bible was finished, he wrote: "The price of our now nearly finished Bible in plain binding with a clasp will be eighteen shillings, but to the poor and needy we have no price." He died in 1758 and was buried in Germantown.

Mr. Saur remembered his obligation to Dr. Luther of Germany,

[8] Hastings, *Dictionary of the Bible,* Vol. I, p. 763.

and sent him twelve copies of his Bible, which fell into the hands of French and Spanish pirates, but after two years came into Dr. Luther's possession.[9] They are now preserved in the libraries of Europe.

Saur's son, Christopher, continued the business, publishing a second edition of 2,000 copies of this Bible in 1763. In 1776 he had just finished the printing of a third edition of 3,000 copies, and had the volumes stitched and ready for the binder, when the Revolutionary War broke out. Germantown was invaded by the British who destroyed practically the whole issue, using the paper as bedding for their horses and for making cartridges. Catherine Saur, his daughter, is said to have rescued ten copies which she had bound, presenting them to her children.[10] The son was accused of disloyalty to the colonies, arrested as a spy, and his property confiscated and sold. His sons were unquestionably disloyal whether he was or not, but feeling toward him softened with the years. His attitude was probably due to his conscientious objection to war and revolutions, and his feeling that the colonies had no chance to win. His business descended to his son, Christopher, and generations of printers came from the family.

There is one interesting story in connection with Saur's arrest that deserves to be told. The controversies of the day had been bitter. The elder Saur and his son had both criticised Pastor H. M. Muhlenberg often and bitterly, and not without cause, but when Saur was arrested he appealed to General Peter Muhlenberg, the son of the pastor, and the general kindly interceded with Washington and saved his life.[11]

Christopher Saur I published the New Testament in German in 1745 and in 1755, and Christopher II published no less than six editions of the New Testament, the last in 1775. While Luther's Bible was not again published in America until 1805, at Reading, Pennsylvania, several editions of the New Testament appeared within this time.

Conrad Beissel, a Pietist from Germany, founded a Baptist community in Lancaster County, Pennsylvania, called Ephrata, in 1732, the members of which never exceeded three hundred; but this colony became quite famous in various ways. They set up the second printing press in Pennsylvania, issuing numerous books, among them

[9] Sachse, in *German Sectarians of Pennsylvania*, repudiates this story. See Vol. II, pp. 57-62. Wright in his *Early Bibles of America* proves it, see pp. 33-42.

[10] Wright, *Early Bibles*, reports owners of 34 copies of the 1776 edition, besides 40 copies in the Saur family. See pp. 382-83.

[11] Sachse, *German Sectarians of Pennsylvania*, Vol. II, p. 67, note.

New Testaments in German. The colony practiced communism and celibacy, though marriage was permitted. Some of them were highly educated. Rev. Peter Miller, the second prior of the monastery, translated the Declaration of Independence into seven languages at the request of Congress, but with the understanding that he should receive no compensation. These were sent to the various courts of Europe. Miller had been recommended to Congress by Charles Thomson, his friend.

Sachse claims that the Ephrata community maintained Sunday schools thirty years before Robert Raikes began his work.[12] According to him, they had schools on Saturday for those who preferred that day, and on Sunday for others. Ludwig Hocker, known among them as Brother Obed, led in this work, and his daughter, Moria, known as Sister Petronella, was the first woman Sunday school teacher of whom we have any record.

Moreover, this community produced numerous hymns, something above five hundred. Franklin printed three collections for them, but the fourth and complete collection, they printed themselves. They are all anonymous, except those by Beissel, such was their modesty. It has been said that among all these hymns "the names of hate or hell or vengeance or emnity are never named."

Michael Billmeyer of Germantown printed many editions of the New Testament, no less than ten issues appearing from 1787 to 1822. He published other parts of the Scriptures also.

Several different firms in Philadelphia published the Scriptures in German. The publication of the New Testament, or other parts of the Bible in German, spread to Baltimore in 1796, and to many points in Pennsylvania—Harrisburg in 1800, Lancaster in 1812, Somerset in 1813, New Berlin in 1819, and Carlisle in 1844. In 1835 the American Bible Society printed Luther's New Testament, and his whole Bible in 1847, following which the publication of German Bibles spread rapidly.

2. THE AITKEN NEW TESTAMENTS AND BIBLE

Three efforts to publish English Bibles in America failed because the colonies were sparsely settled, in an early day, and the difficulties attending such work in a new country were great. Bibles, however, were imported freely from England and Holland, but when the colonies declared their independence, the matter soon became seri-

---

[12] Sachse, *German Sectarians*, etc., Vol. II, p. 310.

ous. Books could not be so easily imported, and there soon followed a general destitution of Bibles, as well as other books, which was keenly felt. How long such conditions would continue nobody could say.

The matter was considered of such importance that it was brought to the attention of the Continental Congress by its chaplain, the Rev. Patrick Allison, D.D., in the form of a petition, others joining him in it. The memorial was received and referred to a committee, which submitted its report to Congress on September 11, 1777. This report suggested that to undertake to provide for the printing of the needed Bibles would be impracticable, under existing circumstances, and then said: "The use of the Bible is so universal and its importance so great, that your Committee refer the above to the consideration of Congress, and if Congress shall not think it expedient to order the importation of types and paper, the committee recommend that Congress will order the Committee of Congress to import 20,000 Bibles from Holland, Scotland, or elsewhere, into the different parts of the States of the Union." [13] Accordingly, Congress resolved to import 20,000 copies of the Bible, which, however, was never done.

While the matter was being agitated, Robert Aitken of Philadelphia published the New Testament in 1777. This was only a small twelvemo. Three more editions were printed in 1778, 1779 and 1781, the one in 1779 being for school purposes.

Mr. Aitken, in 1781, encouraged by the reception of his New Testaments, announced his purpose to publish the whole Bible, and presented a petition to Congress, seeking its support, whereupon Congress adopted the following resolution:

"*Resolved,* That the United States in Congress assembled, highly approve the pious and laudable undertaking of Mr. Aitken, as subservient to the interest of religion as well as the progress of the arts in this country, and being satisfied from the above report, of his care and accuracy in the execution of the work, they recommend this edition of the Bible to the inhabitants of the United States, and hereby authorize him to publish this recommendation in the manner he shall think proper." [14]

The Robert Aitken Bible, published in Philadelphia in 1782, was the King James Version, and the first English Bible printed in

[13] Wright, *Early Bibles,* p. 55.
[14] Wright, *Early Bibles,* p. 58.

America openly and with an American imprint, it being now the rarest of all the early American Bibles.[15] His New Testaments are also rare. Most of the copies of the Bible are more or less defective from excessive use or abuse. This Bible is important because it is a part of our national history, having been the only Bible ever recommended by Congress. The action of Congress in voting to import 20,000 Bibles, and in recommending this Bible to the public, indicates the fact that the founders of the republic were believers in the Bible.

In order fully to appreciate the debt due Mr. Aitken for the publication of this Bible, it must be remembered that it was printed during the Revolutionary War, and with very poor equipment. In the midst of the work, on one occasion, it became necessary to remove the type and materials from the city and bury them under a barn, to prevent destruction by the British soldiers.

A writer in *Freeman's Journal*, published in Philadelphia, in 1781, has this to say about this Bible: "Under all these disadvantages, a complete, an accurate, and elegant edition of the Bible was published in this very city, in four years from the time of its evacuation by the British. The very paper that has received the impression of these sacred books was manufactured in Pennsylvania; the whole book is, therefore, purely American, and has risen, like the fabled Phoenix, from the ashes of that pile in which our enemies supposed they had consumed the liberties of America." [16]

In the publication of this Bible Mr. Aitken lost "more than three thousand pounds specie," which proved a serious financial embarrassment. When the War of Independence was over, it had to compete with imported Bibles that could be sold cheaper. The Synod of the Presbyterian Church, meeting in Philadelphia in 1783, however, resolved to buy his edition exclusively for distribution among the poor, and recommended it to all others. In 1789 Mr. Aitken appealed to Congress to grant him a patent, giving him the exclusive right to print Bibles in America for fourteen years, but this was denied him.

Robert Aitken was a native of Scotland who came to America in 1769, and became a bookseller, later adding book publishing and book binding to his activities.

---

[15] Wright, in *Early Bibles,* pp. 383-84 reports two copies in England and thirty in the United States.

[16] Wright, *Early Bibles,* pp. 66-67.

3. RAPID SPREAD OF BIBLE PUBLICATION

The publication of the King James Version spread very rapidly, twenty editions of the whole Bible and fifteen editions of the New Testament, according to O'Callaghan, being published before 1800. To this number Wright adds two editions of the Bible and three editions of the New Testament. Of these Bibles ten editions had been published in Philadelphia, seven in Worcester, Massachusetts, two in Trenton, New Jersey, three in New York; New Testaments had appeared, seven editions in Philadelphia, two in Trenton, New Jersey, two in New York, two in New Haven, two in Lancaster, Pennsylvania, and one each in Newburyport and Boston. In addition to these, several editions of Commentaries from abroad had been reprinted.

Isaiah Thomas of Worcester, Massachusetts, whom Benjamin Franklin called "the Baskerville of America," was one of the most noted publishers of Bibles in the early days of the republic. At six years of age, he was apprenticed to Zechariah Fowle, a printer of Boston. However, he left his employer at eighteen, working in several places, and returning to Boston in 1770, where he formed a partnership with his former master. Together they started the *Massachusetts Spy,* but within three months he had become the sole proprietor of this newspaper, soon bringing it to have the largest circulation of any paper in Boston. Unhesitatingly he threw the influence of his paper into the cause of the colonies, and, just before the battle of Lexington, he removed his presses and types by night to Worcester, where he long lived and built a large business. He imported type for printing music in 1786, the first of the kind brought to America. He did business in Boston, under the firm name of Thomas and Andrews. In 1791, he published two editions of the King James Version. In his prospectus announcing the quarto, he offers to those not able to pay all in cash, to accept "Wheat, Rye, Indian Corn, Butter or Pork, if delivered at his store in Worcester, or at the store of himself and Company in Boston, by the 20th day of December, 1790, the remaining sum of twenty-one shillings, to be paid in Cash, as soon as the books are ready for delivery."

Thomas took unusual pains to secure a correct text, providing himself with about thirty editions of the King James Version, printed by different firms and at different times, from which he sought to select the text. Every sheet of his edition was examined by clergymen of Worcester, and by others capable of detecting error, who compared it with no less than eight copies.[17]

Boston published early a few editions worthy of special attention. In 1809 there was published a Unitarian New Testament, which had appeared in London a year earlier. This, however, will be discussed under Sectarian Translations.

Men in America were imprisoned for debt, as was once common in England. Rufus Davenport was a successful business man of Boston, who accumulated a large fortune for his day; then lost his property and, for more than three years, was a prisoner for debt. Very naturally his influence was exerted to have all such laws repealed and replaced with legislation more reasonable and just; and perhaps no single man did more to change the laws of our country on the subject. The law of imprisonment for debt, however, was not finally abolished in the United States until 1845.

In 1834 Rufus Davenport published a Bible in Boston with the following title page: "The Right-Aim School Bible; comprising the Holy Bible of the Old and New Testaments, and an Annexment containing the Free-Debt-Rule Petitions, addressed, the First to the Twenty-four States, the Second to the Congress, the Third to the President of the United States of America, and affixed Memorials; the Fourth Petition to three High Officers of the Government of England. Also the Declaration of Free-debtism." The President at that time was Andrew Jackson.

Several pages are devoted to arguments against imprisonment for debt.

Boston published the first "Pronouncing" New Testaments and Bibles in America. Israel Alger of Boston edited what he called "The Pronouncing Testament" in 1822, and the whole Bible in 1825. Other towns in Massachusetts published the Scriptures early— Charlestown, a Bible in 1803, Amherst, a New Testament in 1828, and Brookfield, one in 1829.

The first printing in New Jersey was done at Woodbridge, but the first publication of the Scriptures was at Trenton. Bible printing began here in 1788, when Isaac Collins, a Quaker, published a New Testament. In 1789 he issued a proposal to publish the whole Bible when he had received 3,000 subscriptions. The undertaking was endorsed by the governor of New Jersey, William Livingston. Various Christian bodies also endorsed it, among

---

[17] O'Callaghan, *List of Bibles*, p. 40.

which were the Quakers, the Presbyterian General Assembly, the Protestant Episcopal Convention, and the Baptist Association. His Bible was published at Trenton in 1791, in an edition of 5,000 copies.

Instead of the usual dedication to the King James Version, this Bible is provided with an address "To the Reader" by the Rev. Dr. Witherspoon. This address was printed in numerous Bibles in America by different printers over a period of thirty years.

Collins took unusual care to prevent printer's mistakes. Committees were appointed to correct the proofs, and, in addition to this precaution, the proofs were read eleven times by his own children. It is said that only two errors were ever found after its publication—one a broken letter, the other a punctuation mark.[18]

Hugh Gaine began the publication of the Scriptures in New York in 1790, by issuing a New Testament. He was a successful publisher in that city for more than 40 years, putting out the whole Bible in 1792. O'Callaghan calls Brown's Self-Interpreting Bible, published by another firm in the same year, the first to be composed and printed in New York. Which of these Bibles came from the press first is not known, but Gaine's Bible seems to have been set up and plated in Scotland, and the plates then shipped to the United States.

Daniel Fanshaw's name appears perhaps more frequently on title pages of Bibles than any New York printer of that early day. He printed for the American Bible Society on a ten-year contract, twice renewed, but not for the same length of time, printing also for the American Tract Society for a time. He became a wealthy man but was always eccentric, never wearing an overcoat, no matter the weather. He subscribed for every respectable publication that appeared in the city, paying always in advance, and in his will he provided that his son should be disinherited, if he used tobacco.[19]

Various towns in New York state published Bibles early; Albany in 1813, Utica in 1819, and Cooperstown in 1822.

The first press in Delaware was at Wilmington as early as 1761. Portions of the Scriptures were published there in 1797, the first New Testament appearing in 1802, and the whole Bible in 1812.

New London, Connecticut, set up the first press in that state in 1709; the second press was located at New Haven, where the New Testament was printed in 1790. In 1798 there was published at Hartford a Bible "Appointed to be read by Children," "an ill-

---

[18] Barker, *English Bible Version*, pp. 258-59.
[19] Wright, *Early Bibles*, p. 335.

written paraphrase." Bibles and Testaments soon followed in this city by various printers. Silas Andrus published Bibles here for many years.

Westminster, Vermont, had a press in 1781. In Windsor, Vermont, appeared a Bible in 1812, stating that it was the "First Vermont Edition." Scriptures were published in this state at Brattleboro in 1818, Newberry in 1825, and Woodstock in 1830.

Printing in New Hampshire began as early as 1756. A Bible was published in that state at Walpole in 1815, after having been five years in the press, consisting of 8,000 copies. The New Testament was published at Keene in 1818. Scripture publication began at Concord in 1823, Exeter in 1827, and Claremont in 1830.

Rhode Island published a New Testament at Providence in 1821.

How Bible printing grew the country over may be illustrated by the story of one firm. "H. and E. Phinney commenced printing 4to Bibles August 1, 1822 (in Cooperstown, New York), and published from that time to the winter of 1848, when their establishment was destroyed by fire, 138 editions, of 154,000 copies, averaging about 6,000 copies per annum. About 100,000 of them contained the apocrypha and 14,750 had Brown's Concordance. Only 500 copies were printed in 1822, and 4,475 for the first half of 1848; this will show the ratio of increase from the beginning."[20]

4. THE MORE POPULAR ANNOTATED BIBLES FROM ABROAD

Numerous Bibles or New Testaments with comments and notes which appeared first elsewhere, were reprinted in America. Many of them were published by several different firms in different parts of the country, and had extensive sale. Some of them are still in print, and others find a ready sale in second-hand book stores even today. Certain translations of parts of the Bible made abroad were reprinted in America, not for any notes attached, but for the text itself. We attempt to give only the time and place of the first publication of these.

Bishop Robert Lowth of the English Church made himself famous by his lectures on Hebrew poetry, being the first to state clearly its characteristics. In 1778, in London, he published a translation of Isaiah, giving it a poetic arrangement. Previous to this time the Bible had not been supposed to contain any poetry. This trans-

[20] O'Callaghan, *List of Bibles*, p. 158.

lation of Isaiah was published in New York in 1794, and had considerable circulation in the United States.

John Brown of Haddington was a Scotch Presbyterian, poor and self-educated. His annual income as pastor never exceeded fifty pounds. After 1768 he served as a professor of theology to the Associate Synod of Scotland, but without salary. He prepared what he styled a "Self-Interpreting Bible," which appeared in London in 1778.

In 1790 Hodge, Allen and Campbell of New York decided to publish this Bible. It was thought well to have the endorsement of the legislature of the state, to which a petition was presented. Both the Senate and the House endorsed the project in very cautious words, doubtful of their right to do so. The list of subscribers was headed by "George Washington, Esq., President of the United States of America." The Bible was issued by Hodge and Campbell, Allen having dropped out. This was the first Bible set up and printed in New York. It was two years in the press and appeared in forty numbers. This Bible had a wide use in England, Scotland and America.

"Explanatory Notes" on the New Testament by William Burkitt was published in New York in 1796. He was a minister of the Church of England, his work being a compilation, which appeared in England in 1700-03. Four editions of this appeared before 1800.

Rev. George Campbell, D.D., was a Scotch Presbyterian, long principal of Marschial College, Aberdeen, and later professor of divinity. He made a new translation of the Four Gospels which were accompanied with notes and published in 1789. This was reprinted in Philadelphia in 1796.

Scott's Family Bible circulated more widely in America, in an early day, than any other commentary. Rev. Thomas Scott had no early educational advantages, but managed to educate himself. At first a rationalistic Unitarian, he was converted to Calvinism by the celebrated John Newton, becoming a minister of the Church of England. His Commentary on the whole Bible appeared in London in 1788, proving to be the most popular of its day. From 1808 to 1819 more than 25,250 copies were published in America. Sir James Stephen called this "the greatest theological performance of our age and country." This Bible was first published in Philadelphia in 1804, and often elsewhere.

Cruden's Concordance of the Bible which had a world-wide use, and is still in print, appeared in England in 1737, and was published in Philadelphia in 1806. Several times, in the early part of his life, Alexander Cruden became insane, and was occasionally confined to an asylum. He finally recovered, but was always very eccentric. He regarded himself as divinely appointed to censor the public, especially in such matters as swearing and Sabbath breaking. He styled himself "Alexander the Corrector," and went about London with a sponge which he used to erase obscene words in public places. He paid unwelcome attentions to several women of high station, thereby inviting trouble for himself, but with it all he was a kind-hearted and devoted Christian.

The Family Expositor, an edition of the New Testament by Philip Doddridge, was published at Charlestown, Massachusetts, in 1807, from the eighth London edition, having appeared there first in 1739-56. Rev. Philip Doddridge, D. D. was a non-conformist minister and hymn writer of England, many of whose hymns are still in use. This volume contained a new translation of the New Testament, which was later extracted from the text and published separately.

In 1810 at Boston was published a "Literal Translation . . . of all the Apostolical Epistles" by Rev. James Macknight, D. D., a Scotch Presbyterian, his translation having appeared first in 1795.

Adam Clarke's Commentary was published in New York in 1811, and was advertised in America before it was published in London. The work is Clarke's to Acts; after that the comments are by other non-conformist ministers. Clarke was a Wesleyan minister.

A Bible with notes by the Rev. J. F. Ostervald, a French minister of Switzerland, was published in New York in 1813, the notes being originally in French, from which they were translated for publication in English.

Matthew Henry was a Presbyterian minister of England. His Commentary was practical and devotional, rather than critical, and as such very superior. It was long distinguished for its practical piety and good sense, being published in Philadelphia in 1816.

Rev. G. D'Oyly, B. D. and Rev. Richard Mant, D. D. of the Church of England prepared a commentary in which they consulted something like 160 authors, publishing it in London in 1814, under the sanction of the venerable Society for Promoting Christian Knowledge. This was published in New York in 1818-20, the American edition containing additional notes by Rt. Rev. John Hobart, D. D., Bishop of New York.

Gilbert Wakefield, with Unitarian leanings, made a new translation of the New Testament which was published in London in 1791. The second edition of his New Testament was reprinted at Cambridge, Massachusetts, in 1820.

John Wesley, the founder of Methodism, made a revision of the New Testament which was published in London in 1745, adding very copious notes. This was published in New York in 1837. There is one curious revision of the text made by Wesley that might be told. In the King James Version, 1 John 5:7-8 reads:

"There are three that bear record in heaven, the Father, the Word and the Holy Ghost: and these three are one. And there are three that bear witness on earth, the spirit, and the water, and the blood: and these three agree in one."

Wesley transposes these witnesses, and his text reads: "There are three that testify on earth, the Spirit, and the water, and the blood, and these three agree in one. And there are three that testify in heaven, the Father, the Word and the Holy Ghost, and these three are one." In his notes he assigns no other reason for the change, except that it "is abundantly preferable to the other, and affords a graduation admirably suited to the subject." The "three heavenly witnesses," however, are omitted from modern Greek texts, never having properly belonged there.

Tyndale's New Testament, published in 1525, was reprinted by J. P. Dabney at Andover, Massachusetts, in 1837.

5. THE RHEIMS–DOUAI AND OTHER CATHOLIC BIBLES

Roman Catholics, at the beginning of the Revolutionary War, did not exceed eighteen thousand, and no large numbers came for some time thereafter. It is often supposed that Catholics make little use of vernacular translations, but an edition of the Roman Catholic Bible in English was published in Philadelphia in 1790, and within fifteen years there were published two editions of the whole Bible, and one of the New Testament. By 1829, forty years from the publication of the first Catholic Bible in English, there had been put out no less than ten editions of the Bible, and nine editions of the New Testament. This would seem a rather generous supply, when one considers the comparatively small number of English-speaking Catholics in the country. During this early period a remarkably large amount of Christian literature was published by Catholics. The first Catholic book written by an American Catholic, and published in the United States was, "An Address to the

Roman Catholics of the United States of America" by Most Rev. John Carroll, printed at Annapolis in 1784.[21]

Bernard Dornin was the first Roman Catholic publisher in America, exclusively so. He came from New York to Philadelphia in 1817, and was soon publishing Catholic books exclusively. Eugene Cumminsky was the next, being an eminent publisher in Philadelphia for twenty years. Matthew Carey, who published the first Catholic Bible, printed books of all kinds, and both Catholic and Protestant Bibles.

Matthew Carey, printer, bookbinder, editor, philanthropist and pamphleteer, was born in Dublin, and because of persecution for political reasons fled to Paris, where Benjamin Franklin befriended him. He returned to Ireland, only to suffer further persecution, and finally fled to America dressed like a woman.[22] He landed in Philadelphia in 1784, and in 1786 fought a duel with Colonel Oswald but later they became friends. From 1819 to 1833, he published no less than fifty-nine separate pamphlets on a protective tariff, many of which were reprinted.

Marquis de La Fayette became interested in Mr. Carey soon after his arrival in Philadelphia, and, at his suggestion, Carey visited him, outlining his future plans and hopes. He was greatly surprised, on the following morning, to receive a letter from La Fayette with an enclosure of four hundred dollars. There had been no request for such favor. On this small beginning Matthew Carey built his fortune, first as a journalist, and then as a printer and bookseller. "While it was not the desire of La Fayette that it should be regarded in the light of a loan, but as a free gift, Mr. Carey in after years consigned to him an invoice of tobacco, besides on his arrival in New York, in 1824, repaying him the entire amount."[23]

Mr. Carey, on January 26, 1789, announced his purpose to print the Rheims-Douai Bible, as soon as four hundred subscribers could be secured. He then appealed to liberal minded Protestants to buy the book and encourage the undertaking. The edition was published in 1790, the first quarto Bible in America, it being a reprint of Challoner's second edition of 1763-64. This Bible bears the imprint of Carey and Stewart, being now quite rare. Type for it was cast in Philadelphia by John Baine.

In 1805 Matthew Carey published two editions of the Catholic

[21] Finotti, *Bibliographia Catholica Americana*, p. 67.
[22] Finotti, *Bibliographia Catholica Americana*, pp. 268-83.
[23] Wright, *Early Bibles*, p. 69.

Bible and one of the New Testament, these being reprints of the fifth Dublin edition of Dr. Troy's Bible, which was a revision of Challoner's Bible made by Bernard McMahon, with the approbation of Dr. Troy.

Mr. Carey, under his own name, published large numbers of the King James Version, finally building a very large and prosperous business. He died in 1839, leaving his business to his son, who carried on under the name of Carey and Lea. He had finally abandoned the Catholic faith.

The publication of Catholic literature and Bibles spread rapidly. Eugene Cumminsky began in Philadelphia in 1824. In New York City several Catholic printers soon appeared: J. Leavitt in 1832; J. Dodge in 1833; E. Dunigan in 1844; D. and J. Sadlier in 1844; and Tallis, Willoughby and Company in 1850. P. Donahue began in Boston in 1852. All were publishers of Catholic Bibles, Challoner's translation having the widest circulation.

Roman Catholic translations from the Vulgate in languages other than English were early published in America. The first French New Testament was published in Boston in 1810, this being the De Sacy version of 1667, printed originally at Mons, and copied from the Paris edition of 1759. No notes were included, but the two volumes contained the approbations of Bishop Cheverus of Boston.

The American Bible Society published in New York in 1819, the New Testament in Spanish, and the whole Bible in 1824, and again in 1830; also a Portuguese New Testament in 1839.

The first German Catholic Bible was published in New York in 1852. Dr. Allioli of the Cathedral of Ratisbon edited an edition of the Douai Bible in German. The American issue of this book was prepared by Rev. Gabriel Rumpeler of the Redemptorist Fathers of New York, by abridging the notes of Dr. Allioli. In the preface to this Bible Father Rumpeler says:

"The reading of the Bible has become, among the Catholic population of the United States of America, a general practice, by what authority we shall not stop to inquire. Suffice it, the universal practice hath created a habit we do not praise, neither will we absolutely condemn. The actual want, universally perceptible, of a German Catholic Bible approved by the Holy See, up to this time a desideratum in this country, hath induced us rather to transplant into American soil this truly literal Translation of the Holy Scriptures by Dr. Franz Allioli, which has been received with universal, undivided approbation, is widely dispersed and obtains at present in

Germany an almost exclusive circulation, in order thereby to provide against the erroneous understanding of the word of God, often
occasioned by the use of Protestant, as well as numerous corrupt
Catholic Bibles, especially that of Van Ess . . . The editor thus
hopes to have supplied a pressing want, and to have merited the
gratitude of the public." [24]

Felipe Scio's Spanish Bible was published in New York in 1824;
however, the books of the apocrypha were omitted.

A most interesting edition of the New Testament published in
New York in 1850, has been called the first illuminated New Testament in America. It appeared with the approbations of Rev. John
Hughes, Bishop of New York, and contained nearly one hundred
and fifty woodcuts from original drawings by W. H. Hewitt. The
pages are also ornamented with marginal illustrations and ornate
initial letters. The text is a translation from the Latin prepared by
Rev. James McMahon of New York. Of course, Bibles had used
woodcuts before this, some of them quite extensively; but nothing so
elaborate as this had ever appeared in America. [25]

6. HEBREW AND GREEK BIBLES

Many of the early ministers, especially those of New England, could
read the Bible in its original languages. The first publication of
Hebrew in this country was the Book of Psalms, edited by Professor
Francis Hare and printed at Cambridge, Massachusetts, in 1809.
An effort was made by Mills Day of New Haven, Connecticut, to
publish a Hebrew Bible in 1810, but it failed, though he published
a prospectus announcing it.

A certain Mr. Howitz, in 1812, launched a proposition to publish
a Hebrew Bible, and secured a number of subscribers. However,
in 1813, he sold his interest in the matter to Thomas Dobson of
Philadelphia, who published at Philadelphia the first Hebrew Bible
in America in two volumes, in 1813-14, the preface being in Latin.

The Jewish method of arranging and dividing the books of the
Old Testament is different from that in use among Christians.
According to the Jewish method, the Old Testament contains only
twenty-four books, the twelve minor prophets being counted as one
book, and Ezra and Nehemiah, as one. Christians count thirty-nine
books in the Old Testament, the contents being the same. The Jew-

---

[24] Wright, *Early Bibles*, pp. 164-65.
[25] Shea, *A Bibliographical Account of Catholic Bibles, Testaments*, etc., pp. 36-7.

ish arrangement, always found in the Hebrew, divides the Old Testa
ment into three parts, designated as the Law, the Prophets and the
Writings, or the Psalms, as it is called in the New Testament. The
book of Chronicles is the last book of the Jewish Bible, while
Christians place Malachi last. An occasional Christian Bible arrange
the books of the Old Testament in the Jewish order.

The Pentateuch in Hebrew, edited by Rev. Isaac Leeser, a Jewish
rabbi of Philadelphia, was published in that city in 1846. Following
this in 1849, the entire Old Testament in Hebrew, edited by Leeser
and Joseph Jaquett, was published in Philadelphia, this being the
first Hebrew Bible in America to contain the Massoretic points, that
is the vowels. The Old Testament was written originally with con
sonants only, the vowels being carried in the mind. Somewhere be
tween the seventh and ninth centuries A. D., certain men, known a
the Massoretes, added to the Hebrew Bible the vowels, certain accent
and other points. Hebrew Bibles may be had pointed or unpointed
that is, with or without the Massoretic additions to the text.

The Bible in Hebrew once had manuscripts differing considerably
in their text, but about 100 A. D. the Jews formed a standardized
text. The work was done on what principles we do not know; but
it is this standardized text that has come down to us. It has been so
carefully copied that texts differ very little, much less than in manu
scripts of the New Testament.

Isaiah Thomas, one of the most prominent early publishers of
Bibles, printed the first Greek New Testament in America at Worces
ter, Massachusetts, in 1800. The book purports to follow the text of
Mill, but it is evident that the editor drew from other texts also
In this same year Thomas published the first Greek Grammar in
America.

The New Testament, in both Greek and Latin, arranged in paral
lel columns and edited by John Watts, was published in Philadelphia
in 1806, being a reprint from an edition of John Leusden, published
at Utrecht in 1675. Under the same date in Philadelphia was pub
lished an edition of the Greek New Testament only.

Another New Testament in Greek was published at Cambridge
Massachusetts, in 1809, dedicated to the president and fellows of
Harvard College. This was a reprint of Griesbach's Manual, which
had been published at Leipzig in 1805, being the first publication of
his text in America. It proved upsetting to not a few of the old
time orthodox, because its advanced scholarship had spoiled many
ancient texts that were regarded as vitally essential by certain people

t soon became the standard, however, among the more advanced ninisters. Within a short time a Harmony of the Gospels, based on his text, was in use in the Andover Theological Seminary.

In 1814 an edition of the New Testament in Greek was published n Boston by Isaiah Thomas, Jr., using the text of the edition of his ather, but with a new title page.

George Long of New York, in 1821, published the New Testament n Greek and Latin which followed Leusden's edition.

Rev. Abner Kneeland, a minister of the Universalist Church, edited a Greek New Testament containing Griesbach's text, which was published in Philadelphia in 1822. Two editions appeared. One contained the Greek text only; the other, the Greek, accompanied by a new translation in English.

Dr. P. Wilson of Columbia College published an edition of the Greek New Testament at Hartford, Connecticut, in 1822, at least three editions appearing soon after. This was used extensively in America from 1823 to 1840.

Bloomfield's Greek New Testament was first published in America at Boston in 1837, a reprint of the second London edition, containing a preface written by Professor Moses Stuart of the Andover Theological Seminary.

What was known as the Polymicrian Greek Testament was published at Philadelphia in 1838, edited by Joseph P. Engles, M. A. It had appeared in England in 1829, containing a lexicon prepared by William Greenfield. This lexicon was published in America in 1839, and was later usually printed and bound with the Polymicrian which was several times reissued.

Dr. Edward Robinson's Greek New Testament had a wide use in America, published first in New York in 1842. Many other editions of the Greek New Testament have been published in various places. In the first half of the nineteenth century no less than 52 editions were printed; some were the Greek alone, some contained both Greek and Latin; others the Greek with an English translation. The American Bible Society published in 1833 the first New Testament in modern Greek. The Jews in America have published the Hebrew Old Testament frequently.

7. PHILADELPHIA A CITY OF BEGINNINGS

Boston took the lead in the publication of books in the early colonial era, beginning such work nine years earlier than Philadelphia and seventeen years earlier than New York City, remaining in the lead up to 1760. From this date to the Revolutionary War Boston and Philadelphia each did about the same amount, and then Philadelphia forged ahead.

Philadelphia deserves to be known as "the City of Beginnings" in America, as well as that of brotherly love. It was here that William Penn, in 1782, founded the city, beginning his "holy experiment for all mankind." William Bradford, in 1688, made the first proposal in America to print a Bible in English. In Germantown, a suburb of the city, Christopher Saur published the first German newspaper in America, the first issue appearing August 20, 1739, it being the first religious newspaper in the country. In 1743 he published the first German Bible, which was the first in America in any European language. In 1770 he published the first book in the country on the subject of education. Robert Aitken published here, in 1777, the first New Testament in English and, in 1782, the first Bible in English with American imprints. "The First Day or Sunday School Society" was organized here in 1790, becoming the first society in the United States for promoting Sunday schools. The first publication of the Rheims-Douai Bible was at Philadelphia in 1790, and the first edition of Cruden's Concordance in 1806.

The first Bible Society in the United States, known originally as "The Philadelphia Bible Society," but later as "The Pennsylvania Bible Society," was organized here in 1808. The British and Foreign Bible Society had offered one thousand dollars to the first Bible Society in America, and this sum was paid to this organization.

It was in Philadelphia that Charles Thomson published in 1808, the first Bible translated into English in America, it being the first translation of the Greek Old Testament into English in the world, and, so far as we know, the first and only Bible of America ever printed by a woman.

The first stereotyped Bible published in America was in Philadelphia in 1812, the plates having been imported from England by the Philadelphia Bible Society. The first Hebrew Bible was printed here in 1813-14, and the first Hebrew Bible with the Massoretic points, that is, the vowels, in 1849. The American Sunday School Union, the greatest organization for the promotion of Sunday schools the nation ever had, was organized here in 1824. Isaac Leeser, a Jewish rabbi, published the first Jewish translation of the Old Testament in Philadelphia in 1853, and in 1917, the first Jewish translation of the Old Testament ever made by a committee of

Jewish scholars was published there. In addition to all this, it was Philadelphia that first published in America, the Four Gospels by George Campbell, Scott's Family Bible and Matthew Henry's Commentary.

CHAPTER V

SOME NOTABLE PRIVATE TRANSLATIONS

THE writer has been gathering information, in a quiet way, for considerably more than ten years, concerning versions of the Bible, or its parts, in English, and it has been his hope to compile a list as complete as can possibly be made. Such a list can probably never be made absolutely complete for various reasons; and when the British Museum brings its catalogue of Bibles up to date, and when the Library of Congress finishes making cards for all its Bibles, the list in our possession will doubtless receive several new titles. It is felt, however, that our present list omits little of any considerable importance.

According to the information we have on file now, the whole Bible has been translated into English, or revised, no less than 50 times, 16 of which were made in the United States. In this enumeration, for the United States, is included Kent's Shorter Bible; F. W. Grant's Numerical Bible, not quite complete; L. A. Sawyer's Bible, Genesis lacking; the Swedenborg Bible, which is only the King James Version with numerous books omitted; and the Anglo-American Revision. Since America assisted in making it, it is numbered with American revisions.

The New Testament, independent of the Old, has been translated no less than 85 times, by as many different translators, and these original editions have been revised 15 times, so that the New Testament has been translated or revised independently, no less than 100 times. America produced 32 of these translations, and 5 revisions, making a total of 37 American.[1]

The enumeration of New Testaments includes Evanson's, published in London, and which really contains but a small part of it, but all that the translator accepted. It includes also the version published at Oxford by Anna C. Paues, in 1902, which is from Wyclif's time, but different, and incomplete. Among American New Tes-

---

[1] John V. Madison, in his *English Versions of the New Testament*, published 1925, gives "1850, Spiritual Version, New York, New York. N. T. 'Dictated by the Spirit' ", with a reference to Wright's *Early Bibles*. We have been unable to learn whether such was ever published. The Library of Congress knows nothing about it, and no copy has been found elsewhere.

Madison also lists a New Testament by George Townsend, published at Boston and Philadelphia in 1837, but this is the King James Version. He lists also the University New Testament, published by Townsend Weaver at Philadelphia in 1909, but this is the Anglo-American Revision, rearranged.

taments are included one coyprighted by Leonard Thorn, which omits considerable sections, and that of Hezekiah Woodruff, published in 1852, which omits the Gospels of Mark, Luke and John.

The Psalms have been translated, independently, no less than 85 times, and 19 of these were done in America. In this number it is not intended to include metrical versions, which are simply the English versified, of which there are hundreds. Not being able, however, to examine every book included, a few such may have crept in. The Bay Psalm Book, the Massachusetts Psalter and the Psalterium Americanum, all made in America, have been included, because they are translations from the Hebrew.

The book of Job has been translated, independently, no less than 65 times, America producing 14 of them. Other independent translations have been no less than the following number of times: The Song of Solomon 67, 9 of which were American; Ecclesiastes 49, 6 being American; the Four Gospels 33, 11 produced in America; the Old Testament alone 14, 5 being made in America.

According to the above figures, the different parts of the Bible have been translated or revised in English no less than the following number of times: The whole Bible 50; the New Testament 149; the Old Testament 64; Psalms 149; Job 119; Song of Solomon 121, Ecclesiastes 113, and the Four Gospels 182.

Many other parts of the Bible have been translated, independently. The great majority of all translations and revisions have been private, while a few have been made by committees appointed for the purpose.

1. THE BIBLE

CHARLES THOMSON'S TRANSLATION

The honor of the first translation of the Bible into English made in America, belongs to Charles Thomson, who was influenced in undertaking the task by a letter of Thomas Jefferson.

Thomson was born in Ireland in 1729, and came to America when but eleven years of age. His father died in crossing the Atlantic, leaving the son to land alone and in poverty. A family in New Castle, Delaware, where he landed, thought to make a blacksmith of him, which, however, he escaped by running away, evidently having ambitions for something better at his tender age. On the road, he found a kindhearted woman who offered him a seat in her carriage, and being inquisitive she asked the lad what he wanted to be, to which he promptly replied, "A scholar." She was soon won completely to his way of thinking, cared for him and provided his education.[2] He had a brother in America who may have assisted somewhat. Thomson received the Master's degree from the College of Pennsylvania, later tutoring in the College, which finally became the University of Pennsylvania.

Thomson gave his sympathies without stint to the cause of the colonies, and was elected the secretary of the first Continental Congress by unanimous vote, for which service he declined compensation for the first year. Regularly he was reelected until 1789, when he retired. He married a sister of Benjamin Harrison of Virginia, a signer of the Declaration of Independence; and Congress, in recognition of his patriotism, presented his wife with a silver urn. He was made the first secretary of the United States Congress, and it was he who notified Washington of his election to the Presidency.

In 1789 he retired to devote himself to Biblical study. How he became interested in the Greek Old Testament, resulting finally in its translation, is an unusual story. It is told by Watson in his *Annals of Philadelphia:*

"He told me that he was first induced to study Greek from having bought a part of the Septuagint at an auction in this city. He had bought it for a mere trifle, and without knowing what it was, save that the crier said it was outlandish letters. When he had mastered it enough to understand it, his anxiety became great to see the whole; but he could find no copy. Strange to tell, in the interval of two years, passing the same store, and chancing to look in, he then saw the remainder actually crying off for a few pence, and he bought it. I used to tell him that the translation which he afterwards made should have had these facts set at the front of the work as a preface; for that great work, the first of the kind in the English language, strangely enough, was ushered into the world without any preface." [3]

Thomson spent twenty years in making his translation, copying the manuscript the fourth time. It was published in four volumes in Philadelphia, in 1808. The American committee for the revision of the New Testament published in 1881, used his New Testament. His Old Testament was the first translation of the Septuagint—Greek Old Testament—into English in the world, being made from John Field's edition, Cambridge, 1665. The New Testament makes three

[2] Wright, *Early Bibles of America*, p. 117.
[3] Watson, *Annals of Philadelphia*, Vol. I, p 568.

mportant revisions of the then commonly received Greek text [4] among which the doxology of the Lord's Prayer was omitted, also the "three heavenly witnesses." His revisions are justified by modern scholarship. For clearness, force and felicitous language it would be difficult to surpass Thomson's translation, especially the New Testament. The original manuscript is now in the possession of Alleghany College. The Old Testament was reprinted by S. F. Pells of Hove, England, in 1904 and 1907, and the New Testament in 1929.

Women Printers of the Bible

Jane Aitken was the printer and publisher of Charles Thomson's Bible, and, so far as we have been able to learn, the only woman who ever printed any part of the Scriptures in America. Robert Aitken, her father, had published the first New Testaments and the first Bible in English in America, with American imprints. He died in 1802, and his daughter continued the business, proving herself a capable business woman.

Only a few women have ever printed any part of the Scriptures, the first, of whom we have any knowledge, being "the Wydowe of Christoffel of Endhœ," who printed at Antwerp in 1534, Tyndale's New Testament as altered by George Joye. Her husband had been a successful printer and his wife continued the business. Joye's unwarranted alterations of Tyndale's New Testament broke the friendship between these two men.

Then come several women printers of whom we know nothing, except that they printed certain books. Psalm 136 and a paraphrase of Psalm 104, in verse, by John Milton, were printed in London in 1645, among his "Minor Poems," by Ruth Raworth. The Seven Penitential Psalms, altered from the Douai version, contained in a "Manual of Prayers and Litanies," was printed in 1650 at "Antwarpe, by the Widowe of John Cnobbart." Anne Snowden comes next in order. William Barton left a manuscript of the Psalms in metre, at his death, which she published in London in 1705. Then certain Psalms in English metre by W. Hunnis were published in London in 1851, by the "widow of John Hertforde." The widow of Steven Swart at Amsterdam in 1684, published the King James Version of the New Testament, and also the New Testament in French, and in English and Dutch, the same year. She seems to have done a con-

---

[4] Matt. 6:13 and 1 Peter 3:15 and 1 John 5:7-8.

siderable business. Eadie [5] makes mention of a Mrs. McLean and Company of Glasgow, which printed Bibles, at least, in 1748.

From 1676 to 1711, a Mrs. Anderson enjoyed the exclusive right to print the Scriptures in Scotland. One of her enemies said of her "Nothing came from her press but the most illegible and incorrect Bibles and books that ever were printed in any one place in the world." One example ought to be sufficient. In one of her Bibles dated 1705, we read: "Whyshoulditbethough tathingincredible w' you, y^t God should raise the dead?" [6]

Perhaps no printer of Bibles was ever more careless than Mrs. Anderson, and she had a hard time for years in defending her exclusive right, but succeeded in having a number of people fined for intruding into the business.[7] This makes a total of nine women who have printed the Scriptures in English.

B. NOAH WEBSTER'S BIBLE

Noah Webster, the lexicographer, prepared a revision of the King James Version which was published in New Haven, Connecticut, in 1833, a second and smaller edition in 1841, his New Testament alone being reprinted in 1839, 1840 and 1841. His purpose, so he says, was to remove obsolete words and phrases, to correct errors of grammar, and mistranslations, and to this he added one thing more, which he considered of very grave importance. In his own words: "To these may be added many words and phrases very offensive to delicacy, and even to decency. In the opinion of all persons with whom I have conversed on the subject, such words and phrases ought not to be retained in the version. Language which cannot be uttered in company without a violation of decorum, or the rules of good breeding, exposes the Scriptures to the scoffs of unbelievers, impairs their authority, and multiplies or confirms the enemies of our holy religion." [8] Modern translators conform to this suggestion. Webster's revision, however, was one chiefly of the unimportant, and he was greatly disappointed that it had no wider sale.

Noah Webster was a Congregational layman, who was admitted to the bar in 1781, and taught school for a time. He published his blue-back speller in 1783, and by 1847 twenty-four mil-

---

[5] *The English Bible*, Vol. II, p 322.
[6] Edgar, *Bibles in English*, p 298 and note.
[7] Eadie, *The English Bible*, Vol. II, p 318-321.
[8] Preface to Webster's Bible.

ions of copies had been sold; after that the demand for many years amounted to a million and a quarter copies annually. He supported himself and family twenty years on his income from this speller, while he prepared his famous dictionary.

C. A SWEDENBORG BIBLE

There is one interesting Bible in use in America that does not exactly fit in any classification used in this volume, but must be included somewhere, and here as well as elsewhere. In 1837 Otis Clapp published at Boston what might be called a Swedenborg Bible, since it contained only the books that Swedenborg considered to have "an internal sense" and, therefore, to belong properly to the Bible. It contains the usual books of the Protestant Bible, with Ruth, 1 and 2 Chronicles, Ezra, Nehemiah, Esther, Job, Proverbs, Ecclesiastes and the Song of Songs omitted from the Old Testament, and Acts and all the Epistles from the New Testament.

This Bible was printed originally from plates of the King James Version, the plates being simply cut and the page numbering not altered. In 1865 it was republished in Boston under the title, "The Word of the Lord." This was again a cutting of plates of the King James Version, but more neatly done. Certain pages were reset and the page numberings this time were made consecutive. This was republished in 1869, reset throughout, and in the Old Testament Jehovah was used wherever the King James Version had used the word "LORD" in small capitals. These were all private efforts, and while this is a Swedenborg Bible as to contents, it has never been officially adopted.

D. ARCHBISHOP KENRICK'S BIBLE

Francis Patrick Kenrick was made Archbishop of Philadelphia in 1842, and of Baltimore in 1851. He made the most important revision of the Rheims-Douai Bible ever put out in America, and perhaps the most important in the world since Challoner's revision. He published, first in New York, the Four Gospels in 1849, and the remainder of the New Testament in 1851, these being issued without Catholic approbations. In his notes is nothing uncharitable, and his translation is, in many places, quite unusual for a Catholic, "repent" and "do penance" being used interchangeably. The parts of the Old Testament were published at Baltimore, the whole Bible appearing in 1862. For some reason this Bible has never been very popular, and is now out of print.

E. L. A. SAWYER'S BIBLE

The Rev. Leicester Ambrose Sawyer was one of the first men of America to accept modern views of the Bible. He was ordained to the Presbyterian ministry in 1832, and served as a pastor for several years. Becoming liberal in theology, he went to the Congregational Church, where he hoped to find more congenial quarters. This, however, was not so satisfactory as he had hoped, and he transferred to the Unitarians in 1859. In 1864 he became the pastor of the First Catholic Congregational church (independent) of Boston, and styled himself a Christian rationalist.

Finally giving up regular preaching, he devoted himself entirely to the study and translation of the Bible, being thoroughly dissatisfied with the King James Version. His translation work covered the entire Bible, excepting Genesis, according to one of his relatives, the various books being published separately and in groups. His first translation of the New Testament is perhaps his best known work, and was published in Boston in 1858, the third edition in 1861. This was made from Tischendorf's text, published at Leipzig in 1850. The solemn style was abandoned, except in prayer, and he was the first man to do so in America. He introduced an entirely new set of chapters and verses, chapters becoming logical divisions and verses sensible paragraphs—the old chapter and verse numbers being omitted entirely. This fact injured the popularity of his work. The books of the New Testament were somewhat rearranged, giving the Gospels and Acts, then Paul's Epistles in chronological order, followed by the Catholic Epistles, including the book of Hebrews, and closing with Revelation. His translation provoked considerable criticism. He had the satisfaction, however, of knowing that much of his work, criticised freely at the time, was sustained by the Revisions Committees of 1881.

"The Holy Bible translated and arranged with notes" was published in three volumes in 1860-62, but this did not contain the entire Bible. These volumes did contain, among other things not previously published, the Later Prophets, and the Hebrew Poets. Daniel, with apocryphal additions, was published in 1864, and Isaiah in 1887. Other books were published at different times.

Sawyer's second translation of the New Testament, for it may be called such, was published at Whitesboro, New York, in 1891, under the title: "The Bible; analyzed, translated and accompanied with critical studies . . . New Testament." This contained a new arrangement of the books in chronological order. First Thessalonians comes first and the book closes with the Gospels, Acts and Revelation. The "critical studies" called for in the title are promised in a later volume. In this New Testament he restores the usual chapter and verse numbers, which had been omitted from his former translation. It is said that his studies finally led him to conclude that Jesus was merely a social reformer, and that the only genuine portions of the New Testament were five Epistles of Paul.[9]

His most noteworthy work in the Old Testament field was that devoted to the Prophets, in which he set forth the idea that they contained no reference whatever to Jesus as the Messiah.

E. JULIA E. SMITH'S BIBLE

The only woman in the world's history to translate the entire Bible into any language was Julia E. Smith of Glastonbury, Connecticut, whose version in English was published at Hartford, Connecticut, in 1876, at her own expense.

She claims to have spent seven years in this work, translating the Hebrew twice, the Greek twice and the Latin once. The work finished, she decided to publish it. The books of the Old Testament are arranged in the Jewish order, with Chronicles at the end. She had no assistance from any source. Her translation is very literal, adhering closely to Hebrew and Greek idioms, often making quite unnatural English. Her name is not found on the title page, but is signed to the preface, in which she says: "It may be thought by the public in general that I have great confidence in myself, in not conferring with the learned in so great a work, but as there is but one book in the Hebrew tongue, and I have defined it word for word, I do not see how anybody can know more about it than I do." [10]

Zephaniah Hollister Smith, her father, was a picturesque and versatile character. Beginning as a minister, he was an early abolitionist, then he became a doctor and finally a lawyer. He and his wife belonged to the Sandemanians, a small and obscure sect of Scotland.

[9] *Dictionary of American Biography*, Vol. XVI, pp 393-94.
[10] Preface to her Bible.

Julia was one of the famous five "Glastonbury Sisters," but the most prominent, all being educated in Oriental languages. Julia made herself conspicuous early in a political way, in her champion-ship of the Woman's Suffrage party, rarely failing to attend their conventions, where she took a leading part. A younger sister joined her in refusing to pay taxes until they could vote. They owned a fine herd of Jersey cattle, which the authorities seized and sold for taxes, the matter being contested in the courts and newspapers for years. When all her family were dead, and she had reached her eighty-seventh year, she was married to the Hon. Amos Parker of New Hampshire who was only 86. Strange to say, she lost caste by this action. There was no reason why she should not marry, if she so desired, and she married a man of some standing, but she had been so long an institution in herself, a picturesque character so different from the ordinary, that many of her friends felt that she had be-trayed something sacred in marrying. Many of them did not like it, and said so frankly. One can well imagine what she would have to say to all such.

Women Translators of the Bible

Comparatively few women have translated any part of the Bible into English. Several, however, have made metrical versions of the Psalms, in whole or in part, and some of them have merit: but this does not require a knowledge of the original languages, and is usually made from the English. Therefore, such are not counted as translations.

The first woman to translate from the Hebrew into English was Ann Francis, who published the Song of Solomon, with notes, in London in 1781. It is worthy of remark that this woman should have confined her notes entirely to the literal sense of the book.[11] Almost universally, at this time, this book was considered an alle-gory, but she was plainly ahead of her times.

Elizabeth Smith taught herself Latin, Greek, Hebrew, Arabic, French, Italian, Spanish and German; and then translated the book of Job before she was twenty-six years of age. Dying in 1806, at thirty, the Rev. T. Randolph published her translation of Job [12] with notes at Bath, England, in 1810. She translated other parts of

---

[11] A copy in the University of Chicago Library.
[12] There is a copy in the University of Michigan Library.

he Bible, from Genesis, the Psalms and the Prophets, but these were
never published.

Helen Spurrell of London, wife of a minister of the Church of
England, and a very talented woman, taught herself Hebrew after
she became fifty years of age, and translated the Old Testament
from the unpointed text (without vowels as originally written).
Her translation was published in London in 1885, and sells today
for a rather high price.

Mrs. Agnes Smith Lewis, wife of S. S. Lewis, a distinguished
archaeologist, and her sister, Mrs. Gibson, both of Cambridge, England, discovered in 1892, at a convent on Mt. Sinai, a very ancient
MS. of the four Gospels in Syriac. Mrs. Lewis, in 1894, published a
translation of this MS. in London and New York, and in 1896 she
published at Cambridge a new edition with parts retranslated.
She was highly educated and widely travelled, and was honored by
numerous universities in England and on the Continent.

The Twentieth Century New Testament had among its translators one woman, Mrs. Mary Higgs (nee Kingsland). Mrs. S. Elizabeth Mee (nee Butterworth) and Mrs. Florence Booth both rendered invaluable service in the work, but not as translators. Mrs.
Higgs was one of the two people responsible for the movement that
resulted in this translation. Its publication began in 1898, and the
final revision appeared in London and New York in 1904.

"The Psalms, a new version with notes," was published in London
in 1904. About fifty of these Psalms were translated by Mrs. William Kelly, the wife of a prominent minister of the "Brethren"
Church of England, but death cut short her work, and her husband
finished the translation, and published it. The book appeared anonymously, and these facts have been learned through correspondence.

Charles Foster Kent published a "Shorter Bible" in New York in
1918-1921. One of the translators of this work was Ethel Cutler, religious work secretary of the national board of the Y. W. C. A.

The Centenary Translation of the New Testament, published in
Philadelphia in 1924, was the work of Mrs. Helen Barrett Montgomery of Rochester, New York, a prominent Baptist minister, and
the only woman to translate independently the whole of it into
English.

This makes a total of nine women who are known to have translated at least part of the Bible into English. Some might desire to
add Princess Mary, later known as "Bloody Mary," who translated
paraphrases on John's Gospel in 1549.

The British and Foreign Bible Society, after a careful search of their records, report that not less than 116 women have worked in translations or revisions of the Bible, or its parts, in numerous languages for missionary purposes.

The American Bible Society has published the translations of nine women,[13] eight of whom were missionaries. In addition to this it has published, in Chinese, a Mandarin Gospel of John that had been transliterated into Roman letters by a woman.

2. THE NEW TESTAMENT INDEPENDENTLY

A. JOHN MCDONALD'S NEW TESTAMENT

The first revision of the New Testament, independent of the Old, made in the United States, was the work of Rev. John McDonald, and was published at Albany, New York, in 1813, the title page indicating that it had been "carefully revised and corrected." The Library of Congress, however, does not have a copy, and we have not been able to locate one elsewhere.

B. ABNER KNEELAND'S NEW TESTAMENT

Reference has already been made to the New Testament of Abner Kneeland, containing both the Greek and the English, published in Philadelphia in 1822. He published an edition of the English only in 1823, which is a translation from Griesbach's text.

Kneeland was a minister of the Universalist Church when he made

---

[13] The following are the women who have made missionary translations for the American Bible Society:

Mrs. T. E. Hudspeth, Bolivian Quechua, giving very considerable aid in translating the Psalms.

Mrs. H. D. Peck, Mam (Guatemala), with her husband and native assistants, John, in 1930, and the New Testament is nearly complete in manuscript.

Mrs. A. E. W. Robertson, Muskogee, chief translator New Testament, Genesis and Psalms.

Mrs. H. C. Kramer, Olunyore (Kenya), the New Testament.

Mrs. Eleanor Chestnut, M. D., Sankiang (China), the Gospels.

Mrs. J. Andrew Hall, Samareno (Philippine Islands), the New Testament, now working on the Old Testament.

Mrs. C. H. Crooks, Kamu (Siam) 1 Peter.

Mrs. Daniel McGilvary, Tai Yuan (Siam), assisted in early translation work.

Mrs. C. H. Turner, Peruvian Quechua, the Gospels, Acts and Romans. She was not a missionary.

Mrs. R. Lowrie transliterated John into Roman letters in Chinese, Mandarin.

his translation. He began as a Baptist minister, than joined the Universalists, and ended a deist. In 1830, he established a paper that he called the *Investigator,* and advocated his deistical ideas. He was tried for blasphemy in the Supreme Court of Massachusetts, in 1836, convicted and imprisoned three months, his trial and conviction being utter absurdities, growing out of the narrowness of the day, and being for nothing more than the expression of an honest but unorthodox opinion.

C. J. G. PALFREY'S NEW TESTAMENT

A New Testament was published at Boston anonymously in 1828, but copyrighted by Nathan Hale, from which fact it has been attributed to him. It was simply the King James Version conformed to Griesbach's text, as published at Leipsic in 1805. The work, however, was done by James Graham Palfrey, D. D., professor of Sacred Literature in Harvard University 1831-39.

D. JAMES MURDOCK'S TRANSLATION

The majority of Biblical scholars think the Bible was translated first, in Christian times, into the Syriac, and that the translation was made during the latter half of the second century A. D. What is known as the Peshitta was long thought to be the first Syriac version, but is now generally considered the last of several early versions. The Peshitta, however, is a very ancient text, and quite interesting from several standpoints. It early became the official Bible of the Syrian Church, and holds that position today. Moreover, the New Testament of this version omits five books found in all other New Testaments, namely 2 Peter, 2 and 3 John, Jude and Revelation. These books have never been accepted as inspired by the Syrian Church, which means that the canon of the Syrian New Testament was completed before these books had been accepted generally, these being the last books to be added to the New Testament.

The first translation of the Peshitta New Testament into English was made by the Rev. J. W. Etheridge, and published in London, 1843-49. The first translation of this New Testament in America was made by the Rev. James Murdock, D. D., and published in New York in 1851, other editions appearing in 1855 and 1858. It is regarded as a very accurate translation. The five books not found in the Peshitta are supplied in this book from other Syriac manuscripts.

Dr. Murdock was a Congregational minister, who graduated from Yale in 1797. For a time he was professor of Ancient Languages in the University of Vermont, and later filled the chair of Sacred Rhetoric and Ecclesiastical History in the Andover Theological Seminary, being a well-known linguist.

E.   BENJAMIN WILSON'S EMPHATIC DIAGLOTT

The growing dissatisfaction with the King James Version among scholars was early felt in America and the desire to get back to an older and better text was the main inspiration of numerous revisions and translations. Influenced by this purpose Benjamin Wilson published in New York, in 1864 and at Geneva, Illinois, in 1865, the Emphatic Diaglott, containing Greisbach's text, and a literal translation and a free translation of the New Testament.

F.   GEORGE R. NOYES' NEW TESTAMENT

It was the unsatisfactory character of the King James Version that set George R. Noyes, D. D., a Unitarian, and professor of Hebrew and Oriental Languages in Harvard University, to translating parts of the Bible as early as 1827. In 1869 he published at Boston the New Testament from the text of Tischendorf.

G.   W. D. DILLARD'S NEW TESTAMENT

W. D. Dillard, in 1885, published in Chicago the New Testament, "literally translated out of the Greek," and "dedicated to the poor, illiterate and unlearned", but it has been called "only a halting revision of the King James Version."

H.   R. D. WEEKS' NEW TESTAMENT

Robert Dodd Weeks never attended college and was only a Congregational layman, but for a time he was professor of English in the Agricultural College of Michigan. He published in New York in 1897, a translation of the New Testament from the text of Westcott and Hort, though he occasionally revised this text. This is an imitation of the King James Version, but made from a standard modern text.

I.   H. T. ANDERSON'S NEW TESTAMENT

In 1918 the Rev. H. T. Anderson published in Philadelphia a translation of the Sinaitic manuscript discovered by Tischendorf on Mt.
Sinai, which is recognized as the second oldest and best manuscript
of the Greek New Testament known. The preface is signed by
Pickett Anderson Timmins. Anderson was a minister of the Disciple Church, and at one time a pastor in Louisville, Kentucky.
He made another translation in 1864, which will be treated elsewhere.

J.   THE CONCORDANT VERSION

Adolph E. Knoch of Los Angeles, California, prepared and published
a pretentious revision of the New Testament in 1926, which he
called the "Concordant Version", putting it out originally in in-
stallments, beginning January 1921. The text from which the translation is made is the commonly received Greek text—Textus Re-
ceptus—as modified by the use of codices Vaticanus, Alexandrinus
and Vaticanus 2066, by which he retains much that has been rejected
by modern critical scholarship. The Greek text appears on pages
opposite the English, in a special type which he had cast for the
purpose, and in imitation of the Greek uncial (capital) writing of
the earliest manuscripts. Voluminous notes are appended, by which
we are told that much of the teachings of Jesus are not applicable
today, but will be when He returns in person and establishes His
kingdom. The allegorical method of interpretation seems to be used.
A revised edition was published in 1930. An international edition,
in more popular form, is in preparation, in English, German, Dutch,
Italian and other languages.

3.   THE GOSPELS AND EPISTLES INDEPENDENTLY

The Psalms have been published oftener than any part of the Bible;
but most of these publications have been metrical versions, the English simply versified, and not in any sense tranlations. The Four
Gospels have been translated oftener than any other part of the
Bible, and as a rule independently and alone. The Rev. Samuel
Thompson, pastor of a Universalist Church at Charlestown, Massachusetts, published "The Monotessaron", a harmonistic arrangement
of the Gospels, at Baltimore in 1829. This was made from the text

of Griesbach, it being the first independent translation of the Four Gospels in America.

Alden Bradford was a Congregational minister and served as a pastor for a time. He served also as secretary of the State of Massachusetts, and then as the editor of the Boston *Gazette*. It was evidently his original purpose to publish the whole New Testament. Under the title of "Evangelical History, or the books of the New Testament;" he published the Four Gospels at Boston in 1836, but no more seems to have been issued.

Andrews Norton was a professor in the Harvard Divinity School. He left in manuscript, at his death, a translation of the Four Gospels, using an uncertain text. Charles Elliot Norton, his son, published this at Boston in 1855, the first three chapters of Matthew being omitted. A second volume of notes was published.

Nathaniel S. Folsom, at one time professor in the Meadville Theological School, a Unitarian institution, translated the Four Gospels from the text of Tischendorf, and published it at Boston in 1869. In these translations there is everywhere evident a determination to bring the Bible abreast of the latest and best scholarship.

The American Lutheran Bible Society of Knoxville, Tennessee, published a revised edition of the Four Gospels in 1920, the work being done by a large staff of Lutheran pastors. This society is said to have published translations of other portions of the Bible, but it has long since ceased to exist, and we have been unable to learn more about their publications.

Neander P. Cook published at Los Angeles, California, in 1923, "The Genuine Words of Jesus, according to the Older Documents Underlying the New Testament Gospels." This contained also a sketch of the life of Christ.

The Epistles of the New Testament, or those of the Apostle Paul, have been translated independently many times. A very interesting version of the "Apostolic Epistles," published in New York in 1830, was the work of Judge Egbert Benson, who presided over the Supreme Court of New York from 1794 to 1812. The title indicates that it was published "with amendments in conformity with the Dutch version." For the words *charity* and *bishop*, he substituted *love* and *overseer*.

Rev. William Wallace Martin published at Nashville, Tennessee, in 1929-30, the Epistles of the New Testament in two volumes. His treatment is quite unusual. The book of Romans, for example, is separated into two distinct Epistles, one by Paul, the other by Ap-

JULIA E. SMITH

ollos. Similarly, Hebrews is made into three Epistles, one by Paul, ne by Apollos and another by Barnabas. Several other Epistles are parated in the same fashion.

The Rev. Mr. Martin is a Methodist, and was for seven years rofessor of Hebrew in Vanderbilt University, Nashville, Tennessee. Ie rejects the conclusions of the modern critical school, and offers a ew theory of the origin of numerous Old Testament books, seprating Deuteronomy, for example, into two instead of four sources.

4. PARTS OF THE OLD TESTAMENT INDEPENDENTLY

A. THE PSALMS

The first independent translation of the Psalms in America was the *Bay Psalm Book,* published in 1640. This has already been discussed.

George R. Noyes published at Boston, in 1831, a translation of the Psalms in measured prose, several times reprinted. The Psalms, ranslated from the Peshitta, by Rev. A. Oliver, was published in Boston, in 1861. Rev. John DeWitt, a professor in the New Brunswick Seminary (Dutch Reformed), and a member of the Old Testament revisions committee, 1870-85, published in New York, in 1884, ne of the best translations of the Psalms made in America, which has several times been reprinted. Rev. John G. Lansing, D. D., also a professor in the New Brunswick Theological Seminary, published another revision of the Psalms in 1885. Rev. Emil Lund, a Swedish Lutheran minister, put out a translation of the Psalms at Rock sland, Illinois, in 1908.

A very attractive version of the Psalms was prepared by Rev. Herbert Henry Gowen, D. D., a Protestant Episcopal minister, professor of Oriental Studies at the University of Washington, and published at Milwaukee in 1919. The brief notes appended are splendid. The cover title to this volume is "Biblical and Oriental Series."

Frederick Joseph Bielsky, in 1926, translated the Aramaic Psalms from a sixteenth century Bible, published 1537, which he owns, said to be the only one of the kind in America. The Rev. William Wallace Martin published the book of Psalms in three volumes at Nashville, Tennessee, in 1928. His treatment of the Psalms is also unusual. In fact, he seems to do nothing except from the beaten track. The 150 Psalms are separated into 125 Prayers, 122 Collects and 47 Praises.

B. THE BOOK OF JOB

The book of Job has long been regarded as the greatest poem o
ancient times, but it offers numerous difficulties. Biblical scholar
differ about this book perhaps more than about any other book o
the Bible. It is known that the form in which it appeared originall
in the Septuagint was very much shorter than that found in the
Hebrew. Many scholars reject certain parts of it as interpolations
such as the speech of Elihu. Certain parts seem to have little relation
to the poem, such as the description of Behemoth and the discussion
of Wisdom.

The Rev. Chauncy Lee, under the title, "A Trial of Virtue", pub
lished the first independent translation of Job in America in 1806 a
Hartford, Connecticut, it really being a paraphrase. George R
Noyes, D. D. published a translation of Job, at Cambridge, in 1827
this being his first published version of any part of the Bible. Rev
William Bachelder Green, a Unitarian minister, published a new
version of Job at Boston in 1866.

"The Epic of the Inner Life", a new translation of the book of
Job by John F. Genung, was published at Boston and New York in
1891, accompanied with notes. This was a splendid translation and
among the sanest treatments of the whole subject ever offered.

Rev. Emil Lund, a Swedish Lutheran minister, published a trans
lation of Job, which he writes, Ijjob, at Rock Island, Illinois, in 1903.
He regards the prose parts of the book as historical. New transla
tions of Job were published also by Homer B. Sprague in 1913 at
Boston, Edwin Freegard, at St. Louis, Missouri, in 1914, and H. P.
Shove at Kirkwood, Missouri, in 1915.

Using the Anglo-American Version, Horace Meyer Kallen, Ph. D.,
who was named by William James in 1910 as editor of his unfinished
book, *Some Problems of Philosophy,* published the book of Job in
1918, in Boston and New York, under this striking title, "The Book
of Job as a Greek Tragedy, restored, with an Introductory Essay."
The introduction by George Foot Moore tells us that the most
striking feature of reconstruction offered is, that it provides a reason
for being, and a suitable place for such parts of the book as recent
critics have commonly pronounced additions to the text. In his ar
rangement the poem on Wisdom, chapter 28, and the poems on
Behemoth and Leviathan, chapters 40 and 41, are thought to be
choral odes which belong after the speeches. The speech of Elihu
finds a natural place in his arrangement. It is interesting, in this

connection, to know that Theodore of Mopsuestia, who stood alone in the early church, in his position that the Song of Solomon dealt exclusively with human love, an idea now universally accepted, expressed the opinion that the book of Job was an imitation of Greek tragedy.

William Wallace Martin published at Nashville, Tennessee, in 1929, "The Book of Job in two versions, a Judean Version and Ephramaean, and the book of Ecclesiastes." He regards Job as one of the earliest books of the Bible, consisting of three books combined. He separates the book into two versions, as indicated in the title, and the accounts of Job's disasters and the final recovery of his wealth is considered a midrash, a Jewish school story. It is separated and printed as an appendix.

5. CHILDREN'S BIBLES

Many abridgments of the Bible for the use of children have been published in America. They contain the parts that are adapted to the understanding of the little folks, and generally the language is altered for their use. Many story books have been published for children and youth, in which Bible stories have been entirely rewritten in very simple language. Among the more important efforts to serve the little folks may be mentioned "The Children's Bible," compiled by Mrs. Joseph B. Gilder, with a preface by the Rev. Francis Brown, D. D., and an introduction by the Rt. Rev. Henry C. Potter, published in New York in 1902. "The Child's Bible," by a Lady from Cincinnati, was published in Philadelphia in 1934.

The most pretentious effort to serve the children, and so far as we know the best that has been undertaken, is a Bible now in preparation, it being the King James Version simplified for children, youth and the uneducated, not choice selections, but the whole Bible. In order to make the Bible thoroughly understandable to the young, many words and expressions are paraphrased; and this is done freely where necessary.

This work is being prepared by the Rev. Richard W. Lewis of Siloam Springs, Arkansas. Mr. Lewis was for many years a very popular Presbyterian pastor; then he spent several years in evangelistic work. In more recent years he has been considered a specialist in young people's work, and has delivered numerous lectures and addresses in all parts of the United States to the young people. It was his work among the young people that led him to realize fully the need of a Bible in language that the children, the youth and the uneducated could understand, and thus he began its preparation. It is edited by Dr. David L. Cooper, the founder and president of the Biblical Research Society of Los Angeles, California. The Gospel of John is now in the press of the Eerdman Publishing Company of Grand Rapids, Michigan, to be followed by the New Testament, and then the whole Bible.

This Bible has the enthusiastic endorsement of such Christian leaders as Drs. Biederwolf, Mark A. Matthews, Walter L. Wilson, Gerald B. Winrod, J. E. Jaderquist, Paul W. Rood, President John W. Brown, and many others.

6. BIBLE COMMENTARIES

The Bible has furnished an inexhaustible source of nourishment for faith and the support of Christianity. The religious need of changing times finds in each age and condition the seed-germs of the truths it requires. The critical movement, in the interpretation of the Scriptures, however, was slow in getting under way in America. In early times the population was thinly scattered, and the country had no inherited culture, no stores of learning and no great universities. The Bible alone, since the country was intensely Protestant, counted for more than all else. But the influence of the historical method of interpretation grew with the years. The great Schaff-Lange Commentary, translated and edited by Philip Schaff, and published in 25 volumes in New York, 1866-88, marked a decided advance.

American scholarship has joined with English scholarship in producing the two greatest Bible Dictionaries in the English world; *The Dictionary of the Bible,* edited by Hastings and published in 1899-1904, and the *Encyclopedia Biblica,* edited by Cheyne and Black, and published in 1899-1903. It has also contributed its part to the production of *The International Critical Commentary,* one of the best.

America has used numerous commentaries made in England and Germany, and has produced many at home, critical, devotional and homiletic. They are too numerous to mention. A list of the more important ones published early in America has been given under "The More Important Annotated Bibles from Abroad," in chapter IV.

CHAPTER VI

THE FOUNDING AND WORK OF BIBLE SOCIETIES

THE history of the Bible in America very naturally includes, at least, a brief account of Bible Societies. Hundreds of them have been organized in America, from time to time, their original purpose being to encourage the distribution and use of the Scriptures. The service they render has been enlarged until our national Society is seeking to do its part in providing the translation, the printing and the distribution of the Bible into the various languages and dialects of the whole world, in collaboration with the British, Scottish and other Bible Societies.

1. PRECURSORS ABROAD

Bible and Tract Societies were greatly stimulated as a direct result of the work of John Wesley in England. As early as 1749, Wesley published tracts and books, and his preachers and others became colporteurs. Wesley and Coke, in 1782, organized the Society for the Distribution of Religious Tracts among the Poor. A Naval and Military Bible Society was organized by Wesleyan Methodists in 1779. Speaking on the subject, the Rev. Dr. Dobbin of Dublin University, says, "There were no Bible, tract or missionary Societies to employ the church's powers and indicate its path of duty; but Wesley started them all." [1] This, however, puts the matter too strongly as the following will indicate.

The Society for the Promotion of Christian Knowledge was formed in London in 1648, a hundred years ahead of Wesley, becoming the first society to provide the common people with the Bible. The Society for the Propagation of the Gospel in Foreign Parts, founded in London in 1701, has done a great work in supplying Bibles, both in England and America. The Scottish Society for Propagating Christian Knowledge, founded in 1709, made the matter of circulating the Bible a part of its work, both in Scotland and America. The Canstein Bible Institute was established at Halle, Germany, in 1710, this being the first Society founded with the object of printing the Scriptures at small cost; New Testaments were sold at four cents and Bibles at twelve cents. [2]

In the last half of the eighteenth century numerous Societies

[1] Dorchester, *Christianity in the United States*, p 417.
[2] Norlie, *The Translated Bible*, p 200.

sprang up in Great Britain which distributed Bibles as a part of their work, but all these did not begin to meet the need.

The British and Foreign Bible Society was founded in London, in 1804, by Churchmen and Dissenters, a really union work. This organization, consciously or unconsciously, offered the first definite steps toward a reunion of the Protestant churches; it, at least, caused the various denominations to work together. It has rendered a world-wide service, and is the most powerful and influential Bible Society in the world today.

Bible Societies sprang up everywhere in the early part of the nineteenth century—German, Hungarian, Finnish, Prussian, Russian, Danish, Dutch, Norwegian, Swedish and others.

2. THE AMERICAN BIBLE SOCIETY

The Philadelphia Bible Society, founded in 1808, was the first in America. Its originators immediately sent out an appeal to the leading representatives of the various denominations, urging them to form societies. Within a year, 1809, societies had been launched in Connecticut, Massachusetts, New York, New Jersey, and Maine. By 1816 there were considerably more than 100 Bible Societies in the United States, each independent.

The British and Foreign Bible Society most generously complimented these organizations, and presented each state society with from three hundred to five hundred dollars; so that by 1816 the British and Foreign Bible Society had presented American societies with a total of £3,122. This courtesy takes on a new meaning when it is remembered that it occurred very soon after the Revolutionary War, and the War of 1812. The British and Foreign Bible Society certainly harbored no ill-will against America on these accounts.

A. ORGANIZATION AND PURPOSE

The need of a national society early became evident. The credit for the idea would seem to belong to the Rev. Samuel Mills, who reported, in 1815, the destitution of the West and Southwest. The first active effort in that direction, however, was due to Hon. Elias Boudinot, president of the New Jersey Society, who issued a call on January 17, 1816, for representatives of the local and state societies everywhere to meet in New York on May 8, 1816, to consider the matter. This resulted in a gathering of 60 men, representing 35 soieties. This group organized the American Bible Society,[3] a national institution, electing the Hon. Elias Boudinot as the first president. Mr. Boudinot had rendered distinguished service during the Revolution, and twice had served as president of the Continental Congress.

The British and Foreign Bible Society was the model which America copied, making what seemed necessary changes. That Society immediately sent its warmest congratulations, with the offer of a gift of twenty-two hundred dollars (500 pounds). Almost everywhere the Society received a royal welcome. During the first year 43 existing state and local societies became auxiliaries, and more than 40 new societies were launched as auxiliaries.

The purpose of the American Bible Society, as expressed in its constitution, was to "encourage a wider circulation of the Scriptures, without note or comment," its primary aim being of course, to serve the United States and its territories, and then to extend its help to other countries according to its ability.

It has always been the fixed policy of the American Bible Society, as it has been of the British, to publish the Scriptures "without note or comment." This is no arbitrary or blind groping in the dark for the best methods, but is based on the actual use of notes and comments in the early history of the printed Bible which had proved a hindrance rather than a help.

Wyclif who translated the first Bible into English in 1382, introduced short comments into the margins of his Bible. Tyndale, in his New Testaments, beginning in 1525, added many notes, often controversial in character, some quite bitter, born of the peculiar circumstances of the times. These notes prejudiced many people against his translations. Coverdale was much more inclined to bridge over difficulties than was Tyndale; therefore, his Bible of 1535 contained only a few notes, and these were far less objectionable than those of Tyndale. Matthew's Bible of 1537 once more put the fat in the fire, with notes explanatory and polemic, some of which were resented bitterly. The Great Bible, prepared by Coverdale and published in 1539, did not contain notes, but it was originally intended to include them. The text was put out with pointing hands to call attention to them, but for some reason they were never printed, and these pointing hands were later dropped from the text. The Geneva

---

[3] Much of the information of this chapter is taken from Henry Otis Dwight's *The Centennial History of the American Bible Society*, The Macmillan Company, 1916.

Bible of 1560 was abundantly supplied with notes, many distinctly Calvinistic, and some bitterly anti-Catholic. It was the purpose of Matthew Parker, the originator of the Bishops' Bible, that it should contain "no bitter notes upon any text," but certain notes were distinctly Calvinistic, making it, as the Geneva, the Bible of a party.

The Rheims-Douai Bible of 1582 and 1609-10, especially the New Testament, was well supplied with notes, many being controversial and intolerant, serving only to perpetuate the bitterness of the day. These notes provoked more than one vigorous Protestant reply, and these were none too gentle. Alexander Geddes, a Catholic priest, speaks of them as "virulent and manifestly calculated to support a system, not a genuine Catholicity, but of Transalpine Popery." [4]

When the King James Version was made one rule governing its translators was that no notes or comments should be used, except as marginal translations of certain Hebrew and Greek words, and this proved one cause of its widespread popularity. It contained nothing anybody could object to. Notes inevitably make a version the Bible of some particular party. Consequently the American Bible Society wisely decided to give the world the Scriptures in a form acceptable to all.

B. DEVELOPMENT OF ITS WORK AND METHODS

Naturally enough the American Bible Society felt its way for many years, adapting its work and methods to the needs as they arose. Auxiliary societies were organized at first very extensively, the Society depending upon them to serve their local communities, and to provide a substantial support, in the form of gifts to the national Society. Auxiliaries had worked well in England, and naturally were tried out thoroughly in America.

It was early discovered, however, that auxiliary societies alone were not sufficient; the territory was too large, and many sections too sparsely settled. Something more than a letter was often needed to stir the auxiliaries to do their best, sometimes even to function at all. To meet the needs as they arose it early became necessary to employ agents and colporteurs.

Its work quite appropriately began at home and abroad almost simultaneously. It was soon discovered that Bibles in five or six

[4] Quoted from Hoare, *Our English Bible*, p 234-35.

languages were needed to supply the United States. Accordingly, plates for a French Bible were provided in 1816; and provision was made for Scriptures in German and Gaelic in 1817, and for a New Testament in Spanish. Other languages were provided later. In 1816, the year of its organization, the American Bible Society aided, to the extent of five hundred dollars, the Rev. Ferdinand Leo, a German living in Paris, in printing De Sacy's version of the Bible; this was the first aid granted any foreign country. Very early one thousand dollars was sent to William Carey in India, to assist him and his associates in the work of translating and printing the Scriptures.

Early in its history the American Bible Society began to discover the need of Bibles for foreign missionary work, and this fact was brought before the Society very forcibly in 1827, when from India came the question, "Ought not the American Bible Society supply Bibles needed by American missionaries?" To ask such a question was to answer it, of course. The Bible Society, representing the various denominations, was the agency best fitted to make such provision. The Society, therefore, soon announced its purpose to undertake such work, quickly becoming a clearing house for the needs of American missionaries everywhere. To do this, however, it was soon found necessary to assist in translation as well as in printing. Moreover, it soon developed that it was far better for the Bible Society also to have charge of the distribution of these Scriptures.

It was not long until the American Bible Society was aiding, not only American missionaries, but others as well. In its great service throughout the years, it has worked in harmony with the British and Foreign Bible Society, to the great credit of both institutions.

The work of the American Bible Society has long been world-wide. Service in Latin America began early. Scriptures were sent to South America in Spanish and Portuguese; no less than 3,967 volumes being sent in 1826. Aid has been rendered in Ceylon, the Sandwich Islands, Turkey, France, Germany, Italy, Russia, India, China, Japan, Korea, Cuba, the Philippines, Denmark, Norway, Belgium, Poland, Bulgaria, Greece, Chechoslavakia, Egypt, Syria, Palestine, Arabia, Persia, Siam, Burma, many South Sea Islands, Central, East and West and South Africa, Mexico—the whole world in fact.

C. SOME CONTROVERSIES THAT TROUBLED

The Lord's work can never be done without criticism and opposition; and the American Bible Society was no sooner organized than a certain few began to find fault. Some were opposed to a union effort among the denominations in such work; others regarded it as dangerous to give the Bible freely to the common man without notes and comments to explain it. The Society was even denounced as a dangerous move. It was declared that it was likely, with the great organization that it might build up, to become a positive menace to free government. Such criticism, however, did not last long. Throughout the years there have been occasional criticisms, most of them entirely groundless.

Strange as it may seem, one of the very first difficulties the Society encountered arose over the matter of offering prayer at the regular meetings of the board. Dr. Boudinot, the first president of the Society, was old, often ill and unable to attend frequent meetings. Other members presided in his absence. It was customary at first for the presiding officer, at the beginning of the meeting, to read some selection of Scripture and offer prayer. Various denominations were represented in the board. Some prayed extemporaneously, while others read their prayers. No matter which kind of prayer was offered, certain men were displeased and could not join. The outcome of the matter was the decision of the board, that, at its meetings, the presiding officer would read any selection of Scripture he might choose, but he must offer no prayer. At a Bible Society meeting prayer must be omitted to prevent a row among Christians! And the British and Foreign Bible Society was forced to adopt the same practice. In the first national effort at union work among the various denominations, in both England and America, nobody could be permitted to offer prayer! This story alone is amply sufficient to prove that the good Lord is merciful. Fortunately the Christian men who manage both Societies are now sufficiently civilized that prayer can be offered in board meetings.

Controversies concerning the apocrypha [5] have been the occasion of considerable trouble, in connection with the work of the American Bible Society.

The Roman Catholic church, as has been said, regards the apocrypha as a vital part of the Bible, its books being considered of equal inspiration and authority with any others. While some Protestant churches regard the apocrypha as being a part of the Bible, they assign it an inferior place. Still other Protestants consider it entirely

[5] For the history of the apocrypha, and how it became a part of the Bible, see pp. 63-65.

out of place in the Bible. With such conflicting views among Christians, it is naturally difficult to please everybody.

Roman Catholics have often made trouble with those who would distribute Bibles, and there can be no question that a very large part of such trouble—some have said all of it—has been due to the fact that Bibles have been offered without the apocrypha, or that were not approved by Catholic authorities.

Until 1827 the British and Foreign Bible Society and the American Bible Society both printed the apocrypha, but following a lengthy controversy at this time, they both ceased to print it. Scio's version in Spanish was a Catholic translation containing the apocrypha, and both Bible Societies published it. The American Bible Society was circulating this Bible in South America, where Catholic priests permitted it freely. Later it was printed without the apocrypha, and this resulted in trouble. It was used until about 1841 when a version in Spanish, translated from the originals by Valera in 1602, was substituted. This has been the chief Spanish version used since, though about 1885 an alternative version was prepared by the Rev. H. B. Pratt, D. D.

We do not doubt that the American Bible Society took the wisest and best course in the matter for the Society that it could take, under all the circumstances, but it seems a pity that circumstances were not such that Catholics could have had their choice. In such case much difficulty would have been avoided.

Sectarianism has often shed its blight on Christianity, and perhaps no denomination has been less guilty than any other. One of the most serious difficulties the American Bible Society ever had, and one that threatened its very existence, grew out of sectarian translations for missionary purposes.

In 1835 the Rev. Mr. Pearse, a missionary in Calcutta, and later a district superintendent of the Society in Kentucky, asked the Society to aid in printing the Scriptures in the Bengali language. He had translated, the word *baptidzo* with a Bengali word meaning "immerse." Because of this fact the British and Foreign Bible Society had declined to aid in the printing of his version.

The matter was referred to the Committee on Distribution, which reported that aid could not be given, because of the sectarian character of the translation. Certain objections to this report resulted in the reference of the whole matter to a special committee, composed of one representative from each of the seven denominations making up its board. By a report of six to one the special committee agreed with the former report. Dr. Spencer H. Cone, the corresponding secretary of the Society, and the Baptist member of this special committee, filed a dissent. The board of the Society then adopted a resolution providing that the American Bible Society could use its money in the printing only of such Scriptures as all denominations could use; and this resolution had the cordial support of many leading Baptists, and became the fixed policy of the Society.

Adoniram Judson, an American missionary in Burmah, had made a translation of the New Testament into Burmese, and it had been an "immersion" version. The Bible Society had aided in its printing, but this was done before the question of its sectarian character had been raised. When it was learned that it was an "immersion" version it also figured in the controversy.

In May, 1836 Dr. Cone resigned his position with the American Bible Society, becoming the president of the American and Foreign Bible Society, a new Baptist organization and a rival of the American Bible Society. Its chief purpose naturally would be to provide "immersion" versions for missionary purposes.

The difficulty encountered by the Bible Society in an innocent and honest effort to provide a text free from printer's errors and uniform in spelling has been told elsewhere.[6] This difficulty also threatened the existence of the Society.

D. THE HAND OF GOD IN DIFFICULTIES

During its early history the American Bible Society found headquarters where it could, but in 1822 a building of three stories, with a fifty feet front, was erected at 115 Nassau Street, New York City, at a cost of $22,500, all of which was raised for this particular purpose, the debt for the building being cleared up in 1826. Here the Society housed eleven hand presses, its equipment at that time.

By 1846, however, the Bible Society was stirred with its vision of the possibilities of its work. Accordingly, plans for the coming year were enlarged, the board of managers being directed to print a total of 750,000 copies of the Scriptures by the end of March, 1847, and the following year they hoped to reach a million copies. But they fell short of 750,000 copies by 100,000. It was discovered that the building in use was too small to hold enough presses to do the amount that had been called for.

[6] See pp. 209-11.

More commodious headquarters were necessary, if the Society was to further enlarge its output. Consequently, in July, 1847, the Society contracted for a lot on Chambers Street, where it was expected to provide twice the space contained in their present building. But this property was abandoned through no fault of the Society; among other things because the title was found to be questionable.

Some other suitable place downtown was sought for several years, but simply could not be found. Then the restrictions that confined the search to "downtown" were removed, and a place was sought elsewhere. Finally, in 1852, utterly failing to find anything elsewhere at all suitable, the board bought a small city block of three quarters of an acre at Astor Place. This seemed a foolish thing to do, but the committee explained that it was necessary to buy so large an amount or none, and suggested that any land not needed could be sold. However, it was decided to retain the whole plot.

On this space the Society erected a six story building, with a street front of 741 feet, and a floor space of about three acres, not counting cellars and vaults. With the land the total cost was $303,000. The former headquarters on Nassau Street were sold for $105,000, a handsome profit over its first cost, and $59,000 was given by friends of the work in New York. Then $140,000 was borrowed. Rents from the building enabled the Society, in good time, to pay the entire debt, and not one dollar of money given for the distribution of Bibles was used.

The building of such commodious headquarters, at that time, was a daring thing to do, and could have been done only by men of faith and vision. The board had not thought of such a venture until all efforts at smaller things had been defeated. But without such headquarters the greatly enlarged service during the Civil War period, and the growth and development of the work since, would not have been possible.

When the matter was reviewed by the board, it was found that the land they had bought had been sold three times, before they secured it, and each time the sale had fallen through for some reason. This fact, coupled with the circumstances of their utter failure to do smaller things elsewhere, helped to convince the board that the hand of God had been clearly evident in the whole matter. These men left on record with the Society their conviction that Providence had directed them in the undertaking. Pious Christians will not quarrel with their conviction.

Providing suitable headquarters for the work is not the only place where the hand of God may be clearly seen in the work of the American Bible Society. Institutions distinctly missionary and dependent upon the general public for financial support often face serious difficulty. Perhaps no other institution in America has had a more marvelous record than the Bible Society. While there are those who doubtless will feel that the institution fortunately muddled through many trying times, others will be sure that God in His Providence has provided.

The work of the Society, both at home and abroad, grew from its inception, and by 1837 it had come to do a very considerable volume of business; but this year proved to be one of serious financial stringency everywhere. Definite pledges had been given for aid to missionaries on the foreign field, but the money was not in hand to meet the obligations. Book sales dropped off, and donations to the work greatly decreased. The Society was really in debt to the mission in Ceylon, because the missionaries there had gone forward with their printing as soon as the promise of help had been received. The Society now found itself in a desperate situation. What to do nobody knew. The matter of stopping the presses in New York was considered, but this would involve the dismissal of their workmen. It was also felt that it might be wise to notify the missions, to whom promises had been made, that they simply could not keep their agreements in the matter. But this was a terribly drastic measure. Naturally the Society hesitated at any of these things; its directors could only pray, hope and wait.

Nevertheless, before the end of the year 1838, the dark cloud had completely disappeared. The auxiliaries had sent the largest gifts of their history. Without solicitation and entirely unexpected, Mr. James Douglas of Cavors, Scotland, had sent a draft for a thousand pounds. Legacies came piling in to the amount of $18,000. The crisis had passed and only Providence could explain.

The year 1857 also brought financial panic to America. By August that year business failures had become epidemic, some 5,000 firms failing in a few weeks, with liabilities that totaled $290,000,000. Banks suspended payments, and the income of the Bible Society simply dried up for a time.

The Society was then in the midst of its second effort to supply every family in the United States with a Bible. This work ceased at once, and for a time it seemed as if the presses must be stopped.

In the Providence of God the year 1857 witnessed one of the greatest revivals America has ever known, and this helped. Donations for the year, however, dropped $33,000 below that of the year before, but legacies which had never averaged over $20,000 a year, now jumped to $152,000 over a period of three years, 1856, 1857, and 1858. This saved the day.

The Civil War, for a time, seemed to threaten the Society. Up to that time it had depended largely on the donations of auxiliary societies, but it now lost 653 auxiliaries located in the seceding states. Naturally support of its work suffered heavily as a result.

The Civil War, however, created a situation calling for a greatly enlarged service on the part of the Bible Society, and a larger income was necessary if the increased service was to be rendered. The Bible Society, facing the situation with faith, deliberately proposed to serve both the North and the South during the war, to the extent of its ability, and so notified all its old auxiliaries in May, 1861.

The Bible Society resolved to place a Bible in the hands of every soldier, both North and South. This was done, as far as possible, through the auxiliaries, many soldiers in the North being supplied at camps before going to the front.

The Christian Commission, organized by the Y. M. C. A., received many grants of Scriptures for use among the army and navy, about 1,500 clergymen and laymen assisting in the distribution. The Bible Society furnished the Commission 1,466,484 volumes of Scriptures for such use, and 35,000 volumes of Scripture were given to southern soldiers in northern prisons.

Bibles were sent south directly to the Confederate Army, the generals and guards permitting them to pass unmolested, under a sort of truce. In this way some 300,000 Bibles, Testaments and single Gospels were sent from New York to southern soldiers. Now and then some were held up, but all difficulties in such shipments were removed by 1863, and books were shipped regularly by way of Fortress Monroe.

To render such enlarged service cost money, but somehow it came. Unexpectedly gifts and legacies piled up. People in Turkey sent $1,000. The Jubilee Celebration of 1866 brought in considerable money. Donations from individuals and churches, in 1866, reached $71,874, and not again was so much received from this source for 40 years. The total donations for the war period—1861-1870—from churches and individuals—reached $507,925; the auxiliaries sent in $814,517; legacies mounted to $865,252, larger than ever before. The sale of books totalled $3,053,802 and kept the presses going. Aside from the sale of books, a total of $2,877,694 had been given the

Society for its work. These gifts were unparalleled, but it was a period of unparalleled need. The Society found itself at the end of the period with larger resources than at any previous time in its history.

The attitude of the American Bible Society toward the South during the war, so distinctly Christian, helped marvelously to heal the bitterness when the war was over. The Society could not only work there at once, but its services were sought. No sooner had the war ended, than pitiful appeals for Bibles began to pour in on the Society, and so it was decided that one feature of the Jubilee Year, 1866, should be the resupply of the South with Bibles. The war had created great destitution in this regard. Southern Christians responded to the offer and cooperated freely. Bible societies in the South soon resumed their cooperation with the American Bible Society, and in a short time the South was sending its contributions to the national work. By 1869 a total of 856 auxiliaries existed in the South.

Another financial panic came in 1893, paralyzing business and greatly reducing the income of the Bible Society. At this time legacies for ten years had averaged $126,000 a year; but in 1893, the year of the panic, $247,000 came from this source alone, as if specially to meet the need.

In 1910, 1911, and 1912 there was a loss of the usual income, but during this time the Society received $1,749,000 in legacies, and again the day was saved.

E. THE BIBLE FOR IMMIGRANTS

The thirteen colonies formed but a fringe along the Atlantic seacoast. Settlers, however, soon began to push west into the wilderness, forming a second fringe of colonies which became states in the early history of the Republic. By the middle of the eighteenth century settlements had reached the mountain barrier which separates the Atlantic slope from the Ohio Valley, but at the close of the Revolution the only settlements in the Ohio Valley were in Tennessee and Kentucky.

In 1803, only thirteen years before the organization of the American Bible Society, Thomas Jefferson stretched his theory of government until it cracked, so he said, and bought the Louisiana Territory from the Emperor Napoleon, thus adding about one-third the present area of the United States. The War with Mexico in 1847 resulted

DR. PHILIP SCHAFF

n the addition of territory about equal in area to the thirteen orig-
nal colonies. California had previously declared its independence of
Mexico. About this time the government secured a treaty with Great
Britain which gave it undisputed possession of the territory out of
which the states of Washington, Oregon and Nevada were carved.
Thus the territory of the United States was extended to its present
boundaries.

The Westward Flow of Population

New land laws were enacted in 1820, after which a man could exchange one hundred dollars for eighty acres of government land.
Many took advantage of this opportunity, while many others, without money, simply squatted where they would, and the government
was lax in enforcing the law against them. The fur trade finally
opened up the Far West, the trader often becoming the pathfinder
for the settlers.

Many things contributed to the immense immigration to America in the nineteenth century. It should be remembered that the
century was an age of invention. Steam was applied to transportation and industry. In 1807 Robert Fulton built his steamboat, and
proved it a success on the Hudson. Ocean travel by steam began in
1838, enabling men to cross the Atlantic in fifteen days, eight weeks
less than formerly. By 1851 eight days only were required to cross
the Atlantic. The locomotive made eight miles an hour in 1825, but
by 1829 it had been able to make thirty-five miles. The postage
stamp came into use, and mail facilities were greatly improved.
The Atlantic cable was laid in 1866. Steam, electricity and oil were
being used in many ways to do the work formerly done by hand.
Portland cement came in 1825, friction matches in 1827, the reaper
in 1834, the steam hammer in 1842, the typewriter in 1843, the sew-
ing machine in 1846, and Bessemer steel in 1855. These are but a
few of the epoch making inventions of the first part of the nineteenth
century. The government granted three patents in 1790, but in 1860
it issued 4,778, the total number from 1790 to 1860 being 43,431, and
by 1916 the total was 1,125,000. These inventions encouraged immigration and the vast unoccupied territory of our country invited it.
In 1848 the convulsions which shook Europe drove thousands to
America, and they came from 1849 to 1853 at the rate of a thousand
a day.

During the first five years of the American Bible Society's work

immigrants arrived at the rate of about 10,000 a year. Then abou
1840 the floodgates opened. Immigration became a world movement
never in all history has there been witnessed such migratory move
ments. The population of the United States in 1820 was only 9,638,
453, and 77 per cent of this lived east of the Alleghanies.

The American people from the beginning were migratory
inviting fields luring them west. Many Christians moved west, losing
their church connection, making it necessary to follow them up with
missionary effort, and home missions were born. The immigrant:
pouring into the country were going west, and they required atten
tion. They must be made into good American citizens, and one of
the first necessities in the case was to supply them with the Scripture:
in their native tongues, this being the work of the American Bible
Society, which, indeed, largely led to its creation.

From 1820 to 1880 immigrants came chiefly from western and
northern Europe, and, but for a certain group of Irish, were mainly
Protestant. From 1880 to 1925 they came chiefly from eastern and
southern Europe, and were mainly Catholic.

First in importance among immigrants have been those from Great
Britain. From 1820 to 1920, England sent the United States 2,591,-
231. While this number is much smaller than that of some other
countries, the English have been more influential, occupying con-
trolling positions in every walk of life. The Scotch, Scotch-Irish, and
Welsh have been numerous and influential. Between 1820 and 1920
Ireland sent the United States 4,670,805 people, giving America more
than she kept at home. In the same period came 748,788 Scotch and
262,921 Welsh. During this same time the Dutch sent to the United
States 339,639, the French 352,752. The Germans have poured into
the United States, until, according to some authorities, every fourth
person among the white population is a German.[7] Norwegians began
to come in considerable numbers, beginning in 1825, when the ship
Restorationem arrived in New York with 52 on board. They brought
the New Testament with them. For long the Norwegians had no
Bible of their own, the Danes forcing their Bible on them. They secured their first New Testament in 1819, and the first whole Bible in
1844. Not less than 2,138,000 Swedes, Norwegians and Danes came
to America between 1820 and 1920. During that same time the
United States absorbed a total of 33,803,108 immigrants.

Men finally settled all parts of the West. Thirty years of conflict
ended in the utter defeat of the Indians. The cattle barons, with

[7] Norlie, *History of the Norwegian People in America*, p 81.

their innumerable herds, went from Texas to Wyoming, and at last were driven from there by millions who were bent on founding new homes. Railroads crossed the continent, opening up new and vast empires. Big business was born, grew and developed into giant power, and everywhere those quiet but massive streams of immigration were welcomed, and used.

This influx of immigration laid great and new burdens on the American Bible Society. These millions needed the Bible in their own tongue. Many of them were Christians of the highest order, some only nominally so, and others in no sense Christian. The Bible Society bent itself to the task.

In providing these people auxiliary societies, at ports of entry, in New York, on the Pacific Coast, and at points along the line of travel westward across the country, were supplied with Scriptures for use among them. Provision was even made in France to supply immigrants before they sailed.

Scriptures in German and French were being printed in New York, and other European Bibles were bought from the British and Foreign Bible Society. In 1836 Scriptures were ordered from Europe in Italian, Portuguese, Swedish, Danish, Dutch and Welsh. From 1837 the American Bible Society began a systematic work of enormous proportions to provide Scriptures for immigrants.

The work might be illustrated with a few examples. In 1854 the Southwestern Bible Society of New Orleans secured from the American Bible Society 10,000 volumes in 13 languages and distributed them; and in 1858 the same society placed Testaments or other portions of the Scriptures in the hands of people from 30 nations, speaking 20 languages. The Bible Society of New York, as far as possible, met every man who landed with the New Testament in his own language, obtained from the American Bible Society, and presented by a man of his own nation.

New Testaments were printed in German, Italian, Dutch and Norwegian, in columns parallel with the English, in order to encourage the immigrants to learn the English language.

As a result of investigations made in 1907, the Bible Society increased its number of Bibles in European languages to 42. Thus, with the Indian and other dialects and tongues, at the close of 100 years' work, the American Bible Society offered the Scriptures in the United States in 99 different languages and dialects. In English the Society printed the King James Version exclusively until 1904, when its constitution was revised to permit it to print revisions of this version. The American Standard Bible and the King James Version are now both used.

A national Bible Society naturally had a warm place in the heart of a Christian nation; and it, therefore, grew with the country. Within five years of its organization the Society had more than 300 auxiliaries whose contributions to the work had reached a total of $39,360.90.

At a meeting of the Society in May, 1841, at the end of twenty-five years' work, the Rev. Hiram Bingham, a missionary of the American Board in the Sandwich Islands, who had spent fifteen years in translating the Bible into the Hawaiian language, delivered an address, and presented the Society with a copy of his Bible, made possible by the Society's aid. During these twenty-five years the Society had printed Bibles, or some portions of it, in five American Indian languages, seven European languages, five languages of Asiatic Turkey, seven languages of India, besides the Hawaiian, Chinese and the Grebo languages of West Africa; and it had bought Scriptures for its work in twenty other languages. The total receipts of the Society had amounted to $947,384 and it had printed 2,795,698 volumes. The Scriptures had been circulated in about fifty languages.

Four times the American Bible Society resolved to supply every family in the United States with Bibles, either by sale or gift. The first effort began in 1829, when the Society was only thirteen years old, the proposition provoking great enthusiasm among the 568 local Bible societies of the country. The work covered a period of more than two years, and the Society learned much from this experience as to its responsibilities where there were no auxiliaries.

In 1846 the Society decided to put Bibles into the hotels of the country, on payment of one-half the cost, and many Bibles were provided on this basis.

The second general supply was ordered in 1856, requiring more than four years to complete it, and the distribution of 3,678,837 volumes.

In the midst of its great work following the Civil War, in 1866, the Society decided to make the third general supply of Bibles. At the end of five years a total of 2,990,119 families had been visited and not less than 695,866 volumes had been distributed by all the agencies concerned, which included the American Sunday School Union and the American Tract Society.

The fourth general supply was ordered in 1882. The American Bible Society sent out some 200 colporteurs of its own into sparsely settled fields, supplementing the work of the auxiliaries and volunteers. A total of 8,146,808 volumes were distributed by sale or gift. These figures include grants to the American Sunday School Union and tract societies.

In 1890 the Society decided to furnish a Bible to every child in the United States, under fifteen years of age, and able to read.

The Bible Society is always on hand in emergencies. In the great Mississippi flood of 1927, thousands of homes were swept away. To re-supply the flood sufferers, 2,003 Bibles, 9,141 Testaments, or 12,144 volumes of Scripture were provided.

The World War called for the largest service, in quantity, ever provided by the American Bible Society in any single emergency. Scriptures were distributed through the army and navy chaplains, but chiefly through the Y. M. C. A., to which the Society made a donation of 1,000,000 Testaments, the largest single gift of its history. From April, 1917, to April, 1918, the Society issued 2,231,831 Bibles, Testaments and portions in khaki and navy blue, for the men in our army and navy. It also supplied special editions of the Scriptures in several European and Asiatic languages for the use of other peoples, one unique service "being Russian Scriptures, printed in Germany, by American money sent through British channels, and supplied to Russian prisoners."

One of the most recent outstanding services of the American Bible Society has been its supply of the Scriptures for the Civilian Conservation Camps. A stock of Bibles and New Testaments was maintained at Washington, under charge of the Chief of Chaplains, who arranged for their distribution, the government providing transportation. To December, 1935, 2,000 camp libraries had been provided with Bibles and 125,000 Testaments had been distributed among the men.

At the end of a hundred years of service, or by 1916, the American Bible Society had placed in the United States about 70,000,000 copies of the Scriptures; and some 45,000,000 volumes had been distributed on foreign fields, in many lands and on four continents.

For the year 1934 the Bible Society distributed 343,415 Bibles, 416,842 Testaments, and 6,757,291 portions, making a grand total of 7,517,548 volumes. An average of 14 volumes were issued every minute of every hour, day and night, for the year. During this year it supplied the Bible in 148 different languages and dialects. Some languages have more than one written character. In Turkish, for example, the Bible is printed in Arabic, Armenian, Greek and Roman letters. In addition to the 148 distinct languages the Society provided Scriptures in 28 various characters of different languages, making a total of 176.

From its organization in 1816 to the end of the year 1934, the American Bible Society distributed a grand total of 261,365,086 volumes of Scripture; of these 30,083,975 were whole Bibles. The Bible or some part of it has been printed in 972 languages and dialects. The whole Bible is now printed in 175 languages; the complete New Testament in 208 more; at least one whole book in 514; and translations of less than a whole book in 75 other languages.[8] But it is estimated that there are some 2,000 languages and dialects spoken in the world today, so that the work of providing the Scriptures in the languages of the world has only fairly begun. However, during the past decade some portion of the Bible has appeared in a new language at the rate of one in every five weeks. The British and Foreign Bible Society has been the chief producer, the American Bible Society being next, and then comes the National Bible Society of Scotland.

The American Bible Society once did its own printing and binding, but the work is now done by contract. The Society estimates that during 1934 there were probably no less than 27,000,000 volumes of Scripture issued in the world, 22,647,557 of which were put out by the three leading Bible Societies. The Society further estimates that fully 937,000,000 volumes of Scripture have been issued all told, from the first printed, the three chief Bible Societies having put out 846,077,321 volumes. Those who think the Bible is being outgrown find little to encourage them in these figures, and more especially when it is remembered that there is a hunger for God's Word that is not satisfied even by such an output.

Volumes would be required to tell the story of individual lives, families and even whole communities, that have been transformed into worthy citizens by the presence of the Bible, without note or comment. No other book has ever produced such fruit, and in such quantity.

No more heroic souls ever trod American soil than the colporteurs. Many have been highly educated, often able to speak sev-

[8] These figures were furnished by the American Bible Society.

eral languages. They covered the mountains and the plains, went into lumber camps, mining districts, and out of the way places; endured privation, hardship and often persecution; but they carried the printed Bible wherever men dwelt. Sometimes they sold the Scriptures, often they gave them away. Their labors have borne an abundant harvest.

A few quotations from the One Hundred and Nineteenth Annual Report of the Bible Society printed in 1935, indicating some of the results accomplished, ought to be interesting. The report of the Charlotte Division of work among negroes says: "During the year 1934, jails, chain gangs, hospitals and county homes received special attention. Many were the expressions of joy in receiving the Word. One prisoner, held for murder and protesting his innocence, declared, 'I read where God came to Peter in a prison. I prayed, and now He is with me always.' This prisoner had lost hope and contemplated suicide; but the Word brought him consolation and hope. He was subsequently acquitted, and is now an active member of a church in his city." [9]

From the Houston Division of the work among the negroes comes this story: "I met a preacher, who told me he wanted some Bibles for converts in a meeting he was conducting. I was very much taken off my feet when he said that, before he was converted, he was one of the worst men in the country. He had thirty-two bullet holes in his body that officers of the law, and others, had shot into him while he was living a life of crime. He showed me where one bullet went into his arm and another went through his leg. He believes fully in the power of the Holy Scriptures, and was giving every convert of his meeting a Bible or Testament to read." [10]

In the report of the South Atlantic Agency among the whites we find this bit of information: "A certain magistrate purchased 100 Bibles to give to those arraigned in his court—a most unusual method. He says that the best way to administer law is to put the law and the prophets and the Gospel into the hands of people in trouble. He gives them Bibles to carry to jail when sentenced, and to take home when liberated. Many of the books go into mountain homes where there has never been a Bible." [11]

Many other interesting stories might be told, but we give only one more. This is from the report of the Western Agency. "Come in, brother, and sit down," was the greeting received by a colporteur in response to his ring of the doorbell. The friendly householder

[9] p 57. [10] p 62. [11] p 76.

was an old man, who immediately went into another room and returned with what many years before had been a book. It now consisted of nothing more than a bundle of separate and torn pages
held between two pieces of cloth-covered cardboard, which had once
been the covers of a Bible.

"This," said he, "is the only Bible I've ever owned. When I was
a young man, I was plowing on my father's farm one day, when a
man, who said he had been sent out by the American Bible Society,
came out in the field and tried to sell me a Bible. When I told him
I had no money, he asked me whether I'd promise to read it if he'd
make me a present of one. When I promised that I would, he gave
me the book. That was more than fifty years ago, and I've read it
all this time. My wife and I brought up seven children on that Bible,
and they are all Christians. My wife died five years ago. I'm past
eighty-five and don't expect to live very much longer; so I guess this
Bible will have to do me the rest of my days." [12]

G. MODERN ORGANIZATION

The methods of the American Bible Society have changed with the
needs of the times. Auxiliary societies played a very large part in
its early work, and in 1934 96 auxiliaries are reported active, in
twenty-nine states and the District of Columbia; but in time it became necessary more and more to employ agents and colporteurs.
In recent years agencies have been established in various parts
of the United States, and found highly satisfactory methods of service. The United States has been divided into ten districts, which
are served by district or division secretaries. The colored people
are served by four secretaries, three in the South, at Atlanta, Georgia,
Dallas, Texas and Charlotte, North Carolina, and one in the North
at Cleveland, Ohio. Depositories are maintained at six centers:
New York City, Atlanta, Georgia, Chicago, Illinois, Dallas, Texas,
Denver, Colorado, and San Francisco, California.

The world abroad is served by Foreign Agencies. These Agencies
are maintained for the West Indies at Havana, Cuba; for Mexico at
Mexico City; for the Caribbean at Cristobal, Canal Zone; for the
Upper Andes at Lima, Peru; for the La Plata at Buenos Aires, Ar-
gentina; for Brazil at Rio de Janeiro; for the Levant at Vienna,
Austria; for the Arabic Levant at Cairo, Egypt; for the Philippines

[12] pp 90-91.

at Manila; for Siam at Bangkok; for China at Shanghai; and for Japan at Tokyo.

Cooperating with the American Bible Society are the state societies of Alabama, California, Connecticut, Maine, Maryland, Massachusetts, New Hampshire, Pennsylvania, Rhode Island, Vermont and Virginia.

John T. Manson is the present president of the American Bible Society; the General Secretaries are the Rev. Eric M. North, Ph.D., D.D. and the Rev. George William Brown, D.D.; and the Treasurer is the Rev. Gilbert Darlington.

The American Bible Society has lived throughout its history as did the children of Israel in their wanderings, on manna daily received. The funds held by the Society, some dedicated to certain purposes, do not alter this fact. All the income from invested funds is but a drop in the bucket. The Society lives by faith. Now and then it has been forced to retrench somewhat, but in the end the Lord provides and the work moves forward.

It was a very wise decision when the Society, in years gone by, resolved to aid missions in the translation of the Scriptures in the various languages required in the work, and in printing and distributing them. The Bible Society could do it much better than any other organization in America. And this is a matter that Christian men and women everywhere ought to know. As the missions grow there will be required a constantly increasing income. Unless its support is adequate for a growing work, missions must suffer seriously.

Sales of Bibles bring the Society no profits; books are sold without the purpose of gain; sales only enable the Society to print more Bibles. The money to support the work comes from everywhere—individuals, societies and churches. An analysis of the supporters of the Society for 1934 reveals the fact that almost 57 per cent of the gifts from individuals amounted to less than five dollars each. The strength of the Society lies in the fact that it has an army of supporters who give small amounts, rather than a few rich people who make large gifts. Large numbers of churches, among the various denominations, support the work, and their number is increasing. Annuities are a source of considerable income. For more than eighty years the Society has been writing annuity agreements, a method found highly satisfactory, both to the Society and the annuitants. Legacies have been specially helpful in lean years, and are regularly a source of considerable income. When an endowment of a million dollars was provided a few years ago, an unfortunate result followed, for many thought that a Society with a million in endowment would never again need the gifts of individuals and churches. If it were possible to receive five per cent on such endowment, which is probably not possible now, that would make a yearly income of only $50,000. The annual budget of the Society, however, is almost a million dollars; for 1935 it was exactly $986,100, only $13,900 short of a million. So that an income on a million dollars is but a very small part of the amount required in its work. For every dollar the American Bible Society spends, 40 cents come from the sale of books, one-half cent, from rentals and other miscellaneous sources, 13½ cents, from endowments, and 46 cents, from churches and individuals.

The American Bible Society is the greatest missionary society in America, and the second greatest in the world, serving all denominations, and needs and deserves the hearty financial support of all our churches, and of individual Christian men and women everywhere. No other society has done so much for the native population of the United States; no other has contributed so much to assist in transforming the millions of immigrants coming among us into worthy citizens; and no other is doing so much to make it possible to carry the Gospel to the whole world.

3. OTHER BIBLE SOCIETIES

A. BAPTIST BIBLE SOCIETIES

Reference has already been made to the American and Foreign Bible Society, founded in 1836, by certain Baptists who felt aggrieved at the American Bible Society for its refusal to assist in printing sectarian translations. This society lived only until 1883, when its work was turned over to the American Baptist Publication Society of Philadelphia. Its first Bible was printed in 1838, being a reprint of an Oxford edition of 1833. For a number of years the society published certain editions of the Scriptures, and assisted Adoniram Judson in printing his Bible in Burmese. It supported several native Bible readers and distributors among the Telugus of India and the negroes of the South.

The American Bible Union, to which reference has already been made, also turned over its work to the American Baptist Publication Society of Philadelphia in 1883. It published several tentative revisions of parts of the Old Testament, Job appearing first in 1856, Genesis in 1868, the Psalms in 1869, Proverbs in 1871, and Joshua, Judges and Ruth in 1878. The story of the famous Bible Union New Testament is told elsewhere. The Bible Union assisted in printing missionary translations of the New Testament in Italian, Spanish, Chinese (colloquial Ningpo) Siamese and Squa-Karen.

B. THE CONFEDERATE STATES BIBLE SOCIETY

The Confederate States Bible Society was organized at Augusta, Georgia, in 1862. This society printed at Atlanta, Georgia, one edition of the New Testament, and this was the only publication it ever put out. The edition was small and the book is now very rare. In 1863 an edition of the New Testament was printed at Oxford, England, for the Confederate States.

C. THE CANADIAN BIBLE SOCIETY

Canada is the largest and most populous of the self-governing dominions of the British Empire, with a population in 1831, of 10,376,-786. These figures include about 105,000 Indians and 6,000 Eskimos. While Canada lies immediately north of the United States, the two nations live in perfect unity and harmony, without a single fort on the boundary line, or a single gun-boat on the Great Lakes, such not being needed. Within the territory of the United States and Canada no less than 111 different languages are spoken. There can be no question that the millions of Bibles that have been distributed on both sides of the boundary line, is the chief explanation for their peaceful relationships, and their power to assimilate men and women of "every kindred and people and tongue" that have come from abroad to settle among them. Like other English-speaking people, Canadians generally prefer the King James Version, but the Anglo-American revision and modern speech translations are finding their way among the people.

The first Bible society organized in Canada was in Nova Scotia in 1807, as an auxiliary of the British and Foreign Bible Society. Immediately following this, other auxiliaries were organized in all parts of the Dominion. These Bible societies followed the frontiers everywhere as they served the growing country.

When the Revolutionary War broke out in the United States,

the importation of Bibles was cut off for the States, but not so for Canada. Bibles continued to be imported there, and inasmuch as Canada was not equipped to print Bibles, the people there continued to receive them from abroad; and, for that reason, few Bibles have ever been printed in the Dominion.

In 1904, the centenary of the British and Foreign Bible Society, it was decided that the numerous auxiliaries of this society throughout Canada should federate and form the Canadian Bible Society. Upper Canada, Western Ontario, Perth, Montreal, Quebec, New Brunswick, Fredericton, Nova Scotia and Prince Edward Island united in its formation, and later were joined by Newfoundland, New Glasgow, Pictou, Miramichi, Ottawa and Winnipeg.

The Canadian Bible Society is an auxiliary of the British and Foreign Bible Society, and is the federation of all the numerous auxiliaries in Canada and Newfoundland, with 3,666 branches. Secretaries are maintained in ten districts: Newfoundland and Nova Scotia at Halifax; Prince Edward Island and New Brunswick at St. John; Quebec and Montreal at Montreal; Ottawa at Ottawa; Upper Canada at Toronto; Western Ontario at London, Ontario; Manitoba at Winnepeg; North and South Saskatchewan at Saskatoon; North and South Alberta at Edmonton and Calgary; British Columbia at Vancouver.

The Canadian Bible Society circulates the Scriptures in 111 different languages throughout the Dominion, and offers every immigrant a portion of the Bible in his own tongue; at the port of entrance. Agents of the Society meet every ocean liner at Quebec, Halifax and St. John. Scriptures are sold at modest prices, generally about cost. The Society employs special agents, lay and clerical, and sends out colporteurs who offer the Bible, without note or comment, for sale where it could not otherwise be obtained, and as a gift where necessary. Depositories are maintained in numerous cities across the continent, such as St. John, Quebec, Montreal, Ottawa, Toronto, Winnipeg, Saskatoon, Regina, Edmonton, Calgary and Vancouver.

According to O'Callaghan,[13] in 1835 or 1836, Mr. William Mackenzie purchased from the Bible Society of New York a set of stereotype plates for the whole Bible, in English, and had new plates made for the title pages, substituting his own name and Toronto for the Bible Society's imprint, but for some reason he did not print an edition. The plates were sold to a Mr. Eastwood, who published an edition from them in Toronto, in 1839 or 1840. Only one edition

---

[13] *List of Editions of Holy Scripture*, p XLIX.

was ever printed, after which the plates were resold in New York. This was the only Bible ever printed in Canada in the English language.

Certain Scriptures have been printed in Canada, however. An edition of the New Testament in French was printed in Quebec in 1846. The New Testament in the Cree language was printed in Montreal in 1872, translated by Father Lacombe. In fact, several portions of the Scriptures in various languages were printed in Canada, but most of such work has been done by the British and Foreign Bible Society of London.

The only revision of any part of the Bible in English made and published in Canada, so far as we have been able to learn, was a revision of the book of Job by the Rev. John Fredericton, bishop of Fredericton and metropolitan of Canada, published at St. John, New Brunswick in 1876. He departs from the King James Version only when accuracy requires it. He recognizes the book as one of poetry, but regards it as substantially history. Professor Alek R. Gordon of Montreal and Professor Theophile J. Meek of Toronto aided Dr. J. M. Powis Smith in his translation of the Old Testament, published in Chicago, in 1927.

During the World War not less than 340,000 copies of the New Testament were distributed among the Canadian soldiers by the Canadian Bible Society.

Canada has done a notable work in providing the Scriptures for the Indians in her section, and this matter is treated under the Bible for Indians.

In Canada, as in the United States, the Bible has profoundly influenced the character of her citizenship, her laws and institutions. Her educational system has been greatly influenced by the Bible. The Bible has been kept in the hands of the common people throughout its history, the numerous Bible societies assuming that responsibility. The ideals generated by the use of the Bible have kept Canada in the very van of human progress, in the new status given to womanhood, the new concern for children, the weak and suffering, and the new and ever growing sense of responsibility to the whole world. This it serves substantially by its generous contributions annually to the British and Foreign Bible Society, which prints its Bibles.

The British and Foreign Bible Society in 130 years—to the end of 1934—issued 453,000,000 copies of the Scriptures, at an average in recent years of 21 copies per minute, 1,280 copies per hour and 31,000 copies per day. And yet it does not own a single printing press. It uses the printing presses licensed for the purpose in Great Britain, on the Continent of Europe, as well as in India, China, Japan and Africa; in fact, it uses printing presses wherever one is found capable of producing what it wants under fair labor conditions.

CHAPTER VII

THE BIBLE FOR AMERICAN INDIANS

MAN is a strange bundle of inconsistencies. For one thing, he is incurably religious. If he could be cured, the inconsistencies, sins and crimes of those professing Christianity would have cured him long ago; but he is incurable. While there is always a wide gulf between what Christians teach and what they do, it is not necessarily because they are hypocrites. To begin with, Christians are only sinners under medication; they are the sick only in a convalescent stage, and too much may easily be expected of them. Besides all this, Christianity erects unattainable ideals; no man can reach them no matter how hard he tries. Moreover, it is best that this should be so, for a religion no higher than a man can reach would be worth little.

Man is so constituted that as soon as he reaches any desired goal, he immediately wants to go on. He is, therefore, never satisfied; and it is the divine in him that produces his discontent. But a religion with unattainable ideals gives a man his deepest satisfactions. Christians are not to be blamed for not reaching their ideals; they are to blame only when they do not reach after them, to the limit of their ability. In no field in America have Christian men done less reaching for Christian ideals than in their dealings with the Indians; nowhere has the failure of Christians been more apparent and glaring than in their treatment of the Indians.[1]

The Indian was the original American. He owned this country and roamed it at his pleasure. The white man came among them, deceived them, lied to them, robbed them, and then killed them freely when they questioned the white man's right to do as he pleased. The long and bloody contest between the white and red man can be traced directly to the white man's sins. The manner in which the red man was treated, for the most part, is a sad commentary on the Christianity of the times. Canada managed matters, in dealing with the Indians, vastly better than the United States, and escaped the deadly penalty our nation was required to pay.

Some atonement for the white man's sins, in this connection, however, has been made in the widespread effort to Christianize the Indian. All Christians have not been equally bad. From the very

---

[1] *A Century of Dishonor,* by Helen Hunt Jackson, in the classic indictment of our national policy in dealing with the Indians.

earliest settlements of America effort has been made in that direction. Catholics did much missionary work in an early day, and later the Jesuit priests covered a wide field. In all the thirteen original colonies efforts were made to reach the Indian. Rev. Alexander Whitaker of Virginia, the Rev. John Campanius, a Swedish Lutheran in Delaware, Dominie Megapolensis, a Dutch minister in New York, the Jesuit Father Jogues, in the forests of New York, Rev. John Eliot, Roger Williams and the Mayhews in New England, and many others, early distinguished themselves by their labors in behalf of the Indians. One of the oldest buildings at Harvard College was built for the use of Indian students, and William and Mary College in Virginia, at one time, had no less than seventy Indian students enrolled for advanced education. Everywhere efforts were made to translate the Bible, or its parts, into the various Indian languages.

1. THE DIFFICULTIES IN TRANSLATION

To provide the Indians with the Bible in their own tongues, however, was a labor much more difficult than is generally supposed. The Indian languages all required first to be reduced to writing, which in itself was no mean task. It might be supposed that the Indians of America spoke substantially one language, with varying dialects; but such is not the case. There was found among them an extraordinary diversity of tongues. North of Mexico there are said to have been almost sixty linguistic stocks, differing from one another so radically that the language of one was usually unintelligible to all others. They were structurally so varied that they are said to have differed as widely as English and Russian. To learn all these various languages, reduce them to writing, and then translate the Bible into all of them, was a stupendous and expensive task.

However, the Bible, or some part of it, has been printed in fifty-three languages for the Indians north of Mexico. In five the whole Bible has been printed, the first being the Massachusetts dialect of the Algonquin in 1663, and the Dakota or Sioux in 1879. These were in the United States. In Canada, the whole Bible was printed for the Indian, first, the Plains Cree in 1862, the Eskimo of Labrador in 1871, and the Tukudh, a tribe of the northern Yukon Territory, in 1898. In ten other languages [2] the whole New Testament has

---

[2] Wright, *Early Bible of America*, pp 399, 442, lists a New Testament in Ottawa. No such New Testament is known, and this is thought to have been a mistake. Pilling's *Bibliography of the Algonquin Languages* gives a publication in Ottawa, with a title that covers the whole New Testament, but the volume contains the Gospel of Matthew only. Possibly this fact misled Wright.

been printed: the Micmac, 1874, the Moose Cree, 1876, the Chippe-
vayan, 1881, the Slave, 1891 and the Baffin Land Eskimo, 1912.
These are in Canada. In the United States, the Ojibway, 1833, the
Choctaw, 1848, the Cherokee, 1857, the Muskogee, 1887, the Cheyenne, 1934. The Mohawk will have all the New Testament during
1936, except 2 Corinthians. In 38 other languages some parts of the
Bible have been printed for the Indians in Canada and the United
States, including Alaska. Some of these languages have been spoken
both in Canada and in the United States, and both the British and
the American Bible Societies have often printed Scriptures in the
same tongues. The need for the Bible in Indian, however, grows less
as time passes, since they are rapidly learning to speak English.

Numerous private efforts were made in various places, in an early
day, to give the Indian some part of the Scripture in his own tongue,
but it would be neither interesting nor profitable to name all of
them, and we shall speak only of some of the more important translations.

2. THE FIRST INDIAN BIBLE

The Rev. John Eliot, a graduate of Cambridge University, came to
America in 1631, and soon thereafter became the pastor at Roxbury,
Massachusetts, where, at the age of 42, he began to study the Indian
language. He became a missionary to the Indians in that region,
building fourteen settlements in less than twenty-five years. He
organized twenty-four congregations among them, and trained more
than twenty native preachers from various tribes. In thirty years,
he had won 11,000 converts, "praying Indians" as they were called.
They had schools in fourteen towns. One young man took the
degree of A. B. at Harvard College in 1665, dying in 1690.

John Eliot, known as "the apostle to the Indians," had his hands
full in answering the questions of his Indian converts. According
to the theology of the day, he taught them that they were all naturally
children of the devil, and not children of God. Quite reasonably
they were greatly interested to know all they could about their
father. Among other things they wanted to know:

"Whether ye devil or man was made first?"

"Whether there might not be something, if only a little, gained
by praying to ye devil?"

"Why does not God, who has full power, kill ye devil that makes
all men so bad?"

"If God made hell in one of the six days, why did he make it before Adam had sinned?"

"If all ye world be burned up, where shall hell then be?" [3]

Just what answers these searching questions brought forth from their beloved and devoted pastor is not a matter of record.

Eliot was able to preach to the Indians in their own language in 1646. His first translation consisted of the Lord's Prayer, the Ten Commandments, and certain other passages of Scripture. In 1654 he published a primer or catechism. The book of Genesis and Gospel of Matthew were published in 1655. Eight years were required to finish his translation of the Bible, which was completed on December 28, 1658. The New Testament, dedicated to Charles II in certain copies, was printed at Cambridge, Massachusetts, in 1661, containing title pages in English and Indian. This New Testament was reprinted in 1680. The entire Bible [4] was printed at Cambridge, Massachusetts, in 1663, by Samuel Green and Marmaduke Johnson, and it was dedicated to Charles II, there being title pages in English and Indian for the whole Bible, and for the New Testament. Its title in Indian is, "Mamussee Wunneetupanatamwe Up-Biblum God Naneeswe Nukkone Testament kah wonk Wusku Testament. Ne quoshkinnumuk nashpe Wuttinneumoh Christ noh assoowesit John Eliot," which literally translated, reads, "The Whole Holy His Bible God, both Old Testament and also New Testament. This turned by the servant of Christ who is called John Eliot."

O'Callaghan [5] points out sixty mistakes in the printing of this Bible, mostly the omissions of words and sentences. A very ludicrous blunder, however, was made in the translation of 2 Kings 2:23 where the English has it, "Go up, thou baldhead." The Indian text here translated, reads, "Go up, thou ball-head." The interpreter was probably misled by the pronunciation of the word. Anyhow, the Indian text contains a word here meaning a ball to play with.

Translation into the Indian language was very difficult, with its limited vocabulary, and utter want of abstract terms. Salt was unknown to the Indians, and this word had to be used without translation. They had no word for "amen." Many other terms were wanting. The parable of the Ten Virgins, in Eliot's Bible, is the parable of "the ten chaste young men," because the interpreter did not

---

[3] Dorchester, *Christianity in the United States*, p 176.

[4] Wright in *Early Bibles* lists the owners of 35 copies of Eliot's New Testament and Bible in Europe, and 90 copies in America—pp 376-79.

[5] *List of Bibles*, pp 7-8.

understand that he wanted a noun in the feminine gender. Among the Indians chastity is said to have been a masculine virtue, hence the mistake.

A second edition was printed in 1685, without the English title-page, and a few copies had a dedication to the Hon. Robert Boyle, the governor of the corporation which was established in London by an act of Parliament in 1649, for the Propagation of the Gospel amongst the Indians of New England. This corporation paid the expenses for the printing of this Bible. The errors of the first edition were corrected chiefly by Rev. John Cotton of Plymouth.

The publication of the first Indian Bible was an event of more than ordinary importance both to America and Europe. When the New Testament appeared, forty copies were sent to the Hon. Robert Boyle, governor of the corporation that paid the expenses of the undertaking, to be presented to whomsoever he would. The first copy was presented to Charles II, and other copies given to dignitaries of the country. When the Bible appeared twenty copies were sent to the corporation, in unbound condition, to be given away. These were substantially bound in dark-blue morocco. One copy was presented to Charles II, but to whom the others were given is not known. Pope Clement XI is said to have become alarmed, and to have written the Archbishop of Saragossa, hoping that he might be able to prevent the introduction of the new plague into Spanish America.[6]

In his work of printing, Eliot had the assistance of an Indian interpreter, known as James Printer. He had been taken prisoner in the Pequot wars, and worked in the neighborhood as a house servant. In 1682 when the press work began on the second edition of Eliot's Bible, he writes of James Printer, "We have but one man, the Indian printer, that is able to compose the sheets and correct the press with understanding." He had assisted in printing the first edition.

Eliot's was the first Bible translated and the first to be printed in America; but nobody living can read it today. The last man who could read it was James Hammond Trumbull, who died in 1897. The fact that none can read it, however, does not indicate that Eliot's work was fruitless, "but rather enhances and glorifies that labor which, like a seed dropping into the earth to die, blossomed

[6] Wright, *Early Bibles*, p 15.

forth in due time in many another Bible that today is the comfort and blessing of a multitude of souls." [7]

John Eliot did a marvelous work among the Indians, winning thousands of converts. Men were taught to cultivate the soil, and the women to spin and weave; schools educated their children; but the King Philip War scattered them, and the twenty-four congregations were reduced to four. His noble, self-sacrificing labors will be an inspiration in all the ages to come.

The American Bible Society has done the chief work of printing Bibles for the Indians in the United States, though many volumes have been put out by others. Its first Indian printing was done in 1817. Frederick Denke, a Moravian missionary, offered the society a translation of the Gospel of John in the language of the Delaware Indians. After satisfying themselves of the character of the translation, the managers of the society printed a thousand copies; and thus began a long series of services rendered by it to Indian missions among many denominations.

3. THE NEZ PERCES SEARCH

In all the story of Christian missions, we know of no incident more romantic and graphic than that of the story of the Nez Perces Indians of Idaho. "In the year 1831 four Nez Perce chiefs made their way over the Rockies and were found on the street in St. Louis, asking, 'Where is the white man's Book of Heaven?' General Clark befriended them and showed them everything of interest in the town. Two of the four fell ill and died. Before the remaining Indians departed General Clark gave a feast to them. It was at this feast that, in a farewell address to General Clark, one of the two poured forth his burden of sorrow in words of pathetic eloquence:

" 'I came to you over the trail of many moons from the setting sun. You were the friends of my fathers, who have all gone the long way. I came with an eye partly open for my people who sit in darkness. I go back with both eyes closed. How can I go back blind to my blind people? I made my way to you with strong arms through many enemies and strange lands that I might carry back much to them. I go back with both arms broken and empty! Two fathers came with us; they were braves of many snows and wars. We leave them asleep here by your great water and teepees. They were tired in many moons, and their moccasins wore out. My people sent me to

[7] McClure, *The Supreme Book of Mankind,* p 159.

get the white man's Book of Heaven. You took me to where you
allow your women to dance, as we do not ours; and the Book was
not there! You took me to where they worship the Great Spirit
with candles, and the Book was not there! You showed me images
of the Great Spirit and pictures of the Good Land beyond, but the
Book was not among them to tell me the way. I am going back the
long trail to my people in the dark land. You make my feet heavy
with gifts, and my moccasins will grow old carrying them, and yet the
Book is not among them! When I tell my poor, blind people after
one more snow, in the big council, that I did not bring the Book,
no word will be spoken by our old men or by our young braves.
One by one they will rise up and go out in silence. My people will
die in darkness, and they will go on a long path to other hunting
grounds. No white man will go with them, and no white man's
Book to make the way plain. I have no more words.'

"Such evidence as we have confirms the statement that this speech
was taken down by a clerk in the office and sent to Pittsburg. George
Catlin, the artist who painted the famous portraits of Indians, also
confirmed facts connected with it. This Macedonian cry stirred the
hearts of the people. The apparently fruitless search of the Nez
Perce chiefs resulted in the establishing of the first Protestant mission
west of the Rocky Mountains, the Methodist Episcopal Church furnishing the pioneer in this pathfinding expedition.

"It was in response to a stirring appeal by Dr. Wilbur Fisk in the
Christian Advocate of New York that this far-distant field was entered. The words in which this statesman of the church wrote his
message for the press are of interest today, as the prophecy of his
far-seeking leadership is recalled. This was his summons and his
challenge to faith: 'Who will respond to the call beyond the Rocky
Mountains? We are having a mission established at once. Let two
suitable men, unincumbered with families and possessing the spirit
of martyrs, throw themselves into the nation, live with them, learn
their language, preach Christ to them, and, as the way opens up,
introduce schools, agriculture, and the arts of civilized life. Money
shall be forthcoming. I will be bondsman for the church. All we
want is the men. Who will go? Bright will be his crown, glorious
his reward.'

"The Rev. Jason Lee, a young minister, the son of a Canadian
pioneer, was the servant chosen of the Lord for the task. He was at
the time thirty-two years of age, hardy, experienced in lumber-camp
work, and six feet three inches in height. With his nephew, also an

ordained minister of the Methodist Episcopal Church, and a lay associate, he became the herald of the Gospel, the pioneer worker in the country west of the Rocky Mountains, and the hero of one of the most remarkable transcontinental journeys in the history of American missions. Shipping their supplies around Cape Horn, these consecrated men took the overland journey to Oregon, occupying almost five months. In the Willamette Valley, sixty miles from Vancouver, they located the mission, which developed into an extensive work with twelve ministers and their families, and lay associates of physicians, teachers and farmers. The devotion of the young missionary to his task is expressed in his exclamation: 'Oh, that I could address the Indians in their own language! My ardent soul longs to be sounding salvation in the ears of these red men. I trust I shall yet see many of them rejoicing in the hope of the glory of God.' This was not only the introduction of Protestant missions into Oregon but of civilization among the Indians. Thus the natives of the Willamette Valley received the heralds of the Gospel.

"Jason Lee, by importing cattle from California, making a trip east to interest the people and Congress, and bringing settlers with him, helped greatly to make Oregon a part of the United States. Dr. Lyman sums up the results of Lee's work as follows: 'To Jason Lee more than to any other one, unless we except Dr. Marcus Whitman, must be attributed the inauguration of that remarkable chain of cause and effect, a long line of sequence by which Oregon and the Pacific Coast in general became American possessions, and the international destiny of our nation was secured.'

"The Nez Perces, however, were to wait only a short time for the fulfilment of their hopes, for the following spring the Rev. Samuel Parker, and a young physician named Marcus Whitman, were asked to explore the region and report. Marcus Whitman returned a favorable answer and made preparations to devote himself to the work. This began romantically by his taking Miss Narcissa Prentiss as a wife, and enlisting in the cause the Rev. H. H. Spalding and his bride, the two couples making a honeymoon journey 2,000 miles, lasting seven months. These were the first two white women to cross the Rocky Mountains. On the Fourth of July they reached the Continental Divide, where they raised the flag, and under its folds fell on their knees and took possession of the Pacific Slope in the name of the United States."

"It was in 1871 that the American Bible Society took over the work of printing for the Nez Perces 'the Book that makes the way plain.' Recently these Indians, descendants of the disappointed company that traveled far in search of the white man's Book of Heaven, have been pronounced by a government agent to be the most religious people he has ever known, the most devout Christians of our land." [8]

4. SOME IMPORTANT TRANSLATIONS

A. THE DAKOTA BIBLE

The largest tribe of Indians of the United States is the Dakotas or Sioux. They are found mainly in the Dakotas, Montana, Wyoming and Minnesota. These people have been provided with the whole Bible, and this is perhaps the most important Indian translation ever published by the American Bible Society.

This Bible was translated by Dr. Thomas S. Williamson and Dr. Stephen Riggs, in connection with their exacting and varied labors as missionaries among these people. Dr. Williams gave much of his time for forty years to the work, while Dr. Riggs gave all the time he could to it, each revising the translation of the other. The Rev. John R. Williamson, Dr. Williamson's son, gave a final revision to the work of both.

It is touching to read in the account of Dr. Riggs entitled, "Mary and I, or Forty Years Among the Sioux," this brief statement of the close of their translation work. They had nearly reached the end of their labor of love, when, in 1876, Dr. Williamson's beloved wife, the light of his home, "went over the river to rest under the trees." "He grew homesick and longed to depart, but he said, 'I would like to live until this translation is done. Then there will remain little or nothing for me, an old man and much worn, to do.' At length the work was completed, and soon thereafter he went quietly away, his name to be cherished, his influence to live, the fruitage of his work to increase until time shall end.' " [9]

This work was taken over by the American Bible Society in 1843, and thirty-six years later, in 1879, the complete Bible in Dakota was published, the New Testament having appeared in 1865.

Unfortunately in 1886, a blundering Indian Commissioner issued an order forbidding the Sioux Indians to learn to read their own

---

[8] Moffett, *The Bible in the Life of the Indians of the United States*, pp 8-12. (This is Centennial Pamphlet No. 14, issued by the American Bible Society, 1916).
[9] Moffett, *The Bible in the Life of the Indians of the United States*, pp 14-15

language, and his agents sought to prevent religious worship in this tongue. "I never saw a Dakota, filling a responsible position," said Chief Gray Cloud of Sisseton, "who had not first been educated in his own language and Christianized and so made reliable." The Indians petitioned President Cleveland to revoke this senseless and oppressive order, and in doing so they said: "By learning the Bible a good many of our people have been quieted down in Christian homes and civilized ways. The first scholars of the Dakota language, with the help of a little English, have become the trustworthy men of the different agencies—ministers, teachers, Government clerks, farmers, citizens, and, above all, true Christians." [10]

Rev. Thomas S. Williamson, M.D., was born in South Carolina, and educated at Jefferson College, Cannonsville, Pennsylvania, where he graduated in 1820. Finishing his medical course at Yale College in 1824, he practiced medicine successfully for nearly ten years at Ripley, Ohio. However, in 1834 he was appointed by the American Board to go on an expedition to the Upper Mississippi, where the condition of the Indians, chiefly the Sacs and Foxes, was to be investigated, and it was this work which brought him in contact with the Sioux Indians, in whom he became deeply interested. The exploring party went as far west as Fort Snelling, and from there to Lac-qui-Parle, Minnesota. When the expedition returned, Dr. Williamson offered himself as a missionary, and was appointed to go among the Dakotas. He came back to Lac-qui-Parle, organized a native church in 1837, and as soon after as possible entered upon the work of translation. He died at seventy-nine, and has been justly styled, "The Father of the Dakota Mission."

The Rev. Stephen Riggs, D. D., who joined Dr. Williamson in the mission work in Minnesota in 1837, was born in Ohio, and received his education at Jefferson College, in Pennsylvania, and his theological training at Western Theological Seminary in the same state. He was a devoted servant and a scholarly man.

The war whoop of these savages was once the haunting terror of the life of the plains, but the change wrought among the Sioux tribes has been one of the miracles of missions. Among all the influences that have contributed to the civilization of the Sioux Indians, first place must be given to the Bible. The Indians' appreciation of the service rendered them was well expressed by Rev. Mr. Cook, a Sioux presbyter in the Protestant Episcopal Church, who

[10] Moffett, *The Bible in the Life of the Indians of the United States*, p 14-15.

said, "May God abundantly reward in the day of reckoning his two faithful servants, Dr. Williamson and Dr. Riggs, who gave us the Holy Scriptures in our own tongue, thus helping to make us what we are and what in the future we shall be through His grace."

B. THE CHEROKEE NEW TESTAMENT

One of the most interesting stories in connection with Indian translations has to do with the Cherokee Scriptures. For use in the printing of these Scriptures a new syllabary was invented by an Indian, Sequoyah, or George Guess, a member of the tribe. This Indian displayed unusual genius. He was born in 1763, the son of a Cherokee mother, and of a white father of German descent. He was illiterate, yet he provided himself with birch bark, and began to write characters on it in a crude way, conceiving the idea of inventing characters to represent sounds. He took some of his letters from an English spelling book, others from Greek, working out a syllabary of eighty-six characters. Two years were spent in perfecting his work and then he taught his six year old daughter to spell and read by his new method. Soon the people of his tribe were flocking to him. Thus he became the original Indian inventor of the written language of the red man.

In 1831 the American Bible Society began the printing of Scriptures in Cherokee, using the syllabary invented by George Guess in 1821; and it now issues the whole New Testament, which appeared in 1857, in these characters.

C. THE MUSKOGEE NEW TESTAMENT

One of the notable achievements in the translation and publishing of Scriptures for the Indian, was that of the New Testament in Muskogee, the language of the Creeks and Seminoles, in 1887. Rev. W. S. Robertson and his wife were missionaries among these people, and Mrs. Robertson is credited with having done the larger part of the work of translation, being also the chief translator of Genesis and the Psalms.

The Creeks and Seminoles were long very difficult to manage; they persecuted fiercely any of their number who accepted the religion of the hated white man. But the missionaries were patient, and finally in 1868, when they were provided with part of the Scriptures in their own tongue, the National Council of the Creeks voted that henceforth they would open their sessions by reading the Bible and prayer. This was a landmark in the progress of the tribes.

D. THE NAVAHO SCRIPTURES

For long the Navahos received small attention. They are found in Arizona and New Mexico, and number some 28,000. They are principally shepherds and, therefore, migratory, land among them being owned in common. School and mission work among them is quite difficult. While almost free from intemperance, they are great gamblers, and they are strong believers in witchcraft, being a very primitive people, in what might be called the patriarchal state of development.

Translation of the Scriptures into Navaho was essayed by the Rev. Leonard P. Brink, of Tohatchi, New Mexico, who began with Genesis and Mark in 1910. The final work of putting the translation into shape for printing was done by the Rev. F. G. Mitchell, of Tolchaco, and the Rev. John Butler, of Tuba, Arizona. Other portions of the Bible have been published since.

The missionaries began to make real headway among these people, as soon as they had the aid of considerable portions of the Bible in the Navaho language.

"The results of evangelistic meetings, therefore, during the past few months, have given us much reason for rejoicing. In August the Rev. F. G. Mitchell came here, introducing the advance copies of the Navaho Bible recently received from the press of the American Bible Society. From these he read to audiences on two successive Sundays, closing with an evangelistic message at the morning service. An afternoon meeting was also held each Sunday and opportunity for personal testimony was given, followed by an invitation to begin the Christian life. At least five Navahos took a definite stand and more than half of the audience on the second Sunday came forward to show their belief in the truth as presented. On November 29th Mr. W. R. Johnston and the Rev. F. G. Mitchell conducted meetings morning and afternoon. A large majority came forward at the afternoon meeting and this time signified their purpose to 'take hold of God's way,' as they expressed it, thus making an advance beyond the stand taken at the August meeting." [11]

The Bible is unquestionably the greatest gift of the white man

[11] Moffet, *The Bible in the Life of the Indians of the United States*, p 19.

to the Indian. Said old Monatave, a chief of the Mohaves, "When you read out of that Book I know it is God's Book, for it pulls my heart."

E. THE CHEYENNE NEW TESTAMENT

One of the most recent accomplishments of the American Bible Society, in printing Indian Scriptures, was the complete New Testament in Cheyenne. These Indians are found in Montana and Oklahoma.

The Rev. Rodolphe Petter, D.D., of the Mennonite Church, has been a missionary among these people more than forty years. Beginning before the language was reduced to writing, he prepared first an English-Cheyenne dictionary, then a grammar, then certain portions from both the Old and New Testament were translated, presently the Pilgrim's Progress, and finally a complete New Testament.

Dr. Petter is a man of scholarly attainments and his translation was made from the standard critical text of Westcott and Hort, with which he compared versions in Latin, French and German.

When the translation was completed it was carefully reread by Dr. Petter himself, and then by four different Indians separately. The final typed copy was read to an Indian woman to test the average understanding of the Cheyenne text. Finally, the translator's wife read the copy in a last review before it was turned over to the printer. With such painstaking do missionaries provide the Scriptures for missionary purposes.

The New Testament was published late in December 1934, and at the end of the Christmas Eve program in the mission at Lame Deer, Montana, just before dismissing the congregation, Dr. Petter spoke briefly of the New Testament, and presented gift copies to his Indian associates and fellow workers in the mission.

5. INDIAN BIBLES IN CANADA

In 1931 there were in the Dominion of Canada 105,000 Indians, and 6,000 Eskimos. In Canada missions to the Indians were undertaken early by various societies; and these missionaries have succeeded in translating the Scriptures into every language spoken by Indians in the Dominion. They have generally been published by the British and Foreign Bible Society of London, though a certain amount of printing has been done in Canada. This Society has published, since 1804, for the aboriginal inhabitants of Canada, Scriptures in some twenty different languages; and it has sent to Canada some 90 other different translations of the Bible for use among its people.

A. THE CREE BIBLE

The translation of the Bible for the Cree Indians of Canada has been greatly simplified. The Cree syllabary (later adapted to other Indian languages) was the invention of the Rev. James Evans, a Wesleyan missionary for 18 years among the Hudson Bay Indians. "He whittled out his first types for patterns, and then using the lead furnished by the Hudson Bay Company's empty tea chests, he cast others in moulds of his own devising. He made his first ink out of soot of the chimneys. His first paper was birchbark, and his press was also the result of his own handiwork. Afterwards the W. M. S. supplied him with type, paper and a press, and the sum of 500 pounds, with which he founded a printing establishment." [12]

"The principle on which the characters were formed is the phonetic. There are no silent letters. Each character represents a syllable, hence no spelling is required. As soon as the alphabet is mastered, the student can commence at the first chapter of Genesis, and read on, slowly of course at first, but in a few days with surprising facility . . . The use of the characters has extended much beyond the people for whom they were intended, books having been printed in them in the Eskimauian language, in a number of dialects of the Athabascan, and, in addition to the Cree, in the Chippewa, Santeux, Moose and Moosonee divisions of the Algonquin." [13]

By means of the Cree syllabic form of writing, invented by Rev. James Evans, missionaries without any knowledge of the language, can read the Bible at once to the Indians. This invention of the Cree syllabic gave an idea to the Rev. Samuel Pollard, a missionary in China, and as a result the Scriptures have been and are being produced in the Miao language based on this invention.

The venerable Archdeacon Mackay, D. D. of Prince Albert, Saskatchewan, finally completed his translation of the whole Bible in Cree. It proved, however, an expensive effort. The first edition of 1,000 copies cost the British and Foreign Bible Society a total of 1,800 pounds, or about nine dollars a copy. The book was sold to the Cree Indians, numbering about 15,000, at a very small price compared with the cost. The Cree Indians are nearly all Christians.

[12] *Historical Catalogue of Printed Bibles*, Darlow and Moule, Vol. II, p 272
[13] Wright, *Early Bibles of America*, pp 316-18.

B. THE MOHAWK SCRIPTURES

There is an interesting story of Canada's service to the Mohawk Indians that deserves to be told. The Mohawk Indians lived originally in New York, and were members of the League of the Iroquois.[14] They played an important part in the Indian wars, and in the War of the Revolution were allied with the British. Because of this fact they suffered persecution after the war had closed, to escape which most of them moved to Ontario, Canada. A few are found today at the St. Regis-Mohawk Reservation in western New York.

The Rev. John Stuart was a missionary among the Indians, in the American colonies, when the Revolutionary War broke out. His loyalty to England provoked troubles from which he fled to Montreal, and later to Kingston. Here he resumed his work as a missionary, soon becoming a friend of Joseph Brant, the Mohawk Indian chief. Brant was a loyal Christian, and soon recognized the unselfish service which Stuart sought to render. They became co-workers for the common good.

The Society for the Propagation of the Gospel, in its regular work, found these Indians in Upper Canada, and sought to serve them. It looked on with pleasure and encouraged the joint labors of these men; and they soon translated the Gospel of Mark and the Book of Common Prayer, Brant being a well educated man. This translation was carried to London by Indian hands, and published at the expense of the British Government in 1787.

In the meantime, near Brantford, the Mohawks were establishing the first Protestant Church in Upper Canada. The Bible for their pulpit and the communion plate had been a gift, received in their former New York home, from Queen Anne. Later the British Government presented them with a fine bell for the church tower.

"In Kingston, under Dr. Stuart's inspiration, was built what was probably the first church for Loyalists in the Province (old St. George's), around which came to cluster associations civil as well as ecclesiastical. Thus, in this building, the commissions were read and the oaths administered when Upper Canada became a separate province, July 8th, 1792. In this city, also, Dr. Stuart laid the foundations of the Upper Canada educational system, when he opened schools for the children alike of the Indians and of the whites." [15]

[14] Collier and Son, *National Encyclopedia*, Vol. VII, p 50.
[15] *The Story of the Earliest Scriptures in the Mohawk Tongue,* Canadian Bible Society, p 4.

Captain John Norton was by birth a Cherokee Indian, but from his infancy he had lived among the Mohawks. He became the chief of the Six Nations Indians in Canada; and to him the Mohawks were indebted for the Gospel of John in their own language.

Captain Norton prepared a spirited preface to his translation, recommending it to his people; but the Bible Society, pledged to print the Scriptures without note or comment, could not print this in the volume containing his translation. So the preface to this translation was printed separately.

The British and Foreign Bible Society of London was organized in 1804, and the first book it published was the Gospel of John, translated into Mohawk by Captain Norton, together with the English, in the year of its organization. Thus Canada became the first beneficiary of this old Bible Society. A copy of this publication is preserved in the Canadian Bible Society's museum in Toronto.

CHAPTER VIII

REPRESENTATIVE PROTESTANT TRANSLATIONS

1. WHY THE BIBLE REQUIRES REVISION

MANY people seem to think that those who revise the Bible are only tinkering with it, and making changes that are unauthorized and unwarranted. The amount of ignorance on this subject, in a country as intelligent as America, is astonishing.

The Bible was written originally in Hebrew and Greek, and was copied by hand and kept in manuscript form for long centuries, before printing was invented. It is simply impossible to copy manuscripts by hand without making numerous mistakes. Let those who doubt it copy a few pages of anything, and then see how many mistakes they have made. The first copy made inevitably contained a certain number of mistakes; the next copyist would repeat these mistakes, and add a few more of his own. In this way manuscripts, after long years, came to contain much error. Men sometimes wrote in the margins of their Bible, and when it was copied by somebody, such marginal notes were occasionally transferred to the text, under the supposition that they belonged to it. In this way certain interpolations were introduced. In other ways errors crept in. Such being the case, the older copies of MSS would naturally be nearer the original than later copies. That is why a manuscript from the third or fourth century is considered very much more valuable than one made in the tenth century.

Out of these facts was born what is known as textual criticism, which is wholly an effort to recover, as far as possible, the text as it was originally written. Much material has been gathered within the last few centuries that is found to be very valuable for this purpose.

Revisions of the Bible may be said to be efforts to do three things: first, to provide a text as near the original as possible; second, to give a more faithful translation of the text made possible by the increased knowledge of Biblical scholarship; third, to put the Bible in words and phrases familiar to the people. This is necessary because language is constantly changing, some words becoming obsolete, and others completely altered in their meaning.

The first Greek New Testament published was prepared by Erasmus and appeared in 1516; and since the New Testament of the King James Version was made substantially from this text, it should be a matter of more than ordinary interest to know something in detail about it.

It was prepared in the greatest haste, in an effort to forestall an edition being prepared in Spain. Erasmus used only five MSS, not one of which contained the whole New Testament, and all of which had been written from the eleventh to the fifteenth centuries, and, therefore, were very faulty. On these five MSS he based his text.

But even the five MSS did not contain the whole New Testament, there being but one MS of the book of Revelation among his number, and it was incomplete. The gaps in it were filled in with retranslations from the Latin Vulgate, by which means Erasmus introduced into the New Testament phrases for which no Greek authority has ever been found.

Later Erasmus published other editions of his New Testament with certain changes in his text; but in all his revisions he had no more than a total of eight MSS. Stephens [1] revised the text of Erasmus somewhat by the use of the Complutensian Polyglot and fifteen MSS. Beza, in his editions of the Greek Testament, made a few changes in the text, having access to certain additional MSS, among them a MS of the Gospels and Acts and another of the Epistles of Paul, both from the sixth century. But he did not use these ancient MSS, probably because they differed so much from what he had been accustomed to. Moreover, the changes any of these men made in the Greek text, were made before the true principles of Greek criticism were known, and the text was, therefore, as faulty after being changed as before, because all the texts were made and revised by the use of late MSS. The King James New Testament was made from Beza's text, but it was substantially that of Erasmus.

Very soon after the appearance of the King James Version, however, Biblical scholars began to accumulate MSS of the New Testament more ancient than any previously known. In fact the King James Version had been published only seventeen years when the Codex Alexandrinus, a fifth century MS., came into England; and scholars soon discovered how much it differed from the generally received text. It is recognized as the third oldest and best Greek MS known today. In the years that followed other MSS were discovered or became accessible, some reaching back to the fourth century. Other important discoveries were made which created weighty reasons for Biblical revision.

[1] French, Estienne, Latin, Stephanus. Both forms are frequently used.

2. SUPPOSED BIBLICAL INFALLIBILITY LONG A HANDICAP

No single doctrine ever taught by the church has been fraught with such woeful and disastrous consequences as that of the verbal inspiration and infallibility of the Bible, long held by the church. It blighted everything it touched, and betrayed the church into numerous blunders, some of which were serious. Of course, the Bible is an authoritative source of moral and spiritual truth—an infallible source, if one prefers to state it that way. But in the development of the Hebrew and Jewish people, as set forth in the Bible, there is recorded much that is partial, temporary and passing. Many erroneous ideas were believed and taught. In the ignorance of these primitive people many things are attributed to God that cannot be true. This doctrine of an infallible Bible long hindered a proper and needed revision of the Scriptures.

The idea of an infallible Bible is very old. The Septuagint or Greek translation of the Old Testament was early made infallible, by a story that recounted how it had been made by special inspiration. This was the exclusive Bible of the early church for the first century or so, until the New Testament came to be regarded as sacred and was added to it. And it continued to be the Old Testament of the church for several centuries, because at that time the church was Greek-speaking.

Human nature seems prone to the invention of the miraculous, especially in connection with religion. An old epistle of one Aristeas, from the third century B. C., tells how 72 elders were sent from Jerusalem to Egypt for the purpose of making this translation, doing their work, so the epistle says, on an island far from the noise of the city. Each man worked separately and alone, and then they met to compare results and agree on a final text, completing the Pentateuch in 72 sessions.

This simple story was told and retold, embellished as it was repeated, until it came to be said that these 72 men worked alone, each translating, not the Pentateuch, but the whole Old Testament; and when they met to compare results, each translation was found to be identical with every other. This fact insured the inspiration and infallibility of the whole Old Testament. It should be a matter of interest to know that it was from this story that the version received its name, the Septuagint, the Seventy, generally written LXX. The church for centuries fully believed this story; but it was finally proved legendary, and Biblical infallibility received a setback.

A miracle was early invented, or more likely grew up gradually, to guarantee the infallibility of the Hebrew Old Testament. The early church was of the opinion that the books of the Old Testament had all been destroyed during the Babylonian captivity, from 605 to 536 B. C. It was believed that Ezra, by special divine inspiration, had been enabled to reproduce these books, including the vowel points. We are told that he employed five scribes and, in a period of forty days, he was able to dictate ninety-four books, twenty-four of the number being the books of the Old Testament.[2] This miraculous reproduction guaranteed both their infallibility and their place in the Bible.

This impossible story ceased to appeal to the more intelligent after a time, and during the sixteenth century it was revamped and offered in a new form. It was then said that the canon of the Old Testament had been authoritatively determined by a body of learned men known as the Great Synagogue, over which Ezra presided. The men had been inspired, of course. This new idea, however, was based on a mere conjecture of Elias Levita, a Jewish scholar contemporary with Luther. But long ago it became known that no Great Synagogue ever existed, and the doctrine of an infallible Old Testament received another blow.

The infallibility of the New Testament was early accounted for by miracle, in the days when they were easily invented and readily believed. It is well known that, in early Christian times, numerous books circulated among the churches along with the books of the New Testament, but which were finally rejected as not inspired. Certain of these books were for a time considered sacred, and some of them have come down to us as a part of the ancient New Testament in some of the oldest MSS we have, such as the Shepherd of Hermas and the Epistle of Barnabas. Both of these are found in the Sinaitic MS, discovered by Tischendorf on Mt. Sinai, and considered the second oldest and best MS of the New Testament known.

One Pappus tells us how the books of the New Testament were miraculously selected, and the spurious books rejected. At the Council of Nice, so he says, having "promiscuously put all the books that were referred to the council for determination under the communion table, they besought the Lord that the inspired writings might get upon the table, while the spurious ones remained underneath, and

---

[2] This story is found in 4 Esdras (2 Esdras) 14:44-46.

it happened accordingly." [3] This story, of course, was exploded long ago.

For a time the infallibility of the King James Version was actually held and defended against all adversaries. God was supposed to have played such part in its production as to guarantee it against mistakes of whatever character. Very naturally the idea of revising an infallible book was out of the question to those who considered it such.

Christians long believed that God had not only given His people an infallible Book, but that, through the ages, He had exercised a peculiar providence over the MSS of the Bible, preserving them from all error. The Westminister Confession of Faith contains this old idea, for we read, "The Old Testament in Hebrew . . . and the New Testament in Greek . . . being immediately inspired by God, and by his singular care and providence kept pure in all ages, are therefore authentical." [4]

The first rude jolt dealt this pious opinion was the London Polyglot of 1657, published by Brian Walton. A few of the various readings of the MSS had already been published, creating no serious alarm, however, but when Walton published the various readings of numerous additional MSS, hitherto unexamined, panic seized the leaders of the church, provoking a controversy between Walton and Dr. Owen that became historic. Dr. Owen did what many modern Christians do today; he totally mistook the whole purpose of textual criticism, considering it an unwarranted attempt "to correct the Word of God . . . to amend it at the pleasure of men," whereas it is only an effort to get back to the original text. Roman Catholic writers thought they saw an opportunity for an inning, and, taking advantage of the confusion created by the numerous various readings, urged the necessity of an infallible interpreter of the Sacred Volume. Deists also rejoiced at the confusion created among Christians, and renewed their attacks. The situation seemed critical.

And when John Mill, in 1707, published his Greek Testament with various readings to the number of 30,000, from 100 MSS, it renewed the panic which Walton had created, and left many faithful utterly bewildered. The very foundations seemed to be crumbling. It was Richard Bentley who came to the rescue. He made it clear that the problems created were not theological but purely literary; and he pointed out that neither faith nor morals were endangered in

---

[3] *Apocryphal New Testament*, 2nd ed. published by Henry Altemus, p XII.
[4] Chapter 1, VIII.

the slightest degree by the various readings. He did much to allay the fears of many good people. The contest was long and bitter; yet it was not a question of theory, as some sought to make it, but one of fact; and the MSS spoke for themselves in no uncertain terms. The variations were there for anybody to read. Finally, the church leaders were forced to accept the facts, and readjust their thinking to fit. As MSS continued to be collected the variations mounted higher and higher, until today they are known to number from 150,000 to 200,000. Among the intelligent there is no longer any question of the existence of innumerable mistakes in the Biblical MSS. God has not seen fit to preserve them from error; but that fact disturbs only the timid of faith. Yet, when a discriminating Christian reads his Bible, he prefers a text as near the original as possible.

Another erroneous opinion concerning the Bible that hindered revision of the original text, and precipitated a bitter fight, was concerning the vowels contained in the Hebrew Bible. The Massoretic text, as it has come down to us, contains the vowels, and it was long supposed that God had given them as a part of his original revelation. But when it was suggested that the Hebrew had originally been written without vowels, leaving the reader to supply them, and that the vowels of the Hebrew Bible had been added between the seventh and ninth centuries, by the Massoretes, the theologians were once more alarmed. This seemed to undermine the infallibility and authority of the Old Testament. The first scholar to point out the late addition of the vowels was Elias Levita, as already noted a contemporary of Luther. Then Louis Capel, a French Protestant, finally dealt the oldtime idea a blow from which it never recovered. But the controversy lasted many years. The matter was considered of such importance that the Calvinists of Geneva, at one time, declined to receive any minister among them, until he would publicly confess that these points were a part of the original and, therefore, inspired. Long ago the matter was settled and nobody now doubts that the vowel points of Hebrew are late additions. The revision of the Hebrew text today often consists in supplying vowels different from those in the printed text, and the infallibility of the Old Testament is set further back.

The advocates of an infallible Bible, however, have not abandoned the fight. They have been routed again and again; they retreat each time, reentrench themselves and prepare to fight on. They are no longer concerned as to how the Greek Old Testament was written; they ask nobody to believe that any miracle was concerned in the selection of the books of the Old and New Testaments; the infallibility of the King James Version is freely surrendered; they admit frankly that innumerable mistakes are found in the MSS of the Bible; and they accept the vowels of the Hebrew Old Testament as late additions. But they assure us that the original autographs of the Bible were infallible. Of course, they never saw an original autograph of one of the books, and never expect to see one, because they have all been lost; but they seem to know all about them. Entrenched in their new position they feel they are safe at last, because they know that nobody will ever produce an original MS and prove them wrong again. The only evidence they have of their present position is their unsupported assertions. They now freely admit that the only Bible we have, and the only one we can ever hope to have, contains many mistakes; and at last the work of revision is no longer hindered by the doctrine of an infallible Bible.

3. REVISIONS MADE BY COMMITTEES

A. THE AMERICAN BIBLE SOCIETY REVISION

Before the demand for an authoritative revision of the King James Version had become sufficiently powerful to force it, an incident occurred that illustrated the ignorance and unreasoning prejudice of the masses of Christians, including many supposed to be educated. The episode, a really laughable one, occurred in the work of the American Bible Society.

Scribes who copied the Bible by hand had made many mistakes, thereby greatly corrupting the text, and the same thing occurred in printed editions. Printer's errors soon became very numerous. The Bible Society's attention was called to the many differences in copies of the King James Version as early as 1847, resulting in the appointment of a committee of seven, who employed the Rev. James W. McLane to work as collator in 1848. He compared the standard copy of the Bible Society with copies of the King James Version published in London, Oxford, Cambridge, Edinburgh and the original copy of 1611, his report indicating that he had found some 24,000 variations in these texts.

Naturally enough the Bible Society was anxious to print a text as nearly correct as possible, and, therefore, a committee was appointed to prepare a revision. In the formation of the new text, it was agreed that where four modern British copies agreed, the text would be

adopted. The "great and leading object" of the revision was uni
formity, and a correction of all printer's errors.

In a few instances the text was altered to agree with the Hebrew
or Greek, but none of these changes was of any real importance
Alterations were made in orthography where the forms of words had
become obsolete, or had already been changed in some places and
not in others. Thus "assuaged" took the place of "asswaged," "axe"
was substituted for "ax," "soap" replaced "sope," "didst" was used
for "diddst," "braided" for "broidered," "fetched" for "fetcht,"
"lain" for "lien," etc. The use of the indefinite article "a" and "an"
was made consistent. The spelling of proper names was made uni
form in the Old Testament, except where they differed in the origi
nal. In the New Testament unfamiliar forms were changed; thus
"Korah" was used for "Core," and "Sinai" for "Sina." Special pains
were taken to secure the right use of italics.

In the matter of punctuation the agreement of any three Bibles
examined was considered sufficient, and where there was not sufficient agreement in the copies examined the committee used its best
judgment. In five passages the changes made affected the sense,[5]
but involved nothing of importance.

The summaries of chapters were carefully revised, which consisted
mainly in the removal of the quaint, obsolete, ambiguous and inap-
propriate, and the removal of what constituted comment. The summaries of the Song of Solomon were entirely recast.[6] The summaries
of this book in the King James Version interpret it as an allegory,
which no scholar longer believes.

The newly revised text was adopted as a standard for the Bible
Society, and its publication began in 1851. Everything went well
until 1856, when the Rev. A. C. Coxe of Baltimore, later Bishop
of Western New York, questioned the right of the Bible Society to
make such revisions as had been made. Then in 1857 he published
a pamphlet in which he charged the Society with making 24,000
changes in the Word of God! In his alarm he declared that German
rationalism had completely captured the Bible Society! His pamphlet created great excitement, resulting in much controversy, shak-
ing the foundations of the institution, and even threatening its
very existence. Some fearful souls in the Old School Presby-

[5] Rom. 4:1; 1 Cor. 16:22; 2 Cor. 10:8-11; Heb. 13:8 and Rev. 13:8. See Condit,
History of the English Bible, pp 422-23.
  [6] For a fuller discussion of the revisions made, see *Historical Catalogue of
Printed Bibles,* by Darlow and Moule, Vol. I, pp 362-63.

terian Assembly, in 1857, discussed the subject as if it were a matter of life and death, and instructed its board of publication to print Bibles, evidently feeling that the Bible Society could no longer be trusted!

In 1858 the Bible Society referred the whole matter to its committee on versions. The new and improved text was promptly abandoned, and no more would be printed, so it was said, unless specially asked for. An edition of the New Testament was printed, however, in 1859 and one of the whole Bible in 1860, indicating that there were some who had not caught the contagion of alarm. Whether other late editions were printed is not known.

The new revision had really done nothing of importance except correct printer's errors, and make spellings modern and harmonious. But printer's errors and antiquated spellings had become sacred! The whole episode is only an example of how ignorance often betrays Christian people into making donkeys of themselves.

B. THE ANGLO-AMERICAN REVISION

The King James Version held undisputed sway among English-speaking peoples for more than 200 years, during which many private translations were made, none of which ever had any extensive use. Vast material had finally been accumulated for the correction of the Hebrew and Greek originals; and the King James Version had come to be thoroughly antiquated, with its faulty text, numerous mistranslations, and some 200 words obsolete or completely changed in meaning. These and other considerations finally resulted in a demand for an authoritative revision that could no longer be denied. This demand, however, did not come from the common people, but from the educated. To many of the common people unfortunately the idea seemed little less than sacrilegious, only because they knew little or nothing about the need for such revision.

On February 10, 1870, Dr. Wilberforce, Bishop of Winchester, proposed, before the Upper House of the Convocation of the Province of Canterbury, a committee to report on the advisability of revising the New Testament. It was then suggested that the Old Testament be revised also. The amended motion to revise the whole Bible was adopted. Accordingly, a committee was appointed to consider the matter and report the following May. The report being favorable both houses of Convocation passed a resolution providing that the revision be undertaken. A committee was appointed for the work, and they were "at liberty to invite the cooperation of any eminent for scholarship, to whatever nation or religious body they may belong."

While the Church of England took the lead, the English committee was made up of 54 Biblical scholars from nearly all the existing evangelical bodies, some among them being Congregationalists, Baptists, Presbyterians, Methodists and Unitarians. As an indication of the broadmindedness of the men who launched the work, it was seriously proposed that eminent Jewish scholars be asked to aid in the revision of the Old Testament. This was not done, however, but it was seriously considered.[7] Dr. John Henry Newman, who had left the Church of England, becoming a Roman Catholic twenty-five years before, was invited to assist in the work, but he declined.

It was decided to ask America to assist in the enterprise. Accordingly, in 1870, Dr. Angus visited America, and held numerous conferences with a group of American scholars. A plan of cooperation was worked out, and a committee of thirty American Biblical scholars, representing the various denominations, was organized on December 7, 1871, beginning its work in October, 1872.

Dr. Philip Schaff of New York was made president of the whole American Committee, having taken the leading part in the formation of the Committee, himself being a member of the New Testament section. Theodore Dwight Woolsey, ex-president of Yale University, was made chairman of the New Testament section, and Professor William Henry Green of Princeton University was made chairman of the Old Testament section.

Revision was first made in England, and then submitted to the American Committee, for its criticisms and suggestions, which were used in England in a final revision, where Dr. Harold Browne, Bishop of Winchester, served as chairman of the Old Testament Committee, and Dr. C. J. Ellicott, Bishop of Gloucester and Bristol, as chairman of the New Testament Committee.

The New Testament was completed first, and published in England on May 17, 1881, and in the United States on May 20. Its reception was entirely unprecedented. The University Presses of Oxford and Cambridge received advance orders for nearly two million copies. An agent of the Clarendon Press, in New York, sold 365,000 copies within a year, and other agents at Philadelphia sold 110,000. Several reprints were very early thrown on the market. It is esti-

---

[7] Stoughton, *Our English Bible*, pp 288-89.

mated that 3,000,000 copies were sold in England and America within the first year.

Several periodicals and papers reproduced it, in whole or in part. The Chicago *Tribune* and the Chicago *Times* both printed the whole New Testament in their issues of May 22, 1881. About 118,000 words were telegraphed from New York, and the remainder were taken from copies of the book received in Chicago on the evening of May 21. No such reception was ever accorded any other book in the history of the world.

The Old Testament was not published until May 19, 1885, when both the Old Testament and the New appeared in one volume. This had a generous reception, but nothing to compare with that of the New Testament. There was not the same reason for it.

In making the translation, the Committee revised both the Hebrew and Greek texts, the Hebrew, however, being changed but little. In the New Testament, 5,788 changes were made in the Greek text from which the King James Version had been made. Only one in four of these changes, however, was of any real importance; but that means that 1447 of these changes were important. It has been estimated that the English text of the New Testament was changed in 36,191 places. Most of these were matters of little moment, yet many of them were important.

The Anglo-American Revision marked a very great improvement over the King James Version for those who prefer a Bible as near the originals as possible, and in language more easily understood.

C. THE AMERICAN STANDARD BIBLE

When the Anglo-American version had been published, in 1881-1885, the English Committee, having nothing further in mind, disbanded,[8] but not so with the American Committee. They felt that an American edition should be prepared, and being not entirely satisfied with their former work, continued their efforts. And there was real need for such an edition. The Anglo-American revision, dominated by the English, had retained a large number of words that were entirely obsolete, such as "sith," "holpen," "bewray," "strowed," "hough," "marish," and "pourtray." Then there were many words that do not have the same meaning in England they have in America. In Eng-

---

[8] A committee was formed by the University Presses for the purpose of revising the apocrypha, which was published in 1895.

land "corn" means grain of all kinds, while in America it means Indian corn only. "Chargers" in England means what we in America call "horses," and "chapmen" there are men "traders" with us. Many other distinctly English terms are used. If we should use this version in America it would require a glossary to explain it.

The American Standard Bible, published in New York in 1901, was the result of 30 years of active work by many of the leading Biblical scholars of the world. There can be no question that this Bible represents a riper scholarship than that of the Anglo-American version, and is the most faithful and most accurate, as well as the most American of any version in the solemn style ever made in English. Everything about it is an improvement over former versions, except the mistake of printing the verse numbers mixed up with the text. This was a serious blunder. However, it has already achieved a wide popularity, but not what it deserves.

Its advantages over any other in the solemn style are very great. In the first place, the original text used in the Anglo-American revision was further revised to a decided advantage, especially in the New Testament.

In the King James Version the word Jehovah is used alone only four times, and the Anglo-American revision makes little improvement in this regard; but the American Standard Bible uses this word uniformly as the translation of the Divine Name in Hebrew. It has been said by high authority that this is "the first time in the history of the English Bible, the sacred name Jehovah is given uniformly as the equivalent of the Hebrew name," but this is not correct.[9] Jehovah had been generally used for considerably more than 100 years. When the translators of the American Standard Bible used it, they were only following a well established custom.

The word Jehovah is nowhere found in the Hebrew. Hebrew was written originally in consonants only, the vowels being supplied by the reader. The Hebrew name for God, J H V H, became so sacred to the Jews that they ceased to pronounce it at all, except on certain occasions. When they read a text containing this word they regularly substituted another word, A D N I, which is translated Lord. On this account the correct vowels of the Divine Name have been

---

[9] Lowth used Jehovah in his *Isaiah*, 1778; Blayney, in his *Jeremiah and Lammentations*, 1784; Newcome, in his *Minor Prophets*, 1785. Numerous others did so later. Boothroyd's Bible, 1818, 1824, Julia E. Smith's Bible, 1876, used it regularly. Samuel Sharp's Bible, 1881, used Jehovah and Jah. Even the *Bay Psalm Book* used Jehovah, but whether uniformly or not we do not know; and the Swedenborg Bible of 1869 used it uniformly.

lost. When the Massoretes added the vowels to the Hebrew text, from the seventh to the ninth century A. D., they gave this word the vowels of the word they had used as a substitute. So with the consonants of the Divine Name and the vowels of another name which designated God as Lord, we get Jehovah, and that is how the word was coined.[10] The King James Version substituted LORD (spelled with capitals) wherever the Divine Name is found, except in four cases. While Jehovah was never used among the Jews, it suits far better as a translation than any guess men have made as to the vowels that were probably used originally.

Sheol is a Hebrew word with no English equivalent, meaning simply the place where the dead go, without reference to reward or punishment. The King James Version, however, renders this word "hell" thirty-one times, "grave" thirty-one times, and "pit" three times, all of which are incorrect and misleading. The idea of "hell" is not contained in the Old Testament. Hades is a Greek word meaning the same as Sheol in Hebrew, but the King James Version renders this word "hell" ten times in the New Testament. The Anglo-American revision makes little improvement in these matters, while in the American Standard Bible these are simply made into English words, because neither has an English equivalent. The Bible knows but one devil, but many demons. Therefore, the American Standard Bible speaks of "being possessed by a demon," and not "possessed with devils." "Holy Spirit" is used uniformly instead of the antiquated "Holy Ghost." The American revisers are especially to be commended for their use of euphemisms to avoid expressions that are out of place in modern society. One example may be given. The King James Version reads, "My bowels, my bowels! I am pained at my very heart." [11] The American Standard Bible reads, "My anguish, my anguish! I am pained at my very heart." Many offensive terms are removed. Many unsatisfactory translations are improved. The King James Version reads, "God trieth the heart and the reins." [12] "Reins" means kidneys. The ancients located feeling and thinking in the kidneys and bowels; we locate them in the heart and mind, and translations should be made accordingly.

The chronological dates often found in the King James Version are

---

[10] The use of the word Jehovah cannot be traced beyond 1518 A. D., when Petrus Galatinus, confessor to Leo X, proposed its use. See *Where Did We Get Our Bible?* Robinson, p 179 note 6

[11] Jer.4:19.   [12] Psa.7:9. For a list of offensive terms removed, see *The Bible from the Beginning*, Simms, pp 230-31.

no part of the Bible originally, being supplied by Bishop Lloyd in 1701, and taken substantially from Archbishop Ussher's Annals of 1650-54. These dates have been proved to be utterly worthless, and fortunately no uncertain chronology appears in the American Standard Bible. A complete new set of marginal references appear in this Bible, perhaps the most satisfactory ever prepared for any Bible. Its language is such as can be understood in America.[13]

This Bible with its unquestioned superiority has now been in use thirty-five years, and yet millions, who will have nothing but the solemn style, go right on preferring the antiquated King James Version for themselves and their children.

There is a reason for this, however, as there is for everything else people do. Millions of men and women read the Bible and find it the chief inspiration and comfort of their lives, but who know absolutely nothing about how the Bible was originally written; how it was necessarily copied by hand for many long centuries and inevitably corrupted by the process; how the text has been revised again and again in scholarly efforts to eliminate the corruptions and recover the original text; and how, finally, it has been translated and revised repeatedly in order to keep it in language in familiar use and abreast of the best scholarship. This widespread ignorance is the chief explanation of the continued use of an out-of-date Bible. Of course, long familiarity with the language of the King James Version, in all its sacred associations, very naturally inclines one to continue its use; but, after all, only ignorance can deliberately prefer a Bible with a known corrupted text, with numerous mistranslations that mislead, with many obsolete words that are not understood, and with frequent words, although in familiar use, so changed in meaning that the reader can have no idea what many texts teach.

The history of the effort to recover the original text of the Bible, and to give the world up-to-date translations and revisions, has been pathetic. Origen, one of the early Christian fathers, and one of the greatest men of his day, had little thanks for his effort to improve the Septuagint, the Greek Old Testament of his era. The masses regarded it as tinkering with the Bible.

Jerome, the greatest scholar of his age, at the request of Pope Damasus, revised the Old Latin, badly corrupted by his time, finally translating anew the books of the Old Testament, and so producing the Latin Vulgate. But he was denounced for it on all sides, and

---

[13] For a much fuller discussion of the superiority of the American Standard Bible, see, *The Bible from the Beginning*, Simms, pp. 228-232.

accused of undermining the faith and disturbing the peace of the church. But he was in the right, and his revision finally came into and has since remained in general use.

The men who have spent their lives in efforts to revise the Greek text of the New Testament and get back to the original, as nearly as possible, have generally suffered for their work.

Robert Stephens, the Parisian printer, revised the Latin Vulgate and brought down on his head the wrath of the doctors of the Sorbonne, and when he published a Greek New Testament with 2,174 various readings, the criticisms were such that he felt impelled to leave Paris and take refuge in Protestant Geneva.

J. J. Wetstein spent forty years in preparation, and published a Greek New Testament in 1651-52, for which he was deposed from his pastorate and sent into exile.

John Mill put out a Greek New Testament in 1707, indicating 30,000 variations in the Greek manuscripts consulted, producing a panic among the Christian forces. Death mercifully saved him from bitter persecution.

The saintly Albert Bengel was malignantly assailed for his Greek New Testament of 1738, for which, among other things, he was called a "Bible murderer." Walton, Mill, Bentley, Wetstein, Matthei, Bengel, Lachmann and Tischendorf all suffered for their efforts to improve the Greek text, and yet they were always in the right.

Because Tyndale tried to get away from the Latin Vulgate and give the people the Bible in their own tongue, he was forced to live in exile, hunted like a criminal, his books condemned and burned by the thousands. Finally, he was strangled and burned at the stake.

No revision of the Bible was ever attacked more bitterly than the King James Version when it first appeared; and it required nearly a century for it to acquire the recognition that should have been accorded it on its first appearance.

The Anglo-American Revision of 1881-85 was bitterly assailed, and even men of some scholarship were among its bitter critics. Yet it was unquestionably a great improvement over the King James Version.

Through all these years the scholars have been in the right, constantly seeking to do what was needed, and the critics have been in the wrong. There is this difference, however, today, as compared with the past. Men are no longer persecuted for their efforts to improve the text, or to provide better translations of the Scriptures. Their work is simply ignored by the vast masses. But even this is a gain. Yet what a sad commentary on the intelligence of the masses of Christians is this history!

The American Standard Bible is not perfect. Biblical scholarship continues to learn, and there is felt among the leading scholars of the country the need for a revision of this Bible, to bring it abreast of the scholarship of the day. The copyright has now been turned over to the Religious Education Association, and a committee of the leading Biblical scholars of America have been appointed to revise it. The depression, however, has made this impossible up to the present time.

D. A SPURIOUS AMERICAN EDITION

The American Revision Committee had differed from the English Committee as to the best rendering in English in many passages, as was natural, and it had been agreed that the American preferences should appear as an appendix to the work. The University Presses of Oxford and Cambridge were to have the exclusive right to print the Anglo-American Revision for fourteen years, a period that would expire in 1899. Until this time the American Committee had agreed to sanction no editions of the revision, and like Christian gentlemen they kept their promise. Anticipating an American edition, as soon as the American Committee was free to print one, the University Presses published what they called the "American Revised Version" in 1898, incorporating the American preferences of the appendix into the text, doing this at a time when the American Committee was in honor bound to stand by helpless.

This was manifestly a very unfair thing to do, for various reasons. The American Committee had held together through all these years, and was preparing for publication a further revision for American use. The American preferences, found in the appendix, had never been quite satisfactory. The Committee had been finally compelled to prepare the list in great haste, because the British public had grown tired of waiting for the complete Bible, and were demanding its publication. Working in such haste, an unsatisfactory job had been done. Besides all this, the American Committee, by further study and work, had introduced many changes not contemplated in the former revision. The publication of what purported to be an "American Revised Version" at that time not only would give the public an inferior work, but also affect the sale of the finished American product.

The University Presses had had all the profits of publication for 14 years, and they now sought to preempt the American market with an "American Revised Version." Their action naturally provoked considerable criticism, and the spurious American edition had a small sale, as it deserved.

4. TRANSLATIONS OF THE BIBLE LABORS OF LOVE

There is one thing, in connection with the translation and revision of the Bible, that ought to be deeply appreciated, but about which very little is generally known. Those who have made the various translations and revisions have done their work as a labor of love. Never was more faithful work done without the hope of financial reward. Many have never even received expenses for their labor, and when expenses have been provided, they have usually been quite meager. Wyclif, Purvey and Tyndale worked at their own expense. Certain friends aided Tyndale to live while working. Coverdale, who prepared the first whole Bible printed in English, and later the Great Bible, may have received some slight financial assistance from Thomas Cromwell, but nothing that could, by any possible stretch, be deemed real compensation. John Rogers, who put out Matthew's Bible, worked at his own charges and, like Tyndale, paid for it with his life. Taverner prepared his revised Bible at his own expense. The makers of the Geneva Bible may have had something by way of expenses; anyhow, the English congregation at Geneva provided for the printing of this Bible. The translators of the Rheims-Douai version made the work a labor of love, and it has been said that one of their number greatly hastened his death by the arduous task. The Bishops' Bible was made for the love of the work.

As a sort of compensation for making the King James Version, the king suggested that, when opportunity offered, the translators should be provided with churches, which was probably done in a few cases. He did not propose to put any of his money into the undertaking. Some money was necessary and Bancroft sought to provide a small amount, asking the bishops and deans to make contributions, but there is no evidence that he ever received a single penny.

Somehow the committee seems to have managed without money while the original work was being done. A committee sat for nine months, making a final revision of the whole, for which they each received thirty shillings per week. The work was superintended through the press, a gigantic task, by Dr. Miles and James Bilson. Robert Barker, the king's printer, furnished the money to meet whatever expenses had to be met, to the amount of 3,500 pounds, recouping his advances from the profits of publication.[14]

The University Presses of Oxford and Cambridge furnished the money to provide the expenses of the English Committee, in making the Anglo-American Revision, and reimbursed themselves by the sale of the book. The American Committee assisting provided their own expenses as best they could. For a time it was met by voluntary offerings. A finance committee was finally appointed, which offered memorial copies of the new Bible to all who would give certain amounts. By such methods expenses were provided.

The American Revision Committee, in their preparation of the American Standard Bible, received nothing that could be called compensation. Thomas Nelson and Sons of New York, furnished sufficient money to meet necessary expenses in the preparation of the text, for which they received the copyright to the book.

Luther declined to receive pay for his services as a translator, preferring that the Bible be sold as cheaply as possible. The same general principles apply to the translations and revisions made in all the various languages; nobody has really been compensated, and many have labored at heavy personal expense. Both those made by committees and by private translators have been labors of love.

The only translators of the Bible who have ever received any real compensation for their work—we presume there have been such—are makers of modern translations that have sold in quantities sufficient to bring some worth-while royalty. But even these did their work at their own charge, and had no assurance in advance of any compensation.

The Bible has thus been translated for the world at great personal sacrifice, and watered by the blood of martyrs. These facts ought to make us appreciate it all the more.

[14] Anderson, *The Annals of the English Bible*, pp 481-83.

MAMUSSE
WUNNEETUPANATAMWE
UP-BIBLUM GOD
NANEESWE
NUKKONE TESTAMENT
KAH WONK
WUSKU TESTAMENT.

Ne quoſhkinnumuk naſhpe Wuttinneumoh *CHRIST*
noh aſoowelit

JOHN ELIOT·

CAMBRIDGE:

Printeuoop naſhpe *Samuel Green* kah *Marmaduke Johnſon.*

1 6 6 3.

Facsimile of title page of John Eliot's Indian Bible

CHAPTER IX

JEWISH TRANSLATIONS

THE discovery of America by Columbus resulted in its settlement and development. Great honor is due Columbus, of course, and considerable credit must be given Isabella, the queen of Castile, since she it was who was won to provide the enterprise. The story of her offer to pledge her jewels in order to borrow the necessary money, however, has been called a fable by good authority in recent years.[1]

1. THE CONTRIBUTION MADE BY THE JEWS

The Jews also deserve great credit for the discovery of America by Columbus. Louis de Santangle, the richest man of the kingdom, was Ferdinand's financial secretary, and Raphael Sanchez was his treasurer. Both were Jews, professing to be Christians, however, in order to escape the bitter persecutions of the day, as did many other Jews at that time, thereby taking the easiest way out. But for the influence of these two Jews it is practically certain that Isabella would not have been won to favor the undertaking, in the first place, and to finance it, in the second place. It was Santangle who loaned Isabella the money with which to fit out the first expedition.[2] "Louis de Santangle, Ferdinand's financial secretary, who advanced to Isabella the 16,000 or 17,000 ducats to enable Columbus to discover the New World, was penanced July 17, 1491." [3]

Several Jews accompanied Columbus on his first voyage, among them Louis de Torres, a highly educated Jew, whom Columbus took along as his interpreter. Marco, a surgeon, was a Jew. Numerous Jews also accompanied him on his second voyage, which was financed entirely by money confiscated from the Jews who had been expelled from the country. The national treasury at this time was greatly enriched by a wholesale confiscation of Jewish property.

The first report that Columbus made of the success of his voyage was a letter in Spanish written to Louis de Santangle,[4] and his second report was a letter written in Latin addressed to Raphael Sanchez.[5]

[1] Kayserling's *Christopher Columbus*, translated by Charles Gross, p 74 and note.

[2] Kayserling's *Christopher Columbus*, translated by Charles Gross, p 77.

[3] Lea, *A History of the Inquisition in Spain*, Vol. I, p 259.

[4] This letter was printed in Barcelona in 1493 and a facsimile publication and translation was printed in *The Columbus Memorial*, edited by George Young, Philadelphia, 1893.

[5] An edition in facsimile with translation, etc., was published by the Lenox

By such means Columbus showed his appreciation of the aid given him by these Jews. Both sent their letters to Ferdinand and Isabella, and in this way the latter received their first report of the success of the undertaking.

The first Jews in America, like other faiths, came to our shores to escape persecution, the earliest arrivals being fugitives from Brazil, who landed in September, 1655. From Holland the *Mayflower* had sailed to America freighted with its band of Pilgrims; and from Holland a party of Jews had sailed to Brazil, where they planned to found a colony owing allegiance to the Netherlands. Things went well for a time, but in 1654 Portugal conquered the territory where they had settled, and the Jews fled. A group of twenty-three set sail on the *St. Charles* for New Amsterdam (New York), under the very natural impression that, since they owed their allegiance to Holland, they would be welcome among the Hollanders in New Amsterdam. Holland long had practiced religious toleration, and her colonies would be supposed to do so. They landed, however, only to learn that Peter Stuyvesant, the governor, did not want them. They promptly appealed to Holland against his decision, and he was overruled and forced to receive them; thus they became American citizens. Late in the seventeenth century Jews were found in considerable numbers in New York, Pennsylvania, Maryland, Virginia and South Carolina.

In 1905 meetings were held in many parts of the United States, appropriately commemorating the two hundred and fiftieth anniversary of the first Jewish settlement in America. Many Christian churches, as was befitting, observed the occasion by special sermons that gave the Jews due credit for what they had done. Jews helped to build the nation. To every call of the country they have always responded as good American citizens.

Lyman Abbott, editor of the *Outlook,* on the occasion of this celebration, said, "In my judgment the American people owe more to the ancient Hebrews than to any ancient people. More than to either the Greeks or to the Romans, because to the Hebrews we owe our ethical and spiritual ideas." [6]

"Ever since the day when Columbus first announced in a letter

Library, New York, in 1892. This name is sometimes given as Gabriel Sanchez. Kayserling, in *Christopher Columbus,* uses both names. See p 102.

[6] *The 250th Anniversary of the Settlement of the Jews in the United States,* p 231.

to his Jewish friend, Louis de Santangle, the discovery of America by the expedition fitted out by Jewish gold, manned in part by Jewish sailors, and guided into unknown seas by nautical tables compiled by a Jew, printed by another, and presented to Columbus by a third—ever since that day the Jew has played an honorable and not undistinguished part in the history and development of the Western Continents."[7]

No other race has so influenced the world. From the days of Moses Jews have enriched every age and all civilized nations. Several of them were officers in the Revolutionary Army. The Jews have stood high in the fine arts, conspicuous for poetry, music and the drama, and they have also taken high rank in the sciences. Moreover, they have made a tremendous contribution to the moral and spiritual life of the country.

Their greatest contribution, of course, has been the gift of the Old Testament, the larger part of every Christian Bible in the world, and their gift to the world of Jesus Christ. Jesus was a Jew. Naturally the Christian considers Jesus Christ their greatest gift. The Jews have everywhere set examples of industry, sobriety, domestic peace, philanthropy and reverence. Fortunately for all concerned they are free from persecution in America.

2. TRANSLATIONS OF THE OLD TESTAMENT

The Jews of America have made a rather free use of the King James Version, and also a certain use of the Anglo-American Revision of 1885, interpreting them, of course, in Jewish fashion. Their Bibles have often been revisions of the King James Version. Michael Friedlander published such a revision in London about 1881, under the title, "The Jewish Family Bible." This included the Hebrew text also.

A. ISAAC LEESER'S TRANSLATION

Isaac Leeser was a Prussian Jewish rabbi who founded the Jewish press of America. He made the first Jewish translation of any part of the Old Testament in the United States. About 1838 he announced his purpose to publish the Pentateuch, which was put out in Philadelphia in 1846, under the title, "The Law of God." This edition of

[7] *The 250th Anniversary of the Settlement of the Jews in the United States*, p 63.

five volumes contained the Hebrew as well as an English translation. It was Leeser who published in Philadelphia, in 1849, the first Hebrew Bible in America with points, that is with vowels.

In 1853 he published at Philadelphia an English translation of the Old Testament with the title, "The Twenty-four Books of the Holy Scriptures." In its preparation he spent fifteen years, and the only work in English consulted was Bagster's Bible, a copy of the King James Version. For more than a half century Leeser's Old Testament served as a standard among the Jews, used freely both in England and America. In style he imitated the King James Version, but his work was a new translation.

B. ALEXANDER HARKAVY'S REVISION

Alexander Harkavy a Polish Jew, and a prominent editor and author, published in New York in 1917, "The Twenty-four Books of the Old Testament," a revision of the King James Version. Naturally he changed the parts which the Jews regard as favoring Christian dogma. He sought also to substitute modern words and spellings for what had become obsolete, the whole being done in imitation of the King James Version. This was published with and without the Hebrew text.

C. JACOB LEVI LEVINSKY'S BIBLE

An "Abridged School and Family Bible in Hebrew and English," prepared by Jacob Levi Levinsky, with the cooperation of Dr. H. Vidaver and others, was published in New York; volume I containing the Pentateuch in 1869; volume II, containing the Early Prophets in 1871; and volume III, with selections from the Later Prophets, Hagiographa and Apocrypha in 1871.

D. THE STANDARD JEWISH TRANSLATION

The most important and authoritative Jewish translation made in America was done by a committee of learned Jewish scholars. In 1892 the Jewish Publication Society of America, in Philadelphia, began the preparation of a translation with Dr. Marcus Jastrow, Jr. as editor in chief, and Dr. Kaufman Kohler and Dr. Frederick de Sola Mendes as associate editors. The original plan, however, was revised in 1908, and a new committee named, the altered arrangement giving equal representation to the Jewish Theological Seminary of New York, the Hebrew Union College of Cincinnati and Dropsie College of Philadelphia. Professor Max L. Margolis was made editor in chief and Dr. Cyrus Adler, chairman. The purpose of the translation is stated in the preface to the Old Testament issued in Philadelphia in 1917. "It aims to combine the spirit of Jewish tradition with the results of biblical scholarship, ancient, medaeval, and modern. It gives to the Jewish world a translation of the Scriptures done by men imbued with the Jewish consciousness, while the non-Jewish world, it is hoped, will welcome a translation that presents many passages from the Jewish traditional point of view." [8] This is a splendid translation of the Massoretic text, and naturally has had an extensive use among the Jews.

3. TRANSLATIONS OF SINGLE BOOKS

The Book of Psalms, in a revised edition different from that of the Old Testament of 1917, was published by the Jewish Publication Society in Philadelphia in 1903, the revision being made by Dr. Kaufman Kohler. Dr. Max L. Margolis published in Philadelphia in 1908, a translation of Micah. Dr. Marcus Jastrow published in Philadelphia in 1920, a translation of the book of Job, and in the same place in 1921, "The Gentle Cynic" (Kohelet) or as it is generally known, Ecclesiastes, and also the Song of Solomon. Dr. Jastrow was born in Poland, and was educated for the ministry, but giving this up, he became professor of Semitic languages and librarian at the University of Pennsylvania.

Dr. Moses Buttenweiser, professor of Biblical Exegesis in Hebrew Union College, Cincinnati, has put out a translation of the book of Job which was published in New York in 1925, containing the Hebrew text and notes. It represents a scholarly effort to arrive at a correct arrangement of the text, translation and interpretation.

4. DIFFERENCES BETWEEN JEWISH AND CHRISTIAN TRANSLATORS

Differences between the Jews and Christians in translation were once considerable; but the great differences today are matters of interpretation rather than of translation. Modern scholars, whether Jewish or Christian, differ little in the renderings now chosen. One example will illustrate.

The Jews have always maintained that the Old Testament contained no prophecy of the Virgin Birth of anybody; but for long Christians insisted that Isaiah contained a prophecy of the Virgin

[8] Preface, p vii.

Birth of Jesus Christ. Accordingly, the King James Version reads: "Behold, a virgin shall conceive, and bear a son." [9] But in the standard Jewish translation of the Old Testament, published in 1917, as in all former Jewish translations, this verse reads: "Behold, the young woman shall conceive, and bear a son." Modern Christian scholarship agrees with the Jews in their translation of this verse. Samuel Sharpe's Bible, published in London in 1881, reads, "Behold, the young woman shall conceive, and bear a son." The Improved Edition, published by the Baptists in Philadelphia in 1913, reads: "Behold a young woman will conceive, and bear a son." Kent's Shorter Bible, published in 1918-21, puts it this way: "Behold a young woman will give birth to a child." James Moffatt's Bible, published in 1926, says: "There is a young woman with child, who shall bear a son." The Old Testament, An American Translation, by J. M. Powis Smith, published in 1927, has it thus: "Behold! a young woman is with child, who shall bear a son."

The Anglo-American Revision and the American Standard Bible are the two outstanding exceptions in the translation of this verse, but this fact is easily explained. Translations made by committees, representative of large groups, are always made at a certain disadvantage. Some men on such committees are certain to be very slow in accepting modern conclusions, however well attested; and the committees making such translations know that the general public, always lagging behind, is often not prepared to accept what the best scholarship is known to require. Such committees always feel compelled to make certain concessions to ignorance and prejudice. Therefore, the Anglo-American Revision and the American Standard Bible both use "virgin" in this passage of Isaiah, but both place "Or, maiden," as an alternative rendering in the margin, feeling that they dared not concede more to modern scholarship.

Moreover, it is evidently not certain that the original Hebrew of this text refers to a future conception. According to the translations of J. M. Powis Smith and James Moffatt the "young woman" referred to is already "with child;" and the Anglo-American Revision and the American Standard Bible, while translating "shall conceive" both give in the margin an alternative rendering, "Or, is with child, and beareth."

From the above it is evident that if the scholarship of the most outstanding modern translators of the Bible can be trusted, there can be no question that the Hebrew word used in this text by

[9] Isaiah 7:14.

saiah means not "virgin," but "a young woman" or "maiden"—
ecording simply a matter of age and not one of character.

This text of Isaiah, of course, is quoted in Matthew 1:23 as a
prophecy of the Virgin Birth of Jesus Christ, but it is well known
hat the quotation was taken, not from the original Hebrew, but
rom the Greek Old Testament which contains the word "virgin,"
ut which was evidently a mistranslation.

The Virgin Birth of Jesus Christ must be left to rest wholly on the
tories of such birth found in the Gospels of Matthew and Luke.

CHAPTER X

TRANSLATIONS ECCENTRIC IN CHARACTER OR CLAIMS

FOR some reason no field of human thought and endeavor lends itself so easily and so extensively to the eccentric, the absurd and ridiculous, as religion. It would seem that nothing is too absurd to be believed and practiced among the religious.

The Bible and its various parts have been translated by ministers, scholarly and otherwise, by doctors, lawyers, judges, engineers, teachers, shoemakers, booksellers, fruitsellers and the idle about town, and very naturally every sort of product has been the result.

1. THE ERRATIC IN CHARACTER AND CLAIMS FROM ENGLAND

America, the most polyglot nation of all civilization, would quite naturally be expected, we suppose, to excel the whole world in the eccentric, erratic, unconventional and bizarre in Biblical translation; but in two respects, at least, in this connection, England certainly leads the world. In the utter absurdity of translation, and in the colossal egotism of the translator, England has no equals among those speaking the English language.

A. A FRUITSELLER'S TRANSLATION

The most freakish translation of any part of the Bible in English ever produced, at least so far as we have been able to learn, was the work of an Englishman, and was a translation of the first chapter of Genesis. It is said to have been made by an old man who sold fruit in Clare Court by Drury Lane. Published in London in 1754, it was addressed to the Archbishop of Canterbury. A short quotation of the first part will illustrate its character:

"AELOHIM, beginning, created *lucide* and *illucide* matter. 2. And the *illucide*, void of co-adjunct co-hesion, was unmodified, and distinguishableness was nowhere upon the face of Chaos: And the Ruach of AELOHIM emanated over the periphery of the fluctuation. 3. Until AELOHIM said that *Aether* should coallesce to the production of light. And AELOHIM saw the light was good, when it was become a separation from obscurity. 5. And AELOHIM deemed *this* daylight, and the obscurity was yet as night, which was

light, and obscuration the consummation of the first day." [1] America
has never equaled that.

B. JOHN BELLAMY'S TRANSLATIONS

No history of the eccentric in Biblical translation could afford to
omit mention of the work of John Bellamy, another Englishman,
who abounds both in utter absurdity in translation and in egotism.
The writer owns a copy of his Pentateuch, picked up in London,
published in 1818. Somebody had revised his title-page neatly with
ink, and in quoting it, we italicise the additions: "The Holy Bible,
newly *and wildly* translated from the Original Hebrew: with notes
critical and explanatory *and Ridiculous!*" These revisions are required in an accurate description of the work. He is the only man,
so he says, that has made a translation of any part of the Bible from
the pure Hebrew text only, since 128 A. D.!

Most people smile at the mention of Jonah and the whale, which
is probably what the author intended when he wrote the book; and
Bellamy translated it in his usual erratic style. Jonah 1:17, therefore,
reads, "Now Jehovah had prepared a great barge to remove Jonah:
and Jonah was in the belly of the barge, three days and three nights."
Thus he spoils a whale of a story!

C. FERRAR FENTON'S REVISIONS AND PRETENSIONS

Ferrar Fenton, a wealthy Englishman of rank, and quite proud
of it, published a new translation of the Bible in 1903, the parts
having appeared earlier. He felt the necessity of making Genesis
and geology harmonize. Being familiar with the scientific ideas of
vast "periods" in the creation, or formation, of the earth, his translation originally renders the word "day," in the first chapter of Genesis,
by the word "period." Accordingly, God made the world, not in six
days, but in six periods. But scholars laughed at his translation.
Therefore, in the fifth edition of his Bible "period" becomes "age."
This revised translation has God make the world in six ages. And
he is entirely consistent in his translation elsewhere. The fourth
commandment, in his Bible reads, "Remember the Sabbath day to
keep it holy . . . for in six ages the Ever-Living made the heavens
and the earth and the sea and all that is in them, but rested at the

---

[1] Cotton's *Editions of the Bible*, p 94, quoted from *Gentlemen's Magazine* for
August 1754.

seventh age; therefore the Ever-Living blessed the seventh day and hallowed it." [2]

Fenton's first translation was entitled "St. Paul's Epistles in Modern English," and published both in London and New York in 1884. One specimen from this is worthy of reproduction, "And, indeed, we groan in this, longing to be endowed with our little cottage from heaven." [3]

For colossal egotism, however, Ferrar Fenton, we think, has no equal. In the preface to his Bible, he says, "I contend that I am the only man who ever applied real mental and literary criticism to the Sacred Scriptures." America can never hope to equal that. Our nearest approach to it is the claim of Julia E. Smith, who assured us that nobody knew any more about Hebrew than she did, but that is several leagues this side of Fenton.

2. AMERICAN EXAMPLES OF THE FREAKISH IN CHARACTER

Begrudgingly we concede the highest honors to England in the utter assininity of translation, and in the colossal egotism of a translator, but America must be acknowledged as a very close second. We evidently do not intend that any other country shall eclipse us.

A. BENJAMIN FRANKLIN'S PROPOSAL

Benjamin Franklin was in many ways a very wise and great man. He felt in his day, as many others did, the need for a revision of the King James Version, and used his influence in that direction. He left a model translation of a few verses of the first chapter of Job, indicating thereby the character of revision which, in his judgment, was needed. His letter follows:

"To the Printer of————

Sir: It is now more than one hundred and seventy years since the translation of our common English Bible. The language in that time is much changed, and the style, being obsolete, and thence less agreeable, is perhaps one reason why the reading of that excellent book is of late so much neglected. I have therefore thought it would be well to procure a new version, in which, preserving the sense, the turn of phrase and manner of expression should be modern. I do not pretend to have the necessary abilities for such a work myself: I throw out the hint for the consideration of the learned; and only

[2] Exodus 20:8-11.   [3] 2 Cor. 5:2.

venture to send you a few verses of the first chapter of Job, which may serve as the sample of the kind of version I would recommend." [4]

Here is his model:

"Verse 6. And it being levee day in Heaven, all God's nobility came to court to present themselves before him; and Satan also appeared in the circle as one of the ministry.

7. And God said unto Satan, You have been some time absent; where were you? And Satan answered, I have been at my country seat, and in different places visiting my friends.

8. And God said, Well, what think you of Lord Job? You see he is my best friend, a perfectly honest man, full of respect for me, and avoiding everything that might offend me.

9. And Satan answered, Does your majesty imagine that his good conduct is the effect of personal attachment and affection?

10. Have you not protected him and heaped your benefits upon him, till he is grown enormously rich?

11. Try him:—only withdraw your favor, turn him out of his places, and withold his pensions, and you will soon find him in the opposition." [5]

Few things more ridiculous ever have been proposed in America, and yet some men have made translations almost as impossible as the suggestion of Franklin.

B. SAMUEL SEABURY'S PSALMS

The book of Psalms has been read more extensively, perhaps, than any other book of the Bible. Certain passages in the Psalms, known as imprecatory or damnatory, have long been a source of embarrassment. These passages express naturally the ideas and feelings of an age, the development of which had reached no higher truth than "an eye for an eye, and a tooth for a tooth," and are, therefore, entirely out of place in Christian worship. To read about the righteous rejoicing at the privilege of washing their feet in the blood of the wicked [6] may be of service in showing on how low a plane the best men once lived, but the reading of such a passage in public worship is not conducive to spirituality.

Jesus freely recognized such outgrown elements in the Old Testament, and often said of them, "Ye have heard it said . . . but I say

---

[4] Wright, *Early Bibles*, pp 227-228
[5] Wright, *Early Bibles of America*, p 228.
[6] Psalm 58:10.

unto you." These passages, however, have long made trouble for interpreters of the Scriptures who held the old-time conception of the Bible, and whose ideas of the Bible required them to defend and justify the use of such passages. Verbal inspiration, long accepted, required such methods.

The Rt. Rev. Samuel Seabury, the first bishop of the Episcopal Church in America, first studied medicine, and later entered the ministry, finding his ability to treat disease a great asset in the trying times of his day.

He published in New London, Connecticut, in 1795, "Morning and Evening Prayer with the Psalter," a new translation of the Psalms. The most interesting feature of the book, however, consists in his method of dealing with the imprecatory Psalms. They are softened down greatly, by substituting the future tense for the imperative mood. One example will illustrate: Psalm 5:10, in the King James Version, reads, "Destroy thou them, O God; let them fall by their own counsels; cast them out in the multitude of their transgressions." In Seabury's revision we read, "Thou wilt destroy them, O God; they shall perish through their own imaginations: thou wilt cast them out in the multitude of their ungodliness." This translation, however, seems to have been little used, and the few copies known to exist are only curiosities.

C. RODOLPHUS DICKINSON'S NEW TESTAMENT

The Rev. Rodolphus Dickinson was rector in the Episcopal Church of St. Paul's parish, in the district of Pendleton, South Carolina. He published a translation of the New Testament at Boston in 1833, which was quite out of the ordinary, the language being utterly unsuited for public or private devotions. A few examples will illustrate his style:

"If God so decorate the herbage of the ground, which vegetates today, and tomorrow will be cast into the furnace, will he not much more clothe you, who are of feeble faith?" [7]

"But seek first the empire of God, and the integrity he requires, and all these things shall be superadded to you." [8]

"Beware, that you do not disdain one of the least of these; for I apprise you, that their attendant messengers in the heavens, incessantly survey the face of my heavenly Father." [9]

[7] Matt. 6:30. [8] Matt. 6:33. [9] Matt. 18:10.

"Bring here the fattened calf, and immolate it." [10]

"Be not therefore inquisitive, what you shall eat, or what you shall drink; nor be in unquiet suspense." [11]

"For God has so loved the world, as to give his only produced Son, that whoever trusts in him may not perish, but obtain everlasting life." [12]

"Now to him who is able to do superabundantly above all that we can solicit or imagine, according to the power which strongly operates in us; to him be glory in the church by Jesus Christ through all the successions of endless duration." [13]

D. JONATHAN MORGAN'S NEW TESTAMENT

Jonathan Morgan was a lawyer of Portland, Maine, but he found time to translate the New Testament, which he published in Portland in 1848, using as a text the commonly received Greek. He revised the orthography of his day quite freely; synagog, thru, lik, bro't, tung, thot, and many other similar attempts at phonetic spelling abound. A few examples of his translation will be worth while:

"And he out-cast the spirits with his word." [14]

"And the angel said unto them, Fear not, for, behold, I gospelize unto you great joy, which shall be to all people." [15]

"Since many have undertaken to forthset, in order, a declaration of those things believed among us." [16]

"Why are you troubled, and why do dialogs arise in your hearts?" [17]

"And they were fast standing in the doctrine and fellowship of the apostles." [18]

"Or does not nature herself teach you that if a man has verily hair, it is a dishonor to him?" [19]

"And if any one desires to be contentious, we, nor the churches of God, have any such cohabitation." [20]

"And last of all, he was seen by me also, as an abortion." [21]

E. HEZEKIAH WOODRUFF'S NEW TESTAMENT

At Auburn, New York, in 1852, Hezekiah Woodruff published a

[10] Luke 15:23. [11] Luke 12:29. [12] John 3:16.
[13] Eph. 3:20.
[14] Matt. 8:16. [15] Luke 2:10. [16] Luke 1:1. [17] Luke 24:38. [18] Acts 2:42.
[19] 1 Cor. 11:14. [20] 1 Cor. 11:16. [21] 1 Cor. 15:8.

translation [22] which he called "An Exposition of the New Testament, or New Covenant of our Sovereign Saviour." Why he calls it an "Exposition" does not appear, and seems rather strange, since no notes are appended, nor does he promise any in the future. The Gospel of Matthew is entitled: "The Good News of Salvation according to Matthew." The Acts bears the title, "The Doings of the Commissioners;" the Epistles, "The Letter of Paul (a Commissioner) to the Romans," or Corinthians, etc. The proper name of the Saviour is "the Anointed," the word "Lord" becomes "Sovereign" and the disciples are "pupils." A few examples of translation follow:

"Happy are they; who hunger and thirst for correctness: for they shall be satisfied." [23]

"Unless your correctness shall exceed the correctness of the clergy and the pharisees, you shall by no means enter the dominion of God." [24]

"Whosoever shall divorce his wife, except on account of lustful conduct before marriage, not apparent till after marriage, exposes her to commit adultery; and whoever shall marry her who is thus divorced, is guilty of adultery.[25]

"His pupils came to him and awoke him, and said to him, Sovereign, save us, or we die." [26]

"He, who receives a preacher because he is a preacher, shall receive a preacher's reward." [27]

---

[22] Considerable confusion exists concerning Woodruff's New Testament. O'Callaghan, in his *List of Editions,* described this translation correctly (See p 326). In speaking of Matthew, he uses these words, "the only one contained in the volume." By this he meant that Mark, Luke and John were omitted, Matthew being the only Gospel included. That he had before him the complete work of Woodruff is made clear, because he gives the titles of other parts. Wright evidently took these words to mean that Woodruff's publication of 1852 contained the Gospel of Matthew only, probably not noticing the titles to the other books given by O'Callaghan. Therefore, in his *Early Bibles of America,* See ed. 1894, p. 232, he speaks of Woodruff's edition as containing Matthew only. John V. Madison, in his *English Versions of the New Testament,* See p. 278, repeats this blunder. In *The Bible from the Beginning,* by Simms, it is said (p 289) that Woodruff published the Gospel of Matthew in 1852, and the New Testament, except Mark, Luke and John, in 1853. The facts are that Woodruff published only one book, and that was in 1852, containing the whole New Testament, except three of the Gospels. The author of *The Bible from the Beginning* was misled by Wright and Madison, and the further fact that the copy of Woodruff's book in the Library of Congress bears a copyright stamp dated January 20, 1853, which he now learns is simply the date when the copy, published in 1852, was received in Washington, and not the date of a book published in 1853.

[23] Matt. 5:6. [24] Matt. 5:20. [25] Matt. 5:32. [26] Matt. 8:25. [27] Matt. 10:41.

"Inimical and adulatory people, wish for a token; but there shall be no token exhibited to them except the token of the prophet Jonah." [28]

"When the day of the feast of pentecost (five ribs) has arrived, they assembled by appointment." [29]

"Many wonderful signs were exhibited by the Commissioners." [30]

"And Philip ran thither; and heard the bachelor reading the prophecy of Isaiah." [31]

3. THE ABSURD AND IMPOSSIBLE IN PRETENSIONS

Translations or revisions of the Bible accompanied with unusual claims may be eccentric in character also, and generally have some such peculiarities; but certain Bibles or parts have appeared with claims so extraordinary as to completely overshadow other things out of the beaten track.

A. JOSEPH SMITH'S BIBLE

We come now to consider the most astonishing claims ever made in connection with the Bible, and the most peculiar alterations of any Bible in English ever published—that of Joseph Smith, the founder of the Mormon Church. Smith was killed by a mob in 1844, following which the Mormons broke up into several factions. Brigham Young led one faction, by far the largest, into Utah, and this group have always used the King James Version and now, more or less, some revision of it.

The factions repudiating Young's leadership united to form the Reorganized Church of Latter Day Saints, with headquarters at Lamoni, Iowa. Joseph Smith, the son of the founder of the original church became the first president of the Reorganized Church and his mother, the widow of the original founder, also went with the new church. The younger Joseph Smith indignantly denied that his father had ever taught polygamy, and whether this be true or not, it is true that the Reorganized Church repudiated polygamy from its beginning.

The widow of the founder of the movement claimed to have in her possession a manuscript of the Bible, which the original Joseph Smith had prepared, as he claimed, under a direct revelation from God, it being a revision of the King James Version. This Bible was first published at Lamoni, Iowa, in 1867, and is the favorite Bible of

[28] Matt. 12:39. [29] Doings of the Commissioners (Acts) 2:1. [30] Doings of the Commissioners (Acts) 2:43. [31] Doings of the Commissioners (Acts) 8:30.

the Reorganized Church, though the King James Version is permitted, and presumably revisions of it also.

The Book of Mormon, which the Mormons of Utah and the Reorganized Church both accept as divinely inspired, says, "For behold, they have taken away from the Gospel of the Lamb, many parts which are plain and most precious; and also many covenants of the Lord have they taken away; and all this have they done, that they might pervert the right ways of the Lord." [32] Joseph Smith's revelations were supposed to restore the parts of the Bible that had been taken away or altered.

The differences of this Bible from that of the King James Version consist in numerous additions, deliberate alterations, words transposed and often the addition of words that make clearer the meaning of the text.[33]

Those believing the Bible to be, in every part, the very Word of God, and, therefore, infallible, have had a rather difficult time of it, being frequently forced to justify God in doing many things morally objectionable. The enemies of religion have often pressed their advantage at this point, parading such things as acts of God, on the authority of the Bible. Men with modern views of the Bible have no such difficulty, since such Scriptures are assigned their proper place as representing opinions expressed by primitive men who were simply mistaken. Joseph Smith, however, relieved the situation, in a measure, by deliberate alterations of the text of Scripture. According to his Bible, God never repents, such evidently being considered beneath the dignity of a being of his character. Consequently where the King James Version says, "It repented the Lord that he had made man on earth," [34] Smith's Bible reads, "It repented Noah and his heart was pained that God had made man on earth." "It repenteth me that I have set up Saul to be king," [35] is altered to say, "I have set up Saul to become king, and he repenteth not." Other texts are dealt with in like fashion.

According to Smith's Bible, God hardens nobody's heart, such being unthinkable. "I will harden his heart," [36] is made to read, "Pharaoh will harden his heart." In like manner, "The Lord hardened Pharaoh's heart," [37] becomes, "Pharaoh hardened his heart." Speaking of Saul, the king, it is said, "An evil spirit from the Lord

---

[32] 1 Book of Nephi, 3:40.

[33] For a comparison of numerous texts, see *The Bible From the Beginning*, Simms, pp. 157-47. [34] Gen. 6:6, (Smith's Bible Gen. 8:13). [35] I Sam 15:11. [36] Ex. 4:21. [37] Ex. 9:12.

ALEXANDER CAMPBELL

troubled him," [38] but Smith puts it, "An evil spirit which was not from the Lord troubled him." "The Lord hath put a lying spirit in the mouth of these thy prophets," [39] in Smith's Bible, reads, "The Lord hath found a lying spirit in the mouth of these thy prophets." Similarly, "If the prophet be deceived . . . I the Lord have deceived that prophet," [40] is changed to read, "If the prophet be deceived . . . I the Lord have not deceived that prophet." In the Lord's Prayer of Smith's Bible, we read, "And suffer us not to be led into temptation, but deliver us from evil," [41] and it cannot be inferred, as might be from the usual text, that God ever leads men into temptation.

Could this Bible have been in exclusive use in an early day there would have been no witch hunting, since the famous passages relied on for authority to put them to death, in Smith's Bible, reads, "Thou shalt not suffer a murderer to live."[42]

Great controversies over the Lord's Supper would have been avoided had we never had any but Smith's Bible. "This is my body," "this is my blood," is not found in it; instead we read, "Behold, this is for you to do in remembrance of my body—this is in remembrance of my blood." [43]

Joseph Smith's Bible relieves the author of Second Peter from a possible charge of ignorance. According to the King James Version, Peter says, "The heavens shall pass away with a great noise, and the elements shall melt with fervent heat," [44] because of which it has been suggested that the author of this Epistle shared the ancient opinion that the firmament or sky was made of metal, or ice, capable of being melted. But according to Smith, "the mountains shall melt and pass away, with a great noise, and the elements shall be filled with fervent heat."

The most numerous and extensive changes in the text, perhaps, are found in a few of the first chapters of Genesis, these being literally filled with New Testament ideas—Jesus Christ, the Only Begotten, the Lamb of God slain from the foundation of the world, the resurrection of Christ and all men, and the necessity of being born again. Even the trinitarian formula for baptism was given Enoch, who preached and practiced baptism freely in his day. God himself preached baptism to Adam, who was unmistakably baptized by immersion, for he was "carried down into the water, and was laid under the water, and was brought forth out of the water; and thus he was

[38] 1 Sam. 16:14. [39] 2 Chron. 18:22. [40] Eze. 14:9. [41] Matt. 6:13, (Smith's Bible Matt. 6:14.)
[42] Ex. 22:18. [43] Mark 14:22, 24, (Smith's Bible, Mark 14:21, 23). [44] 2 Pe. 3:10.

baptized." [45] It is also made clear that when Jesus Christ preached to the spirits in prison, he offered them salvation, "for which cause also, he went and preached to the spirits in prison."

Nobody of course believes that Joseph Smith had any revelation on the subject, except members of the Reorganized Church. It is very evident that he deliberately made any text read as he pleased. He relieves God of the responsibility of much that is objectionable, but why did he not make a clean sweep? He leaves God responsible for a war of extermination on the Amalekites [46] which included women, children and the cattle. This was a revengeful reprisal on these people, because when invaded 400 years before, they had defended themselves, as any other people would have done under like circumstances. Not one of those punished could have had any responsibility for what their ancestors did, even if it had been wrong. Yet God is said to have ordered the war.

David had a census taken, and one Scripture tells us that God himself moved David to do it, while another attributes it to Satan.[47] For this act God deliberately destroys 70,000 people, not one of whom could have had any responsibility for the act, but Smith's Bible leaves God responsible for this butchery. Numerous other acts, attributed to God, but utterly repugnant to Christian principles, are left unrevised.

Joseph Smith, being the founder of the original Mormon Church, taught many doctrines entirely new and different. He did not hesitate to alter the Bible and make it read to suit his own pleasure. Naturally we wonder why he did not slip in a few passages at least that would favor his peculiar doctrines. There seems to be no such. He did make immersion certain, by an addition to Genesis,[48] and he made the text clearly imply that Jesus gave a second chance of salvation to the imprisoned spirits,[49] but these are not doctrines peculiar to his church.

Smith's Bible, in the books it contains, is identical with the usual Protestant Bible, except that the Song of Solomon is omitted. The apocrypha was never included.

B. LEONARD THORN'S NEW TESTAMENT

A New Testament was published in New York in 1861, copyrighted by Leonard Thorn, professing to be a correction and revision made

---

[45] Smith's Bible, Gen. 6:67.   [46] 1 Sam. 15:1-4.   [47] Sam. 24:1; 1 Chron. 21:1.
[48] Gen. 6:67 (Smith's Bible).   [49] 1 Pe. 3:19.

by the Spirits, as revealed through mediums, Jesus Christ being the Great Medium through whom God has spoken to the world. According to the claims of this volume Jesus Christ and His apostles were freely at the beck and call of certain mediums. As stated in the "Introductory Remarks," the Apostle Paul corrected his Epistles and Acts; but it was Jesus Christ himself who corrected the Four Gospels and Revelation. James, Peter, John and Jude all came freely when called, and corrected their writings, except that Jesus Christ corrected Revelation, He being better fitted to do it. John was permitted to write the book originally, but could not be trusted to correct it. For some reason Luke was not permitted to correct Acts. Several books are shortened, some very considerably. Romans contains only seven chapters, Revelation only three, Hebrews being omitted without explanation. Several pages of entirely new matter were added by Jesus Christ. This, of course, is intended for spiritualists.

We have said that translations of the Bible in English have been honestly made, and we believe they have. Joseph Smith's Bible, and Leonard Thorn's New Testament, however, do not come under the head of translations, or even revisions in the ordinary sense. They are both deliberate, unauthorized and unwarranted changes of the text, made at the whim of their authors, and under claims that are preposterous and impossible.

4. THE FANCIFUL AND VISIONARY IN CLAIMS

A. SOME ANCIENT CASTLE-BUILDING

In every age pious souls have vied with one another in the discovery and invention of fanciful meanings concerning the Bible. The Jews count only twenty-four books in the Old Testament, and this is easy when several are put together and counted as one. But for long it was insisted among the early Christians that there were only twenty-two books in the Old Testament, so planned by the Lord to correspond with the 22 letters of the Hebrew alphabet. To get twenty-two from the Jewish enumeration, it was only necessary to add Ruth to Judges, and Lamentations to Jeremiah. In the Hebrew alphabet, however, there are five letters that have a different form when they occur at the end of a word, and by counting these the Hebrew alphabet may be said to contain twenty-seven letters. In keeping with this fact, some people insisted that there were twenty-seven books in the Old Testament, an arrangement easily made.

Origen, an early Christian father, would seem to be the first to call attention to the fact that by counting only 22 books in the Old Testament, the number of books was made to correspond with the 22 letters of the Hebrew alphabet. Many of the leading fathers of the early church accepted the idea. The number of books could easily be made anything one pleased, even when the apocrypha was included, by the simple expedient of adding any number of books to others and counting them one.

Jerome, one of the greatest of the early fathers, gives two enumerations of the books of the Old Testament, one of 22 and one of 27, and probably wavered between them. Still others insisted on 33 books in the Old Testament, which could easily be arranged. With 33 books in the Old Testament and 27 in the New the total became 60, which corresponded with the "three-score" queens mentioned in the Song of Solomon.[50] This book was at that time a happy hunting ground for fanciful meanings, since it was considered an allegory, and the idea of sixty books in the Bible powerfully appealed to certain people.

For centuries the Song of Solomon was interpreted as an allegory, representing the love of Christ for the Church, and every fanciful interpretation possible to the ingenuity of man was put forth as taught by this book. Theodore of Mopsuesta stood alone in the early history of the church, in his insistence that the poem treated of human love only; and was condemned by the Council of Constantinople in 533 A. D. for his interpretation. Sebastian Castellio was banished from Geneva in 1544, and one count against him was his refusal to give this book an allegorical interpretation. But nobody today regards the poem as an allegory. The makers of the King James Version, however, so regarded it, and the headings of the chapters of the Song of Songs in this Bible so interpret it.

B. F. W. GRANT'S NUMERICAL BIBLE

The element of human nature, however, which fabricated the fanciful speculations and theories of ancient times, would seem to be as powerful today as ever. The Rev. F. W. Grant, a very earnest minister among the Plymouth Brethren, made one of these fanciful discoveries, which he regarded as profoundly important, it being that a peculiar numerical structure pervades the Scriptures everywhere.

[50] Song of Songs 6:8.

This, in his mind, was sufficient to establish the infallibility of the old Book, and answer the arguments of all sceptics and unbelievers. A thing so valuable was, of course, too good to be kept to himself, so he immediately published it to the world, about 1876.

Some fifteen years later, in 1891, he began the publication of a revision of the King James Version, the Pentateuch appearing first. The Old Testament of this version includes Genesis to 2 Samuel inclusive, and the Psalms, while the New Testament is complete; the whole in six volumes, the last of which appeared in 1903. The death of the author prevented its completion.

The style of the King James Version is imitated, and voluminous notes are appended. The title indicates that the various books have been "arranged, divided, and briefly characterized according to their numerical character." He has worked out definite meanings for numerous numbers found in the Scriptures, and by such means interprets the Bible, his scheme being a matter of interpretation.

"Numerical structure" is explained in the volume containing the Pentateuch. "It is this: That if, for example, in the Pentateuch we find plainly a series of five books,—that is, five divisions of Moses' whole work, this five-fold division has a meaning intimately connected with the subjects of the books themselves. The numerals of Scripture all students of it believe to have (in many cases at least) definite meanings,—as, for instance, in the number 7 we have 'completeness.' The view that I am advocating simply applies this symbolism to such a series as we have here, and affirms that Genesis, which stands first among these, has for its special line of truth what would be suggested by the number 1: Exodus, similarly, a line of truth connected with number 2; Leviticus, with number 3; Numbers, with 4; Deuteronomy, with 5. To take these, perhaps the simplest, the number 4 stands as the number of the world, and the symbol for weakness (which may come out in failure), trial, experience; and so the book of Numbers will be found to be characterized by these thoughts." [51]

In defense of his scheme, he says, "Nor can you afford to despise it, when you remember how all the natural sciences in the present day are ranging themselves under arithmetical law, when, as Herschel says, every law of nature tends to express itself in terms of arithmetic; while astronomy preaches it to you from the starry spheres, the plants in the arrangement of their leaves and the division of their flowers . . . the crystal talks mathematics from the windowpane.

[51] *Numerical Bible,* Vol. I, p. 8.

Why should not a law of numbers pervade Scripture also, and link God's work and His Word together,—or show His Word also to be His work?" [52] We know of no Bible that abounds in more pious but harmless nonsense.

C. W. B. GODBEY'S NEW TESTAMENT

The Rev. W. B. Godbey, was a minister in the Southern Methodist Church, and a member of the Kentucky Conference at his death. having been for many years a very prominent "holiness" preacher. He was always known as a most eccentric character. His translation of the New Testament, dedicated to the holiness people of all lands, was published at the "Office of God's Revivalist" of Cincinnati, Ohio, in 1902. The Gospels are printed in a harmonistic order, modeled after the arrangement of E. Robinson.

The translation was made from Codex Sinaiticus. "In this translation I have used the text of the sainted Tischendorf, which God in His mercy hid away in a Christian convent on Mt. Sinai . . . God in His great mercy kept a complete copy of the New Testament, safely hidden through the long, dark, and dreary centuries, from the apostolic age down to A. D. 1859, when He revealed it to His faithful servant, the learned Tischendorf." [53]

Because the Sinaitic MS is the only complete New Testament in uncials (all capitals) known in the world, the Rev. Mr. Godbey regarded it as a copy of the original, without interpolations or other mistakes of copyists, but the one and only copy prepared by the Lord's inspiration, hidden and providentially preserved to us. In speaking of the matter, he says, "I have nothing before me but the inspired original, which is precisely what the Lord gave us." [54] This text he regarded as absolutely infallible.

This MS., however, was made long after the apostolic age, and had been revised several times by different hands before it was "hidden" by the Lord, but whether Mr. Godbey ever learned these facts does not appear. In any event, they did not disturb his sublime faith in the infallibility of the text. Then again, this MS. contains two apocryphal books, the Epistle of Barnabas and the Shepherd of Hermas, which were evidently considered a part of the New Testa-

---

[52] *Numerical Bible*, Vol. I, pp. 10-11.
[53] Godbey, *New Testament*, p. 372.
[54] Godbey, *New Testament*, p. 6.

ment by whoever made the MS. Why Mr. Godbey did not insist on
including these books in his New Testament, since they were part of
the infallible MS., especially prepared and preserved by the Lord, we
do not know. Perhaps entire consistency is too much to expect of any
man. This MS. also has a peculiar arrangement of the books of the
New Testament, and it would seem that he should have insisted on
the same order, but he did not.

D. IVAN PANIN'S NUMERIC NEW TESTAMENT

Ivan Panin was born in Russia and graduated at Harvard University. He published a new translation at New Haven, Connecticut, in
1914, under the title, "The New Testament from the Greek Text as
Established by Bible Numerics." In the preface, he promises a second
volume which will explain "Bible Numerics" to the public but, so
far as we can learn, this was never published. His theories, however,
have been set forth rather extensively in certain monographs that
have appeared, so that we are by no means left in the dark concerning
them. Panin, in his opinion, had discovered one of God's pro-
foundest secrets, which is, that the whole Bible is constructed on a
numeric plan. In fact, the whole universe is so constructed; and God
has only done in the Bible, in this regard, what He did everywhere
else in creation.

Panin's discovery has no relation and bears no resemblance to the
numeric principles discovered by Rev. F. W. Grant, and worked out
in his Numerical Bible. Grant's system is one of interpretation,
while Panin's system affects interpretation only by its infallible determination of the original text. It would seem that they might be
combined to a great advantage. One would provide an infallible
text, and the other a very superior if not an entirely infallible interpretation, both expressly provided for by the Lord himself; but unfortunately neither seemed to give credit to the other's pet scheme.

An example of how Panin's system works may be seen in a quotation:

"The Bible of the Roman Communion omits Jesus in Matthew
1:18: apparently a trifling difference between *the birth of Jesus
Christ* and *the birth of Christ*. But the Scripture cannot be broken.
The words in I:18-25 are 161, or 23 sevens; their vocabulary is 77 or
eleven sevens; their forms 105 or fifteen sevens; the numeric value of

the entire passage is a multiple of seven. But omit this name and the most elaborate numeric scheme thereof is destroyed." [55] Therefore, the Catholic text is wrong.

This system works equally well in the Old Testament, as the following will indicate:

"Mr. Panin calls every numeric phenomenon a 'feature.' Thus, in digging below the surface of Psalm 110, he discovers the first feature to be: 'The number of words (without the title) is 63, or 9 sevens.' Then he uncovers thirteen more 'features' of sevens dug out of the Psalm. He ends what he has to say upon this Psalm thus:

"These 14 features of sevens in nowise exhaust the numeric phenomena of this Psalm. But the chance for even these 14 features of sevens being accidental, undesigned, is only one in seven multipled by itself 14 times: one in 678,223,072,849, less than one in some two-thirds of a million millions. With a chance so small in its favor to merely happen, its being accidental is usually declared in such cases to be practically impossible. These numeric phenomena are therefore—designed." [56]

By such methods Panin established, in his own mind, the original Greek text of the New Testament, and its consequent infallibility, because only a divinely inspired text could possibly contain such numerous "features" as he finds. Since his system works equally well with the Old or New Testament, the whole textual criticism of Biblical scholarship is unceremoniously dumped into the ash can.

Panin also determines the number of the books of the Bible to be exactly 66. He discovers that "Moses . . . foreknew the number of books in the Bible, their order numbers, the number of times his name was to occur in each book." [57] And he thinks it very highly probable, though he modestly declines to say for certain, that "the number of the books in the Bible may have thus been planned with special reference to the diurnal revolution of the earth and its neighbor Mars." [58] Let us hope so.

Bible numerics determines the divine order of the Bible also, indicating that the Jews have arranged the Old Testament correctly, with Chronicles at the end. The New Testament by this method is rearranged, with the Catholic Epistles immediately following the

[55] King and Others—*Panin's Scientific Demonstration of the Inspiration of the Scriptures*, p. 77.

[56] King and Others, *Panin's Scientific Demonstration*, pp. 11-12.

[57] King and Others, *Panin's Scientific Demonstration*, p. 59.

[58] King and Others, *Panin's Scientific Demonstration*, p. 91.

Acts. The authorship of many books is also determined. Biblical chronology is tested and rendered infallible, but all scientists have not yet accepted his conclusions on this point.

Biblical numerics is equally valuable in correcting many conclusions of the scientists, especially in the matter of the diameters and revolutions of the earth and the planets. Panin is generous about it, too, offering data of his system, in manuscript form, to astronomers and other scientists who are really anxious to get things straight. He does not say who shall pay the postage.

Such are some of the silk purses made from sow's ears. Further comment would seem to be superfluous.

CHAPTER XI

SECTARIAN TRANSLATIONS

Many translations and revisions of the Bible, or its parts, have been made to favor certain doctrines by means of notes. This was true of most of the early versions in English previous to the King James Version; but with such we are not here concerned. When we speak of sectarian translations we have in mind those in which the original text is deliberately rendered to favor certain doctrines. Many of these have been accompanied with sectarian notes. It is not meant to imply that these translations are in any sense dishonest; they are due to differences of opinion.

Charges of tampering with the original text in the interest of party or doctrines, were made very early by both Jews and Christians. The Jews charged the Christians with such, in connection with the Septuagint or Greek Old Testament, which was in general use in the early Christian church; Christians paid them back in their own coin by charging them with dishonesty in handling the Hebrew Old Testament. Through the succeeding centuries many charges of duplicity in translation were made; Protestants and Catholics made such charges against each other; but proof of such in any of these cases is lacking. Men have differed, of course, as to how certain words should be translated, this being but perfectly natural and normal. Men have always interpreted the Bible differently, and always will. But in the exigencies of bygone days, times of more or less bitter theological controversy, there have always been those ever ready to charge dishonesty for difference of opinion.

1. EARLY METHOD OF BIBLICAL TRANSLATION

The most important sectarian translations ever made are what are known as "immersion" versions. To understand the situation in regard to these particular versions, it is necessary to go back to the beginning of translations. The New Testament was translated into Latin, probably, in the latter part of the second century. In this work the Greek word *baptidzo,* and its cognates, were not translated at all, but transliterated, that is, adopted as Latin words. We need not inquire why this was done, it is enough to know that it was done. Jerome later revised the Old Latin, producing the Latin Vulgate, which became the most influential of all the early versions. He did the same thing.

When Wyclif, the first to put the whole Bible into English, and later Tyndale, made their translations, the first from the Latin, the second from the Greek, they both followed the same method, simply making English words of *baptidzo,* and its cognates, rather than translating them. Following Tyndale all the standard versions in English have adhered to the same practice. In this way the English language comes to have the words "baptize" and "baptism."

This practice proved a great practical benefit, at least, for while Christian people have long differed as to the proper mode of baptism, the same version could be used by both sprinklers and immersionists, leaving each to interpret the words to suit themselves.

2. *BAPTIDZO* TRANSLATED AS INTERPRETED

A. NATHANIEL SCARLETT'S NEW TESTAMENT

The first "immersion" version ever made, so far as we have been able to learn, was put out in England by Nathaniel Scarlett, a bookseller in the Strand. He published in London in 1798, a new version which was based on a manuscript translation by James Creighton, an Anglican minister. William Vilder (Universalist), John Cue (a Sandemanian) and Creighton (an Anglican) met once a week at the home of Scarlett and revised this work. Scarlett was successively a Methodist, a Universalist and a Baptist, and his New Testament reflects his Baptist opinions in the text, and is rendered distinctly Universalistic by its notes.[1] This translation is peculiar in its arrangement. The dialogue of the New Testament is exaggerated by placing before every utterance, in italics, the name of the speaker, as is done in Shakespeare's plays. Historical matter is also so indicated.

B. J. M. RAY'S BIBLE

The next "immersion" version, if it may be socalled, was made by J. M. Ray,[2] a licentiate in the Scotch Presbyterian Church. He published a new version of the whole Bible, probably at London, though some think it was at Glasgow, in 1799, but it is certain that he published an edition at Glasgow in 1815. In the New Testament of the edition of 1815, we read, "In those days John the Baptist (dipper) came, preaching in the wilderness . . . and were baptised (dipped)

---

[1] See 1 Tim. 2:3-4 and Appendix p. II.
[2] He left his name in several forms, David McRea, McRay and J. M. Ray.

by him." [3] Having thus delivered himself at the first appearance of these words in the New Testament, he follows the usual custom afterward.

C. JOHN BOWES' NEW TESTAMENT

The Rev. John Bowes was a Methodist minister in England, and did much itinerant preaching. He represented England in the Brussels Conference in 1848, being a man of influence. He published an "immersion" version of the New Testament at Dundee in 1870. None of the above were ever used in America.

D. J. B. ROTHERHAM'S EMPHASIZED NEW TESTAMENT

Only one other such version has been put out in England, but it has been used frequently in the United States in the Disciples Church Rev. Joseph Bryant Rotherham, first a Wesleyan minister, then a Baptist, and finally a minister of the Disciples Church, published in 1872, what he called an "emphasized" New Testament, it being an "immersion" version. In 1901-03 he published in London the whole Bible "emphasized." While the whole Bible has been used in America, the New Testament has had a much wider use, it being made first from Tregelles' text, but conformed to the text of Westcott and Hort in 1897. The Old Testament has been conformed to the text of Christian Ginsburg.

E. ALEXANDER CAMPBELL'S NEW TESTAMENT

Whatever America attempts is usually done on a rather generous scale, and sectarian versions have, therefore, flourished among us. The first issued in the United States was put out by Rev. Alexander Campbell at Buffaloe, Virginia, in 1826, he publishing his final revision in 1832.

Rev. Alexander Campbell was born in Ireland, educated in the University of Glasgow, and came to America a Presbyterian minister, soon becoming widely popular. He was a Baptist for a short time, and then became the founder of the Disciples Church, one of the very few native American churches.[4] Most of our denominations

---

[3] Matt. 3:1-6.

[4] Frank S. Mead, in *Like A Mighty Army*, published in the *Christian Herald* for December 1935, says that the Disciples Church is the only native American

have been imported. Campbell, in his early ministry, caught a glorious vision of the possible union of all Christians on a non-sectarian basis, with no creed but the Bible; but in the exigencies of the times, he became finally one of the most powerful sectarian controversialists of his day, founding a church fully as sectarian as any then in existence.

He did not make a new translation of the New Testament, but used the Four Gospels by Dr. George Campbell, published originally in Edinburgh in 1778; the Epistles of Dr. James MacKnight, first published in London in 1795; and the Acts and Revelation as they appear in the New Testament of Dr. Philip Doddridge, published in London in 1765. These had previously been published together making a complete New Testament, in London in 1818. The whole was slightly revised, the emendations being little more than enough to make it an "immersion" version.

Campbell was a man of scholarly attainments, and it was the unsatisfactory character of the King James Version chiefly that inspired his effort to provide a better text, and while at it he translated *baptidzo* as he interpreted it. This was unquestionably the best New Testament in use at that time, and while it circulated for years among the Disciples, its use was naturally confined to immersionists.

F. DAVID BERNARD'S BIBLE

In 1842 the Lippincotts of Philadelphia published a Bible for David Bernard, the preface to the New Testament indicating that the Rev. A. C. Kendrick, D. D., a noted Baptist scholar, was responsible for that part of the work. Who prepared the text of the Old Testament we have been unable to learn, except that Dr. George Ripley Bliss was among the number. The New Testament is an "immersion" version.

G. N. N. WHITING'S NEW TESTAMENT

Joshua V. Himes of Boston printed a New Testament in 1849, the preface being signed by N. N. Whiting of Williamsburg, Long Island, who doubtless was responsible for the translation, made from Tittman's text, as published by E. Robinson in 1842.

hurch. But this is hardly correct. The Christian Church, recently united with he Congregational Church, was a native church, and the Cumberland Presbyerian Church was another. There are others.

It has been called a "Millerite" New Testament, for no reason we have been able to find in the text. Probably Whiting was a "Millerite." This is an "immersion" version.

H. ADONIRAM JUDSON'S NEW TESTAMENT IN BURMESE

Two "immersion" versions in foreign languages have been the occasion of considerable trouble in America, one of these being made by Adoniram Judson in Burmese, and the other, by Rev. Mr. Pearse in Bengali.[5]

In all the history of sectarian and religious controversy, we know of nothing more pathetic than the story of Adoniram Judson. He had been reared in the Congregational Church in the United States, and was sent to India as a missionary by the Congregational Board of Missions. All his sympathies, affections and life-long associations were bound up with this church, in which he hoped to spend his life.

On his long voyage to India, lasting many months, he restudied the question of baptism, and reached the conclusion that immersion was the proper mode, concluding also that children should not be christened. In other words, he became a full-fledged Baptist in his opinions on these points.

Neither the Baptists nor the Congregationalists regarded baptism by any mode as essential to salvation or Christian character; but this change of doctrinal position unfitted him utterly, so it was considered, for service as a Congregational missionary. There being no board of missions among the Baptists in America to assume his support, he and his wife were simply left stranded in far away India. The heartache and suffering involved in the whole matter were intense. The thing that makes it so exceedingly pathetic is that it was all so utterly useless and foolish.

Judson had lost none of his Christian faith, none of his zeal or interest in missions. God could still use him, and did use him, and perhaps the world has never known a more devoted and valuable missionary in all its history; but the Congregational Church could not use him! What a commentary on the values set by sectarianism! Fortunately, one good thing resulted; the Baptists in America were, in time, thereby impelled to take over his support and thus they began to do foreign missionary work.

---

[5] The story of the refusal of the American Bible Society to assist in printing the Bengali translation, and its consequences, have been told in a previous chapter. See pp. 167-68.

Judson translated the New Testament into Burmese, and *baptidzo* was translated by a Burmese word, meaning "immerse." Being an American he naturally looked to the American Bible Society to aid in the printing of his translation. It was published in 1835, and the American Bible Society furnished some money to assist in the work.

Judson spent twenty-four years in making his translation of the whole Bible, and the last sheets went to press October 24, 1840. It ranks as one of the best missionary translations ever made, and the best in India, notwithstanding its sectarian character.

I. CONE AND WYKOFF'S NEW TESTAMENT

When the American Bible Society declined to use its money gathered from all denominations to print sectarian translations, the Rev. Spencer H. Cone, D. D., the corresponding secretary of the Society at that time, as has been said, resigned his position in 1836, and became the president of the American and Foreign Bible Society.

Now that the question had been raised and the controversy had grown bitter, a certain element of the members of the American and Foreign Bible Society demanded an "immersion" version in English. On this question, however, the Baptists were divided, many preferring that the English Testament be left as it was, and had always been. While Adoniram Judson had made an "immersion" version in Burmese, he was opposed to making one in English.[6] In 1849 a controversy arose in the American and Foreign Bible Society over the matter, the issue was forced, and the Society definitely refused to put out such a version.

Dr. Cone now led in the organization, in 1850, of the American Bible Union, becoming its president, this organization being formed by the Baptists who insisted on an "immersion" version in English. While men were promptly set to work preparing such a version, it would necessarily require several years to do what was contemplated. Dr. Cone was evidently impatient in the matter, and he and W. H. Wykoff published an "immersion" version of the New Testament in New York in 1851, under the title, "The Commonly Received Version . . . with several hundred emendations." This, of course, was intended to serve until a more satisfactory revision could be provided.

[6] *The Life of Adoniram Judson,* by his son Edward Judson, pp. 408-409.

J. AMERICAN BIBLE UNION NEW TESTAMENT

It was well known among scholars everywhere that the King James Version was badly in need of revision, and the Bible Union proposed to revise both Testaments. They engaged the services of such men as the Rev. Drs. H. B. Hackett, A. C. Kendrick and J. C. Conant, all Baptist scholars of distinction.

The tentative revisions prepared by the Bible Union were published from time to time, the New Testament being finished and published in three volumes, as a "first revision", in New York in 1862, 1863 and 1864, and in one volume in 1864 and 1865. A further revision of the work appeared in New York in 1865, as "second revision," which became the famous and widely used Bible Union New Testament. Both revisions, as well as the parts published previously, were the work of Drs. Conant, Hackett and Kendrick.

The Greek text from which this was made was revised considerably, in keeping with the best scholarship of the day, and there can be no question that this was the best translation of the New Testament in English in its day, but its use was naturally restricted to immersionists.

In 1891 this New Testament was revised again by a committee consisting of Drs. A. A. Hovey, John A. Broadus, and H. B. Weston, all noted Baptist scholars. This revision, however, appeared in two editions, one with "immerse" in the text, and the other with the Anglicized word "baptize." Only a part of the Baptists had ever been in sympathy with the idea of an "immersion" version in English, and so two editions were now issued that both parties might be pleased.

K. H. T. ANDERSON'S NEW TESTAMENT

The Rev. H. T. Anderson, a minister of the Disciples Church, published at Cincinnati, Ohio, an "immersion" version of the New Testament in 1864, an edition appearing in England in 1867. It was made from an uncertain text.

L. JULIA E. SMITH'S BIBLE

Julia E. Smith published a new translation of the whole Bible at Hartford, Connecticut, in 1876, the New Testament being an "immersion" version, made from the commonly received Greek text.

M. SAMUEL WILLIAMS' NEW TESTAMENT

When the Anglo-American revision of the New Testament appeared in 1881, the Rev. Samuel Williams, at one time pastor of the First Baptist Church of Pittsburg, Pennsylvania, published it in New York in the same year, in an amended form. He supplied, in the text, the renderings preferred by the American Committee, found in the appendix, and added such emendations as were required to make it an "immersion" version.

N. J. W. HANSON'S NEW TESTAMENT

Rev. John Wesley Hanson, D. D. was a Universalist minister, being the pastor of the New Covenant Church of Chicago in 1869-1884. He published at Boston a revision of the New Testament in two volumes, the first of which contained the Four Gospels, appearing in 1883, and the second containing the remainder of the New Testament in 1885. The Four Gospels are arranged in a harmonistic order. The second volume contains a chronological arrangement, modeled after that of Conybeare and Howson, in their *Life and Epistles of St. Paul*. The solemn style is abandoned, except in prayer. He uses the Greek text of Westcott and Hort slightly modified. This is an "immersion" version, and the notes make it distinctly Universalistic.

O. A. J. WORRELL'S NEW TESTAMENT

A. J. Worrell, A.M. published a quite vigorous translation of the New Testament in 1904 in Philadelphia, from the text of Westcott and Hort. His theological opinions evidently made it impossible to accept this Greek text unrevised. Believing in the possibility of present day miracles, he restores Mark 16:9-20, this probably being supposed to support the idea. The Greek word *ecclesia* is never translated church, but always "assembly." This is also an "immersion" version, but the chief inspiration for the work was dissatisfaction with the antiquated King James Version.

P. IMPROVED EDITION OF THE BIBLE

The American Bible Union revised tentatively and published several books of the Old Testament, and when the work of the Union was turned over to the Baptist Publication Society in 1883, it finished this work, and revised again the New Testament of the Union, publishing in Philadelphia an "Improved Edition" of the Bible in 1913. The Old Testament was based, in part, on the work of the Bible Union revisions, being prepared by Drs. Bernard C. Taylor, J. R. Sampey, Ira M. Price and W. R. Harper, each revising

certain parts. Dr. J. M. Powis Smith read and corrected the proofs
for Dr. Harper's part. The New Testament was now revised for
the fourth time by Dr. J. W. Willmarth. All these men were scholars
of the highest rank. This New Testament restores, in the text,
the Anglicized form, baptize, etc., followed by "immerse," etc. as a
comment in parenthesis. The Old Testament is made from the
Massoretic text, and the New from the commonly received Greek
text, as revised by the translators.

Q. GEORGE N. LEFEVRE'S NEW TESTAMENT

The last "immersion" version put out in America was printed
by George N. LeFevre at Strasburg, Pennsylvania, in 1928, the
translation being made chiefly from the Sinaitic and Vatican MSS.
While it was published anonymously, the printer was also the
translator. He is known as a very eccentric character and belongs
to no church. "In this translation 'Jehovah' is used where God
the Father is exclusively referred to." He uses "Holy Ghost" and
"a holy spirit," and seeks to discriminate between the two uses.
Rather frequent notes are appended, and they are filled with pious
eccentricities. He defends the verbal inspiration and infallibility of
the Bible; Jesus was crucified on Wednesday and "he remained in
the earth '3 days and 3 nights'—Thursday, Friday and Saturday",
"exactly as Jesus said," so he claims, but he overlooks the fact that
this keeps Jesus in the tomb four nights. The wine that Jesus
made was not wine at all, but grape juice; and Mark wrote the last
twelve verses of his Gospel as found in the King James Version,
regardless of the fact that the oldest Greek MSS. do not contain
these words.

This completes the list of all the "immersion" versions ever made,
so far as we have been able to learn. The day of bitter theological
controversy is probably over, most modern men being interested
in things of more importance. The trend of the day may be seen,
we think, in the history of the famous Bible Union New Testament.
It was published in the days of bitterest controversy in a "first
revision" and a "second revision," in one edition with "immerse" in
the text. The third, however, was issued in two editions, one with
the Anglicized "baptize" in the text, and the other with "immerse."
In the Improved Edition of the Bible, where the fourth revision of
the New Testament appears, there is but one edition, which restores
the Anglicized word "baptize" in the text, with "immerse" following
in parenthesis. While we are told that both words are considered

a part of the text, and that the reader may take either word or both, "immerse" serves only as a comment. This does not mean, however, that the Baptists believe any less in immersion, but it does mean that the stress of theological controversy grows less among the Baptists, as it grows less among other denominations. We have possibly seen our last "immersion" version. If so it will be because the spirit of the times does not require them.

3. TRANSLATIONS MADE IN THE INTEREST OF OTHER DOCTRINES

A. A UNITARIAN NEW TESTAMENT

The one sectarian translation which provoked perhaps the most bitter controversy of any ever published, was a Unitarian version of the New Testament, put out in London in 1808, and reprinted in Boston in 1809. The type of Unitarianism represented by the makers of this version, however, was never very popular in America, and only one reprint of it ever appeared in the United States.

The Rev. Thomas Belsham, a very prominent Unitarian minister in London, was the leading spirit in preparing this revision, he being responsible for the introduction and the major part of the notes at least; and he also superintended its publication. Just who made the revision is not known.[7]

The Unitarians first sought to adopt the translation of the New Testament made by Gilbert Wakefield, which had appeared in London in 1791, but his contract with his publishers prevented. Failing in this, they appointed a committee, of which Belsham was a member, to prepare a revision for their use. This committee chose as the basis of their work, a new translation made by Archbishop Newcome, printed in London in 1796, but published later, which had been made from Griesbach's text.

The version this committee put out was pronouncedly Unitarian. Everything that might be used to teach the divinity or deity of Jesus Christ is swept away in some manner. The narratives of the Virgin Birth and infancy of Jesus [8] are printed in italics, and pronounced additions to the original text. The introduction to John's Gospel, however, could not so easily be dealt with in this manner; therefore, the day is saved by translation and notes.[9]

---

[7] Belsham, *The Epistles of the Apostle Paul*, Vol. I, p. IX-X.
[8] Matt. 1:17–2:23; Luke 1:5–2:52. [9] John 1:1-10.

The introduction to John's Gospel reads as follows: "The Word was in the beginning, and the word was with God, and the word was a god. This Word was in the beginning with God. All things were done by him; and without him was not any thing done that hath been done . . . He was in the world, and the world was *enlightened* by him, and yet the world knew him not."

Comments admit that *Logos* or "Word" found in the introduction to this Gospel refer to Jesus Christ, but the "beginning" mentioned here is "the commencement of the gospel dispensation or the ministry of Christ." According to this translation the "Word" was only "a god," spelled without capitals. Lest this imply too much, we read further, "All things were done by him; and without him was not anything done that hath been done," that is, says a note, "all things in the Christian dispensation were done by Christ; i.e. by his authority." Further on the version reads, "He was in the world, and the world was *enlightened* by him."

Newcome's translation reads: "The Word was in the beginning, and the Word was with God, and the Word was God . . . All things were made by Him and without Him was not anything made that was made . . . He was in the world and the world was made by Him."

This version provoked a furious storm of criticism from many sources, and the controversy was long and bitter. "Blasphemous," and "pestilential" were hurled at it, accompanied with numerous charges of deception, falsehood and deliberate fraud. The bitterest criticisms were charges of deliberate dishonesty in trying to palm off on an unsuspecting public a version of the New Testament as substantially that of Archbishop Newcome, when, in fact, it had been emptied of almost every doctrine that he deemed essential to Christianity.

It had been promised that where the new version departed from the text of Newcome, that fact would be indicated in the margins, but this was not done in numerous and important instances, thus provoking the bitterest criticisms. The new version created the impression, whether intended or not, that Archbishop Newcome was responsible for numerous renderings of the New Testament most favorable to Unitarianism, causing, as it did, no little embarrassment to the Archbishop's many friends.

When attention was called to these omissions, the revisers replied that they had been entirely accidental. This explanation might have been accepted, even in that day of bitter controversy, had these failures been few; and even a large number might have been excused, had they been doctrinally unimportant; but the omissions of notes indicating a revision of the text occurred frequently, and in many of the very passages where some of the most vital changes had been made to favor the Unitarian position. They appeared to many to be entirely too numerous and too important to have been accidents; therefore, the charge of deliberate dishonesty.

A few further examples of this translation should be interesting. "Therefore that holy child also who shall be born of thee, shall be called a Son of God," [10] whereas Newcome's version read, "the Son of God." Any man might be "a Son of God." Newcome's version read, "For ye know the gracious goodness of our Lord Jesus Christ, that though he was rich, yet for your sakes he became poor, that through his poverty ye might be rich",[11] which was changed to read, "that while he was rich, yet for your sakes he lived in poverty, that through his poverty ye might be rich," [11] Trinitarians have always understood this text to imply that Jesus Christ had been rich in His preexistence, and that He became poor by becoming a man, and Newcome's version was in harmony with that idea. The Unitarian translation implies that Jesus was rich here on earth, but chose to live in poverty, and leaves no room for any preexistent state.

Again, Newcome's version read, "See that ye refuse not him who speaketh. For if those escaped not who refused him that uttered the oracles of God on earth, much more we shall not escape, if we reject him who was from heaven," [12] but the new version has it, "See that ye refuse not *God* who speaketh. For if those escaped not who refused him when he uttered oracles on earth, much less shall we escape, if we reject him speaking from heaven." Here the word "God" is deliberately added to the text as a substitute for "him," without any authority whatsoever, and the text is otherwise completely changed. Such were the liberties taken in making this version.

The particular texts we have quoted from Newcome's version all had important doctrinal implications, and they were all changed to favor the Unitarian position, yet only two changes were noted in the margins.[13] This illustrates the ground for the charges of dishonesty. Many more such examples might be given.

Among all the versions in English ever made this is doubtless the

---

[10] Luke 1:35.

[11] 2 Cor. 8:9.　[12] Heb. 12:25-26.

[13] Notes indicate that "The world was made by him" (John 1:10), and "See that ye refuse not him who speaketh" (Heb. 12:25) were changed.

most open to the charge of deliberate unfairness and duplicity; and those who made such charges felt that they offered evidence and an argument that were unanswerable; but we do not believe that there was any dishonesty in the case. The explanation of the revisers, we think, should have been accepted. Bellamy, and those associated with him, were undoubtedly good men, and it seems too much to charge deliberate falsehood and double-dealing. That an utterly impossible scholarship was responsible for the revision, probably nobody today would hesitate to admit.

B. A REINCARNATION BIBLE

A curious book with a strange title was published in Philadelphia in 1881, edited by the son and daughter of Robert Hare and his wife, containing the Four Gospels and a part of the first chapter of Acts, from the King James Version, woven into a continuous narrative, together with much other matter, both poetry and prose, with the following title page: "Christian Spiritual Bible, containing the Gospel of the Type of the Emanation and God, the only ubiquitous Son; being the Gospel of our Lord in his four Incarnations. Together with the Gospel of our Lady, his altruistic Affinity. Given through the angel Robert by his intelligences, Robert Hare, M. D., late emeritus professor of Chemistry, etc., and Harriett Clark Hare. Edited by their son and daughter, Philadelphia, A. D. 1881. In Heaven, 1901." This is intended as a Bible for those who believe in reincarnation. Much of the peculiar matter it contains can be understood only by one well schooled in the ideas of the sect.

C. A CHRISTIAN SCIENCE NEW TESTAMENT

A new translation under the title, "The People's New Covenant (New Testament) Scriptural Writings, translated from the Metaphysical Standpoint" was published by Arthur E. Overbury at Monrovia, California, in 1925, containing considerable introductory and explanatory matter. While in no sense official, nobody being responsible for any part of it except the author, it is professedly made in the interest of Christian Science, and Mary Baker Eddy is frequently quoted. On the title page it is said that it "recognizes healing as well as teaching as a component part of true Christianity." The "Explanatory Index" states that it "is based on the premise of 'The Scientific Statement of Being,' as given in 'Science and Health.' "

Considerable of the translation is incomprehensible to those outside the charmed circle. A few examples might be of interest:

"In original being the Word, or GOD-Idea existed; and the GOD-Idea existed in at-one-ment with GOD; and the GOD-Idea was GOD-manifest. The same existed in original being, at-one with GOD. All things came into being in this GOD-conception, and apart from it came not anything into being that came into being. In the GOD-Idea Life, GOD, was manifest, and Life, GOD, was the *Light* of men. And the *Light* shineth in darkness; but the darkness comprehendeth it not." [14]

"The same is he who baptizeth with the holy SPIRIT-truth." [15]

"Whatsoever is born of GOD overcometh the mortal world." [16]

D. A LABOR DETERMINATIVE VERSION

The Old Testament teaches, without qualification, that taking interest for money or anything loaned by the Hebrews and Jews, among brethren, is morally wrong,[17] and this was well understood among the Jews. The old prophets explained some of the sufferings of the nation as God's punishment for a violation of this very law.[18] For more than a thousand years the Christian church taught that taking interest on loaned money was wrong. When capitalism arose, however, men began to borrow money with which to do business, whereas formerly they had borrowed money to relieve distress; and there developed in the church a change of opinion on the subject, interest taking coming to be considered legitimate and right. When the King James Version was made the word "usury" meant simply "interest." Modern translations of the Bible use the word "interest" where the King James Version has "usury." [19]

In 1924, at Jackson, Michigan, the Rev. Dubois H. Loux published a translation of the Gospel of Matthew, containing brief notes, which he calls "a Labor Determinative Version." A translation of the Gospels, in a harmonistic order, was published at the same place in 1926, and Mark's Gospel in iambic pentameter appeared in 1930.

Loux believes that interest taking is condemned by the New Tes-

---

[14] John 1:1-5. [15] John 1:33. [16] 1 John 5:4. [17] Deut. 23:19-20. [18] Isa. 24:2-3.
[19] Psa. 15:5.

tament, and so translates it. Two quotations will indicate his method:

"Give to him that asks you, and from him that would obtain a loan without interest, turn not you away." [20]

"Love your enemies to bring about utmost good, and create good, and lend without interest, despairing of no man." [21]

Rev. Dubois H. Loux is an earnest and faithful Presbyterian minister, with a splendid record as a pastor, but he seems singularly unfortunate in the choice of numerous awkward terms to express his ideas, frequently making of his translations very unsatisfactory English. This feature greatly mars what might have been quite readable translations.

[20] Matt. 5:42.   [21] Luke 6:35

CHAPTER XII

SOME NOTABLE DEVELOPMENTS AND SPECIAL EDITIONS

PRINTING in raised letters for the blind owes its origin to M. Valentin Hauy of Paris, who printed his first book in 1784. This was introduced into England by Sir C. Lowther, who, in 1832, printed the Gospel of Matthew and other portions of the Bible later, from types obtained in Paris. Then, in 1834 James Gall of Edinburgh printed the Gospel of John from a type of letter thought to be an improvement on the original.

According to the census reports there were in the United States in 1835 more than 5,000 blind. Dr. Samuel G. Howe of Boston became greatly moved by the condition of these people, and went to Paris to study the best methods of educating them. Returning to Boston, he opened a school for the blind, his most famous pupil being Laura Bridgman. He promptly began experimenting to find a more practical system of raised letters for the blind, and succeeded in cutting down the bulk of the book by one-half, and the expense of printing to one-fourth what it had been previously.

The American Bible Society naturally became deeply interested in this work, and granted Dr. Howe a thousand dollars at one time, and other sums later, to assist in the printing of the New Testament for the blind in 1836, the work being done at what is now known as Perkins Institute. Money was contributed also by the Massachusetts Bible Society, and by the New York Female Bible Society. Plates for the whole Bible were finally finished in 1843, at a total cost of $10,000. Within the next ten years 400 volumes of the Scriptures were distributed to the blind, reaching thirteen states, while some went to the West Indies, and some to Turkey. Dr. Howe's system is known as the Boston Line Letter.

Mr. William B. Wait of the New York Institution for the Blind, was also interested in providing improved methods of serving the sightless, and, in 1874, invented a new system known as the New York Point, printing a single Gospel in 1874, the whole Bible in 1894. In 1915 he presented the American Bible Society with a printing press of his own invention, for printing the New York Point system.

The arbitrary point character for the blind was the invention of Charles Barbier, a Frenchman, arranged in its present form by

Louis Braille, one of the blind professors at the Institution Nation-
ale of Paris. This is the leading system in use today; and one advantage is that it can be used in writing as well as in printing. There
are several modifications of the Braille.

There is still another system of printing in English for the blind
used by the American Bible Society, known as the Moon. When the
blind become old and their fingers have lost their sensitiveness of
touch, they can no longer read the Braille; and when people do not
become blind until they are too old to learn the Braille, which often
happens, the Moon system can be used. This is the most expensive
system in use, the whole Bible requiring 58 bulky volumes. This
Bible, however, has the disadvantage of being illegible to people who
can see.

The American Bible Society's service to the sightless has been a
noble one. No less than 5,069 volumes of embossed Scripture
were distributed in 1934, in 14 languages and systems, at home;
abroad, 939 volumes were distributed in 9 languages, making a total
for the year of 6,008 volumes.

The year 1934 marked the centennial of the Bible Society's service
to these unfortunates. During these hundred years no less than
100,393 embossed volumes of Scripture have been distributed, at
home and 15,590 abroad. The whole Bible is now accessible to the
blind in Japanese, Arabic, English, Welsh and German, and parts of
it in several other languages. During its hundred years of service to the sightless the Bible Society has provided at home and
abroad a total of 115,983 volumes for their use, and is furnishing
them Scriptures today in 25 languages and systems.

Mr. Jonathan Burr of Chicago, on one occasion, saw three persons
from one family, a sister and two brothers, taking part in the exer-
cises of a Sunday school by means of a Bible in raised letters. On
inquiry he learned that such Bibles were supplied by the American
Bible Society. He provided in his will a legacy for the Society, the
interest from which is to be used forever to print Bibles for the blind,
and this fund has largely met the expenses of the Bible Society in its
work.

2. THE MODERN READER'S BIBLE

One of the most interesting as well as most valuable Bibles ever
published in English is known as *The Modern Reader's Bible,* arranged and published by Richard G. Moulton, a professor in the

University of Chicago. This is not a new version, but a new arrangement of the Anglo-American Revision, in which Dr. Moulton sometimes prefers the marginal rendering to that of the text; and occasionally the wording is sufficiently changed to adapt the language to modern literary structure.

The first consideration in an intelligent interpretation of the Bible is to determine the character of literature the section under consideration happens to be; for different forms of literature are interpreted in different ways. The Bible, whatever else it is, is literature, consisting of lyrics, epics, dramas, essays, sonnets, treatises, history, epistles, etc.

No book on earth has been so uniformly and universally printed in a fashion to misrepresent it as the Bible. It has been cluttered up with chapter and verse divisions, which though convenient for reference, have been confusing and misleading. Then, until quite recent times, it has been printed in such fashion as to give no idea of its character or literary form and structure. The King James Version is printed as if it were all prose history, or a monumental collection of proof-texts.

Dr. Robert Lowth was the first to make clear the characteristics of Hebrew poetry, publishing his translation of Isaiah, arranged as poetry, in 1778. Certain modern Bibles have been so printed as to indicate poetry; but this is only the beginning of the recognition of literary forms.

The purpose of Professor Moulton in *The Modern Reader's Bible,* was to give the exact literary form and detailed structure of the books of Scripture, using all the devices of modern printing to indicate such structure to the eye of the reader; and he prepared and published the most complete arrangement of the Bible, according to the character of its literature, in existence. In this fact is found its chief value. Subjects are announced, and such headings, where needed, as will enable the reader to understand what he reads. Ample notes are appended where required; and the book is provided with sufficient additional explanatory matter to enable the reader to profit by his arrangement.

This Bible was published first in twenty-one volumes, beginning in 1895, the whole being published first in one volume in 1907. The *Modern Reader's Bible* is the most outstanding contribution in existence toward methods of printing that make the Bible both attractive and intelligent.

3. THE POLYCHROME BIBLE

The Polychrome Bible had its origin in Germany, and the German publishers were Deutsche Verlags-Anstalt of Stuttgart. It was planned to cover the whole Bible in about twenty volumes, to be prepared by eminent scholars of both Europe and America, Dodd, Mead and Company of New York being the American publishers. Professor Paul Haupt of Johns Hopkins University was the editor, and he had the assistance of Professor Horace Howard Furness. This was to be an entirely new translation of the Bible.

Modern Biblical scholarship accepts what is known as the documentary theory of the origin of much of the Old Testament. The Hexateuch, for instance, is understood to be composed of excerpts from four different sources, put together something after the fashion of a scrapbook. It is now possible for scholarship to separate these different sections, and when those of like character are put together, they are found to make four continuous stories, each with its own distinct viewpoint and literary characteristics, and designated as J.E.D. and P. The text of this Bible reads continuously as any other Bible, but the sections taken from their separate sources, J. E. D. and P, are printed in different colors—hence the name Polychrome Bible. By this means the composite structure of such portions of the Old Testament as was formed in this way is exhibited to the eye at a glance.

Six volumes were published in 1898-1899—Judges, Psalms, Isaiah, Leviticus, Ezekiel and Joshua. The sale of the work, however, was not sufficient to justify a continuance of the undertaking, and the project was abandoned. These six volumes were republished in 1904 in America and in Germany.

4. THOMAS JEFFERSON'S BIBLE

Thomas Jefferson's relation to democracy, his authorship of the Declaration of Independence, and the fact that he was President of the United States, are widely known; but comparatively few, perhaps, know anything about what is called "Jefferson's Bible."

It does not deserve, however, to be called a Bible, since it contains only a selection from the Four Gospels. It would seem that he had in mind, at one time, to prepare a small book of excerpts from the Gospels, containing an account of the life and moral teachings of Jesus, for the Indians, consisting of such matters only as would be of easy comprehension to them, but this idea was abandoned.

What he prepared finally was for his own use, and consists of excerpts from the Four Gospels containing the life and teachings of Jesus, using the Greek, Latin, French and English, these clippings being pasted into a scrapbook, side by side, for purposes of comparison, and bound in red leather, with gold tooling. His only copy is now in the Library of Congress.

It was published in 1904, in a photographic reproduction, in an edition of 9,000 copies, at the direction of Congress, and bears the title: "The Life and Morals of Jesus of Nazareth, Extracted Textually from the Gospels in Greek, Latin, French and English, by Thomas Jefferson. With an Introduction;" the introduction being written by Dr. Cyrus Adler. An edition containing the English only was published privately in St. Louis and New York in 1902.

The religious controversies of Jefferson's day were quite bitter, and he was often branded as an "infidel." He was reticent about his theological opinions, feeling that they were a matter of his own private concern only; but he finally promised Dr. Benjamin Rush, a very devoted and distinguished Christian of that day, that he would put his religious creed on paper. This he finally did, and this Jeffersonian creed, and the letter to Dr. Rush that accompanied it, are printed in the English edition of "Jefferson's Bible." In this letter, he said: "I am a Christian in the only sense in which he wished anyone to be; sincerely attached to his doctrines, in preference to all others; ascribing to him every human excellence, and believing he never claimed any other." [1] Such men today are known as Unitarians.

Jefferson made no war on other men's religious opinions, believing that every man should be free to adopt such religious beliefs as he himself chose, without hindrance or molestation. He was clearly in advance of his age in Christian charity and toleration, and his purity and uprightness of life were never called in question.

In a letter to Charles Thomson, speaking of what is now called his Bible, Jefferson had this to say: "I, too, have made a wee-little book from the same materials (the Gospels) which I call the Philosophy of Jesus. It is a paradigma of his doctrines, made by cutting the texts out of a book and arranging them on the pages of a blank book, in a certain order of time or subject. A more beautiful or precious morsel of ethics I have never seen. It is a document in proof that I am a real Christian, that is to say, a disciple of the doctrines of Jesus, very different from the Platonists, who call me infidel and themselves Christians and preachers of the Gospel, while they draw all their

[1] Jefferson, *The Life and Morals of Jesus of Nazareth*, (English edition), pp. 11, 17

characteristic dogmas from what its author never said nor saw. They have compounded from the heathen mysteries a system beyond the comprehension of man, of which the great reformer of the vicious ethics and deism of the Jews, were he to return on earth, would not recognize one feature." [2]

5. HARPER'S ILLUMINATED BIBLE

The most pretentious illuminated Bible ever published in the United States was put out by Harper and Brothers in New York in 1846, appearing in about fifty parts, the first in 1843. It was embellished with 1,600 engravings by J. A. Adams, more than 1,400 of which were from original drawings by J. G. Chapman, the artists being engaged in the work more than six years. Mr. Adams is credited with having made, in 1841, the first electrotype in America from a wood cut. The expenses attending the publication of this Bible ran to more than $20,000. It was reprinted in 1859.

6. THE COLUMBIAN EXPOSITION BIBLE

A very special edition of the Bible was prepared for the Columbian Exposition held at Chicago in 1893, serving to show the mechanical attainments of the southern states in bookmaking at that time.

This Bible contains 836 pages and weighs sixty pounds. When open it measures 23 x 40 inches, closed it measures 23 x 17 inches. It is printed on genuine sheepskin in letters of pure gold, each page having a border of about three inches, beautifully illuminated in colors, different colors following each other on succeeding pages. The finest Russian leather was used in its binding, which is elaborately tooled in gold and leather of various hues. The front cover shows a Maltese Cross, inter-set with a scene from Solomon's Temple, heavily embossed on the outside, while inside there is deeply impressed a picture of Christ before the doctors.

To produce this Bible cost approximately $1,700, and required many months of painstaking labor. It is now in the possession of the Southern Methodist Publishing House of Nashville, Tennessee, and its most prized possession. It was prepared by this publishing house, Barbee and Smith, agents. It was highly praised by the World's Columbian Commission in its Certificate of Award, which was accompanied by a "Medal for Specific Merit." This Bible was also exhibited at the Tennessee Centennial Exposition, held in Nash-

[2] Jefferson, *The Life and Morals of Jesus of Nazareth,* (English edition), p 18.

ille, Tennessee, May 1 to October 31, 1897, where it was awarded
he highest honors.

7. THE BRUCE ROGERS BIBLE

Bruce Rogers hails from Indiana, and is recognized today as Amer-
ca's premier designer of books. His peculiar talent in this direction
became manifest while he was still in college. He spent a number of
ears with the Houghton-Mifflin Company, where he developed the
Riverside Press editions. He has served as Advisor to the Cambridge
University Press, and the Harvard University Press. During the last
sixteen years he has designed and printed over one hundred books,
mostly for the Rudge Press, of Mount Vernon, New York, dis-
playing an amazing versatility.

Mr. Rogers, in collaboration with the University printer, set out
few years ago to produce at the Oxford University Press a Lectern
Bible, suitable for church or library use, spending six years in its
production.

The text of this Bible is the King James Version, including the
Apocrypha and the original preface to this version, now universally
omitted. It is set in paragraphs, but the usual verse numbers are
given. Metrical portions are distinguished by a typographical arrangement.

Two editions were printed from the same type; one with small
margins on Wolvercote paper, the other with wide margins on
Bechelor's hand-made paper. Of the hand-made paper edition only
200 copies were printed, 40 for sale in America.

In 1930 Mr. Rogers visited the paper mill of J. Bartham Green
and Son of Maidstone, Kent, where he found a small quantity
of unusually beautiful paper, hand-made from fibre imported from
Japan. He bought it and sent it to Oxford, England, for use in
printing a special copy of his Lectern Bible for a gift to the Library
of Congress. This Bible cost about $1,200. Not feeling financially
able to assume the whole expense, Mr. Rogers sought subscriptions
from his friends, of ten dollars each, with the promise that the name
of each would be printed on a special presentation page and bound
in Volume I. Sixty names of such contributors appear in the list.

This Bible is now in the Rare Book Room of the Library of Congress, where it has attracted admiring attention. While Mr.
Rogers has to his credit many marvelous productions, this is considered his masterpiece. This Bible is in two volumes, with duplicate title pages, and suitable half-titles, containing 1,259 pages num-

bered consecutively. It is printed in a special Centaur type, 22 point cast on a 19-point base, and in double columns. The type page measures 9 x 13 inches on a leaf of 13 x 18¼ inches, and is beautifully bound in a deep cream-colored pig-skin. No decorative scheme is used, except capital letters for headings, upper and lower case letters as subheads, and initial letters starting off the various books and chapters.

CHAPTER XIII

MODERN SPEECH TRANSLATIONS

THE Greek found in the New Testament offered a peculiar problem for centuries, because there was no other known exactly like it. It was clearly not classic Greek, or Greek used for literary purposes, and it was different from that of the Septuagint. Certain pious souls, always ready to invoke the marvellous, imagined that the Lord had created a special kind for exclusive use in the New Testament; "the language of the Holy Ghost," it was called. Others, however, who did not accept this easy explanation could only wait, and hope that some day an explanation might be found. Until quite recently the world has known only that the Greek of the New Testament was unlike any other.

It is interesting, in this connection, to know that Dr. Lightfoot, then a young instructor in Cambridge University, said to his students in 1863, that if letters written by ordinary people to their friends, in New Testament times, could be recovered, they would help to understand New Testament Greek. This, of course, was only a shrewd guess at that time, but it proved to be prophetic, for it has turned out to be literally true.

Papyrus was the common writing material of Egypt and the Eastern Mediterranean world for many centuries, and during New Testament times, but it is easily perishable, and for long it seemed that little of it had been preserved. Within recent years, however, in regions of Egypt where the unusual dryness of the climate has made possible the preservation of such things, large quantities of papyrus have been discovered. Fortunately these discoveries include many kinds of private documents, such as letters, bills, invitations, petitions, leases, contracts, deeds, birth notices, wills, marriage agreements, and such like. Fragments of many books and new sayings of Jesus have been found.

The most interesting and valuable contribution these discoveries have made, perhaps, has been to determine the character of the New Testament Greek. The Greek of the papyri and that of the New Testament are found to be exactly the same, which means that the New Testament Greek is simply the speech of the common people in their everyday life, there being no longer any question in regard to the matter. The first man to point out this fact was a young German scholar, Adolph Deissmann.

This fact has a very important bearing on the translation of the New Testament. Since it was written originally in the common vernacular, it should be translated into the common vernacular, and any other character of translation misrepresents it, by making it what it is not in the original. When the New Testament was written it said things in an easy and natural way, plainly and directly, in the kind of speech the people used daily at home and in business. To translate it properly it must be put in exactly the same style. To do so is not to foist something new upon the New Testament, but is to return to the ancient and original style of the writing.

It was Tyndale who set the style of Biblical translation to which we have been so long accustomed, more than 400 years ago, choosing, as he did, a style then antiquated, feeling that it added a sort of dignity to the Scriptures. Once begun this solemn style has been continued down through the ages, and many people imagine the Bible was originally written so.

Since it has been discovered that the New Testament was written in the everyday language of the common people, and not in a literary tongue, there have been numerous New Testaments published, known as "Modern Speech Translations"—efforts to put the New Testament into the language of the common man.

Even before the discovery of papyrus had established the character of the New Testament Greek, there were those who felt that the Bible should be put into modern English. Rev. Leicester A. Sawyer, in his New Testament of 1858, abandoned the solemn style, except in prayer, and, as far as we know, he was the first to do so.

1. MODERN SPEECH BIBLES

Strictly speaking perhaps modern speech translations, those consciously colloquial under the influence of the revelation of papyrus findings, are confined to the New Testament; but since the Old Testament was written originally, not in a literary language, but in that of the common people, it has come to be common to translate it also in the language of everyday life. The reasons underlying this practice, are equally as sound as those determining the style of the New Testament.

A. C. F. KENT'S SHORTER BIBLE

There was published in New York in 1918-21, in two volumes, what was called *The Shorter Bible,* by Charles Foster Kent, Woolsey

Professor of Biblical Literature in Yale University. This contains those parts of the Bible only, that are of the most vital interest and practical value to the present age, and without duplication. The work was translated by Charles Foster Kent, with the collaboration of Charles Cutler Torrey, Henry A. Sherman, Frederick Harris and Ethel Cutler.

This was printed without any indication, of chapters and verses, and it was difficult to know what parts of the Bible were included and what omitted. This fact doubtless restricted its use.

B. JAMES MOFFATT'S BIBLE

Dr. James Moffatt published *The Historical New Testament* in Edinburgh in 1901, the chief features of this work being its arrangement in chronological order, its prolegomena, historical tables and critical notes, there being no effort at a modern speech translation.

His modern speech New Testament, published first in 1913, in New York in 1917, was an entirely new translation. It was published again in 1922, when printer's errors were corrected. The Old Testament appeared in two volumes, the first in New York in 1924, and the second in 1925, the complete Bible in one volume being published first in 1926.

Dr. Moffatt is a Scotchman, but he came to the United States in 1927, since which time he has been the Professor of Church History in Union Theological Seminary, New York City. He held several important positions in Scotland, and is the author of many books, being recognized as one of the outstanding Biblical scholars of the day. While his translation was made in Great Britain, and contains certain distinctly English terms, it has had a wide circulation in America, and ranks as one of the best modern speech versions that has appeared.

The New Testament is a translation from the text of von Soden, one of the best modern critical texts, differing little from that of Westcott and Hort. The Hebrew of the Old Testament was revised quite frequently, by means of material suitable for such purpose, which had accumulated through several centuries; and perhaps no other translator of the Old Testament has been quite so free to revise the Hebrew text.

It is well known among scholars that the Hebrew is often quite faulty and needs considerable amendment, the chief difficulty in the matter being that there has not yet been accumulated sufficient material for a thorough-going revision, such as is needed. Dr. Moffatt, however, has made such correction as he felt the evidence required. Sections of the Biblical text have been disarranged in the ages of the past, and Dr. Moffatt rearranges many of them. In the Old Testament, he follows the French method, originated by Olivetian, of using "the Eternal" [1] as the equivalent of the Divine Name. Chapter and verse numbers are printed in the margins, and quotations from the Old Testament are printed in italics.

C. THE SMITH AND GOODSPEED BIBLE

Dr. Edgar J. Goodspeed, a professor in Chicago University since 1915, occupying the chair of Biblical and Patristic Greek, widely recognized as one of the best Biblical scholars of the country, and the author of several books, published in Chicago in 1923, a modern speech version under the title: *The New Testament: An American Translation,* which has proved one of the best and most popular produced in America, being made from the standard critical text of Westcott and Hort. One most attractive feature of this translation, as the title indicates, is that its language is wholly American. In this work Dr. Goodspeed has done for America what The Twentieth Century, Weymouth and Moffatt did for England. The solemn style has been abandoned, even in prayer. Chapter and verse numbers have been printed in the margins of certain editions only. Quotations from the Old Testament are distinguished by being set apart, and properly enclosed.

Dr. J. M. Powis Smith published a modern speech translation of the Old Testament in Chicago in 1927. In this work he had associated with him Professor Alex R. Gordon of the United Theological College of McGill University, Montreal, Professor Theophile J. Meek of the University of Toronto, and Professor Leroy Waterman of the University of Michigan, each translating certain books. Dr. Smith translated part of the work and edited the whole. These men were all outstanding Biblical scholars.

Dr. Smith was a professor in the University of Chicago from 1915 until his death in 1932, being associate editor, at various times, of such publications as the *Biblical World,* the *American Journal of Theology,* and the *American Journal of Semitic Languages and Literatures.* He was the author of several books.

---

[1] The only other Bible in English to use "the Eternal" as an equivalent of the Divine Name is that of J. M. Ray, or David McRea, whose Bible was published at Glasgow or London in 1799, and Glasgow 1815.

Dr. Smith and his colleagues did not hesitate to revise the Hebrew, and an appendix of ninety pages contains a list of the textual revisions made. On its title page this is called "An American Translation," which means that its language is wholly American. The solemn style is abandoned except in prayer.

The word Jehovah, used uniformly in the American Standard Bible as the translation of the Divine Name, was used alone by the King James Version only four times; and wherever else the Divine Name occurs, its translators followed the Jewish custom of using the word LORD. Dr. Smith's version also uses the word LORD uniformly. This, at least, gives the people, in this regard, what they have been accustomed to in the King James Version. Chapter and verse numbers are in the margins, and subjects are announced freely.

A quite happy thought was carried out in 1931, when the Old Testament of Dr. Smith and the New Testament of Dr. Goodspeed were combined to form a complete Bible, which was published in a single volume by the University of Chicago Press.

The Short Bible published by the same press in 1933, consists of the most vital and essential parts of the Smith and Goodspeed Bible; and this makes decidedly the most attractive short Bible to be had today. The books of the Short Bible are arranged in chronological order, chapter and verse numbers are in the margins, and each book is accompanied with a brief but exceedingly helpful introduction.

There is one quite interesting feature of the New Testaments of Dr. Moffatt and Dr. Goodspeed that should be mentioned, and that is their agreement in the revision of the Greek text of 1 Peter 3:18-19. This passage in the American Standard Bible reads:

"Because Christ also suffered for sins once, the righteous for the unrighteous, that he might bring us to God; being put to death in the flesh, but made alive in the spirit; in which also he went and preached unto the spirits in prison, that aforetime were disobedient, when the longsuffering of God waited in the days of Noah, while the ark was a preparing."

This passage has always made trouble for the orthodox. It seemed to say that Jesus, between his death and resurrection, went somewhere and preached to imprisoned spirits. It did not seem possible that he could have gone to announce the irretrievable doom of these spirits; that would be poor preaching. On the other hand, to admit that he went to offer salvation to these spirits, long since condemned for their wickedness, was more than orthodoxy could concede, but just how to escape the apparent implications of the text was a problem.

Dr. Rendell Harris, some years ago, suggested that the word "Enoch" had been dropped from the text at this point by some copyist. To understand this, however, it must be remembered that the oldest Greek of the New Testament that has come down to us is written all in capitals, and without the separation of words. Using English equivalents, the Greek text originally, at this point, according to Dr. Harris, read, ENOKAIENOK. When these words have been separated, we have EN O KAI ENOK, which translated gives us, "In which also Enoch." With ENOK left out, we have to translate "In which also he," referring back to Christ. Dr. Harris suggests that some copyist saw the second ENOK in the text, imagined it an accidental repetition by a former copyist, such repetitions being common, and omitted it, with the result that the text coming down to us makes Jesus preach to the imprisoned spirits. Both Dr. Moffatt and Dr. Goodspeed accept this conjectural emendation of the text, and in both translations it is Enoch and not Jesus who preaches to the spirits in prison.

This conjectural emendation is greatly strengthened by the well known fact, that the book of Enoch was extensively used in New Testament times; and that it contains a lengthy story of how Enoch preached to the spirits in prison, they being the spirits of the giants who lived before the flood and corrupted the world. There can be little doubt that these words of first Peter contain a reference to that story. Forty-four separate footnotes to the *Twentieth Century New Testament* indicate the powerful influence of the book of Enoch on the writers of the New Testament.

The writer does not hesitate to say that the Bibles of Dr. Moffatt and of Drs. Smith and Goodspeed are by far the two best in English today, for any and every purpose. In the first place, they are made from texts nearer the originals than any other Bibles; second, they represent more nearly than any others the style of language in which the Bible was originally written; and third, they are couched in beautiful, simple, chaste, normal modern English, such as is in use everywhere in America. If one reads the Bible to learn what its writers have to say, these Bibles present it in a manner most easily understood. While there are other modern speech New Testaments that justly take high rank, there are no other whole Bibles in their class.

These Bibles are not paraphrases, and in no sense commentaries, as has been suggested, but are faithful idiomatic translations of the original languages, entirely suitable for private devotion and public reading in religious services. We have used them regularly since they first appeared; and the common people have been delighted. Those who prefer the antiquated "solemn style" are unfortunately bound by a false education.

Furthermore, scholarship has never been so well equipped to translate the Scriptures as within the last quarter of a century. A very important event in connection with Biblical history and translation was the publication, in 1881, of the Greek New Testament of Westcott and Hort. These scholarly men, fully equipped for the task, spent almost thirty years in the preparation of their text, consulting every known source of information; and their text is that based on the most ancient authorities. The most pretentious effort at the revision of the Greek text since, was the Greek Testament published by H. von Soden in 1913. He worked on slightly different principles, and whether they will be accepted ultimately remains to be seen; but his text differs only slightly from that of Westcott and Hort. These are certainly the best texts available today, and both were used in making these two Bibles.

For the preparation of a Greek text today there are known some 4,000 Greek MSS., including lectionaries and fragments, some dating back to the third and fourth centuries. Hundreds—possibly a thousand—copies of the ancient versions, made from the second century on, are now available. The early Christian fathers wrote extensively, and quoted the Bible freely. Their quotations have all been extracted and can now be used in determining the text of their day.

Likewise, scholarly men have been busy through the centuries on the text of the Hebrew Old Testament. Certain of the ancient versions, such as the Septuagint, the Syriac and the Old Latin, are found to contain material for a revision of the Hebrew text. The Targums, now accessible, contain valuable material for the same purpose, also the Samaritan Pentateuch.

Moreover, translators today understand the Hebrew and the Greek better than those who made earlier revisions and translations, and are far better equipped for the work. They now have an endless number of grammars, lexicons, concordances, commentaries and previous translations. Comparative philology has rendered valuable service in the study of languages, and modern men have a historical sense that greatly aids their work.

The translators of the King James Version had none of these

things. Their equipment for the Old Testament consisted of the Massoretic Hebrew text, the Septuagint, and Latin Vulgate; for the New Testament they had the Greek texts of Erasmus, Stephens and Beza, and the Syriac. They had also certain modern translations of the Latin, C. B. Bertram's French, J. Diodati's Italian, and Casiodore de Reyna's Spanish Bibles. Possibly also the Dutch Bible. They had the best possible equipment for their day, but little compared with what may now be had.

The translators of the Anglo-American Revision of 1881-85, and the American Standard Bible of 1901, were neither so well equipped as the men who made these two Bibles. The text of Westcott and Hort had not been published in 1881, though its authors were both members of the committee making this revision; and, while it was published long before 1901, the American committee was not prepared to accept it fully. Still more important, neither of these committees had any benefit of the new knowledge of the character of New Testament Greek, as revealed in the papyri discoveries. This knowledge was unknown to the Anglo-American committees, and whatever the committee making the American Standard Bible may have known on the subject, they did not profit by it. These matters all have an important bearing on the comparative values of the Moffatt and the Smith and Goodspeed Bibles.

In addition to all this, the best translations are always made by one man, rather than by a committee, provided the one man has proper qualifications for the work. He knows that his reputation for scholarship is at stake, and does the best work of which he is capable. Committees are always hampered by a diversity of opinion. There is certain to be on any committee men too conservative to accept the best results of scholarship, no matter how well attested. Then, committees, representing large constituencies, very naturally fear what the public will have to say, and they are given to putting their best work in the margins. That is exactly what was done in the Anglo-American Revision and the American Standard Bible. If the primary purpose of a new version is to please the masses that always lag behind, then let a committee make it; if the purpose is a revision or translation that is accurate and abreast of the best scholarship, let one man do the work. While several men were concerned in making the Smith and Goodspeed Bible, each man was responsible for the part with which he dealt.

There is another highly important reason that insures superiority in these two Bibles, but it is not claimed that this reason applies to no other modern translations. It is not until very recent times that Christian men have come to seek the truth fearlessly, regardless of where it may lead them. Previously, almost everybody sought confirmation of what they thought ought to be true, whether conscious of it or not. This created an unwholesome atmosphere, vitiating their translation work in a measure.

The King James Version, for example, was mode in such an atmosphere, and the unconscious prejudices of the times naturally led the men who made it into translations that did injustice to the thought of the writer. These men were bound hand and foot by their theological system, and inevitably their work was colored by it.

An example of the influence of such atmosphere may be seen in certain forced interpretations of the Bible. The Old Testament unquestionably teaches that interest taking is morally wrong; but when men came to believe, as they did, that there could be no wrong in accepting interest, they immediately forced a brand new meaning into the word "usury," which had always meant interest and nothing more. "Usury" was now made to mean "exorbitant interest," simply because men could not permit the Bible to teach anything they thought it ought not teach. Such atmosphere vitiated translation.

Today men seek the truth in Biblical study with the same fearless detachment that the chemist watches his test tube, and the biologist uses his microscope. Today translators reproduce what the writer said, regardless of their own opinion of what was said. This attitude, almost wholly modern, insures a grade of faithfulness in translation work impossible without it; and these two Bibles were made in this modern atmosphere.

2. MODERN SPEECH NEW TESTAMENTS

A. F. S. BALLENTINE'S NEW TESTAMENT

The Rev. Frank Schell Ballentine was rector of the Protestant Episcopal Church and chaplain at the Naval Home Hospital, Philadelphia, during the World War. His inspiration for translating the New Testament came, not from the revelations of the papyri, but from reading the Four Gospels in modern French, translated by Henri Lasserre, a good Catholic, and published in Paris in 1887. He sought to do in English what Lasserre had done in French.

He published first the Four Gospels in Scranton, Pennsylvania, in 1897, under the title, *Good News. The Four Gospels in a Modern American Dress.* This had extensive notes and an appendix containing three sermons. At Scranton, Pennsylvania, in 1902, he published the whole New Testament in five volumes, revising the part previously published, using the title, "The American Bible." This was reprinted twice. In 1909 he published the New Testament in one volume anonymously at Perkiomen—the name of his parish and not a town—in Pennsylvania, under the title of *The Modern English New Testament,* but this was so poorly printed that the edition was finally withdrawn, after selling 3,000 copies. In 1922 this New Testament was further revised and published at Jersey City, New Jersey, under the title, *A Plainer Bible for Plain People in Plain American.* This was an improvement over previous editions, but the volumes were ruined by storage in a damp place before being bound, and no copies were ever sold. Fifty or sixty copies, however, were bound and given away.

For much of his arrangement he was indebted to Moulton's *Modern Reader's Bible.* His translations were all made from the commonly received Greek text, now thoroughly out of date.

B. THE TWENTIETH CENTURY NEW TESTAMENT

The *Twentieth Century New Testament* was an English product, published simultaneously in London and New York, and has had a wide use in America. This was the first really influential modern speech translation to appear, being made from the text of Westcott and Hort. The translators had before them the manuscript of the New Testament of Richard Francis Weymouth, which was published later.

There is more romance connected with the Twentieth Century New Testament, perhaps, than any translation of any part of the Bible in modern times. More credit is due Mrs. Mary Higgs, now of Oldham, England, for this version, than any other one person.

She was first set to thinking about the need for such a work when on a visit to St. John's Vale, Keswick, where she was asked by a farmer, "Why is not the Bible written so that we can understand it?" This question he supplemented with, "Why does not someone translate it into English again?" These questions lingered with Mrs. Higgs long after being asked; she often found them in her mind. And then a personal experience in her own home some time later greatly reenforced the farmer's questions.

In Mrs. Higgs' own words: "Reading the first chapter of Mark to my little lad of three or four years of age, I came to the verse about the 'Holy Ghost.' A look of fear came over the child's face, as he said, in a whisper: 'Mother, what is the Holy Ghost?' "

"I saw instantly that the child had been alarmed by some talk about 'ghosts,' and explained that it meant God's Holy Spirit, that came into men's hearts to make them good."

"With a look of evident relief, he said, 'Mother wouldn't it be better if the men that made the Bible said Holy Spirit?' " [2]

She was now fully convinced of the need of putting the Bible into common every day speech. Others matters intervened later to strengthen the conviction. The matter soon assumed such proportions in her mind that Mrs. Higgs wrote to W. T. Stead, then editor of the *Review of Reviews*, suggesting the need for a new translation of the New Testament.

A year later, in 1891, Mr. Ernest de Merindol Malan, a busy railroad engineer, was having difficulty in reading the Bible to his children, and struck by what he regarded as the superiority of Lasserre's Four Gospels in modern French, which he was able to read, wrote Mr. Stead, advocating the necessity of a new translation of the New Testament in English.

Mr. Stead put the two correspondents into communication. Mrs. Higgs had already translated the first chapters of Mark's Gospel for her own children, and the engineer, who was himself a Greek scholar, now agreed to join her in translating the Gospel of Mark, each doing one-half, for exchange between themselves.

The outcome of the matter was that these two people resolved to provide a New Testament in modern speech. By means of a notice in the *Review of Reviews* the work of finding volunteer translators began.

A company of about twenty, from various denominations, was organized, and the work launched by setting aside November 1, 1891, for a communion service and as a day of special prayer. The committee contained men of proved scholarship, several of whom occupied responsible positions.

Mrs. Mary Higgs was a daughter of the manse, her father being a Congregational minister, a Sunday school teacher at thirteen, educated at home and in private schools. She finished at Girton College, Cambridge, the first woman to take a science degree, and remained two years at Girton as assistant lecturer. She taught for a time. Then she became the wife of Rev. T. K. Higgs, a Congregational minister,

[2] *A Twentieth Century Romance,* published by the National Sunday School Union ,London. p. 5-6

taught Sunday school twenty-one years, became a social welfare worker, a leader in establishing the first summer schools in England for social study, and in many of the most worthwhile movements of her country, being known today as "Mother Mary" the friend of the tramp. Several books have been published from her pen. She is now (1936) in her eighty-second year, but still a very busy woman, deeply interested in social welfare work. Her husband died in 1907. When the *Twentieth Century New Testament* was launched, she was the busy wife of a minister and mother of four children, two under five years of age, but she found time to translate Mark's Gospel, and first and second Timothy, rendering other valuable service to the work.

It was decided early that this New Testament should be published anonymously, and, for that reason, no public call was made for funds to meet the necessary expenses. The translators did their work without pay, it being agreed in the beginning that not one of them should ever receive a penny in compensation. To have done so, in the minds of these workers, would have been to taint their "labor of love." Many serious personal sacrifices, however, became necessary in order to keep things going. A clergyman sold his horse, used to travel his wide parish, in order to do some printing that required to be done. Several times it seemed as if the effort was doomed to failure for the want of funds. A more beautiful story of personal sacrifice would be hard to find. Following the appearance of the first tentative edition in 1898, the profits from the sale of copies provided necessary expenses, five editions of the first volume being sold. No more heroic devotion was ever exhibited in any Christian work. One old man wore out his eyesight, but prolonged his usefulness to the committee as long as possible by the use of colored inks.

The *Twentieth Century New Testament* is a splendid translation, and the first modern speech version to feel the influence of the papyri discoveries. Chapter and verse numbers are in the margins, frequent subjects are announced, quotations from the Old Testament are set apart and printed in smaller type, and footnotes indicate frequently the influence of the books of the apocrypha and the book of Enoch. A new arrangement of the books has been provided, and within each section they are placed in chronological order. Conversational matter is enclosed in quotation marks. In England the publication of this work was turned over to the Sunday School Union, the profits to go to religious work.

The names of translators have been denied the public until recently, when Mrs. Mary Higgs gave to the John Rylands Library of Manchester, England, a box of old papers and letters, concerning the translation work. Most of the names may now be had. Only two or three still live.

The following are known to have taken part as translators of the *Twentieth Century New Testament:* [3]

Henry Bazett, T. Sibley Boulton, W. Tucker Broad, John A. Barrow Clough, W. Copland, E. Bruce Cornford, William M. Crook, Peter William Darnford, George G. Findley, Edward Deacon Gilderstone, Mrs. Mary Higgs, J. K. Homer, A. Ingram, Ernest de Merindol Malan, and R. O. P. Taylor.

C. R. F. WEYMOUTH'S NEW TESTAMENT

Richard Francis Weymouth was a Baptist layman of England. He left at death a translation of the New Testament in modern speech, which was revised somewhat by certain scholars and published in London in 1903, being made from the *Resultant Greek Testament,* a text of no critical value. This was further revised in 1924, and again in 1933. Chapter and verse numbers are in the margins, all conversational matter is enclosed in quotation marks, subjects are announced freely, and brief notes appended. This version has had considerable use in America.

D. W. G. BALLANTINE'S RIVERSIDE NEW TESTAMENT

William G. Ballantine, D. D., a Congregational minister and prominent educator, was president of Oberlin Theological Seminary, 1891-1906, having previously been a teacher in the institution for ten years. He is the author of several books. He published the *Riverside New Testament* in Boston and New York in 1923, being a translation from Nestle's text. This is more literal than other modern speech versions. For example, when eating, in New Testament times, the people reclined. This is so stated in the stories of the feeding of the five thousand, and when Jesus ate in the Pharisee's house. It has been customary to translate these passages in keeping with our method of sitting at meals, but the Riverside New Testament tells us that they "reclined." Numerous other literal renderings appear. Chapters are retained, but verse numbers are omitted entirely.

[3] Bulletin John Rylands Library Vol. 19, No. 2, July 1935, p 471.

Quotations from the Old Testament are appropriately enclosed.

E.   MRS. HELEN BARRETT MONTGOMERY'S CENTENARY TRANSLATION

Mrs. Helen Barrett Montgomery was licensed to preach in the Baptist Church in 1902, and was made the president of the Northern Baptist Convention in 1921, a position no other woman ever held. She labored extensively and effectively in the interest of missions, and was the author of several books. She published at Philadelphia in 1924, the *Centenary Translation of the New Testament,* made from an uncertain text, not differing greatly, however, from that of Westcott and Hort. It appeared in two volumes and in a one volume edition. This was published to signalize the completion of the first hundred year's work of the American Baptist Publication Society. This is the only modern speech translation of the New Testament into English ever made by a woman. Chapters are retained and verse numbers are in the margins. Numerous subheads appear. Quotations from the Old Testament are printed in italics.

3.   THE FOUR GOSPELS IN MODERN SPEECH

The Very Rev. Francis Aloysius Spencer, O. P. published in New York in 1898, a translation of the Four Gospels, from an uncertain Greek text, with a preface by His Eminence James, Cardinal Gibbons, this being the first effort at a modern speech translation in America by a Roman Catholic. While it was made from the Greek, the Lord's Prayer reads, "Give us this day our supersubstantial bread."

Dwight Goddard was educated as an engineer, but left the profession and became a Congregational missionary to China, which he abandoned after a few years to reenter his profession, later becoming a trader. He made a modern speech paraphrase of the Four Gospels under the title, *The Good News from a Spiritual Realm,* which was published by the Ann Arbor Press in 1915, a revised edition appearing in New York in 1916. This is a most delightful paraphrase. Goddard is now an enthusiastic Buddhist.

Perhaps the most revolutionary claims published within recent years concerning any part of the New Testament, are those of Dr. Charles M. Torrey, who is professor of Semitic Languages at Yale University, and a man of scholarly attainments. He published the Four Gospels in New York in 1933. He maintains that the Gospels were first written in Aramaic, the language in which it is generally understood that Jesus spoke, and then translated into Greek. If this be true, the Gospels were written originally much earlier than has been previously supposed, probably within twenty years after Pentecost; and they become the first part of the New Testament to be written.

All scholars freely admit that there are certain awkward spots in the Greek text, from which it is difficult to get an intelligent meaning. Dr. Torrey translates the Greek of these passages into Aramaic, and finds, so he says, that they become respectable idioms of the Aramaic, which may then easily be translated into intelligible English. By such a process, he removes difficulties from about 250 passages of the New Testament.

We give two examples. The usual translation of the Greek of Matthew 5:48, reads: "Ye therefore shall be perfect, as your heavenly Father is perfect." This seems an exhortation to the utterly impossible; besides it does not fit the context any too well. Dr. Torrey renders it: "Be therefore all-inclusive (in your goodwill) as your heavenly Father includes all." This would seem to be in perfect keeping with the context, to say the least. Then, Mark 9:46 is usually translated, "Every one shall be salted with fire." This, however, seems to make no sense at all. Dr. Torrey renders this, "Whatever would spoil, is salted," which certainly makes sense, whether or not there is any justification for such translation.

There is much more involved in the new idea, however, than appears on the surface. If accepted it will require a complete rewriting of the early history of Christianity, and will throw into the discard much that has been supposed to be established. Not a little controversy has been provoked on the subject among champions of both sides, and the experts must be left to settle the matter.

Rev. George M. Lamsa, a minister of the Episcopal Church, was born in Assyria and educated abroad. He published at Philadelphia in 1933 a translation of the Four Gospels from the Syriac Peshitta. He maintains the position, as does Dr. Torrey, that our Greek Gospels are translations, and that they were first written in Aramaic. From his language it would seem that these two men were in perfect accord, but not so. Lamsa made his translation from the Syriac, which he strangely calls Aramaic. His position is, therefore, that the Gospels were originally written in Syriac, while Dr. Torrey thinks they were written in Aramaic. Both translations appearing about the same time, and both apparently maintaining the same position, has caused confusion concerning the two publications.

4. OTHER PARTS OF THE NEW TESTAMENT IN MODERN SPEECH

Rev. George Barker Stevens was Dwight Professor of Systematic Theology in Yale University and a Presbyterian minister. In 1891 he published in New York *The Epistles of Paul in Modern English,* calling it a paraphrase. The Epistle of Hebrews is included. The text is that of the translator.

Dr. Ernest A. Bell, then minister of the Night Church of Chicago, about 1922 published, *The Gospel of John, translated and arranged for American Readers.* This was in pamphlet form. We have been unable to examine a copy of this, but it was only one of the numerous expressions of the feeling that the Scriptures should be put in plainer English for ordinary people.

Rev. Ray Allen, D. D., the instigator of the Methodist Episcopal Church's invitation to the Presbyterian Church U. S. A. to unite, published a translation of the Gospel of Mark at Rochester, New York, in 1927. First published under the title of "Mark," it has been revised several times, the eighth edition appearing in 1935, under the title, *Jesus, That Wonderful Man.* One striking translation may be quoted by comparison. Mark 1:8, is generally rendered, "I baptize you in water, but he shall baptize you in the Holy Spirit." Dr. Ray's version reads: "I baptize you with water, but he will baptize you with a saintly spirit."

Something entirely new and yet old in Biblical translation may be seen in *The Memoirs of St. Peter,* a new version of Mark's Gospel by the Rev. James A. Kleist, S. J., professor of Classical Languages at the St. Louis University, published at Milwaukee in 1932. The translation is printed in colometric style, or in "sense-lines." This has been followed by the publication in 1936 of "The Gospel of St. Mark," which is principally the Greek text from which the translation was made, arranged in "sense-lines," this being accompanied with considerable matter introductory and explanatory. The translation is from Greek text of Dr. H. J. Vogels, D. D., professor of New Testament exegesis at the University of Bonn, Germany, the second edition, published in 1922.

Father Kleist has given considerable attention to Greek papyri, discovered in such abundance in recent years, and which sheds so much light on the character of New Testament Greek.

Writing in "sense-lines" was a common custom among Greek authors, both of prose and poetry, before the time of the New Testament, during New Testament times and long afterward. Whether

THOMAS JEFFERSON

any part of the New Testament was written in this style is not known, but it is known that Jerome put the Latin Vulgate in "sense-lines."

Dr. Kleist says that the ancients composed their writings in "sense-lines" whether actually written in such style or not, and that reproducing them in such style is only to make clear to the eye their inner structure.

The writer finds this a most interesting and delightful translation and arrangement.

CHAPTER XIV

THE INFLUENCE OF THE BIBLE ON NATIONAL LIFE AND INSTITUTIONS

1. ITS MAJOR INFLUENCES HAVE BEEN BENEFICENT

A MATERIAL civilization is built on the sand, as history has demonstrated. America has made a marvelous material progress, but if the settlement of America results only in the development of material forces, then it will suffer the fate of Babylon, Egypt and Rome. Unless we have some saving element in our civilization, not found among the ancients, then we can have no hope for permanency. But we have something that ancient civilizations did not have—Christianity with its Bible. It is the influence of this book alone that promises us permanency and a glorious future.

The Bible has profoundly influenced art, music, sculpture, architecture, literature, and, in fact, every worth-while human interest; but the limits of this volume forbid the discussion of a field so wide. However, it is now proposed to point out something further of the blessings which the Bible, as the chief agency, has brought to the six primary social institutions of our country. They are the family, the church, the school, the state, industry, and the associated life.

A. THE HOME AND FAMILY

The family is the fundamental social unit of civilization; it is the necessary underpinning of the state. The sanctity of marriage and the marriage relation, derived from the Bible, makes the cornerstone of American society and civilization. It is from the home and family that go forth the streams of national greatness.

To know fully what the Bible has done for the home and family in America, it would be necessary to know what these institutions were before Christianity came, and what they have been since, and are today, where Christianity is not the dominant religion. This is a long story. But it may be said in general that the elevation and improvement of these institutions, due to Christianity, have been stupendous. It was Drummond who said: "Show me ten square miles in the whole earth without Christianity, where the life of man and the purity of women are respected, and I will give up Christianity."

Marriage Made a Sacred Thing

Early Christianity lifted family life to a new sense of dignity and worth; it demanded purity in family relations, even in thought, and discouraged the needless and reckless breaking up of homes. A new sacredness was attached to the union of marriage. The stability of the family was interpreted in terms of God's original purpose, in the creation of the sexes. Races, religion and civilization itself, can be rated by the position given to woman. It was Jesus who first gave her the place God intended; in his thought marriage became an institution of God, a holy, sacred thing. The elevation of marriage inevitably elevated woman, for it is impossible to have high ideas of marriage and low ideas of woman. And these fundamental conceptions of Christianity were a pronounced advance over Jewish and pagan ideas of the day.

It is more difficult to realize what the Bible has done for the home and family in America, because Christianity had already greatly blessed these institutions before America was settled; but that the original colonists brought with them high ideals of family life, does not alter that fact that such ideals came from the Bible. It should be remembered that the highest form of family life is found only where Christianity prevails; where woman is accorded her rightful place as the equal with man; where husband and wife are one in affection, honor and influence; and where children are the common bond of love.

Jesus the First to Discover Children

It should also be remembered that it was Jesus **Christ** who discovered children. According to him they have value as children; and he used them to teach some of his most beautiful lessons. Nobody else had ever seen anything in children previously, except what they might become when matured. Jesus gave them an entirely new value and a new place; according to him they belong to the kingdom of God. No higher exaltation could be given them. Outside of Christianity children had no such honorable place. The exposure of children, before and after Christ, by those not under the influence of the Bible, was common. Children who were not wanted, and there were many such, might be abandoned to die of the elements, or to be devoured by wild beasts. Men even as high in the world as Roman senators exposed their children. Boys, if of sound body and mind, were usually held in a certain veneration; but girls were often not wanted. Jesus wiped out any distinction. The early church fathers stigmatized child exposure as murder; and the church early took care of exposed children. The chief influence in giving children their rightful place is Christianity, for no other influence has done so much to ameliorate their condition. It is Christian influence today that seeks to abolish the scandal of child labor—a sacrifice to the greed of impersonal wealth. Children could not have the position they occupy in America but for Jesus Christ.

Community Transformations Wrought by the Bible

The value of the Bible to the individual, the home and family, and to the whole community as well, may be seen in the lives of individuals, families and communities without the Bible, in contrast with those which have it. In an early day in America many communities were established where the prevailing opinion opposed the Bible and the church, and where concerted efforts were made to keep the church out. It was boasted that the Sabbath should never cross the Mississippi. All such communities were morally terrible without exception, but completely transformed when the church came in with its Bible. It is a fact that cannot be denied that the further men get away from the ethical teachings of the Bible, the nearer do they approach the jungle life.

A settlement in Wake County, North Carolina, called Flat Rivers will illustrate this character of town. This place, for many years, was as infamous as Sodom, moral conditions being terrible. In 1830 a colporteur of the American Bible Society visited the town. He called on 34 families, gave away 33 Bibles, having found one home with a Bible, and received forty cents in return. Thirteen years later the place was completely changed, and in every home where a Bible had been left someone at least had become religious. The moral transformation had been marvelous.[1]

In the New England and eastern states in modern times, many towns have ceased to have any church or religious worship, followed with moral conditions that are deplorable.

[1] Dwight, *Centennial History of the American Bible Society*, p. 206.

Through a better understanding of the Bible, Christianity in America has been restored to something of its primitive condition, where good morals and a genuinely Christ-like spirit are recognized as essential marks of the Christian. The work of the Reformation has been carried much further afield, and the full rights of the individual as to liberty of conscience have been recognized and provided. In this advanced step America set an example to the whole world.

Character Building the First Consideration of the Church

If a state is to prosper, it must be built on foundations of moral character. Such character is the principal element of its strength, the only guarantee of its permanence. Moreover, morality, to be worth anything, must have an enduring foundation. Some have resolved morality into self-love; others find a basis only in civil law; and still others would base all moral laws only on what is useful and expedient. But can anything be called morality when it asks, not what is right, but what is profitable? Christianity alone furnishes an enduring basis for morality, and grounds it in principles that are eternal. It was Emerson who said, "The true test of civilization is, not the census, nor the size of the cities, nor the crops, but the kind of man that the country turns out."

While character is a matter of first importance to the state, character building is the first business of the church. It begins with the child, and continues its efforts down to old age. What America owes to the Bible for the character of its manhood and womanhood cannot even be estimated.

Christianity Begins With the Individual

Christianity is social and would save man's environment, but it rightly begins with the individual; and while it has powerfully influenced the laws, customs and institutions of mankind, its entering wedge has always been personal. Individual victories have accompanied Christianity throughout its history. However, one man "born again," alive with the spirit of Jesus Christ, is enough anywhere to begin the change of the social order. Christianity has often changed the world's worst, conspicuous among such being Augustine of the early church. Norbet of the twelfth century, utterly reckless and dissolute, was changed into an apostolic preacher. John Newton, engaged in the slave trade, and sunk to the lowest depths of degradation, was set on fire with the love of God, to become one of the world's noblest and most useful ministers. We still sing hymns written by him.

Conspicuous among the abandoned of America, who have been redeemed, is Jerry McAuley, who was one of the most notorious river thieves New York ever knew; yet he was lifted out of it all, and became one of the noblest of men. He established a mission on Water Street, New York City, that still operates. It has rendered a marvelous service in saving the utterly abandoned. Henry M. Hadley, drunk for years and an all-around tough, was redeemed in this mission, to become one of God's noblemen, succeeding to the head of the Water Street Mission on McAuley's death.

Hadley told a thrilling story of his conversion. After having been drunk for years when the Lord found and saved him, he declared that he had never wanted a drink since. A physician once took him to task for telling such an impossible story, explaining, as only one versed in the matter could have done, how alcohol inflamed the stomach and created an abnormal and growing appetite for drink, which could not be removed instantly, without a new stomach. Hadley had heard him patiently, and then exclaimed, "Thank God! I always knew God gave me a new heart when he saved me; and now I know that he gave me a new stomach also."

Melvin E. Trotter was bound hand and foot by drink. While from home his little child died, and was prepared for burial by charity. When he returned and learned the sad news, he was so helpless and crazed for drink, that he stole into the room where the dead child lay, took the shoes from its feet, and pawned them to buy liquor. Yet Christianity laid hold on this man, and lifted him out of it, to make him one of America's noblest and most successful evangelists.

Rev. Sam P. Jones, certainly one of the greatest evangelists America has produced, was lifted from degradation and ruin, and made into a prince among men. Jones was a genius who never attempted to prepare a sermon in advance, though he was careful to have always a text and subject in mind when he entered the pulpit. He then trusted to the occasion for what he would say. For years, in all parts of America, he held vast audiences literally spellbound with his boundless fund of quaint and pungent sayings, which seemed to flow like water from an artesian well. Thousands of his sermons were reported in the daily press, but he did not repeat himself as most ministers do.

Sam Jones had many a tilt with men of prominence, and rarely came off second best. The newspapers chided him at one time for something, and bluntly claimed the honor of having made him what he was. He replied by saying, "Prove it by making another." They had no reply to that.

In the city of Memphis, Tennessee, there came a scourge of yellow fever in the seventies. Panic stricken thousands fled the city, where conditions soon became terrifying. The sick, dying and dead were everywhere. Forces for caring for them were utterly inadequate, because everybody was afraid. Nurses were needed, badly needed, for few would take the risk. But out of a sporting house in the red light district walked a woman who offered to nurse and help. She made no effort to disguise herself. Day and night she toiled, week after week, a ministering angel wherever needed. Nobody seemed to remember her days of sin and shame. When the scourge began to lift, almost gone, in fact, she took the fever and died. Her body lies in Elmwood Cemetery, marked by a monument erected by those who appreciated her services. On it is a lengthy inscription, the essence of which is an exhortation to charity in judging Fannie Walker, and to remember her heroism in giving her life for others.

While Christianity saves the worst, it also changes the best. Captain Thomas Ryman of Nashville, Tennessee, a wealthy and prosperous business man, cultured, refined, gentlemanly, and one of the most splendid citizens of the city, was converted in one of Sam Jones' meetings, held in a great tent in 1885. Being the owner of a line of steamboats on the Cumberland and Ohio rivers, he immediately closed every bar on his boats, had the liquor poured into the river, and had painted on the wall of each stateroom a verse of Scripture. Following his conversion, he promptly began a notable work of charity and philanthropy, among other things, establishing a mission on Broad Street near the wharf, for the river men and the downs and outs. Many lives were completely changed as a result of this work.

The city of Nashville had no auditorium suitable for such large audiences as came to hear Sam Jones preach, and soon after his conversion, Captain Ryman proposed the erection of a tabernacle for such purpose, taking the lead in raising the money, for which purpose he himself gave a large sum. With a seating capacity of ten thousand, it was known at first as the Union Gospel Tabernacle.

Captain Ryman died a triumphant Christian, and Sam Jones conducted his funeral in the Union Gospel Tabernacle, suggesting during the service that the building should be renamed and called the Ryman Auditorium, which was done. The building still serves the city. Sixteen times Sam Jones held meetings in Nashville, never more than a year apart, and sometimes after only six months, many of them being held in this building.

Captain Ryman was as completely changed as was Jerry McAuley and Henry M. Hadley. These are all examples of the power of Christianity on individual lives; all trophies of the Bible. And from changed lives come changes in laws, customs and institutions.

Charles Bradlaugh unfortunately became an opponent of the Bible. On one occasion in England he challenged Hugh Price Hughes to a debate on the question of the Bible's value. Mr. Hughes knew that a public discussion of the kind would accomplish no real good, so he issued a challenge in return. He said, "I propose to you that we bring some concrete evidence of the validity of the Bible's purpose in the form of men and women who have been saved from lives of sin and shame. I will bring a hundred such men and women saved by the Bible, and I challenge you to do the same saved by atheism that denies the Bible. If you cannot bring a hundred to match my hundred, I will be satisfied if you will bring fifty men and women who will stand and testify that they have been lifted up from lives of shame by the influences that deny the Bible's teachings. If you cannot bring fifty, I challenge you to bring twenty people who will testify with shining faces, as my hundred will, that they have a great new joy in a life of self-respect as a result of your teachings. If you cannot bring twenty, I will be satisfied if you bring ten. Nay, if you cannot bring ten, I challenge you to bring just one man or woman who will make such testimony regarding the uplifting influences of your teachings." [2] It is needless to say that the challenge was never accepted.

Outstanding among the influences in character building, derived directly from the Bible, may be mentioned the great revivals of America. The story of the Great Awakening of the colonial period has already been told. It definitely lifted the moral standards everywhere, and gave America its first sense of religious unity. This revival was nothing short of a providential preparation for the

[2] McClure, *The Supreme Book of Mankind*, pp 209-10.

peril involved in the coming Revolution, and made a contribution to America's wellbeing that was incalculable.

Pioneers pushed on westward in all our early history, to found new settlements. By 1800 a great population existed in what is now Kentucky and Tennessee, where French freethought covered the region like a blanket, and was widely felt elsewhere. Wherever it went it had been accompanied with a decided lowering of moral standards and character.

The great revival of 1800 began in Kentucky and Tennessee, and spread more or less over the whole country. The results of this revival, during a period of thirty years, increased the Congregational Church two-fold; the Baptist Church three-fold; the Presbyterian Church four-fold; and the Methodist Church seven-fold.[3] An entirely new denomination, the Cumberland Presbyterian, was born in this revival. The whole country was lifted morally, and French freethought, with its demoralizing tendencies, was greatly checked. A powerful impetus was given Bible Societies, Tract Societies, and Sunday school and missionary interests and work everywhere.

In 1857 hard times appeared. Men had been so busy and prosperous for years that they had neglected religion, but now, in the business stagnation, they had time to think and to pray. As always happens in difficult times, the people generally turned to religion and the Bible, for comfort and guidance. As a result a great revival swept the entire country. Previous to this time the secular press had given little attention to distinctly religious news, but now this was all changed. Enterprising journals everywhere, with sensational headings, began to report "Revival News." Pithy sayings and pungent words, from the noon-day prayer-meetings and evening sermons, were culled out and scattered broadcast in leading dailies. It has been estimated that not less than a million new members were added to the churches; and the general moral conditions were greatly improved. Out of this revival grew a new era in the religious life of America. It proved to be a sort of training school for a force of lay evangelists who did a great work, chief among whom may be mentioned Dwight L. Moody. This was a needed preparation for the great struggle involved in the Civil War, so soon to burst upon the country. These great revivals were all due entirely to the Bible.

The debt of America to the pioneer preacher and missionary, who carried their Bibles and hymn books wherever they went, is

---

[3] Dorchester, *Christianity in the United States*, p 373.

enormous. They pressed on everywhere, following the adventures and settlements of men. They rode through the primitive forests and over mountains and plains, waded swamps and streams and were often required to swim; they lay out all night, wet, weary and hungry, slept with a saddle blanket for a bed, a saddle or saddle-bags for a pillow, and a great coat for a covering, if they had one. They plowed their way through storms of wind, rain, hail and snow, or blistering heat, sometimes all day; and many were the times when they rode all night in the dark. They often bivouacked among the wolves, coyotes, other wild animals, poisonous serpents and Indians; suffered from chiggers, ticks and mosquitos; and were often stricken with violent fevers. But they were making footpaths of love. Everywhere their text was, "Behold the Lamb of God!" They carried a message of salvation to camps and cabins wherever they went.

The Methodist circuit rider is an example. For years his salary was sixty-four dollars a year, and then it was increased to eighty, but he did not always get it. The hardships of the period took such deadly toll that it has been said, that the first seven hundred and thirty Methodist preachers in America died at an average age of thirty-five years.

The Daily Ministrations of the Church

The churches, in their daily ministrations, have always made a silent but constant and powerful contribution to national well-being and prosperity. Their services keep before the people the highest ideals of manhood and womanhood. Many institutional and social service churches render a wide variety of service. And the church with its Bible is the chief inspiration of the vast social service rendered the world, both inside and outside the church. The church keeps before the public constantly the necessity for men to be consciously related to God; that man must love God and also his brother; and that there is no genuine love to God apart from the love of one's brother.

These daily ministrations have contributed mightily to the education of the general public. The world is governed much more by public opinion than by its laws; public opinion is a sort of second conscience to the nation. Statutes are only milestones telling us how far public opinion has traveled. With us law is nothing, unless close behind it stands a living, throbbing public opinion. That fact was illustrated in the days of prohibition. It is not the judgments of the courts, but rather the moral judgments of the masses of men and women which constitute the chief defense of life and property. It is public opinion that moulds our laws and institutions; and one of the greatest forces for moulding this opinion has been the church with its Bible. In fact, Christianity is today the most deep-seated and powerful influence in its formation. Thus it is that Christian principles, by slow degrees, are helping toward divine justice as the fundamental basis of all human law.

The temperance movement is an example. This work is religious and has drawn its chief inspiration from the Bible. The first conspicuous efforts in its behalf came from ministers; the first organizations were in consequence of formal action by ecclesiastical bodies, and through committees which they named. It is Bible-inspired Christians who support the work.

In 1785 Dr. Benjamin Rush, a devout Christian, wrote a famous essay on "The Effects of Ardent Spirits Upon the Human Mind and Body," which was used widely to produce great results. Inspired by it the Rev. Ebenezer Porter of Washington, Connecticut, preached a temperance sermon in 1805, the earliest to be printed. Inspired by the same essay, the Rev. Lyman Beecher, in 1808, at East Hampton, Long Island, preached a temperance sermon. The subject was more fully developed later in six sermons preached at Litchfield, Connecticut. These sermons were published in 1826.

Prior to this the Methodists had taken action. Their conference in 1783 declared against the making and selling of spirituous liquors, as "wrong in its nature and consequences." This, however, was only in keeping with the "General Rules" which the Wesleys had set forth in 1743, for the direction of the "United Societies." [4]

The liquor business presents one of our most difficult problems. In the past it has always allied itself with vice and crime; it has controlled legislatures, purchased immunity, debauched courts and corrupted politics generally; and there is not the slightest indication that it has any intention of reform in any of these respects. In the United States prohibition was undone chiefly as a result of lying propaganda, giving a setback to the cause, which may in the end prove a boomerang. Signs are not wanting that the business will once more thoroughly disgust the American people. It is an inherently unclean business, and has hitherto proved incapable of any sort of reformation and decency.

It must be admitted that prohibition was established in the United

[4] Buckley, *The Methodists*, Appendix pp 688-89.

States on an inadequate educational foundation; and, when it had been established in law, the churches made the mistake of thinking that further education on the effects of alcohol were not necessary.

Just what is the wisest course to take in the matter at the present time is a problem that puzzles many good men, but it is certainly one that only enlightened Christian men can work out. Some day a satisfactory solution will be found, dictated by the principles of the Bible. The primary need of the moment is education on the subject, which the church and the school must supply.

Christianity gave the world and America Sunday as a sacred day. To the Puritans, a part of whom were Presbyterians, we are indebted for Sunday as a legal rest day, as has been said. It was New England that was the first to regulate the observance of Sunday by statute. But to the Christian Sunday is more than a legal rest day; it is the Lord's Day, so called in the New Testament. It is a sacred day, the day on which his Master arose from the dead. In commemoration of that event he keeps it. The Puritan idea of its observance, which made it a terror to children and a burden to adults, is gone. Our ideas today are much nearer those of Jesus: "The Sabbath was made for man, and not man for the Sabbath." It is a day for rest for those who need it, a day of rebuilding, recreation, change, the companionship of friends, the beneficent influences of nature, music,. meditation, religious worship and doing good. Common sense and an enlightened conscience should determine its use.

The Most Important Institutions of the Church

One of the mightiest influences for righteousness in America has been its Sunday schools. The modern Sunday school grew out of the effort to provide religious instruction for poor and neglected children, founded by Robert Raikes, Jr. He started his first Sunday school in Sooty Alley, Gloucester, England, in 1780, paying a Mrs. Meredith for teaching such poor and ragged children as he could persuade to come to her kitchen. After passing the experimental stage, he published the results and methods of his work, and it was taken up and soon spread everywhere.

Many claims for the existence of Sunday schools prior to Robert Raikes have been made, in England, Scotland and America, but none of these perhaps were wholly parallel to the modern Sunday school, which is devoted to the study of the Bible. The earlier work was catechetical in its nature.

In 1790 there was founded in Philadelphia "The First Day, or Sunday School Society," for the establishment of schools, and this is said to be the oldest existing Sunday school society in the world. It has rendered a noble service. Other organizations sprang up and many schools were soon organized.

The American Sunday School Union was formed in Philadelphia in 1824. The first national convention met in Philadelphia in 1832, with delegates from fifteen states. In 1872 the uniform lesson system was adopted; the committee appointed that year to provide lessons has been continued since, being enlarged and made international in 1875. The movement has been world-wide since 1889. Graded courses were first offered by the International Lesson Committee in 1908.

The growth of the Sunday school in America was phenomenal. In 1824, the year of its organization, the American Sunday School Union reported in its connection 1,150 Sunday schools, with 11,295 teachers and 82,697 scholars, estimating the number of scholars in all America at 143,697. By 1829, a period of only five years, the Sunday schools in the American Sunday School Union had increased to 5,901, with 52,663 teachers and 349,202 scholars. It was determined in 1830 to plant a Sunday school in every needy community, estimated at from 8,000 to 10,000, in all the newly settled Mississippi Valley. About eighty missionaries were engaged to do this work. Within eighteen months 2,867 new Sunday schools were organized and 1,121 revived. Within a very short time not less than 20,000 adults and 30,000 scholars professed conversion, reaching as many as 17,000 in a single year.

The Sunday school missionary pushed on everywhere, planting, reviving and nourishing Sunday schools, which often provided the only religious services many communities had. Out of such schools grew innumerable churches. Through them thousands were won to Christianity and the highest citizenship.

The Sunday schools of America have taught the Bible to millions of children, youth and adults, and have been one of our most powerful Christian influences. In addition to this, the church is teaching the Bible in Christian associatons, Bible conferences, older boy and girl conferences, community training schools and vacation Bible schools.

On February 2, 1881, the Rev. Francis E. Clark, young pastor of the Williston Congregational church in Portland, Maine, organized the Young People's Society of Christian Endeavor. Young people's organizations had been launched before, but none had lived or spread. Such societies had been organized for purposes largely social. While Christian Endeavor provided these, it was primarily a spiritual movement and definitely Christian. This fact has been the secret of its success.

Organized first to meet the needs of the young people of an individual church, the plan was so successful that it immediately spread to other churches and denominations. Requests for information about the society poured in upon Dr. Clark in such numbers that he was unable to meet the demand. This led to the organization of the United Society of Christian Endeavor in 1885, the name of which was changed in 1927 to the International Society of Christian Endeavor. In 1895 the World's Christian Endeavor Union was organized.

From its small beginning Christian Endeavor has, in little over half a century, grown from one society of fifty-seven members in a single church, to a union of some 80,000 societies in eighty-nine different denominations of one hundred and thirteen countries and island groups, comprising some 4,000,000 members. It is estimated that not less than 25,000,000 young people have been trained in Christian Endeavor to take a large place in the leadership of the church.

Strange as it may seem few religious movements have received as much criticism as has Christian Endeavor. Its phenomenal growth, fellowship and cooperation at first alarmed sectarians, who, though there was not the slightest danger of such happy outcome, feared that denominational walls might crumble. Leaders in several denominations persuaded their churches to withdraw from the movement and organize similar young people's work for their own particular churches.

In 1889 the Methodist Episcopal Church organized the Epworth League to be their official young people's organization, but many pastors and churches resisted the pressure brought to bear and retained Christian Endeavor. With the exception of the Methodist Episcopal Church, practically all branches of Methodism are included in Christian Endeavor, so that today there are more Methodist Christian Endeavor Societies around the world than those of any other denomination.

In 1891 the Young People's Baptist Union of America was formed, an independent organization recognizing, in the independence and autonomy of the local Baptist church, its right to choose whichever form it desired. This Union gained recognition especially among Southern Baptists, but many of the churches of the Northern Convention continue to have Christian Endeavor.

Among German speaking Lutherans, the Luther League is generally organized, but among English speaking Lutherans there are many Christian Endeavor societies. The United Brethren at one time had a denominational young people's organization, but soon returned to the Christian Endeavor. An attempt on the part of certain Presbyterian pastors to substitute the Westminster League in that church failed, and nowhere is Christian Endeavor more heartily received than by Presbyterians, who have more societies in the United States than any other denomination.

The criticisms and controversies of an early day are only memories now; and while there has been no organic union of all these denominational organizations, they are united in a common purpose. "Christian Endeavor has continued, however, as the one society working among young people of many communions, and today is recognized as having the largest number of local units and members of any organization in this field." [5] It has been a most powerful influence in the creation of a spirit of interdenominational fellowship and cooperation, yet without weakening denominational loyalty.

From a young people's prayer meeting, with an occasional social and missionary meeting, the movement has grown to embrace juniors, intermediates, seniors, and adults as well. Its influence has enlarged until its activities cover the whole field of evangelistic, missionary, civic and social endeavor. From it have been born many great movements.

There is the Quiet Hour, with its simple covenant: "Trusting in the Lord Jesus Christ for strength, I will make it the rule of my life to set apart at least fifteen minutes every day, if possible in the early morning, for quiet meditation and direct communion with God," a covenant into which scores of thousands have entered. There is the Tenth Legion, a vast body of youth whose covenant is the simple promise, "As a Christian whose practice it is to dedicate one-tenth or more of my income to the Lord's work, you will please enroll me in the Tenth Legion," and which has greatly enriched missionary and other giving in the church. There are the Life Work Recruits—a group of young men and women who, feeling them-

[5] *A Concurrent Statement Concerning the Present Place of the Young People's Society in the Program of Christian Education.*

selves called to full-time Christian service, accept the challenge of the ministry or mission field.

In 1893 at Montreal, Dr. Clark challenged the youth to an expression of their religion in terms of Christian citizenship. As the years have passed the movement has taken an increasingly larger part in the crusade for civic righteousness and social justice. The International Convention at Atlantic City in 1911 enthusiastically adopted the slogan, "A Saloonless Nation by 1920." This was sent broadcast by the Associated Press, only to be met with the sneers of the liquor interests, but a year in advance of the time set, the eighteenth amendment was adopted. The contribution Christian Endeavor made to its passage is inestimable. And today, with prohibition repealed, the movement stands, as it always has, bone-dry!

Being international in its scope, it has from the beginning interpreted literally Christ's words, "One is your Master, even Christ, and ye are brethren." Not only has it insisted upon racial goodwill as a principle, but it has practiced it. Thus has Christian Endeavor been responsible for the finest Christian contribution yet made to a better understanding between the white and negro races in America.

International as it is, Christian Endeavor stands as a powerful force for international goodwill and peace. Here it faces untold opportunities. At the International Convention held in Philadelphia in 1935 the movement declared: "This is the faith: That mankind is one great brotherhood, indivisible alike by social position, religion, nationality or color, God being the Father of all, and Jesus Christ, his Son, the Redeemer of all mankind. This is the aim: To destroy those barriers which separate man from man; to substitute for them a Christian comradeship, and to foster the spirit that does away with the occasion of wars." Following this convention Dr. Daniel A. Poling, president of the World's Christian Endeavor Union, and Ernest Bryan, executive secretary of the World's Peace Fellowship, attended the ninth World's Christian Endeavor Convention in Budapest, and then toured thirty-four nations in the interest of peace.

The largest gatherings of Christian youth in America have been the International Christian Endeavor conventions—the largest, in fact, in the world.

In 1892, when Christian Endeavor was only eleven years old, it was decided to invade New York City with a convention, which many considered foolhardy. No religious gathering could stage a suc-

THE

HOLY BIBLE

Containing the Old and New
Testaments : Translated out
of the Original Tongues and
with the former Translations
diligently compared and revised by His Majesty's special
Command

Appointed to be read in Churches

OXFORD
Printed at the University Press
1935

Title page of Oxford Lectern Bible

cessful meeting in the greatest metropolis of America, so it was said. But fortunately the lusty infant was not yet old enough to take advice from the worldly wise; so Madison Square Garden was engaged for the occasion, and New Yorkers and the country gasped in amazement. This auditorium seated fifteen thousand people and was the largest in America at the time.

The manager of the Park Avenue Hotel, one of the largest in the city, was sure he could entertain the whole convention, and said so boldly; but when the final report of more than thirty-five thousand delegates was presented to him, he decided that other hotels might have some of the business.

The newspapers of the city practically ignored the convention up to the time of the arrival of the United Society officers, on the very morning the meeting was announced to open. That morning frantic telegrams poured in from Buffalo and Niagara Falls, stating that a dozen or more special trains were literally stalled at these places, because the New York Central did not have sufficient engines to bring them in. The newspapers woke up and decided that here was one religious gathering that it might be well to look into. Within an hour every metropolitan newspaper had its special representative at the headquarters of the United Society officers, in the Fifth Avenue Hotel, begging humbly for information about Christian Endeavor.

Naturally these officers were busy on the opening morning, but they did their best to accommodate. Even leaflets explaining the plans and methods of the movement were eagerly seized and republished as news. The demand for Christian Endeavor news soon became such that two of the leading dailies put out special editions, devoted exclusively to the convention and its work, with verbatim reports of addresses. The regular editions of the papers would not sell, and the newsboys spent their whole time supplying the public with these Christian Endeavor numbers.

Madison Square Garden was packed to the doors long before the hour set for the opening session, and an impromptu overflow meeting was held in Union Square, where thousands of enthusiastic young delegates from everywhere gathered. Such was the jam in attendance that nobody was admitted to these meetings without the official badge, and on the second day the officers were literally overwhelmed with applications from the most prominent people of the city, eager to attend and share the enthusiasm of a religious gathering that had shaken New York from the Battery to the Bronx.

Madison Square Garden could not accommodate the convention. Carnegie Hall, the Metropolitan Opera House, and the largest churches of the city were requisitioned to house the vast crowds, and even then many outdoor meetings were necessary.

The metropolitan newspapers of New York City, through their world-wide circulation, scattered news of the convention and the work of the society to the ends of the earth, giving great impetus to world-wide Christian Endeavor.

In 1895, when the movement was only fourteen years old, the Boston convention registered 56,425 delegates. This convention secured special permission to erect two great tents, that would each seat 10,000 people, on the Boston Common, a concession never before nor since granted to any other organization. More than twenty-five different auditoriums were used and eight hundred and twenty-five meetings held. The San Francisco Convention of 1897 so congested traffic that the railroads commandeered all their locomotives from the freight service for use in hauling passenger trains. Many delegates were never able to secure their trunks, because of the congestion, and lived with their hand-baggage and local purchases.

Nor have conventions lost their power. The International Convention of 1935, held in Philadelphia, "was regarded by some as the most wholesome and potential of all such gatherings in the last quarter of a century." Fifty thousand young people marched in the parade, and three thousand and two hundred declared their intention to enter full-time Christian service; and this in the day of "modern youth!"

America and the Christian church owe a tremendous debt to the Christian Endeavor movement. It turned the face of the American Protestant church from doctrines to be propagated, toward the lives and careers of its youth. It was largely instrumental in saving the Christian youth of the last generation to the service of the church. To Christian Endeavor, more than to any other agency, the church owes the training of its leaders for the past half century. It has led the way in the whole field of organized young people's work. It is helping to keep the young people of the present generation loyal to the church. It has blazed the way in the whole modern movement of interracial and international service and fellowship. Finally, it offers the church its one great chance to reach the unchurched youth of the present generation.

Christianity is essentially missionary; the church that ceases to be missionary dies. Charity may begin at home, but Christian charity soon ceases to be, if it remains at home. Accordingly, in their efforts to obey the great commission, the churches of America have built vast organizations and raise and spend annually millions of dollars, in an effort to carry the Gospel to the nations of the world. The home field is not neglected, and vast sums are spent annually in efforts to provide every American community and people with the Gospel. This great interest in missions, both at home and abroad, has had a profound influence in its reaction on the home church; it is this that has so powerfully built the home church. And this missionary interest has been one of the influences that has enabled America to assimilate so successfully the vast hordes of immigrants that have settled among us.

The Christian character of America may be seen in its power as a "melting pot." This country has received and assimilated millions of immigrants from all parts of the world, the story of which is almost incredible. They have poured into America from east and west; various nationalities, with differing languages and creeds, many of them none too desirable. That America has been able to assimilate them into the body politic, making good citizens of most of them, is one of the most marvelous feats of all history. And the mightiest influences in this transformation have come from the Bible. None but a genuinely Christian nation could have accomplished it, as America has done.

The Student Volunteer missionary movement originated at the first International Conference of Christian Students, held at Mt. Vernon, Massachusetts, in 1886, at the invitation of D. L. Moody. Before this conference closed one hundred of the two hundred and fifty delegates recorded their "purpose, if God permit, to become foreign missionaries." The movement was definitely organized in 1888. Its effect has been tremendous, both in America and in England. Through its influence thousands of young people have given their lives to missionary effort; and many others have had their spiritual lives quickened for service at home. Every individual won for foreign missions became a center of beneficent influence in America, thereby rendering great service at home as well as abroad.

The Bible has the most satisfactory answer to the world's questionings after truth; it alone brings us a knowledge of Jesus Christ and his kingdom. Other religions are not entirely destitute of truth, because God has given to all peoples so much of his truth as they could understand and assimilate. An early type of missionary felt it to be his first duty to destroy other faiths utterly; and this type of missionary may still be found. But today men understand the Bible and Christianity better, and their studies of comparative religions have revealed their elements of value. The more thoughtful missionary would now assimilate the best of the world's systems of religious thought, and then provide them with that which completes their own, Jesus Christ, the peculiar and superior contribution of Christianity. It is this advanced knowledge that is responsible for (Rethinking Missions), which originated in America, and which, though by no means perfect, points the way to a greater service to the Master.

The most outstanding weakness of the church is its divisions; but there is today a growing fellowship and cooperation, and even an occasional happy union among its forces. Especially is this true of the larger denominations. Certain denominational families are showing a disposition to get together. This is true among the Lutherans. The Cumberland Presbyterian and Presbyterian Church U. S. A. united some years ago. The Congregational and the Christian Church have united. A notable union occurred in Canada, where the Presbyterian, the Methodist and the Congregational churches united to form one big body. The plea for Christian unity holds a large place today in religious thought and literature. The Federal Council of the Churches of Christ in America, representing the larger part of the Protestant forces, is rendering a powerful service in bringing these denominations together in cooperation and fellowship based on what they have in common.

C. EDUCATION AND SCHOOLS

True Christianity has always sought to lift the masses into higher intelligence, and has, therefore, been a leader in education. In the Middle Ages practically all education was in the hands of the church. Charlemagne gave the first impulse to popular education by inviting Alcuin of York, England, to come to France to direct his educational activities. It was he, a devout Christian, who inspired Charlemagne to provide general education. "The name Alcuin might well be inscribed over the doorway to every free school, every private school, every college and every university, yes, and every Sunday school, too, of the entire English-speaking race, for he it was that started the movement that eventually led to their existence." [6]

Education had been in the hands of the church, but with the Reformation came a change, and its secularization began. And in emphasizing the right to private judgment, and that each soul should have direct access to the Bible for himself, the Reformers put a premium on education for the common man that made it necessary. Protestant principles that threw responsibility on each individual, in deciding matters of the highest moment, furnished the additional inspiration necessary to provide for modern universal education.

Education in America Christian in Origin, Growth and Development

Education in America was religious in its beginnings. It flows naturally out of the Christian recognition of the value of human life as such, the essential dignity and worth of the individual man. How schools originated and spread over the colonies has already been told. We have also pointed out the fact that of the first ten colleges founded before the Revolution, nine were planted by religious bodies, and the other grew out of a school for orphans. And as the Republic grew it was Bible-trained men who organized schools and colleges everywhere; the higher education of the entire country was launched by men with Bibles in the hearts and often in their hands. The denominational college was everywhere the pioneer. Its inspiration was the Bible; and it prepared the way and made possible the numerous state universities and independent institutions of higher learning. So that the primary influence behind the whole educational system of the United States is the Bible, not only in its origin, but in its growth and development. The same is true of Canada.

One of the great contributions the Bible has made to America has been the teachers it has furnished for the educational institutions of the country. They have been an army of heroes and heroines, serving in self-denial and humility; generally with the consecration and devotion of ministers of the Gospel, feeling that teaching was their calling from God; and their chief compensation often has been the consciousness of having rendered a Christian service. The vast majority of all our teachers in schools of every sort are and have always been Bible-inspired men and women.

[6] McClure, *The Supreme Book of Mankind*, p. 90.

Professor T. H. Huxley, with certainly no prepossessions in favor of Christianity, bears eloquent tribute to the value of the Bible in the education of the world. He has this to say: "I have always been sturdily in favor of secular education, in the sense of education without theology; but I must confess that I have been perplexed to know by what practical measures the religious feeling, which is the essential basis of conduct, was to be kept up without the use of the Bible. The pagan worship lacks life and color, and even the noble Stoic, Marcus Aurelius, is too high and refined for the ordinary child. Take the Bible as a whole: make the severest deductions which fair criticism can dictate for shortcomings and positive errors; eliminate, as any sensible lay teacher would do if left to himself, all that is undesirable for children to occupy themselves with; and there still remains in this old literature a vast residuum of moral beauty and grandeur. It is written in the noblest and purest English, and abounds in exquisite beauties of mere literary form; it forbids the veriest hind who never left his village to be ignorant of the existence of other countries and other civilizations, and a great past, stretching back to the farthest limit of the oldest nation of the world. By the study of what other book could children be so much humanized and made to feel that each figure in this vast historical procession fills, like themselves, but a momentary place in the interval between two eternities; and earn the blessings or curses of all time, according to the efforts to do good, and hate evil, even as they are earning their payment for their work?" [7]

Secular Education Dominated by Christian Ideals

New theories of both education and the state have assisted in the secularization of education. The old theory of the state was that its citizens existed for its benefit; the modern idea is that the state exists to serve its citizens. The old time idea of an education was that of assisting people to prepare for the world to come; the modern idea is that an education is primarily to prepare people for this life. Schools are now more and more considered civil affairs, the great constructive instrument of the state in preparing its citizenship for the highest service. The fight to secure free education for the masses as a right, and not as a privilege, is due very largely to Horace Mann and Henry Barnard.

[7] *The School Boards, What Can They Do, and What May They Do?* In the Contemporary Review, December 1870.

While there are numerous schools and colleges in America under church control and distinctly Christian, education is rapidly passing to the state. Since the middle of the nineteenth century there has been a great world movement in that direction; and in the forefront of this movement has been the United States. But secular education, now so widespread, is inspired by motives that are essentially Christian. In the new system the child is regarded as of first importance. Education is considered as the birthright of every child in the land. It puts a premium on the value and capacity of the individual; and it is also based on the idea that each student is capable of development and worthy of it. The teaching of our secular schools, in helping boys and girls, men and women, to make the best of themselves, is done that they may make the best possible contribution to society. In addition to the educational provision for the normal, there has been, more especially since the World War, an extensive attempt to provide such advantages for those suffering from various disabilities—the deaf, the feeble-minded, subnormal and delinquent. All such is essentially Christian. And the vast majority of those in charge of secular education are Christians.

The struggles of the sixteenth and seventeenth centuries gave religious toleration and freedom; those of the eighteenth and nineteenth centuries gave political freedom and political rights; and this leaves to the nineteenth and twentieth centuries to provide universal education. The World War ended "the divine right of kings" in Europe and established democratic types of government. The great problem of the future is to make democracy safe for the governments of the world. This can be done only by universal education, and the state alone can provide it.

One profoundly important matter in connection with secular education remains to be solved. Education that does not produce character is a failure; and the highest character requires a religious basis. There is grave need of religious instruction, which in reality forms the basis of all instruction. This the state cannot provide. In some way the church must supply the deficiency. Small beginnings have been made in that direction.

The importance of religious liberty, as guaranteed by the Federal Constitution and as practiced all over the country, in its relation to education, cannot be overestimated. This provision had a profound influence not only on religion, but on the educational policy of the nation. On no other basis could the United States have laid the foundation of a free, common, public, tax-supported school.

It could not have been established, with any degree of satisfaction, on a religious basis, with the numerous competing sects. A non-sectarian basis only was possible.

But it is easily possible to oversecularize education, and this has been done; but fortunately the pendulum is now swinging back toward better conditions. Legal restrictions and prohibitions of state institutions are meant only to shut out sectarian influence, and not religious teaching. There is already in evidence a return in the direction of a larger use of the Bible in education. One of the first steps in the correction of this oversecularization in public education has been Bible reading in the public schools. According to Government Bulletin No. 14, 1930, Bible reading is definitely required by statute in eleven states, and by order of the Board of Education in the District of Columbia. Furthermore, it is specifically permitted by law in five states, and, while twenty states are legally silent on the subject, this silence is interpreted as legal permission, and the Bible is being read in their schools. No state has direct legislation against the use of the Bible in the school, and those with negative attitude are in the small minority.

Another movement that promises much for the future is the modern practice of giving credit for Bible study by public educational institutions. North Dakota and Colorado began the practice and were quickly followed by Washington and Indiana. This new movement gives high school students credit for Bible study done outside. Originating in 1910, the movement had spread by 1925, according to the survey of W. A. Squires, until schools in nineteen states were authorized to accept such credits. Without official backing ten other states were following the plan. The number of states giving credit for Bible study had risen to twenty-six by 1927, and seven others were including some type of Biblical education.

State colleges and universities are increasingly recognizing the value of religion in the curriculum. There is a widespread feeling among our educators that religion has been neglected, and that it should have a place in education. The churches have established many schools of religion and church foundations, located at state universities, where courses in religion are offered for credit or on a non-credit basis. State universities have welcomed this provision. They have done more than that. Thirty-three state universities, within a dozen years past, have increased the number of hours of credit courses in religion from 384 to 693 hours, a gain of eighty per cent. From a survey of thirty-three state universities reported in *School and Society,* March 11, 1933, we have this information: "It is interesting to note that courses having to do with the Bible, both Old and New Testaments, are usually included in the curriculum. In the group of thirty-three surveyed, only two institutions were found where no distinctly Biblical courses were offered. There is a general feeling that the Bible challenges the attention of both scholars and students, not only because of its recognized authority, but also because of its influence on law, literature, and the progress of the race generally." [8]

D. THE STATE AND GOVERNMENT

America a Christian Nation

It was the influence of the Bible that led Columbus to discover America. "According to his own assertion, the incentive that impelled him to plan his discoveries was not the love of science, but his interpretation of the prophecies of Isaiah." [9]

The religious history of America begins with the landing of Columbus in 1492, on San Salvador, where his first act was to erect the flag of Castile and Aragon, and by its side the banner of the Cross, thus dedicating the New World to Christianity. His first discovery was named San Salvador in honor of Jesus Christ. America early became an asylum for the persecuted for conscience's sake in all the world. The Bible moulded the life, customs and laws of the colonists as no other influence did. The early charters make clear that colonization had a Christian purpose; and early constitutions recognize the Christian purpose of the colonies. The United States is a Christian nation.

The Declaration of Independence appeals to the "Supreme Judge" of the world and recognizes the "protection of divine Providence." It declares that all men are free, that they are equal before the law and in the sight of God, and endowed with certain inalienable rights —a Christian doctrine. This document was an expression of the very soul of Jefferson. It is a declaration not only of American independence, but of human brotherhood. Its power lies not in the fact that it was something new, for it was as old as the dream of

---

[8] *The Bible and the Life and Ideals of the English-speaking People,* pamphlet No. 3, in commemoration of 400 years of the printed English Bible, p. 13, American Bible Society.

[9] Kayserling, *Christopher Columbus,* translated by Charles Gross, p. 15.

Jesus of Nazareth, who first preached effectively the brotherhood of man. Jefferson's democracy, his faith in the common man, is strangely akin to the teachings of Jesus. Representatives of every shade of religious belief were found among those who signed the Declaration of Independence, from the Deism of Franklin to the Catholicism of Carroll. It became the ritual of a new political faith, the faith in humanity.

The Constitution of the United States is a Christian document, framed by men who believed in God and who represented a God-honoring and God-fearing constituency. The Christian spirit of justice and fair play pervades it.

The Constitution was necessarily a compromise; it was that or no constitution at all. Every man could not have exactly what he preferred. Progress is made only by such concession, conciliation and compromise. The Church of England is a compromise, halfway between Geneva and Rome. The English Constitution is a series of concessions. Even Moses permitted a very free divorce as a concession to the hardness of men's hearts. And so the Constitution of the United States protected slavery; yet its provisions were as thoroughly Christian as could be provided at that time.

The Constitution recognizes the Lord's Day, given the world by Christianity, in its expression "Sundays excepted.' The President must approve all bills passed by Congress, or veto them. If a bill is not returned within ten days, "Sundays excepted," it becomes a law. And Sunday is recognized by law everywhere, whether municipal, state or national. The spirit of Sunday legislation, however, is protective and not coercive.

"The men who effected the American Revolution were not all of them believers. In different degrees, Jefferson, Franklin, Gouveneur Morris, John Adams, were free-thinkers, but without intolerance or display, without ostentatious irony, quietly, and almost privily; for the masses remained believers. Not to offend them, it was necessary to speak with respect of sacred things; to produce a deep impression upon them, it was requisite to appeal to their religous feelings; and prayers and public fasts continued to be instruments resorted to whenever it was found desirable, whether by agitators or the State, to act powerfully on the minds of the people." [10]

Admittedly several of the men who assisted in framing the Con-

[10] G. Adolph Koch, in *Republican Religion; The American Revolution and the Cult of Reason*, p 284, quotes this from Cornels de Witt, *Jefferson and the American Democracy*, translated by R. S. H. Church, p 17.

stitution were not orthodox; but that fact does not alter the character of the document. They embraced the doctrine of Deism, which grew up in Italy and France, in opposition to Christianity. Many men of that day rejected historic Christianity, under the supposed veneration for the one true God. From France the idea came into America. Such ideas in general are held today as Unitarianism. While not agreeing with their theological position, it must be said that many of the best Christians of the world have been Unitarians. There never would have been a doctrine of Deism but for the Bible; every idea of the Deists of any worth came from the Bible. Even Rousseau defended the fundamental values of Christianity; the belief in God, future life with its rewards and punishments, and the sacredness of social laws. It was his veneration for the Bible that provoked him to ask, "Is it possible that a book at once so simple and sublime should be merely the work of man?"

But it has been said that no prayer was offered during the Constitutional Convention, though Benjamin Franklin proposed it; and that the word God is nowhere found in the document. Public prayers have an important place in religious assemblies; but, while not out of place, they can hardly be said to be essential in civic and secular meetings. And those who insist on such trivialities as that the addition of the word God would change the character of the document, only need to grow up. They might console themselves with the fact that it does recognize Jesus Christ; it is dated "in the year of our Lord."

"In the constitutions of all but one of the American states God and the true religion are recognized, and in twenty of them his worship is guaranteed, and in not one of them is any other worship guaranteed. It matters not that the Federal Constitution forbidding establishment of religion as a legal national institution has not 'God' written in it, for that Constitution is but an instrument to provide a union of several states, all but one of which constitutionally recognizes God".[11]

The Supreme Court of the United States formally declared the United States to be a Christian nation.[12] State courts, where the occasion has arisen, have declared the states to be Christian; and the dominating influences and ideals of the country are Christian. If we were to remove the Christianity and the morality it teaches from the civil government, there would be little left worth preserv-

---

[11] *The New Schaff-Herzog Encyclopedia of Religious Knowledge*, Vol. XI., p 149.
[12] In the case of Holy Trinity Church VS United States. 143 U. S. 471.

ing. The United States has a national Thanksgiving Day, in recognition of the blessings of the Christian's God, instituted by the Pilgrims, and now observed on proclamation of the President and the concurrent action of the various governors. In addition to all this, the vast majority of the people of America are professing Christians.

The Bible the Chief Inspiration of Progressive Legislation

Law is a form of social control; it is both a product and a prop of civilization. Many influences have contributed to the making of our laws, but the most powerful has been the Bible. Christianity had its influence on Roman law. Puritanism, a product of the Bible, powerfully influenced American law in its formation and early development, which influence continues even today, giving color to legal enactments.

No example is more telling than the influences that set up our chancery court, a court of equity. It is intended that the law of this court shall be the law of God; its whole purpose is to make Christian morals and ideals into law. Another example is the modern juvenile court. Jesus Christ discovered children, and gave them a new place. This court, with its new methods, recognizes the fundamental values that Jesus pointed out. In the history of penology the influence of Christianity has made itself distinctly felt. Human life has become more and more sacred; and as a result capital punishment has grown less and less. Once England punished with death considerably more than two hundred crimes. Until 1894 twenty-five offenses were made capital under the military code of the United States; twenty-two under the naval code, and seventeen under the penal code. Under federal laws the number was finally reduced to three.[13] Many states abolished capital punishment altogether. Recently, due to the hysteria caused by the unusual prevalence of serious crime, there has been a tendency to restore the death penalty. It will probably last but a short time. The modern theory of the reformation of offenders, the indeterminate sentence, probation and parole are all due very largely to Christian influence. Productive labor for prisoners, and the support of his family from his earnings, and many other tendencies are chiefly Christian in origin.

[13] *The New Schaff-Herzog Encyclopedia of Religious Knowledge,* Vol. II, pp. 406-07.

Much modern legislation provides forms of social control that increasingly recognize the rights of men, rather than those of property; and a higher order of justice is everywhere being sought. The laborer's condition has been greatly improved by shorter hours, the introduction of safety devices and more sanitary conditions. The agitation for widow's pensions, old age pensions, unemployment insurance and other proposals of social security are thoroughly Christian. In fact, the whole trend of modern legislation is an effort to apply more and more the principles of the brotherhood of man.

Dueling in the United States received its death blow as a result of the death of Alexander Hamilton, one of the greatest statesmen the world has ever known. And it was the church chiefly that brought about such result.

Aaron Burr, a man of powerful ability, occupying the second highest office within the gift of his country, paid a terrific price for his vindictive deed. He was finally compelled to flee and became a wanderer, often penniless, in a foreign land. He returned to America hoping to practice law; but he was a ruined man, in spite of talents and former social advantages. His moral character was rotten, and he was classed with Benedict Arnold. The penalty he suffered was due to the fact that where the Bible rules, a man whose fundamental moral character is bad, is doomed. Men may have defects, faults, weaknesses, yet stand high; Christianity is merciful, and no man is expected to be perfect. But where Bible influences dominate no power can save the fundamentally bad.

The indignation provoked by the wanton murder of Hamilton was such as often evaporates into thin air. It doubtless would have done so in this case, but the churches and ministers pressed their advantage; they struck while the iron was hot. They applied Christian principles, pressing the matter on the heart and conscience of the nation.

Among those whose influence was powerful in abolishing this evil was the Rev. Lyman Beecher, then young and unknown. He preached a sermon on the subject, one of the most powerful ever delivered on any subject. Other pulpits took it up. Very soon a situation was created that made it very difficult for men who had fought duels to be elected to public office. When Henry Clay was a candidate for the presidency, the Democrats printed an edition of forty thousand copies of Lyman Beecher's sermon, and scattered them all over the North, where it hung like a millstone about Clay's neck. Anti-dueling societies were formed in the churches, and the politicians finally took the hint. In time it was abolished by church influence.

The Liberty of the United States Marks the Nation as Christian

The religious liberty granted in America marks a decided Christian advance. At the time it was provided, our country was far ahead of the nations of the world in this respect. The idea of religious liberty developed very slowly; but the kingdom of God comes without observation. God was preparing for a signal advance in his kingdom in the establishment of America. The most influential element in its settlement represented the various sects into which the church had been shattered. The division of the church into competing and unfriendly sects has had its disadvantages; but it has not been wholly evil. Denominationalism made an enormous contribution to the establishment of religious liberty; Christians learned from experience that it was a practical necessity.

The Edict of Constantine, in 313 A. D., would seem to be the only ancient proclamation of any civil government providing absolute religious liberty. This was issued in behalf of the Christians. Throughout the ages following, persecuted minorities occasionally pled for liberty, but they were not heard. The Reformation did not provide religious liberty, and had no thought of such. The Lutheran Church, the Reformed Church, the English Church and the Presbyterian Church originaly had no thought of liberty of conscience, or even toleration.

At the outbreak of the Revolution, the colonies were in three classes, in the matter of church organization. One group consisted of New York, New Jersey, Delaware, Maryland, Virginia, North Carolina, South Carolina and Georgia; in these colonies the English Church, without a resident episcopacy, was more or less completely established by law. A second group consisted of Massachusetts, New Hampshire and Connecticut; here the Congregational form of church organization was established by law. The third group consisted of Rhode Island and Pennsylvania; in these there was no church established by law.

During the colonial period extensive dissent had resented the legal establishments, especially any system of taxation for their support. The whole idea was growing increasingly unsatisfactory everywhere. After the Revolution had been won there developed a widespread demand for the entire separation of political and ecclesiastical affairs.

One needs to be familiar, at least briefly, with the history of the church, in order to understand fully why the separation of church and state was so long delayed, and why so much difficulty was encountered in securing it. Among the Hebrews the church and state were one; and the Old Testament which contained this record exercised a profound influence as a model in government, especially in New England. The church and state were one in Greece and Rome, and Rome dominated the world for centuries. The Reformation proposed no change in this regard, concerning itself solely with the kind of religion the state should foster. When America was settled, only in Holland and in sections of Switzerland was there anything known but state churches.

By this union of church and state, the religious and political elements were identified. Accordingly, ecclesiastical non-conformity and theological heresy seemed to be political disloyalty, to be punished as any other crime or rebellion. This explains why force was so long used in connection with religion; the religious and political had not been differentiated. When Separatists appeared they broke across the universal Protestant principle; and that they suffered for it is the most natural thing in the world.

In Virginia the Baptists and Presbyterians, with the aid of such free-thinkers as Jefferson and Madison, waged an uncompromising war on the established church, and secured religious liberty to the state in 1785. Several religious bodies, scattered here and there, made varying contribution to the liberty of conscience, but the larger influence was exerted by the Quakers and the Baptists. The Baptists were everywhere, and they did more active work than any other denomination. To them belongs the chief credit. While Virginia did much for the cause, it hardly equals that of New York whose constitution of 1777 provided liberty of conscience. In this New York owed much to the Dutch, and the special charter granted them by William III.

Two chief influences gave liberty of conscience to America; humanism and the Bible. Humanism was represented by such men as Jefferson and Madison; but all the free-thinking influence in the country could not have secured it, either in Virginia or the nation, but for the enormous assistance of the Biblical influences that were in the majority.

The Constitution of the United States, as originally adopted, contained these words: "No religious test shall ever be required as a qualification to any office or public trust under the United States." [1] The first amendment to the Constitution, adopted in 1791, makes further provision in these words: "Congress shall make no law respecting an establishment of religion, or prohibiting the free exercise thereof." This amendment, together with the article of the original Constitution, quoted above, provide for religious liberty, and what is commonly called "the separation of church and state."

Contrary to much popular opinion, the Federal Constitution, as originally adopted, and its first amendment, places limitation on the power of Congress only. Congress can make no law establishing a national religion, nor can it make any religious tests, as qualifications for holding office or positions of trust under the Federal Government; but the Constitution does not provide that the various states of the Union may not do so. Religious affairs are left entirely to the control of the states. Certain states had established churches when the Constitution was adopted, and continued to maintain them for some years. Connecticut removed all restrictions to a free exercise of religion in 1820, and Massachusetts did so in 1833. But New Hampshire today does not permit Roman Catholics to teach in her public schools.

The growth of public sentiment favorable to liberty of conscience and the separation of church and state, when the Constitution was formed, was making the state churches increasingly unpopular; no state without one dared to establish any church; while the states with such churches soon abolished them. In the gradual development of the relations of the church to the various states of the Union, the principles of liberty of conscience have prevailed. Many states have laws, constitutional or statutory, that govern; and where no law forbids state churches, public opinion, stronger than any law, governs. In the American political system all church relations are voluntary and without political penalty. The various states are expected to see that it is so. "This obligation of American civil governments is now confirmed by a public opinion which has been gaining strength through four generations and is now generally accepted without controversy. It is now expressed in a series of guarantees and limitations contained in the organic law of several commonwealths, in a well-developed system of statute legislation providing definite legal procedure covering many ecclesiastical relations, and in a body of notable judicial decisions rendered by

[14] Article VI, Sec. 3.

the civil courts of last resort defining under ever changing circumstances what shall be the relation of the church and state." [15] This situation is the logical outgrowth of liberty of conscience. The same influences that provided this, gave us also the separation of church and state, the religious predominating.

America has not only separated church and state, but it has demonstrated that those who enjoy Christianity will best sustain it with their voluntary offerings; claims for its support are based solely on its own excellence. And we have also learned that man's opinions cannot be coerced; his professions only may be forced, and to do so is only to make him a hypocrite.

"The organized hostility to foreigners and Catholics which for a few years thrust itself upon state and national politics was a localized episode due primarily to the economic menace of masses of ignorant immigrants and to the belief that the Catholic Church was a political as well as a religious power, and before the Civil War the agitation had disappeared." [16]

Another advance in the government of America was its guaranteed freedom of speech and the press. In 1732 the *Weekly Journal*, published in New York, ventured to criticize the arbitrary acts of the governor and the assembly, in imposing illegal taxes. This was the first time a newspaper had dared to criticize political measures. Governor Crosby imprisoned the editor, John Peter Zenger, and prosecuted him for libel. The editor was defended by the liberty loving and Christian lawyer, Andrew Hamilton, from Philadelphia, who was a Quaker. In spite of great odds against him, he won a verdict of acquittal; and freedom of the press was started on its way.[17] This was thirty-seven years before such principle was established in England. The first amendment to the Federal Constitution, adopted 1791, provided that Congress could pass no law "abridging the freedom of speech or of the press."

Freedom of religion protects the conscience; the freedom of speech and the press protects the mind; and freedom of the ballot, which America also enjoys, protects the suffrage. These are all, in their deepest essence, thoroughly Christian. In fact, our whole political system is based on the equality of all men, a Bible doctrine. It was General Grant who said, "Hold fast to the Bible as the sheet-anchor of your liberties." Horace Greely bore similar testimony, when he

---

[15] *The New Schaff-Herzog Encyclopedia of Religious Knowledge*, Vol. III, p. 110.
[16] MacDonald, *Three Centuries of American Democracy*, p. 299.
[17] Jackman, *History of the American Nation*, Vol. I pp 221-22.

declared that "the principles of the Bible are the groundwork of human freedom."

International Relations Increasingly Christian

The moral principles of Jesus Christ are making themselves felt more and more in our international relations. The Monroe Doctrine is an example. While much of the foreign policy of the United States cannot be defended, other parts of it mark a decided improvement in a Christian direction. The Monroe Doctrine has been a vast benefit to South and Central America, and has served to protect them from the fate that befell Africa. While some incidents in connection with it are indefensible, it is one of the established policies of our country that has almost universal approval.

America's treatment of Cuba and Porto Rico, while not all it might have been, has been outstanding as an advance in Christian principles and ideals. Our treatment of the Philippines has been something entirely new under the sun. President McKinley, in annexing these islands, announced America's purpose: "The Philippines are ours not to exploit but to develop, to civilize, to educate, to train in the science of self-government." And under American rule marvelous advance has been made in these islands, in every field of activity—public health, agriculture, justice, finance, self-government. An outstanding service has been rendered by the American educational system. In 1900 no children were in school; today the first building of every village and town is a school house. Now final provision has been made for their complete independence. In its dealings with the Philippines the United States has displayed an impressive sense of stewardship and brotherhood.

In its treatment of China, at the conclusion of the Boxer insurrection, in 1901, the United States government did something entirely new in such matters, dealing most generously with China, while other nations demanded their pound of flesh and took it to the limit. After a reasonable award had been made, the United States Senate passed a resolution, January 15, 1908, remitting $13,000,000 of the indemnity, and in June, 1924 all further payments were remitted—an entirely new note in international diplomacy.

Under a misapprehension of the real character of war, it has long been felt to be necessary. It has been supposed that war was simply the use of force for worthy ends; and it cannot well be denied that it is sometimes necessary to use force for righteous purposes.

But whatever may be said of the past, modern war is not the use of force, but its flagrant abuse. It is a resort to brute force, reinforced by cunning and guile. These are essential; war can not be waged successfully today without deceiving the people with lying propaganda.

The Christian conscience of the world is now so developed that few nations will longer admit responsibility for war; usually they are very careful to put the blame on others. Everywhere there is lying and deception. This is because the nations recognize the increasing sensitiveness of men's consciences on the subject, and are afraid of what might happen if the truth were known. Nations are afraid of what their own people might do; and they usually have some regard for their standing among other peoples. Therefore, they deceive their own people and mislead the rest of the world, to the extent of their ability. That such is felt necessary by those who would wage war, is an indication of great moral progress among the masses.

Perhaps the church never made a greater blunder than when it threw itself into the World War and made itself, next to the daily press, the most powerful agency in repeating the lying propaganda that fed the flames of hatred, and without which modern war cannot be successfully waged. Possibly just this was needed to show the church the utter depravity of all war. Anyhow, one of the most recent and powerful tendencies of Christianity is its growing hostility to war. Until recently only Quakers and Mennonites had set themselves against it resolutely; but the World War has opened the eyes of the world to the fact that war is utterly unchristian. Both Protestants and Catholics have declared that international affairs should be settled on principles of the Gospel. Ministers and churches everywhere are renouncing war. Nowhere is the influence of Christianity showing itself more today than in this growth of opposition to all war. We see it in the sentiment favoring arbitration in international disputes, the Hague conferences, the establishment of the Permanent Court of International Justice, the demand for the reduction of armaments, the Bryan treaties and the Kellogg Pact.

The highest achievement in this direction in modern times was the establishment of the League of Nations. President Wilson's advocacy of the idea during the last year of the war, made him the dominant moral leader of the world. But personal and political enemies defeated the entrance of America into the League. So far

America has been denied participation in either the League of Nations or the World Court, by a group of United States senators who are quite anxious always to demand equal privilege; but who are not willing to accept commensurate responsibilities. Rights alone concern these men; they feel no sense of duty or responsibility for others. Such selfishness is wholly unchristian.

The League of Nations is a daring and Christian experiment, in an effort to end all war. It is not perfect, but it can be improved as nations learn. Its full power can never be known until all nations take part. The idea for which it stands is growing. Some day war will be abolished, and Christianity and the Bible will be chiefly responsible.

If we would get back to the beginning of the idea of abolishing all war, we will find it in the Bible—the Old Testament. No less than three outstanding prophet-statesmen of that ancient day predict that the implements of war will some day be made into the implements of peace, and that war will cease, as a triumph of righteousness and goodwill.[18] For ages these prophetic ideas have been thought to be visionary and impractical. Only since the World War has mankind, in any considerable numbers, come to realize the real character of war, and the absolute necessity for its outlawry, if modern civilization is to be preserved.

E. INDUSTRY AND LABOR

Wherever the Gospel went it found the laboring man a slave. Mommsen calculated that three-fifths of the Roman population were slaves—human beings without families, without possessions, without rights.

It is true that Jesus Christ said no word about the evils of slavery, and the early church made no effort to end it, a fact that has puzzled many good people. But Jesus showed His superior wisdom in the course He took. He might have led an anti-slavery agitation; but it could have accomplished little or no good then; and it would inevitably have invited needless embarrassment in matters of more importance, at that time. Even if He could have liberated all slaves in His day, they were in no sense ready to profit by their freedom. It was not the method of Jesus to launch programs, but to plant principles. Accordingly, He left a new sense of human values and a new spirit of brotherhood—a little leaven that would eventually

[18] Isaiah 2:2-4.; Micah 4:2-5; Joel 3:9-13.

leaven the whole lump. Programs must be changed from time to time, to fit new conditions; they are soon out of date. Principles live forever; that is why Jesus is never out of date.

In the new society which Jesus founded all the old disabilities were abolished. As the Apostle Paul conceived it, "There can be neither Jew nor Greek, there can be neither bond nor free, there can be no male and female; for ye are all one." The new unity transcended all the old distinctions.

Slavery involved a contempt for labor; Jesus dignified labor. He was himself a carpenter, several of the apostles were fishermen, and Paul was a tentmaker. The first dignity ever conferred upon labor was by those under the influence of the Old Testament; nowhere is Christianity and paganism in sharper contrast than here, for one dignified labor, and the other made it a disgrace.

Christian Principles Aided by Humanism Abolished Slavery in Europe

It was once supposed that Christianity alone abolished slavery. In reaction from this extreme view, many came to conclude that it was wholly an economic process, with which Christianity had nothing to do. Both views are incorrect. Economic influences have had a part in the matter; both Stoicism and Humanism made their contribution; but Christianity was the more powerful influence.

Those under the influence of the Bible have always shown a marked contrast in their attitude toward the slave. Among the ancient Hebrews and Jews slaves fared better than anywhere else in the world at the time. Christianity mitigated their condition from the very beginning. There was a change in spirit; masters displayed a new kindness, and slaves became more faithful. The early influence of Christianity may be seen in the fact that by 140 A. D., one Pius, the bishop of Rome, had risen from slavery; and he was not the only slave-bishop Rome ever had. The cynic Lucian said, "The legislator of the Christians has persuaded them that they are all brothers." The process of the slaves' elevation was slow and not uniform; but monasticism finally assailed it, and made the chief contribution to its overthrow in the Middle Ages. Monasticism was influenced by the Bible.

Near the middle of the eighteenth century two distinct new movements arose, both of which had powerful influence. In France slavery was attacked on philosophical grounds; Rousseau's philosophy of the rights of man did much. Under his influence the French Convention, in 1794, decreed that negro slavery should be abolished in all the French colonies, the first European country to take such action. About the same time there arose in England a powerful movement that attacked slavery on purely Christian grounds; and under this influence England abolished slavery in all her dominions.

The Bible the Chief Influence in Abolishing Slavery in America

The history of African slavery is a blot on American Christianity; yet it was opposed in America from the beginning. Georgia, in her early history, has the distinction of being the only colony that was anti-slavery. The Massachusetts legislature condemned it in 1641. John Eliot, the Indian missionary, opposed it, and the Mennonites and Quakers condemned it. As it grew all the churches everywhere came to array themselves against it, and slavery had no defenders in the church until about 1820.

In 1820 Missouri was admitted to the Union as a slave state. The matter had been agitated for two whole years, and slavery was defended only by extension politicians on the ground of expediency and convenience or for constitutional reasons. American Christianity immediately took alarm, and began a vigorous opposition. Having made Missouri slave territory, the politicians thought to sweep the country. They resolved to introduce it into Illinois, Indiana and Ohio; but were defeated largely by ministers of the Baptist and Methodist churches. This plan of the politicians provoked Christian people to action everywhere, and efforts to thwart it became widespread. This work was led in Tennessee and Kentucky by Presbyterians and Quakers. In North Carolina and Maryland the church people were aroused; in fact, abolition sentiment became widespread through the influence of the churches. In Virginia, as late as 1831, a memorable debate was held in the legislature on the question of abolishing it in that state. Up to this time there was no division in the church on the question,[19] and there was an utter absence of sectional division. Everywhere the church unitedly opposed slavery.

Then a strange thing happened. Somewhere about 1833, the Rev. James Smylie, a Presbyterian minister, made the remarkable "discovery" that slavery was a divine institution, so set forth in the Scriptures. He proved it, to his own satisfaction at least, and to the satisfaction of many others, by his skillful interpretation and manipu-

[19] Bacon, *History of American Christianity*, pp. 268-85.

lation of certain parts of the Bible. In some strange way, but in an incredibly short time, the whole church of the South accepted Smylie's conclusions, with some exceptions in Tennessee and Kentucky. Slavery was vindicated; and Bible defenses of slavery poured from the press. In the South dissent from the new view was suppressed with the vigor of the Inquisition.

This sudden and almost complete "Southern Apostacy" is not easily explained. How so large a constituency of Christian people could so completely reverse themselves in so short a time, is difficult to understand. Bacon,[20] thinks the chief cause was the fear of negro uprisings. It was felt that the continued agitation in favor of abolishing slavery encouraged them. In 1831 an insurrection had been led in Virginia by Nat Turner, a crazy negro; and this had been followed by a bloody vengeance on the part of the whites. The South wanted no more uprisings, and were terrified at the danger. So when Smylie offered his supposed proof of the divine right of slavery, the whole southern church adopted it, in justification of their action in stopping agitation on the subject. Perhaps there is much truth in this explanation.

The North now began to develop a certain opposition to abolition, partly out of sympathy with the South, in its danger of insurrection, and in part due to the fear of disunion, now freely talked, if the agitation was continued.

In abolishing slavery, as in all great reforms, many forces made their contribution. The wrath of man as well as the love of God is sometimes intermingled; and so it was with slavery. The matter was badly managed. The northern abolitionists used bad judgment and pressed their cause with more heat than light, needlessly engendering much bitterness. Reformers are often in too big a hurry and nowhere did they ever blunder more in this respect. They created a situation out of which the Civil War came, resulting finally in abolishing slavery as a "war measure." In estimating the influences responsible, however, the chief credit must be given Christianity, for it was the anti-slavery feeling, based on the supreme value of every soul and the brotherhood of man, Bible doctrines, that made possible the final result.

Capitalism Not Sacrosanct

Capitalism with its modern methods goes back only to the Refor-

[20] *History of American Christianity*, pp. 277-85.

mation, and is, therefore, comparatively young. It marked a distinct advance in the onward march of the race, bringing a marvelous development and consequent widespread prosperity. In 1769 James Watts harnessed steam and set it to work for humanity. Previous to this manufacturing had been done in villages and in the homes of the people wherever they lived. Large factories now began to spring up in the cities, drawing men from the country to do their work. The cities at once showed an amazing growth. This soon reshaped the conditions under which the masses of humanity lived; two classes were created, with a wide gulf between them, the employer and the wage earner. Great evils resulted, for strange to say, modern poverty begins just here. It originated when man, for the first time, had really made it possible to escape poverty. Large scale organizations, entirely impersonal, sprang up everywhere for conducting business and hiring labor, "soulless corporations"; and individualism ran riot. The most serious evils of the system were not felt so keenly in America, as long as there was plenty of new land to be taken up; but when the country had been settled from coast to coast, the more glaring evils began to appear.

A society where a few men, with little effort or none, have all the blessings of life, while the great mass have little but squalor and misery, regardless of how much effort they put forth, is not ideal. Wealth concentrated in a few hands possesses enormous power, and may easily dominate the life of the nation. Moreover, it is dangerous. Some day a limit will be set to the amount of a man's wealth; justice and the brotherhood of man will require it, as will the very safety of the nation.

The greatest menace to our country today is not the radical and the "red," so systematicaly and regularly played up in specially prepared propaganda, as a smoke screen, but the respectable and predatory rich, whose greed has blinded them even to their own best interests. The liquor business of the United States brought prohibition by its own recklessness and utter disregard for the rights of others; and capital, by its stubborn disregard for human values, justice and fair play, threatens the safety of the nation more than any other present danger.

The feudal system belonged to a stage of human development; and capitalism, with its industrial and commercial systems, may be stages of development only. In any case, there is need for wise measures to curb the present system, or to modify it. If these are not sufficient then it must be supplanted, in the interest of the masses. The economic struggles of modern society are religious struggles, which must find their solution in the principles of Jesus Christ. There is need, however, for something more than economic change; the spirit of Jesus Christ is required. Nothing else takes the selfishness out of men.

Democracy Grows as Christian Principles Are Better Understood

The Reformation gave a new and powerful impulse to modern democracy, which may be said to have been completely born in the Declaration of Independence in 1776, and in the French Revolution of 1789. But democracy, first considered wholly political, is found to be social as well. In fact, it is found to be as broad as life itself. Democracy grows directly in proportion as Christian principles are better understood. For long years industry and labor were regarded as matters entirely of private concern; men were considered to have the right to do as they pleased with their own. But society is now rapidly coming to realize that industry is one of the major social institutions of the land. The whole trend of modern thought and legislation is a recognition of this fact. Democracy has some of its roots in the Renaissance, and in the doctrines of the rights of man, as popularized by such men as Voltaire, Rousseau and Thomas Paine; but Christianity, with its emphasis on individual responsibility, and the brotherhool of man, must be accorded the profounder influence. It is certainly the better understanding of Christian principles that gives its broader application today.

Christianity Committed to Principles Rather than Programs

Christianity, like its founder, is not committed to programs, but rather to principles. Communism is a definite program that seeks to right the evils of the present economic and industrial order. As a theoretical system it appeared first among the Greeks, the "Republic of Plato" being the most famous example.

The New Testament has been supposed to teach communism; but to understand the early church at Jerusalem as a communistic society is a grave mistake. Only such as desired to do so, sold their possessions for the benefit of others. The idea of communism, however, has had more or less place among Christians from very early times; it was a common idea throughout the Middle Ages. The Waldenses and certain other religious bodies had strong tendencies in that direction. Many Anabaptists held communistic views, especially the Moravian Anabaptists.

America from its very beginning has abounded in communistic experiments. Jamestown in Virginia began with a common storehouse; the Pilgrims, for a time, maintained some communistic features. The Shakers, the Harmonists, the Icarians and the Amana Society were transplanted from other countries. Owenism, Fourierism, Cabetism and Marxism have all been tried here, and Brook Farm left its imprint on literature. Religion was made the center of some of these experiments, while others were only social and economic. Of early organizations only the Shakers and the Oneida Community remain. The Amana Society in Iowa has now completely changed the fundamental character of its experiment. Communism has always failed in the United States.

Socialism also seeks to right existing wrongs. While many men have tried to present socialism as basically Christian, the popular literature of the movement is very largely anti-Christian. Both socialism and communism, which is socialism in its extreme form, have become largely antagonistic to the church as in Russia.

"Christian Socialism" is a term that was first used in 1848 by J. F. D. Maurice, a clergyman in the English Church. He considered socialism as an outcome of Christianity, which to be effective required a Christian basis. Under the leadership of Maurice and Charles Kingsley, the ideas they taught made considerable headway in England. Out of their efforts numerous cooperative societies were developed, which prospered in a remarkable degree; and their teachings have been the seed of many valuable reforms in England.

The influence of these men bore some fruit in America. An organization called the Society of Christian Socialists was launched in Boston in 1889, due largely to the leadership of W. D. P. Bliss. Its constitution emphasized the stewardship of property, the fatherhood of God and the brotherhood of man, and criticised the present social order. Though the idea took little root in America, such journals as *The Outlook, The Kingdom* and *The Christian Statesman* all advocated Christian Socialism more or less.

One difficulty with both socialism and communism is that they expect entirely too much from purely economic changes. Man does not live by bread alone. The socialistic and communistic experiments that had a religious foundation always lasted longer than those which did not. Those who do battle for a just social system make a mistake when they push religion aside. If the Bible be true, no economic

change alone will save this world; and programs that lack adequate
spiritual foundations are, therefore, necessarily unsatisfactory. Christianity must preserve certain spiritual values generally ignored in
the literature of these movements.

The world, however, dreams of social and economic reconstruction,
both saint and sinner, and it is coming. No power can prevent it.
The alternative that faces the world today is socialism in some form,
or the kingdom of God. If the church will not build the kingdom,
the other will ultimately be forced on us.

Christianity is not committed to any definite system of betterment
or social control. Institutions grow and change and pass. What concerns Christianity is the spirit that animates these institutions; with
the right spirit, institutions will shape themselves to fit the spiritual
needs of the age. Christianity, therefore, instead of committing itself
to definite programs, would provide principles to guide in their
formation. One of the greatest contributions to a social interpretation and application of Christianity ever made by any man, was made
in America, by Walter Rauschenbusch of the Rochester Theological
Seminary. His books have contributed powerfully to a better understanding of the Bible and Christianity. No other one writer has done
so much to popularize the "social Gospel."

The church is rapidly recognizing its social obligations. Such marvelous progress in this direction has been made within recent years
that today practically the entire church—Protestant, Catholic and
Jewish—is officially committed to principles that must inevitably lead
to a reconstruction of the social and industrial order.

In 1908, the Federal Council of the Churches of Christ in America,
representing thirty denominations with a constituency of some 24,-
000,000 Christians, adopted a "Social Creed" at the first Quadrennial
Meeting held in Philadelphia; and since the World War this "creed"
has been made broader and more explicit. This "Social Creed" may
be said to be the platform of practically the entire Protestant Church
in the United States.

A group of Roman Catholic bishops in America published a joint
statement that was outspoken in its championship of the workingman. Pope Leo XIII, in 1891, issued his historical Letter on "The
Condition of Labor." Pope Pius XI, in 1931, issued an Encyclical
Letter on "Reconstructing the Social Order." These are highly important documents, indicating the increasing social mindedness of
the Roman Catholic Church.

No people among us has shown more progress in social thinking than the Jews. Their social ideas have been expressed by the Central Conference of American Rabbis, the Union of American Hebrew Congregations, and the Rabbinical Assembly of America.

In all its history the church has never been so thoroughly committed to a reconstruction of the social order on the principles of Jesus Christ. Political economy, somebody has said, is being rewritten on the principles of the Sermon on the Mount. It was the advanced thinking of the church—Protestant, Catholic and Jewish—that made it possible for the Federal Government to pass a Social Security Act, one of the greatest forward steps ever taken in American legislation. This act, now the law of the land, provides unemployment compensation, old age pensions, aid to dependent children, state maternal and child-welfare services, aid to the blind, the extension of public health services and vocational rehabilitation. It is highly significant that federal legislation for more than three years past has touched almost every modern pronouncement of the churches, seeking to make them operative in the nation's life. That there should be opposition to any advanced social program on the part of the government is inevitable; progress has always been denounced as a prodigal son.

The church has often been accused of utter inability to understand social wrongs and hopes, of leaving the under-dog to fight his battles alone. There has been much truth in the accusation in the past, but such is no longer the case. There has been for several years, in the church, a steadily rising curve of active interest in social problems, and a widening and deepening of social consciousness. There has been a rediscovery of the inherently social nature of the Christian religion. On all sides the social thinking of the church has become vocal with demands for social change in the ethically vulnerable areas of social life. Much of the criticism of the church since the steel strike of 1919, has come from a very different source. Many rich reactionaries have become alarmed at what the church might do, and at what they know the church must do, when it once sets itself fully to the task of making this world into the kingdom of God. From many sources it is now thought the church is too radical; many resent the fact that ministers have anything to do with politics, simply because they stand for the application of Christian principles to our social and industrial relations.

The church, true to ideals of the Master, will rely on evangelization, education and the irresistible leavening power of cooperative Christian fellowship, and will not be betrayed into the short-range methods of coercion and violence in its work of building the kingdom of God, relying rather on the long-range methods of persuasion, education and fellowship which always win in the end.

The church has often blundered. It has been slow to learn. Valuable years were largely wasted in unhappy and fruitless controversies. It has set undue value on the relatively unimportant. But at last the church is coming to see that its real mission in the world is to transform the social order into the kingdom of God. It is, therefore, today that the Bible is beginning to win its most enduring success, in its contribution to the problems of the social order. The very ability of the church to readjust itself and its message to the changing thought and conditions, in order to meet new needs, is one of the evidences of its vitality.

F. COMMUNITY AND ASSOCIATION

Community and associated life in America is abundantly provided with institutions both secular and religious that render a wide variety of service. Nowhere has non-ecclesiastical Christianity made a greater growth and development.

There were no philanthropic institutions in pre-Christian times, likewise no organized charity. Institutions for charitable purposes developed slowly among Christians, because there was no early need for such; the various Christian congregations were able to meet their need in such matters without them. These conditions, however, were all changed in the fourth century, as a result of the adoption of Christianity by Constantine. A widespread need soon arose; and institutions then sprang up to meet it, and so continued through the succeeding ages.

Basil the Great founded the most complete hospital up to his time, 330-379 A.D., providing even the leper and the stranger. At Antioch, during Chrisostom's activity, about 380 A.D., there existed a hospital for the sick and a house for the poor. The first person to build a hospital in Rome was Fabiola, a convert of Jerome. Jerome had previously built one at Bethlehem. In every well arranged monastery there came to be a hospital, and cathedrals everywhere came to have them. The Roman Catholic church has made, and continues to make, a tremendous contribution to such work. Protestant churches also render a splendid hospital service.

As early as the ninth century a brotherhood for nursing the sick was formed in Italy, and during the crusades their numbers increased greatly and spread all over Europe. In the seventeenth century there was created at Breese, France, an organization for the relief of suffering, called "Servants of the Poor." Others formed were known as "Lazarites," "Sisters of Charity," etc. Women had been trained to deeds of charity even before this time, and the great sisterhoods devoted to such work today began to be formed as early as the twelfth century. Woman, as symbolized by the trained nurse, has proved the greatest humanitarian of modern times. Modern nursing originated with Florence Nightingale.

Christianity Has Fructified the World

Law, state-craft and diplomacy, medicine, literature and philanthropy, as well as education, were all once the almost exclusive work of the church. Four have already passed into other hands; and education and philanthropy are passing to the state. These are examples of how Christianity has overflown its original bounds and fructified the world. Today poor relief is largely the work of the state or city, but is greatly supplemented by public charity. This work assumes gigantic proportions in America. Hospitals are provided extensively by the state and municipality, while many distinctly Christian hospitals continue to serve. The genuine Christianity of the world outside the church gains in volume and momentum as time passes. It is the humanitarian spirit generated by the Gospel of Jesus Christ that furnishes the chief inspiration for the numerous philanthropic and social efforts that bless the modern world.

Institutions Originating in America

In America the church took the lead and set the example of philanthropic and humanitarian work and reforms. Many today engaged in such work decline to be known as Christians; but most of them were cradled in the church.

While hospitals did not originate in America, a distinct contribution in this work has been made here; the field of such endeavor in America is the broadest and most promising in the world, because here it was not hampered by historic evolution as it was elsewhere. In Europe the old monastic institutions required to be adapted to modern work. The modern hospital—an institution devoted exclusively to the care of the sick—was developed in the eighteenth century. Until then even London's only hospitals had been adapted from medieval monastic establishments, institutions that did much more than care for the sick. Its function, however, is being greatly enlarged. It now trains the hospital personnel—laboratory workers, nurses, physicians, dieticians, and others. The modern hospital is being made a powerful factor in the program of social improvement.

America has the distinction of founding the first hospital in the world for the treatment of the insane; this was done by the Quakers in Pennsylvania in 1768. In 1791 such work was begun in England by William Tuke and by Pinel in France. Previous to this the insane had been considered to be devil-possessed and treated as such.

Hospitals abound in America. In most of the large cities of the United States are institutions under city control, and used for the city poor. Such are the Massachusetts General Hospital and Boston City Hospital of Boston; the Philadelphia Hospital of Philadelphia; and Bellevue and Allied Hospitals of New York city. There are many state hospitals where the poor receive service at public expense. Many hospitals exist for the treatment of particular diseases—for diseases of the eye, ear, nose and throat; cancer hospitals; maternity hospitals; hospitals for the diseases of women; for the diseases of the skin; for tuberculosis and various other ailments. Asylums, almshouses and homes are everywhere, for the insane, the feeble-minded, the epileptic, orphans, foundlings, the aged and helpless, and the incurable. All are distinctly Christian in origin. Numerous other institutions exist to serve the country; homes for the rescue and reformation of fallen women, for truant boys and girls, and for drunken men before prohibition.

It was Bible-inspired America, the "half-brother of the world," somebody has called it, who created the Near East Relief, to serve the Armenians in their hour of supreme need. This is the most outstanding instance of private and Christian charity in the world's history. The United States raised among its own people more than one hundred millions of dollars, and more than ten millions elsewhere, for this glorious work; the money being given for this important service by the whole American people. Canada responded generously, and other countries in a small way. Never was money raised in such fabulous amounts in a private charity, with such ease and at so little expense; never did the world see such an army of cheerful givers. It was all because the Bible had prepared America for such service.

The charity of the United States government has been unparalleled, and possible only in a Christian nation. Feeding the Belgians and others of war-torn Europe may be called a government charity. At the outbreak of the World War, the American Relief Commission in Belgium was organized with Herbert Hoover at the head. Depots for the collection of supples were established in every state in the Union. It is estimated that more than 9,000,000 people in Belgium and northern France were clothed and fed by this Commission, which raised a total of approximately $500,000,000 to November 1918. The money was given by the people of America and other nations.

After the armistice Mr. Hoover returned to Europe, at the request of President Wilson, to confer with the various governments as to the best methods of providing provisions for the allied and enemy countries. The American Relief Administration was established, and this organization, through the European Children's Fund, established by Mr. Hoover, fed more than 6,000,000 children, providing also housing, etc. In 1919 Mr. Hoover was requisitioned again to feed the dependent children of Europe, and expended over $100,000,000 in this work.

Great credit is due Mr. Hoover for these services, which covered a period of about nine years, and for which he received no compensation. Only a genuinely Christian man would have played the part he did; and only a nation inspired by the Bible would have backed him so extensively in the work.

The Volunteers of America is a philanthropic, social and Christian movement organized in New York in 1896, whose work is primarily in the poorer sections of our cities. It does much for prisoners on their release from confinement through its "Hope Halls," and renders a wide variety of much needed service. Released prisoners are also served by the Society for the Friendless, which has done much to rehabilitate thousands of men.

No institution is more distinctly American, and none more thoroughly Christian than the Chautauqua, which had its inception in the fertile brain of Dr. John H. Vincent, a bishop of the Methodist Episcopal church. The work began at Chautauqua, New York, beside a lake from which the movement took its name. Originating as a Sunday School Teacher's Normal Institute in 1874, it was so rapidly expanded that within four years a complete system of popular education was developed. It always provided a summer assembly, but soon extended its work throughout the year.

In a modified form it became a traveling institution and was carried to all the United States and Canada, held generally in tents at suitable seasons; thus becoming the most characteristic institution

J. M. POWIS SMITH

of American civilization. It became a public forum for the discussion of moral, social, religious and political questions; the one platform accessible alike to the Jews, Roman Catholics and Protestants. It contributed greatly to a better understanding of social problems, broader toleration and higher ideals. Bacon, in his *History of the American Christianity* [21] traces the traveling chautauqua to the backwoods camp-meeting, another distinctly American institution, that rendered a noble service in its day. There is, however, no connection between these, only a certain similarity.

The traveling chautauqua had a phenomenal growth, confined chiefly to towns of five thousand population or less. At one time its programs were put on in no less than ten thousand communities. Many of them drew attendance from fifty miles away; the people coming to camp on the grounds for a period of days, during which sessions were held mornings, afternoons and evenings. Lectures on the Bible held an important place. In fact, the chautauqua originally consisted of a well organized and balanced group of lectures on the most vital themes, Biblical, moral, social, economic and political. These lectures were garnished with a bit of music and other forms of entertainment as preludes, with few hours of program that did not contain a lecture.

Why a movement so popular and so valuable as chautauqua should have died is not generally understood. Radio did not kill it; it was dead before radio came in any satisfactory form. Neither did the depression end it. The story of its death is interesting, and it throws a side-light on American character.

As has been said, the lecture constituted the heart of the movement. The most popular of its lecturers were men, or even women, with messages in advance of the times. These lecturers were utterly unfettered in their delivery; they spoke their minds freely without let or hindrance, regardless of whose ideas were contradicted. Nothing delighted the average audience quite so much as the lecturer, often a galvanic battery on two legs, who tore into cherished notions ruthlessly, and who presented something new, but too far in advance of the times to be acceptable then. It provided a peculiar thrill to be able to discuss such lectures with members of the audience afterward, and often to refute its argument and cuss the lecturer; and the people gladly paid their good money year after year for just such thrills. This was in the days of the original and independent chautauqua, a time when each town selected its own talent. These were the palmiest days of the movement.

[21] pp 233-34.

Then came the circuit chautauqua. The bureau now selected the talent, which was unfortunate. It lessened the town's interest a bit to be unable to select talent for its own programs. But the circuit chautauqua provided a program of equal merit at half the former price, because they abolished so much loss of time for the entertainers, and ended the long and expensive travel. Naturally it soon won the field. Contracts for chautauqua had always been signed only a few months in advance of their dates; and the bureaus now discovered that they could save considerable expense, if they could sell the chautauqua for the next season while in session. The superintendent, therefore, sought his contract for the next year while the people were enjoying their annual thrill of cussing and discussing the lectures that had criticised the present order, and advocated advanced steps. Nobody cared to sign a contract a whole year in advance; they had never been asked to do so previously, and could see no reason why they should be asked to do so now. There was plenty of time for that. Besides, they were having the time of their lives, telling one another how rotten certain lectures had been, and they did not want to be bothered with matters of business. With great difficulty signatures were secured, and not infrequently the effort resulted in complete failure. This non-plussed the superintendent, whose interpretation of the situation was that the people declined to sign the new contract simply because the lectures had proved utterly unsatisfactory. They so wrote the bureaus, which unfortunately accepted such explanation, and immediately set about to change the character of the lectures.

Certain types of lecture were discarded at once. Lecturers thought to be safe were now required to hand in their lectures, in typewritten form for suggestions. They were generously blue-penciled and handed back, with instructions to deliver them as corrected. Soon the chautauqua was provided with lectures that contained no single idea or expression to which anybody could possibly take an exception. When they had thus been emasculated, nobody would cross the street to hear one of them. Very soon hundreds of chautauquas were put on without a single lecture during the session; music and other forms of entertainment providing the whole program. Chautauqua promptly died—because the very heart had been taken out of it.

The same characteristic of the American people may be seen in the radio audiences of today. Outside the President of the United States, who would naturally have a large audience in any event, the biggest radio audiences of America have heard such men as Bob

Shuler of California, Father Coughlin of Detroit, and Huey Long of Louisiana. Many people hear such men, not because they believe what they say, but because they are live wires with something to say, and speak unhampered. America likes the unconventional.

Only one other major influence was concerned in the death of the chautauqua, but it was by far the lesser of the two. During the days of the independent chautauqua numerous big assemblies had been developed, drawing support from a wide territory. Thinking to increase its popularity, and incidentally to augment the profits, the circuit chautauqua bureaus soon put out programs suited in price to every little village and cross roads in the country. Three day chautauquas were sold as low as one hundred and fifty dollars. Naturally the talent of every sort offered on such programs was greatly lowered in quality. When nearly every little village had its own chautauqua, the people no longer patronized the larger assemblies further away as formerly. That injured them. This lowering of the grade of talent on so many programs helped to destroy interest in the whole institution. Thus the movement was killed by the mistakes of its friends. If chautauqua ever returns, it will be in something of its original form, chiefly a group of lectures that mean something. The American people are always glad to hear any man who really has something to say, and is on fire to say it.

Institutions Originating Elsewhere

One of the most powerful examples of non-ecclesiastical Christianity originating elsewhere and transplanted to America, may be seen in the omnipotent Red Cross. The Swiss government, in 1864, invited the representatives of several nations to hold a convention at Geneva, at which the Red Cross was launched, and promptly adopted by the civilized world. It was organized in the United States in 1881, with Clara Barton, who served until 1904, as president. This organization not only ministers to the army and navy, but gives relief in peace time, in national and international disasters. The whole movement is simply an expression of Christian sympathy and service.

No nation on earth has given such a splendid example of willingness to help in times of trouble as America—all due to the public sentiment created by the Bible. One needs but to recall the great disasters of the past: fire in Boston and Chicago; famine in Russia, China, India and elsewhere; epidemics of cholera and yellow fever; earthquakes in the Carolinas, Japan, Greece, San Francisco and Italy.

America has sent shipload after shipload of food stuff for free distribution among the starving of the world.

The Young Men's Christian Association originated in England in 1844 through the efforts of Sir George Williams, but its first Association in America was formed in Boston in 1851. This was rapidly followed by organizations in the other principal cities of the country, until today the movement covers the whole land.

Notable among its services was the part it played in the formation of the United States Christian Commission, which cared for the religious needs of the soldiers of the Civil War. This was first proposed by Vincent Colyer of New York in 1861, and taken up the same year by the Association. A commission was organized. Bibles, hymnals, tracts, religious books and newspapers were distributed through the armies, and much personal work done. The outstanding service it rendered during the World War can never be forgotten. Although seriously criticised, and for the most part unjustly, or for the acts of individuals, the organization proved true to its ideals.

The Young Woman's Christian Association had its beginning in the United States in 1858. Known under several different names for some years, it was at Boston in 1866 that it first took the name Young Woman's Christian Association. It arose in England in much the same way, beginning in 1855; it was first called the Young Woman's Christian Association in 1877; and the first international meeting was held in London in 1892. First called a "Prayer Union" in England and a "Union Prayer Circle" in America, the movement was distinctly Christian in origin, and has rendered an outstanding service in the development of a well-rounded Christian womanhood. Like the Young Men's Christian Association, it builds the body, trains the mind and strengthens the moral and spiritual forces of the young. No estimate can be placed on its value.

Among the institutions that have been transplanted to America is the Salvation Army. William Booth was a minister of the Methodist New Connection Church of England. He left this church to devote himself to evangelistic work, and in 1865 founded the Christian Mission in London. This work developed, in 1878, into the Salvation Army. It has had countless conversions among an element not reached by the churches; and its social salvage operations have won it a favorable place in the estimation of the whole world. The Army has done a splendid work in America.

Samuel Barnett, founder of Toynbee Hall, began the movement of Social Settlements in London in 1884. The object of this work was not charity, but Christian friendliness, its whole service animated by the spirit of Jesus Christ. The work has accomplished splendid results in America. Notable in the United States is the Social Settlement of Hull House, Chicago, opened by Jane Addams in 1889—America's first. The Social Settlements have done much to assist in the problems created by the large additions of European immigrants to our cities.

Non-ecclesiastical Christianity has had a phenominal growth in America; everywhere helping to make life worth living. All of it is based on the supreme value which Jesus Christ placed upon individual life, and the brotherhood of man. Societies by the hundred have been launched, for the prevention of cruelty to children; the prevention of cruelty to animals; the suppression of vice. Bible Societies, Tract Societies, and missionary societies abound.

Christianity has created in modern society "a great fund of altruistic feeling," which finds expression in public charity. To this extent the state has been Christianized. The burden of such work is larger than the church could carry; but the church has educated the masses to where there is a public demand for such things. It is all a triumph of Christian civilization, a testimony to the value of the Bible.

2. SOME INFLUENCES OF THE BIBLE HAVE BEEN UNFORTUNATE

The influence of the Bible on the whole has been profoundly beneficial, but it must be admitted that it has sometimes been quite unfortunate. It is not the fault of the Bible, however, that such has been the case. A pocket knife is a valuable instrument, but one may cut his finger with it. Very naturally the Bible has often been misunderstood and misapplied. Many mistakes have been made in its interpretation, both by individuals and by churches. What is known as the allegorical method of Biblical interpretation once held almost universal sway. It professed to see in every Scripture a three-fold sense—the corporeal, the physical and the spiritual. Scripture could be made to teach anything one wanted it to teach. Accordingly, for ages, the Bible was systematically tortured into teaching every conceivable fancy that men could conjure up. Fortunately most of such interpretations were entirely harmless, but wide of the truth. Many have given the Bible a very literal interpretation, disregarding the character of its literature, especially apocalyptic utterances. Naturally they missed the truth.

A. DANGER IN PRIVATE INTERPRETATION

The Roman Catholic Church and the Protestant Church differ in many things, but nowhere more widely than the place they assign the Bible, and in the right of its private interpretation. Roman Catholics consider that there is grave danger in giving the Bible to the people freely, especially without proper notes to guide in its understanding, and in the granting of the privilege of private interpretation. The New Testament recognizes this danger. Peter, in speaking of Paul's Epistles, says, "Wherein are some things hard to be understood, which the ignorant and unsteadfast wrest, as they do also the other Scriptures, unto their own destruction." [22]

The Roman Catholic Church, therefore, denies the right of private interpretation to its membership. By this means they think to avoid the dangers involved. They permit their people to have the Bible freely, in the vernacular, provided the translation has been properly approved by competent authorities, and proper notes accompany the text.

They do not regard Bible reading as a means of grace, on the same scale that Protestants do. Roman Catholics find Christ in the Mass; with them it is only through the sacraments that any soul can approach God. The Mass and the confessional are considered the chief means of grace. As they are everywhere within reach of all Catholics, from their standpoint, this is sufficient.

Protestants are not less aware of the danger of private interpretation than are Roman Catholics, but they accept the danger frankly and freely. They regard private interpretation as an individual right, which no man may deny his brother, and as having the best results in the end. While recognizing private interpretation as a grave risk, the Protestant believes that in that way only lies the highest development of the race. All life is fraught with danger; and religion can be no exception in the economy of God. It is all right to tell children what to do, but when manhood arrives childish things should be put away. God would develop our personality and character; He would have us become men; but we can become men of the highest type only by doing our own thinking, and making our own decisions. Many foolish things will be believed, even by the highest ecclesiastical authorities. Many mistakes will be made, but time tends to correct them. God in His infinite wisdom will continue to lead into truth those who honestly seek it. So reasons the Protestant.

[22] 2 Peter 3:16.

Protestants find Christ everywhere in the Scriptures, as the central fact of the Bible. Therefore, they regard Bible reading as one of the chief means of grace; for that reason they give the Bible to the people freely, without note or comment, expecting every man to use his best judgment in its understanding.

B. SOME EXAMPLES OF UNFORTUNATE USES OF THE BIBLE

The old time conception, once held well-nigh universally among Christians, that the Bible is the very Word of God, verbally dictated by the Lord himself and infallible in its every statement, has been responsible for more misuse of the Bible than all other influences put together. It was once supposed to contain the final word of revelation on every matter of which it spoke; and all its parts were supposed to be properly applicable to every age—certain ceremonial affairs only excepted.

The Bible Used to Support Glaring Evils

Therefore, with entire consistency, "Thou shalt not suffer a witch to live," [23] was made the basis of the persecution of witches, with all its horrors. This Scripture was the chief authority for the execution of witches everywhere; and it is only a modified conception of the Bible that can release the church from the obligation of witch hunting today. Changing the translation to "sorceress" does not affect the authority of the commandment. In the beautiful parable of the Great Supper, when they all began to make excuse for failure to attend, we read, "Compel them to come in." [24] This Scripture became the chief authority for the Inquisition, with all its horrors. The stories of the persecution of witches and that of the Inquisition could be written only with a pen dipped in blood and tears and yet it came legitimately from the old time conception and interpretation of the Bible. All the persecutions of Christians in America, as elsewhere, were supported always by quotations from the Bible.

Because the Bible has been supposed to contain a message for all ages, in all its parts, it has been used as a bulwark of war. Although Christianity was founded by the Prince of Peace, among the religions of the world, with the possible exception of Mohammedan-

[23] Exodus 22:18.
[24] Luke 14:23.

ism, none has been more devoted to Mars. The Old Testament with its war God, Jehovah, the holy wars of Israel, the imprecatory Psalms and other Scriptures, has provided a defense of war that has been powerful. Instead of seeing these things in their historical perspective, as belonging naturally to primitive times, what is said on the subject of war has been used to justify and glorify it, even down to modern times. But as the world better understands the Bible, it is changing its interpretation and application of these Scriptures.

One of the most surprising discoveries of the modern world was that slavery was a divine institution, so set forth in the Bible. By a skilful manipulation of certain Scriptures there was presented an argument in support of this novel position that powerfully appealed to slave owners. For a few years the idea held almost universal sway over the whole South; today it is relegated to the museum for the curious.

Among the unfortunate influences of the Bible has been its use in support of the idea of celibacy; the idea that there is something inherently unclean in married life. No more detestable and pernicious doctrine was ever advanced, nor could anything be further from the teachings of the New Testament.

The New Testament nowhere forbids marriage, nor does it anywhere even intimate that marriage is in any measure unholy. Some of the apostles were married,[25] and Paul recommended marriage to the heads of churches,[26] though there were circumstances under which he thought it best not to marry.[27] Legitimately interpreted, the New Testament nowhere exalts celibacy above marriage, because it is a purer state of mankind. However, very early in the church there developed such an idea, which grew into a perfect contempt for marriage. The idea that God's only provision for the reproduction of the race is by methods inherently unclean is a slander on God himself. As a matter of fact no relationship in life has so much power to ennoble and exalt as marriage; God created them male and female that they might find their highest and noblest development in union. It is only necessary to know the history of celibacy, the evil and scandal it has caused, to know that it is not of God.

The Bible Used to Oppose Normal Progress

The old time conception that the Bible contains the final word of revelation on every matter of which it speaks, equally applicable to

[25] Matt. 8:14; 1 Cor. 9:5.   [26] 1 Tim. 3:2.   [27] 1 Cor 7:26-28.

every age, betrayed the church into opposition to practically every advance of science for ages. The shape of the earth, whether inhabited on the other side; the antiquity of the earth and man; the Copernican theory and gravitation; the nature and origin of comets, the nature and origin of fossils, the origin of languages; the agency of demons in disease, storms, lightning and drouth; anatomy, surgery, and the use of inoculation, vaccination, anesthetics and sanitation; the existence of witches, and whether insanity was demon possession or disease; God's method of creation, whether by fiat or by evolution, are only a part of the questions on which theologians arrayed themselves against science on the grounds of Biblical teachings.[28]

The scientific position on all these questions was declared to be contrary to the Bible, and it was further declared, in numerous instances, that if the teachings of science were true the Bible was false and utterly worthless. Those who accepted the position of science on most of these questions were called "atheists" and "infidels." No soul could even be saved, so it was said, who believed many of the doctrines of science.

By the opposition of theologians surgery was held in disgrace for a thousand years. It might embarrass the resurrection; if the surgeon cut a man's leg off, what would he do for one when raised again? People were actually executed for using anesthetics; but James Y. Simpson finally floored the theologians by pointing out that, according to the Bible, God himself used the first anesthetic, when he put Adam to sleep to remove his rib with which to make his woman.

Exactly the same arguments, couched in exactly the same language, were used against practically every advance of science for fifteen hundred years; but in every fight science has won. Its conclusions are now accepted universally by theologians, except the few who do not yet accept evolution. Instead of throwing their Bibles away, as consistency would have required—having declared that if the scientific position was true the Bible was false—the theologians in each case simply revised their theology and Biblical interpretation to fit the new truth, and moved forward with the world; but the spectacle has been humiliating in the extreme. Nobody can deny that each new advance of science has ennobled religion; what was feared in each case as an enemy proved a friend.

[28] White, *History of the Warfare of Science with Theology in Christendom,* 2 vols. tells the whole story.

One serious evil growing out of such use of the Bible has been that many men of superior intelligence and ability have been betrayed into rejecting historic Christianity because of it. The church, in its interpretation of the Bible, needs to be in harmony with the great intellectual, social and scientific movements of the day. All truth, in whatever realm, is God's truth; in His truth there are no contradictions. Therefore, theologians cannot afford to ignore or contradict well established truth in other fields of knowledge. Here is found one of the marked advancements of our age; men no longer fear the truth about anything. Any other attitude is no longer respectable.

The Bible has been used to retard woman's elevation. Unfortunately for woman, the early chapters of Genesis, which record the story of her being deceived and leading Adam astray, were long regarded as literal history. Poor Adam! He could not be expected to help himself. Doubtless this early story powerfully influenced Paul, who calls attention to that fact,[29] and who further says, "Neither was the man created for the woman; but the woman for the man."[30] Many of Paul's sayings stood in her way: "The head of the woman is the man;"[31] "the woman is the glory of the man;"[32] "I permit not a woman to teach, nor to have dominion over a man;"[33] and "let the women keep silence in the churches: for it is not permitted unto them to speak; but let them be in subjection . . . if they would learn anything, let them ask their own husbands at home; for it is shameful for a woman to speak in the church."[34] What the old maids were to do Paul does not say; they seem to be left to "burst in ignorance."

And yet, notwithstanding these Biblical handicaps, it was to other elements of Christianity that woman owes her elevation. It is among the Christian nations only that she has been elevated. The ennobling influences of Christianity have greatly enlarged men's hearts and minds, and finally lifted woman to something of her rightful place, in spite of any Scriptures that seemed to stand in her way.

The Bible Used to Support Erratic Movements

One of the most melancholy misuses of the Bible has been by those who find in it a plan for the ages, an almanac for all time. The apocalyptic utterances of Daniel, Revelation and those attributed to

[29] 1 Tim. 2:14. [30] 1 Cor. 11:9. [31] 1 Cor. 11:3. [32] 1 Cor. 11:7. [33] 1 Tim. 2:12. [34] 1 Cor. 14:34-35.

Jesus, have been, again and again, fitted into the times, more especially in periods of calamity. Often the public have been assured that these prophecies were all then receiving their final fulfilment, and that the personal return of Jesus might be expected shortly.

America has had her full share of such use of the Bible. Beginning in 1831, a thoroughly honest but sadly mistaken Vermont farmer, William Miller, began to urge upon the people, in pamphlets and lectures, the rapidly approaching advent of Christ to Judgment. The date was set for April 23, 1843. The excitement became intense as the date drew near. Great meetings were held, in the open air and in tents; thousands were won to the idea. Great preparations were made for the event. Men parted with their money freely, believing they would no longer need it, paralyzing business in many sections. But Jesus did not return. The utter failure of the whole scheme did not dampen the ardor of many good men; a monument to that delusion exists among us today in our Adventist churches.

History is literally strewn with the set times for Christ's return, though many no longer fix the exact day. During the World War the public were once more deluged with the idea. Prophecies were all once more receiving final fulfilment; so we were told, and Jesus could be expected most any time, certainly very soon. It was said frankly that it was useless to talk about reconstruction following the war, since Christ would be here so shortly to make things over in his own way. But Jesus did not return.

This sort of thing has now gone on for more than a thousand years. One thing is self-evident; those who have so applied the Scriptures in the past did not know what they were talking about. Jesus has not returned personally. And it would seem that intelligent men might begin to suspect that the whole method of Scripture interpretation used to reach such conclusions is wrong. Why the idea has not been more extensively exploited during the present world depression remains a mystery, unless it be that fingers were so badly burned when Jesus failed to return, in connection with the World War, that, for once, the advocates of the idea have learned caution.

Modern spiritualism appeals to the Bible in support of its claims. Without discussing the question of whether communication with the dead is possible, it cannot be denied that the general effect of spiritualism has been unfortunate. No religious movement of history so lends itself to imposition and fraud; and no other has been so extensively shot through with fraud.

This movement arose in America, though something like it has existed from very ancient times. In 1855 the adherents of the cult were estimated at around 2,000,000 in the United States. There has been a great falling off in the movement, and nothing has done more to curtail it than the exposure of the frauds connected with it.

The Bible has been used to support numerous erratic movements, all of which have been unfortunate, and some of which have done much evil. Among them was that of John Alexander Dowie, who persuaded many good people that he was Elijah II. Pastor Russell, at whose Watch Towers the faithful, properly robed, patiently awaited the Lord's return, deceived multitudes of good people. The Maid of Angelus Temple, with her flair for newspaper notoriety, belongs in this class. Mormonism, the House of David, Shakerism, New Thought and Unity are all of this character. Christian Science, with its conglomeration of philosophical and theological thinking, and its utterly impossible method of Biblical interpretation, is another example. Christian Science, however, would probably never have arisen, had not the church neglected an important part of its divinely ordained service. It is doing a good work to the extent that it is calling attention to the place of healing in the Christian scheme.

The Bible Used Superstitiously

The Bible has often been prostituted to superstitious uses; it has often been regarded as a fetish, charm or talisman, rather than as a revelation of God's will to intelligent men. Bibliomacy is a term used to describe a method of divination, once very common, which consists in opening the Bible haphazard, and considering the first passage the eye rests on as a guide in a particular situation. This has often been used in modified forms. Some people, on entering the church, marked the first words of Scripture read, as an indication of duty, or prophecy of future good or ill.

Bibliomacy was freely used in ancient days in the consecration of bishops. In the Gallican church it was long practiced in the election of bishops, children being used to draw slips of paper containing Scripture quotations. The passages considered the most favorable determined the choice; but nimble wits had the advantage in the interpretation. It was used also in the Greek Church. In fact, bibliomacy became so rife early that several church councils condemned it, on pain of excommunication. Still it persisted. In the Middle Ages this method was used to detect heretics. In England a

modified form was used to detect witches, the suspect being taken
to the church and weighed against the church Bible, and guilt or
innocence thereby determined. Some very eminent Christians, such
as John Bunyan and John Wesley, used bibliomacy freely. Tennyson
makes use of the custom in Enoch Arden. The practice long persisted
among the pious and is probably not entirely dead today. The
method was derived from paganism; pagans used Homer and Virgil
in the same way.

Something of the same character was in vogue in Tennessee in
our boyhood days; many of the ignorant used it. We knew personally a Baptist farmer-preacher who practised it. He was well-to-do,
reared a large family, and preached regularly here and there, without a stated pastorate. He often thanked his God that he had never
"rubbed his back against a college wall," an expression frequently
heard in those days. Ministers did not need an education, we often
heard it said in our boyhood; all they needed was to open their
mouths and God would fill them. Our farmer-preacher declared that
texts taken at haphazard served his purpose as well as any others.
Some of his neighbors did not agree with him, however. So to prove
his contention in the matter, he announced his purpose to preach in
a local church, naming a certain Sunday, promising that he would
make no previous preparation and no effort to provide a text. He
proposed to open the Bible in church at haphazard, and take as a
text the first passage that caught his eye. From a text so selected, he
assured the people that he could preach as good a sermon as he could
preach from a carefully selected text, with weeks of preparation.
And perhaps that was the truth.

The day came and the church was filled to overflowing. Considerable interest had been aroused, for not everybody entertained such
opinions; but all were anxious to see how well the farmer-preacher
could acquit himself. Therefore, an eager audience awaited the
hour, several preachers being in attendance.

Most churches in that region were provided with old fashioned
family Bibles, big and heavy, regular pulpit Bibles being unknown.
The hour finally arrived, and for once the preliminaries dragged
heavily, or so it seemed, but at last they ended to the great relief of
everybody. The farmer-preacher arose with a broad smile, as he
confidently surveyed the splendid group before him. Deliberately
he opened the big Bible haphazard, glanced at it a moment, and
stood for once non-plussed. His smile evaporated. He hesitated a
moment, and then turned to one of the ministers present, and said,

"Brother Smith, you'll have to preach; I opened the Bible at the family record, and it is blank!" He sat down and his brother minister took over the service.

The farmer-preacher never again attempted to preach. A few years afterward, however, he confided to some of his most intimate friends, that he had come to think that he had acted foolishly in giving up the ministry; and said that had he been clever enough to see it, he had had before him on that occasion the finest text possible. The blank pages to which he had turned has been intended to suggest to him that from nothing God had made the world, and all that was in it; but he had failed to catch the suggestion and thereby lost his opportunity. No amount of urging, however, would induce him to preach again. Such are some of the foolish and superstitious uses that have been made of the Bible.

The Bible has been woefully misused and abused; more so than any other book in all the world. Out of this fact has come its unfortunate uses. Most of these have been due to a mistaken idea of the Bible and its consequent misinterpretation and misapplication. But a new conception of the Bible is rapidly displacing the old; and this new view reduces to a minimum the danger of its misuse.

The modern conception of the Bible recognizes it as a sort of moving picture of the moral and spiritual development of the Hebrew and Jewish peoples, the growing revelation of God to humanity which culminated in Jesus Christ. The modern approach to the Bible puts each part into its historical environment, and determines the character of literature represented in its various parts. The Bible contains tradition, story, fable, history, epistle, parable, apocalypse, poetry and prose, and each different character of literature requires its own method of interpretation. The temporary and the passing is separated from the permanent in Christianity, and Jesus Christ is made the supreme authority.

Now if the Bible is a book of such value as to produce the marvelous results that we have pointed out, when so extensively misunderstood and misapplied, what may we expect from it in the future, freed from so much that handicapped and hindered?

3. THE GOLDEN AGE OF THE BIBLE YET TO COME

Many people seem to think that the Bible is being outgrown; that the church and religion are losing their hold on the public. We are told that the modern world and even the church is in a mad race for amusement, that church attendance, proportionately speaking, has been lessened, and that the Bible is not read as formerly. To many the church seems to be on its last legs. But so it has seemed to many of the fearful from the very beginning, because they see only upon the surface.

A. THINGS FEARED NOT ALWAYS EVIL

The world does seek amusement as never before, but not because it is hell bent. This is the most strenuous age in the world's history; the grinding exactions of modern business and labor, in the campaign for efficiency, are terrible. When the day is done multitudes are literally exhausted, and in need of recreation, entertainment, amusement. They must be able to laugh and forget. By such means nature rejuvenates them and prepares them for the stress of tomorrow. This is largely the explanation of the world's mad craze for amusement. The world needs it to carry on. One other factor enters into the explanation; our age has more leisure than any age in the world's history, due largely to the shortening of working hours. This constitutes one of our modern problems, how best to provide for the people's leisure time. Amusements serve a valuable place here. Under such circumstances as face the modern world, recreation is as necessary and sacred as prayer. Each has its place.

It is freely admitted that church attendance is not as great proportionally as once in America; but this is not the evil it is sometimes supposed to be. In the early colonies people were often compelled by law to attend church; such was the case in Massachusetts, Connecticut, Georgia, South Carolina and Virginia. For long the church furnished the chief means, often the only means, of social life; people, even those not religiously inclined, attended largely because there was nowhere else to go. Today the people find social life and entertainment abundantly provided without church attendance; thus those who attend do so from choice, and for the spiritual benefits its services bring. The crowd has been cut, but the church finds itself with an audience more genuinely interested in what it is doing, and more conducive to a spiritual atmosphere. This is not the first army that was ever reduced to advantage; Gideon, of Biblical fame, began with an army of 32,000 which was finally reduced to 300, with great gain.

To be able to remain away from church has often been a blessing to those so favored. People may be genuinely religious and have little care for the service of the church, and especially of some particular church which they would most naturally attend, and they should be permitted their choice. All people have not the same temperament. God may even be found outside the church house, as well as inside. Many find God in nature—in the fields, along the streams, or in the mountains. Some people get more out of such places than in a church service. The church, however, during the nineteenth century, while attendance was declining, gained in membership several times faster than the country did in population, proving that the church is growing and not dying.

That the Bible is no longer read so universally and extensively as once, cannot be denied. This fact, however, is not due to any loss of interest in genuine Christianity, and is another positive gain.

So long as Christianity was supposed to consist in religious observances as was so universally the case in the Middle Ages, the Bible was read very little, because it was not needed. The church was supposed to hold the keys of heaven and hell, and all one needed to do was to obey the church. But the Reformation set the Bible up as the supreme authority in all matters social, civil and religious, which led to its being read extensively for direction in the whole round of human thought and activity. It was once read for authority in persecution, and for direction in dealing with the devil-possessed. It was read extensively throughout the ages to disprove science. The cosmology of the ancient Babylonians, modified somewhat by that of Egypt, with its flat earth and metal sky, was defended by Biblical quotations for centuries. It was read in America as an infallible guide in setting up governments, some of which were modeled after the Old Testament pattern; for the enactment of all sorts of laws, and for authority in dealing with witches. In more recent times it has been read in America by a few who sought to disprove evolution. Such Bible reading is not very profitable, and it is a positive advantage that it has about ceased.

The Bible has been read extensively for theological controversy. People have ransacked it again and again for some text that could be used in the interest of a favorite doctrine that was of little value, or to answer an adversary. Men have read it for definite sayings that applied to evils of their day. One of the old preachers of the South, in an early day, became quite indignant at the women who had begun to do up their hair in a ball or knot on top of their heads. He could not approve the new fashion, and hoped to be able to check it, but felt the need of a "Thus saith the Lord" that applied directly. He read his New Testament several times in search of it.

And he found it, as such men always found what they were looking for, in the place where Jesus had said, "Let him which is on the house top not come down." Next Sunday morning he was ready with his sermon, using the text: "Top not come down." This illustrates the character of much Bible reading in the past.

Then again, people often read the Bible from a sense of stern duty, being afraid not to read it. When so read the daily portion was something to be gotten rid of as quickly and easily as possible, rather than as an opportunity to gather fresh insight and renewed strength. Such reading is of doubtful value.

Today the Bible is read from choice and with delight. More men and women proportionally read the old Book now seeking to find the secret of living victoriously, in a world of sickness, sorrow and disappointment, than ever before. More people than ever before read it seeking to learn the principles of the kingdom of God, that they may apply these principles in their own lives, and to the problems of the social order. Many read it in the vast Christian literature of our day that would explain and apply it. In other words, the Bible was never read profitably so much as it is in our day.

What if much unprofitable Bible reading has ceased? The world is better off for it. What if certain classes who once attended church never darken a church door today? They made no real contribution to its services and received little benefits when they did attend. The Bible and the church may be neglected at times by the faithful, but never permanently. Something always happens to bring people back—a personal crisis or a national disaster, anything; then the old Book shows its power again.

The Bible is read far more than the average pessimist imagines. Charles I. Blood, during his thirty years as a city editor, came to know something of the modern interest in the Bible. He has this to say about it:

"Back in 1904, when I first became city editor, a choleric citizen telephoned me one night and proceeded to tear his newspaper to bits in front of the mouthpiece, so I could hear the ripping sound.

"Having called me a number of names, he informed me he was canceling his subscription because our paper ran race-track results on the front page.

" 'But thousands are interested,' I explained. 'It's a public service to print them. What do you want us to print?'

" 'Something uplifting,' he snarled. 'Why don't you run something from the Bible?'

"I have known newspapermen who would have roared with laughter at the idea. But an idea should not be laughed at. On the editorial page next morning we published a verse of Scripture . . . and the next morning . . . and the next.

"Every night for more than thirty years now I have copied down a text from the Bible for the editorial page. I have copied down all the Bible, verse by verse, with a lead pencil. Now I am copying it again, verse by verse, to be printed in tomorrow's paper. I think it the most fascinating serial ever published.

"There is drama in writing that verse every night. Who will read it? In what crisis will it come to the eyes of men—like a finger pointing? Never a week passes that I do not receive a telephone call or a letter from some person whose life has been affected by that little verse I pencil every night from my worn-out Bible. I wonder why more editors do not run that serial." [35]

The Press-Radio Bible Service does a unique work. Through its influence it has come to be quite common to find a text of Scripture on the editorial pages of the dailies of the country. Few people know anything about how the press of the country was induced to begin such service.

Addison Y. Reid is a layman of Cincinnati, Ohio, and a very devoted Christian. In 1919 he conceived the idea of providing a press-sheet, consisting of suitable quotations from the Bible for the daily use of newspapers. He felt that if such press-sheet could be furnished free, editors could be induced to print a text in their papers from the Bible daily.

Naturally he talked the matter over with his friends, but they thought him visionary and impractical. Only two friends, among a wide circle, gave him any encouragement whatever. One of these said, "If you proceed on lines you have indicated, and make your work free from commercialism, non-sectarian and undenominational, I feel that you will find some editors who will give a bit of Holy Writ a preferred position on their editorial page."

Accordingly, a press-sheet was prepared, printed and sent out; and on January 1, 1920 the first verse of Scripture, as a result of this service, was printed by a daily paper. For the next six months the work grew very slowly, but it grew. The example set by beginners encouraged others. Editors saw, in this appeal for free space, something different, something designed to help people, and without the trace of commercialism. Soon Scripture passages began to appear

[35] 30 Years as a City Editor, *American Magazine,* July 1935. p. 99.

all over the country on editorial pages, often at the head of the editorial column—a priceless position. Today newspapers in all sections of the United States, and more or less over the whole world, regularly use this service.

It is estimated that the secular press gives annually more than a million dollars' worth of space, at advertising rates, for the publication of these brief passages from the King James Version; and yet this service is rendered on an annual budget of less than $5,000. The Press-Radio Bible Service may be called a team-mate of the American Bible Society. Each in its own way is spreading abroad the Bible throughout the world.

In the year 1933 the Bible Society published 323,109 Bibles, 413,826 Testaments, and 7,064,043 Portions. During the same period of time the Press-Radio Bible Service served newspapers having a daily circulation of more than 14,000,000 copies; or during the year 4,382,000,000 copies of papers were printed, including those of the United States, and its possessions, Dominion of Canada, England, Ireland, Scotland, Union of South Africa, Manchuria, China, New South Wales, Australia, and even far-away New Zealand, each of which carried a helpful verse from the Bible.

Hardheaded editors would not continue this service year after year, as they do, if it did not bring a response that fully justified; and it would require volumes to tell of the good accomplished by this simple service.

A man in Pittsburg had serious domestic trouble, and made up his mind that his best way out was to take his own life. He picked up one of the great dailies, and there on the editorial page was a verse of Scripture, which sent him to his knees. The outcome was a reconciliation in the home. A few weeks after this occurred, the editor of a paper in Harrodsburg, Kentucky, wrote to say that, "A man was in my office today and said that I have been the means of saving his life, and explained by saying, 'Ten days ago I made up my mind to take my own life, but that day you had a verse of Scripture in your paper which gave me a new vision of life'." The Press-Radio Bible Service receives hundreds of letters annually bearing testimony to the value of the service.

Dr. Robert Watson of Boston has served for sixteen years as president of the Press-Radio Bible Service, but Addison Y. Reid has done the work of selecting the passages of Scripture, printing the press-sheets and mailing them to the newspapers, and often at great personal sacrifice. The service is furnished free, and Mr. Reid sells nothing. The expense of maintaining the service has been provided by friends interested in the work. It lives by faith and from hand to mouth.

The Press-Radio Bible service maintains an office at 603 Southern Ohio Bank Building, Cincinnati, Ohio, and the Crosley Radio Corporation broadcasts for the organization a weekly religious program that includes a sermonet every Sunday.

This amazing record of service, however, covers but a small part of the total number of publications that would gladly use the daily text of Scripture, if they could be furnished them; and the only thing that stands in the way of a greatly enlarged service is the want of money sufficient to enlarge it.

People who think the Bible has played out know little about what goes on in this old world. To outgrow the Bible would be to outgrow the one really hopeful book in all the world's literature, the one book out of which all other optimisms have come. So long as "hope springs eternal in the human breast" this cannot be.

The tremendous power of the Bible is evidenced nowhere better than by the fact that Soviet Russia has banned the Book. A great Russian Christian, D. Merezhkovsky, tells why. "That is why all those who wish to enslave the spirit seize on the Gospel, to them the most terrifying of books, the need for the destruction of which they regard as the most urgent of all needs."

B. GRAVE DANGER FACED BY AMERICA

The writer is an optimist; he believes in God, and does not see how one can believe in God and be anything else. But he does not live in a fool's paradise. He does not believe in an automatic and inevitable progress, guaranteed to any nation. What will happen to America in the end, like what happened to numerous nations of antiquity, will depend upon whether America uses her opportunity while she has it. The only kingdom of God that will ever be on this earth will be such as the followers of Jesus Christ build, with God's help. It is easily within the power of America to throw away her opportunity, and have the kingdom of God taken from her and given to others, as has been done in the past.

We see grave danger ahead. There is much to alarm the Christian when he considers the present state of international peace, unemployment and economic injustice, and the power of selfish wealth concentrated in a few hands.

We of the twentieth century have the most amazing possibilities that have been known in all history . We now know how to produce everything the world needs, in quantity sufficient for all; we have the machinery and ability to do more to end poverty than any previous generation. It is evident that capitalism unrestrained will destroy itself, and our civilization with it. Our hope and faith that it will not do so is based on what God can do with even a small group, a vital and creative minority, genuinely consecrated to his work. Remember what he did with a few ignorant fishermen.

Today America has her chance to help build a decent world, an advance in the kingdom of God; tomorrow her children may be paying the penalty of her failure. Our nation, and even our present civilization, may go to pieces, as did Babylon, Egypt and Rome, and she will if she betrays her trust. The outer husk of our civilization may have to be destroyed in order to preserve the spiritual values. Only spiritual values are permanent, and our Christianity is our only hope of national permanence.

We can put an end to war if we will; the chance is not yet lost, but it does not seem as good as it did a few years ago. The League of Nations and the World Court are doing what they can; but the attitude of America is disturbing, to say the least. In 1890 the United States spent about $25,000,000 on its army; and the navy in the same year cost about $22,500,000. But for 1934 our government expended on its army more than $243,000,000, and on its navy more than $297,000,000. This same character of increase of expenditure for such purpose is going on all over the world, notwithstanding the world depression. We are traveling precisely the same road that led former civilizations to utter ruin. While our boys in the World War fought and bled and died in France for a dollar a day, 21,000 men who stayed at home piled up fortunes sufficient, as a result of the war, to make themselves millionaires. A civilization that continues to permit such things does not deserve to live.

We had religious liberty in America once, but the Supreme Court has crippled it. Today, in order to become a citizen of Christian America, one must give his conscience into the keeping of Congress. If this means anything, it means that Congress has the keeping of the consciences of all our citizens, whether born or naturalized. The whole fight for religious liberty, it would seem, must be waged to a finish once more in America.

There is still a chance to reconstruct the economic order into something equitable and humane, although the outlook is not as good as we could wish. Communism, with its utter destruction of religion and liberty, on the one hand, and capitalism, with its power and propaganda on the other hand, are not a hopeful outlook.

Individualism had its place in the development of our civilization, as did capitalism. But the world changes. The personal welfare of the individual may once have been in his own hands, but it is no longer so. It depends today upon world-wide conditions, which are beyond his control. Things now must be cooperatively handled for the good of all; and nothing short of this will solve the problems of our day. Capitalism is on trial because it has broken down. Something is wrong with an economic system that turns millions upon millions out of work, men and women who want work and must have work to live. And any system that concentrates such large fortunes in a few hands is wrong. Capitalism, therefore, must be modified or displaced. If our civilization will not do it, one more worthy will. The only system that can prevail in the end will be one that has at heart the welfare of the whole people. Possibly capitalism may be so modified as to do that, but if not it must give place to something better.

But there is one thing that most people seem to overlook. If the kingdom of God is ever built on this earth, somebody must pay the price in suffering. Progress can be made in no other way. Christianity brings its joy and its victories, but it brings its troubles as well. "If any man will come after me let him take up his cross," the Master said. Jesus said frankly that he came "to send not peace but a sword", or as Luke put it "but rather division". Brother will be arrayed against brother. This world is full of people, rich, powerful and selfish and people who are poor, selfish and determined to be rich, whose interests, they think, are bound up with the existing othodoxies, theological and political, and who are ready to make war on anybody that threatens their selfish interests. Men who profit by war want war and will fight for it. The armament makers want war. Men who enjoy any selfish advantage will fight to retain it. They spend vast sums to spread propaganda about "patriotism," "100 per cent Americanism," "the menace of the reds," all for the purpose of befogging the issue and deceiving the public, in order to insure the continuance of their advantages. And they fight unscrupulously; there is no weapon they hesitate to use. And followers of Jesus who cannot resist them can never build the kingdom of God, and are not worthy to be called disciples.

Yes, America has a glorious opportunity. Millions in this world have been won to devote their lives unselfishly for the common good. Ministers and teachers have always done so. We expect it of them. But today doctors by the thousands are doing the same thing; scientists are doing it. No more thrilling story was ever told than that of Banning and Best discovering insulin. Here was an opportunity to make millions of profit; but it was given the world unselfishly. Dr. Reed, an army doctor on small pay, abolished yellow fever in Cuba, and showed the world how to do it elsewhere, for the common good. No better efficiency has ever been shown by capitalism than that of Colonel George W. Goethals, who, on the small pay of the army, built the Panama Canal for the common good. Men enter the army and navy for what they believe to be the common good and at small pay. Statesmen serve on small pay for the common good. Why cannot business and professional men be won to give unselfish service for the common good, on small pay? The future of our civilization depends upon it.

C. CHRISTIANITY LOOKS TO THE FUTURE

While other religions look backward, Christianity looks forward for its golden age; thus has been the inspiration for all worthy endeavor that would build the kingdom of God. It is the only religion that sets a definite goal to all history. The Bible inspired the chief early settlements of America; molded the early life of the Republic; and has been the chief inspiration of its most enduring progress. Today it stands prophetic of untold blessings for the future.

Christianity is not decadent. Intelligent and profitable interest in the Bible was never so great; never have the teachings of Jesus had such hold on the world. There is always present among us, however, those who glorify the past and belittle the present. In every age the young people are supposed to be going straight to ruin, simply because they do things different from what their parents or grandparents did. But the good old days of long ago were not nearly so good as they are often represented; nor is the present so bad as it is often pictured by the fearful.

The processes of God work slowly. Worthy ideals are not reached quickly. God's plans are too big to move swiftly; with Him a thousand years "are but as yesterday when it is past, and as a watch in the night." It is man who gets in a hurry. Millions of years were required in forming the earth, in fitting it for man's habitation. Man has been here tens of thousands of years, possibly hundreds of thousands. In the same slow but sure way God is building His kingdom. The forces whether physical or moral, which are shaping the world, require long periods of time. The principles which Jesus planted will ultimately remake the world into His kingdom.

D. THE WORLD GROWS BETTER

Those who read only the daily press and take account only of the evil that is rampant in the world, are prone to think that the world grows constantly worse. It is only when we study cross sections of society a hundred, or five hundreds years apart, that we are able to see clearly a steady moral and spiritual advance throughout civilization. Thus the kingdom of God comes without observation. We should remember that Jesus "came not to send peace, but a sword." His sword is peculiarly busy today. It is stirring the nations of the world as never before. The world depression is being used, in God's providence, to teach the world more in a few years than could be learned in a century of normal times. Much of what men fear are only growing pains. The reaction against democracy since the World War is only temporary—a hangover from the hysteria of war time, reinforced by the depression. The remedy is more democracy and not less. Truth develops pendulum like; there is always action and reaction, but in the end the truth wins. The chief evils from which we suffer are the work of minorities. Wars are forced by a few people. My old grandmother was a pacifist before the days of pacifists. She had a saying about war that fits perfectly, "Broadcloth makes 'em, and cotton breeches must fight 'em out."

The horizon is full of dark clouds, but when was it ever otherwise? Great evils abound; baleful influences would destroy the Bible, the church, and all that stands for holiness and justice. Small minorities are responsible for it. But the church has weathered the storms for near two thousand years; and the gates of hades have not prevailed against it. They will not now. God must be busy in his world. How otherwise could the early church have served the generation in which it was born? A petty Jewish sect, despised and cast out by their contemporaries, they went everywhere proclaiming the utter absurdity of a Leader who had died on the Cross, and then risen from the dead. The church could never have gained its amazing triumphs in that early day had there not been divine interference in its behalf. The same God leads and defends the church today.

The kingdom of God has been rediscovered within modern times.

It is not the church, neither is it heaven, nor wholly spiritual and within. It is simply this world, in all its departments of activity, put on a Christian basis—the basis of social justice and brotherhood. It is spiritual but it is also social. Several sections of modern life have already been put on a Christian basis. In the home every one contributes according to ability and receives according to need. The public school is on such basis. The rich man without a child pays taxes according to his ability, while the poor widow with nothing but ten children has them educated at public expense. The next great department of modern life that must be put on a Christian basis is the economic order. John in his vision on Patmos saw it, "the holy city, new Jerusalem coming down out of heaven from God" to dwell among men. "The seventh angel sounded; and there followed great voices in heaven, and they said, The kingdom of the world is become the kingdom of our Lord, and of his Christ; and he shall reign for ever and ever." [36]

Unconscious prophecies of the golden age of Christianity are about us on all sides, if one only has the discernment to see them. The dream of a time when every citizen would loyally play his part is as old as human history. It must be God inspired. Plato and Aristotle dreamed of it. The old prophets and poets have sung about it.

Every plan of social reconstruction is a prophecy of the kingdom of God. Among the notable books forecasting a new social order may be mentioned Plato's *Republic*, Campanella's *City of the Sun*, More's *Utopia*, Bacon's *New Atlantis*, Harrington's *Oceana*, Cabet's *Icaria* and Bellamy's *Looking Backward*.

Every communistic society is a prophecy—Brook Farm near Boston, the Amana Society in Iowa, and dozens of others. Socialism is a prophecy of God's kingdom. These are all dreams of the reign of God on earth. It helps to meet God in a dream; it is better than not to meet Him at all. Much of what they teach is impossible, even foolish; but nevertheless it has its value. They are all forecasts of social salvation; men feel the injustice of the present order, and believe a better possible. Some day it will be realized, and the chief agency in bringing it will be the Bible.

E. THE SPIRIT TO GUIDE INTO ALL THE TRUTH

Among the promises of Jesus was one that has, in the past, impressed the church very little. "It is expedient for you that I go away; for if I go not away, the Comforter will not come unto you.

[36] Rev. 11:15

. . . I have yet many things to say unto you, but ye cannot bear them now. Howbeit when he, the Spirit of truth, is come, he shall guide you into all the truth." [37] This Spirit was to abide forever. This is a deliberate provision and promise of progress. But the church has made no place for this promise, except to suppose that all truth was given the apostles, and that when they were all dead, God ceased to speak.

Yet throughout the ages, the Spirit has been guiding the church into all the truth, exactly as Jesus promised, a fact which has often proved a disturbing element. Augustine evidently thought he had the last word in theology; Calvin thought there was nothing of real worth beyond his system; creeds have all been supposed to be final—among them the Westminster Confession of Faith. Yet they require revision from time to time, often at sore expense in sufferings, all because the church has not expected progress.

This attitude is now changing; the church is beginning to expect progress. John Robinson, the saintly pastor of the Pilgrims before they came to America, a man far ahead of his day, shared the hope of this progress, when he said, "I am persuaded that God has yet more truth to come to us, which will break forth in time out of his holy Word."

The philosophies of the world have failed—those of paganism, materialism, rationalism and commercialism. It is evident that they have no solution for the world's problems. As a result the world is turning more and more to Jesus of Nazareth, in hope that He does have the cure for the world's ills. Benjamin Franklin, who understood his Bible better than many of his day, said, "He who shall introduce into public affairs the principles of primitive Christianity, will revolutionize the world." The issue of world peace, the race question, the labor question, the distribution of wealth, industrial slavery and democracy in industry, are all problems to be settled on Christian principles.

The position of Jesus is secure. Whatever our differences of opinion as to his divinity, he stands supreme among men. Renan closes his life of Christ with these words: "Whatever the unexpected phenomena of the future, Jesus will never be surpassed. His worship will constantly renew its youth, the legend of his life will bring ceaseless tears, his sufferings will soften the best hearts; all the ages will proclaim that amongst the sons of men, none has been born who is greater than Jesus."

[37] John 16:7-14.

How marvelously strange! A Galilean, so very poor that He had not where to lay His head, isolated, uneducated in the schools of His day, untraveled and unknown in the centers of the civilization of His time, served but three short years in His ministry, and then died at thirty-three the most disgraceful death known. But He has influenced the world as no other man. That He is divine millions have learned from personal experience of His power to transform their own lives. Faith in Him goes hand in hand with the highest civilization, and His influence now reaches all parts of the globe.

BIBLIOGRAPHY

Full Information Concerning Each Book Given Only at Its First Mention.

INTRODUCTION

HOW ITS BOOKS WERE SELECTED

Ryle, H. E., *The Canon of the Old Testament*. 2nd ed. London: Macmillan and Co. 1909.

Westcott, Brooke Foss, *General Survey of the History of the Canon of the New Testament*, 3rd ed. rev. by W. A. Wright. London: Macmillan and Co. 1905.

Gregory, Caspar Rene, *Canon and Text of the New Testament*. New York: Charles Scribner's Sons, 1907. (All three very fine).

For the exact contents of the various Christian Bibles in use, see Simms, P. Marion, *The Bible from the Beginning*. New York: The Macmillan Co., 1929. pp. 128-48.

SOME CHANGING CONCEPTIONS

Fosdick, Harry Emerson, *The Modern Use of the Bible*. New York: The Macmillan Co., 1924. (Splendid).

Peake, Arthur S., *The Bible; its Origin, its Significance, and its Abiding Worth*. New York: George H. Doran Co., 1913. (Well worth reading).

Gordon, A. R., *The Early Traditions of Genesis*. Edinburgh: T. and T. Clark, 1907.

Bewer, Julius A., *The Literature of the Old Testament in its Historical Development*. rev. ed. New York: Columbia University Press, 1933.

Jones, Maurice, *The New Testament in the Twentieth Century*. London: Macmillan and Co., 1924.

Moffatt, James, *The Approach to the New Testament*. London: Hodder and Stoughton, 1921.

I. THE SETTLEMENT OF AMERICA

1. FIRST COLONIZATION OF AMERICA A FAILURE

A. SPANISH SETTLEMENT AND WORK EPHEMERAL

Bacon, Leonard Woolsey, *History of American Christianity*. New York: Charles Scribner's Sons, 1900. pp. 1-15. (Splendid short account).

Lowery, Woodbury, *The Spanish Settlement within the Present Limits of the United States, 1562-1574*. New York: G. P. Putnam's Sons, 1905. pp. 211-314.

Fiske, John, *The Discovery of America*. New York: Houghton and Mifflin Co., 1899. Vol. II, chap. 12.

B. DREAM OF FRENCH EMPIRE BLASTED

Bacon, Leonard Woolsey, *History of American Christianity*. pp. 16-29. (Splendid).

Marquis, Thomas Guthrie, *The Jesuit Missions*. (4th Vol. Chronicles of Canada). Toronto: Glasgow, Brook and Co., 1916.

Lowery, Woodbury, *Spanish Settlements in the Present Limits of the United States, 1562-1574*. pp. 3-186.

Parkman, Francis, *Pioneers of France in the New World*. Boston: Little, Brown and Co., 1865.

2. GENERAL CHARACTER OF FIRST PERMANENT COLONISTS

Chitwood, Oliver Perry, *History of Colonial America*. New York: Harper and Bros., 1931. pp. 516-49.

Macaulay's Essay on Milton (A splendid estimate of the Puritans).

Calhoun, Arthur Wallace, *Social History of the American Family*. Cleveland: The Arthur H. Clark Co., 1917-19. Vol. I, Chap 7 (Moral conditions in New England).

3. SETTLEMENTS ALONG THE ATLANTIC SEABOARD
    A. COLONIES FOUNDED BY DISTINCT GROUPS

Bacon, Leonard Woolsey, *History of American Christianity*. pp. 30-126.

Andrews, Charles McLean, *Our Earliest Colonial Settlements*. New York: New York University Press, 1933. (Very fine). Also *The Colonial Period of American History*. New Haven: Yale University Press, 1934. (Fine for the English side of the story).

Usher, Roland Green, *The Pilgrims and their History*. New York: The Macmillan Co., 1918. (Sympathetic).

Ellis, G. E., *The Puritan Age and Rule of Massachusetts, 1629-1685*. Boston and New York: Houghton and Mifflin Co., 1888. (Favorable).

Richman, Irving Berdine, *Rhode Island: its Making and its Meaning*. New York: G. P. Putnam's Sons, 1902. 2 vols. (The best on the subject).

Fiske, John, *Dutch and Quaker Colonies in America*. New York: Houghton and Mifflin Co., 1903. 2 vols.

Howell, Clark, *History of Georgia*. Chicago-Atlanta: The S. J. Clarke Co., 1926. 4 vols.

    B. NUMEROUS GROUPS FOUND IN OTHER COLONIES

Hirsch, Arthur Henry, *The Huguenots of Colonial South Carolina*. Durham, N. C.: Duke University Press, 1928.

Johnson, Amandus, *The Swedish Settlements on the Delaware, 1638-64*. New York: D. Appleton and Co., 1911. 2 vols.

Ford, H. J., *The Scotch-Irish in America*. Princeton, N. J.: Princeton University Press, 1915.

Hanna, Charles Augustus, *The Scotch-Irish*. New York: G. P. Putnam's Sons, 1902. 2 vols.

Faust, Albert Bernhardt, *The German Element in the United States*. New York: Houghton and Mifflin Co., 1909.

Cohen, George, *The Jews in the Making of America*. Boston: The Stratford Co., 1924.

4. IDEALS AND INSTITUTIONS OF THE COLONISTS
    A. PERSECUTIONS

Chitwood, Oliver Perry, *History of Colonial America*. pp. 141-48. (Good short account).

Adams, C. F., *Three Episodes of Massachusetts History*. New York: Houghton and Mifflin Co., 1892. Vol. I, pp. 381-406.

Jones, R. M., *The Quakers in the American Colonies*. London: Macmillan and Co., 1911. Chaps 3-6.

Osgood, Herbert Levi, *The American Colonies in the Seventeenth Century*. New York: The Macmillan Co., 1904-07. Vol. I, pp. 269-89.

Richman, Irving Berdine, *Rhode Island: its Making and its Meaning*. Vol. II pp. 60-102.

WITCHCRAFT

Adams, J. T., *The Founding of New England*. Boston; The Atlantic Monthly Press, 1921. pp. 451-56.

Kittredge, George Lyman, *Witchcraft in Old and New England*. Cambridge, Mass.: Harvard University Press, 1929. (Very fine).

Taylor, John M., *The Witchcraft Delusion in Colonial Connecticut, 1647-1687*. New York: The Grafton Press, 1908.

Fiske, John, *New France and New England*. Cambridge: The Riverside Press, 1904. Chap. 5.

B. LAWS

Farrand, Max, Ed., *The Laws and Liberties of Massachusetts*. Cambridge, Mass.: Harvard University Press, 1929.

Chitwood, Oliver Perry, *Justice in Colonial Virginia*. Baltimore: The Johns Hopkins Press, 1905.

Bruce, Philip Andrew, *The Virginia Plutarch*. Chapel Hill: The University of North Carolina. Vol. I, Chap 4 (Favorable to Dale).

Force, Peter, *Tracts III*, 1905. (For text of Dale's laws see pp. 9-27).

C. STATE AND INDEPENDENT CHURCHES
TOLERATION AND RELIGIOUS LIBERTY

Chitwood, Oliver Perry, *History of Colonial America*. pp 516-49.

Bacon Leonard, *The Genesis of the New England Churches*. New York: Harper and Bros., 1874. (Old but good).

Bacon, Leonard Woolsey, *History of American Christianity*.

Felt, J. B., *Ecclesiastical History of New England*. Boston: Congregational Library Association, 1855-62. 2 Vols.

Cobb, S. H. *The Rise of Religious Liberty in America*. New York: The Macmillan Co., 1902.

Lauer, Paul E., *Church and State in New England* (Johns Hopkins Studies, 10th Series; also, Petrie, George, *Church and State in Maryland* (10th Series). Baltimore: Johns Hopkins University Press, 1892. Also, Weeks, Stephen B., *Church and State in North Carolina*. (11th Series).

Shea, John Gilmary, *History of the Catholic Church in the United States*. New York: J. G. Shea, 1886-92. (Vol. I is The Catholic Church in Colonial Days).

HALF-WAY COVENANT

Chitwood, Oliver Perry, *History of Colonial America*. pp. 538-39.

THE GREAT AWAKENING

Adams, J. T., *Provincial Society, 1690-1763*. New York: The Macmillan Co., 1927. pp. 279-86 (Fine short account).

Bacon, Leonard Woolsey, *History of American Christianity*. pp 127-80 (Fine account).

Tracy, Joseph, *The Great Awakening*. Boston: Tappan and Dennet; New York: J. Adams, 1842.

Gewehr, W. M., *The Great Awakening in Virginia, 1740-1790*. Durham, N. C.: Duke University Press, 1930.

Maxson, Charles H., *The Great Awakening in the Middle Colonies*. Chicago: University of Chicago Press, 1920.

D. SCHOOLS AND COLLEGES
SCHOOLS CHRISTIAN IN ORIGIN

Dexter, E. G., *History of Education in the United States*. New York: The Macmillan Co., 1904. (Very fine).

Small, Walter H., *Early New England Schools*. Boston: Ginn and Co., 1914.

Griffis, W. E., *The Story of New Netherland, the Dutch in America.* Boston and New York: Houghton, Mifflin Co., 1909. Chap 18.

Goodwin, Maude Wilder, *Dutch and English on the Hudson.* New Haven: Yale University Press, 1921. Chap V.

Woody, Thomas, *Early Quaker Education in Pennsylvania.* New York: Teacher's College, Columbia University, 1910.

Smith, Charles Lee, *History of Education in North Carolina.* Washington: Government Printing Office, 1888.

McCrady, Edward, Jr., *Education in South Carolina Prior to and During the Revolution.* Charlotte, S. C.: South Carolina Historical Society, 1883.

Steiner, Bernard C., *History of Education in Connecticut.* Washington: Government Printing Office, 1893. Also, *History of Education in Maryland.* Washington: Government Printing Office, 1894.

COLLEGES CHRISTIAN IN ORIGIN

Quincy, Josiah, *History of Harvard University.* Boston: Crosby, Nichols, Lee and Co., 1860

Heatwole, Cornelius Jacob, *History of Education in Virginia.* New York: The Macmillan Co., 1916. For history of William and Mary College, Chap. 6.

Dexter, F. B., *Documentary History of Yale University.* New Haven: Yale University Press, 1916.

Dexter, E. G., *History of Education in the United States.* Princeton University, pp. 245-50; University of Pennsylvania, pp. 250-52; King's College, pp. 253-57; Rutgers College, pp. 263-65; Dartmouth College, pp. 265-67.

Bronson, Walter Cochrane, *History of Brown University.* Providence: The University, 1914.

Washington and Lee University, see *Historical Papers* Nos. 1-6, Lexington, Va.: Washington and Lee University, 1890-1904.

E.   THE GROWTH OF DEMOCRACY

Glover, T. R., *Democracy in the Ancient World.* New York: The Macmillan Co., 1927.

Borgeaud, Charles, *The Rise of Modern Democracy in Old and New England,* translated by Mrs. Birbeck Hill. New York: Charles Scribner's Sons, 1894.

MacDonald, William, *Three Centuries of Democracy.* New York: H. Holt and Co., 1923.

F.   SOURCES OF COLONIAL INSTITUTIONS

Campbell, Douglas, *The Puritans in Holland, England and America.* 4th ed rev. New York: Harper and Bros., 1916. 2 Vols. (Almost everything worth while traced to Holland).

King, James M., *Facing the Twentieth Century.* New York: American Union League Society, 1899. pp. 13-174. (Splendid brief account).

Greene, E. B., *Foundations of American Nationality.* New York: American Book Co., 1922.

Faust, Albert Bernhardt, *The German Element in the United States.*

Knauss, J. O., *Social Conditions among the Pennsylvania Germans in the Eight-eenth Century.* Lancaster, Pa.: New Era Printing Co., 1922. Chap. 6.

Ford, Henry Jones, *The Scotch-Irish in America.*

Hanna, Charles Augustus, *The Scotch-Irish.*

Rosengarten, Joseph George, *The French Colonists and Exiles in the United States.* Philadelphia: J. B. Lippincott Co., 1907.

Hirsch, Arthur Henry, *The Huguenots of Colonial South Carolina.*

Fosdick, L. J., *The French Blood in America.* New York: The Baker and Taylor Co., 1911.

Cohen, George, *The Jews in the Making of America.*

Peters, Madison C., *The Jews in America.* Philadelphia: J. C. Winston Co., 1905.

CAUSES OF THE AMERICAN REVOLUTION

Andrews, Charles McLean, *The Colonial Background of the American Revolution.* Rev. ed. New Haven: Yale University Press, 1931. (Fine on indirect causes).

Schlesinger, Arthur Meier, *Colonial Merchants and the American Revolution.* New York: Columbia University Press, 1918. Chap. 7 (Interesting observations).

Beard, Charles Austin and Mary Ritter, *The Rise of American Civilization.* New York: The Macmillan Co., 1927-28. 2 vols. (Deals with social phases of the Revolution).

Jameson, John Franklin, *The American Revolution Considered as a Social Movement.* Princeton: Princeton University Press, 1926.

Van Tyne, C. H., *Causes of the War of Independence.* Boston and New York: Houghton, Mifflin Co., 1922.

SOME ESSENTIAL ELEMENTS OF PURITANISM

Flynn, John Stephen, *The Influence of Puritanism on the Political and Religious Thought of the English.* London: John Murray, 1920. (Exceptionally fine).

II. *PRINCIPAL BIBLES BROUGHT TO AMERICA*

1. LATIN PROBABLY THE FIRST LANGUAGE TO FURNISH A BIBLE

A. NORSEMEN PROBABLY BROUGHT LATIN BIBLES TO AMERICA

Norlie, Olaf Morgan, *History of the Norwegian People in America.* Minneapolis, Minn.: Augsburg Publishing House, 1925. pp. 36-72 (Very fine)

Fischer, Joseph, *The Discoveries of the Norsemen in America.* St. Louis: B. Herder, 1903.

Gathorne, Hardy, *Norse Discoveries in America.* Oxford: Clarendon Press, 1921.

B. SPANISH FATHERS DOUBTLESS BROUGHT LATIN BIBLES

Bolton, Herbert Eugene, *Spanish Exploration in the Southwest, 1542-1710.* New York: Charles Scribner's Sons, 1925. (Original narratives).

Lowery, Woodbury, *Spanish Settlements within the Present Limits of the United States, 1513-1561.* New York: G. P. Putnam's Sons, 1911. See also, *Spanish Settlements within the Present Limits of the United States, 1562-74.* Same Pub. 1905.

HISTORY OF THE LATIN VULGATE

Hoare, H. W., *Our English Bible.* London: John Murray, 1911. pp. 317-20. (11th ed of *The Evolution of the English Bible*)

Eadie, John, *The English Bible.* London: Macmillan and Co., 1876. Vol. II, pp. 107-10.

Hastings, James, Ed., *Dictionary of the Bible.* New York: Charles Scribner's Sons, 1901-02. Vol. IV., pp. 873-90.

Pope, Hugh, *The Catholic Church and the Bible.* New York: The Macmillan Co., 1928.

THE APOCRYPHA

Simms, P. Marion, *The Bible from the Beginning.* New York: The Macmillan Co., 1929. See pp. 95-106, 130-99 for character of its books, influence, etc.

Hastings, James, Ed., *Dictionary of the Bible.* Vol. I, pp. 110-23.

2. FRENCH BIBLES BROUGHT TO AMERICA

Parkman, Francis, *Pioneers of France in the New World*. Boston: Little, Brown and Co., 1865. Part I, pp. 33-181.
See under "Dream of French Empire Blasted" in Chap. I.

HISTORY OF FRENCH TRANSLATIONS

The New Schaff-Herzog Encyclopedia of Religious Knowledge, New York: Funk and Wagnalls Co., 1908-12. Vol. II, pp. 142-3.
Darlow, T. H. and Moule, H. F., *Historical Catalogue of Printed Editions of Holy Scriptures*. London: The Bible House, 1903-11.

3. GERMAN BIBLES BROUGHT TO AMERICA

Sachse, Julius F., *The German Sectarians of Pennsylvania*. Philadelphia: Printed by the Author, 1900. 2 vols.

HISTORY OF LUTHER'S BIBLE

Norlie, Olaf Morgan, *The Translated Bible, 1534-1934*. Philadelphia: The United Lutheran Publication House, 1934. pp. 11-113.
Reu, Johann Michael, *Luther's German Bible*. Columbus, Ohio: Lutheran Book Concern, 1934.

4. ENGLISH PROBABLY THE FOURTH LANGUAGE TO FURNISH A BIBLE.

THE ENGLISH BIBLE IN GENERAL, REGULAR LINE OF TRANSLATIONS.

FROM ANGLO-SAXON TO THE KING JAMES VERSION OR ANGLO-AMERICAN REVISION

Eadie, John, *The English Bible*. (Voluminous and detailed)
Hoare, H. W., *Our English Bible*. (11th ed of *The Evolution of the English Bible*) (Fine)
Mombert, J. I., *English Versions of the Bible*. New and enlarged ed. London: Samuel Bagster and Sons, 1906. (Splendid account).
Moulton, W. F., *The History of the English Bible*. New rev. ed. London: Charles H. Kelly, n.d.
Heaton, W. J., *Our English Bible*. 3rd ed. London: Francis Griffiths, 1913. 3 Vols.

FROM WYCLIF OR TYNDALE TO THE KING JAMES VERSION OR ANGLO-AMERICAN REVISION.

Westcott, Brooke Foss, *A General View of the History of the English Bible*. 3rd ed rev. by William Aldis Wright. London: Macmillan and Co., 1905. (One of the best).
Stoughton, John, *Our English Bible*. London: Religious Tract Society, 1878. (Old, good).
Edgar, Andrew, *The Bibles of England*. London: Alexander Gardner, 1889.
Conant, Mrs. H. C., *The English Bible*. London: Arthur Hall, Virtue and Co., 1859.
Lea, John W., *The Book of Books*. Philadelphia: The John C. Winston Co., 1922.
Dore, J. R., *Old Bibles*. 2nd ed. London: Eyre and Spottiswoode, 1888.
Anderson, Christopher, *The Annals of the English Bible*, Rev. Ed edited in one vol by Hugh Anderson. London: Jackson, Walford and Hodder, 1862. (Old but very good).
Lovett, Richard, *The Printed English Bible, 1525-1885*. London: Religious Tract Society, 1909.
Pollard, Alfred W., *Records of the English Bible; the Documents Relating to the Translation and Publication of the Bible in English, 1525-1611*. Oxford: Oxford University Press, 1911.
Ayers, S. S., and Sitterly, C. F., *History of the English Bible*. London, 1898.

Pattison, T. Howard, *History of the English Bible*. Philadelphia: American Baptist Publication Society, 1894.

Milligan, George, *The English Bible: A Sketch of its History*. New York: A. D. F. Randolph and Co., 1895.

Copinger, W. A., *The Bible and its Transmission*. London: H. Sotheran and Co., 1897.

Barker, Henry, *English Bible Versions, with Special Reference to the Vulgate, the Douay and the Authorized and Revised Versions*. New York: E. S. Gorham, 1907.

Hunting, H. B., *The Story of the Bible*. New York: The Macmillan Co., 1915.

Guppy, Henry, *A Brief Sketch of the History of the Transmission of the Bible*. Manchester: The University Press, 1926.

McComb, Samuel, *The Making of the English Bible*. New York: Moffatt, Yard and Co., 1909.

Scriverner, F. H. A., *The Authorized Edition of the English Bible; its Subsequent Reprints and Modern Representatives*. Cambridge: University Press, 1884.

Margolis, Max Leopold, *The Story of the Bible Translations*. Philadelphia: Jewish Publication Society of America, 1917.

ACCOUNT OF VARIOUS VERSIONS AND THE MSS IN ADDITION TO HISTORY OF ENGLISH TRANSLATIONS

Simms, P. Marion, *The Bible from the Beginning*.

Kenyon, Frederic G., *Our Bible and the Ancient Manuscripts*. 4th ed. London: Eyre and Spottiswoode, 1903.

Price, Ira Maurice, *The Ancestry of the English Bible*. Philadelphia: Sunday School Times Co., 1907.

Robinson, George L., *Where Did We Get Our Bible?* Garden City, N. Y.: Doubleday, Doran and Co., 1928.

Smythe, J. Patterson, *How We Got Our Bible*. New York: J. Potts and Co., 1931.

ACCOUNT OF PRIVATE TRANSLATIONS AS WELL AS REGULAR LINE OF TRANSLATIONS.

Simms, P. Marion, *The Bible from the Beginning*.

Goodspeed, Edgar Johnson, *The Making of the English New Testament*. Chicago: The University of Chicago Press, 1925.

Mombert, J. I., *English Versions of the Bible*. New and enlarged.

Condit, Blackford, *The History of the English Bible*. 2nd ed. rev. New York: A. S. Barnes and Co., 1896.

ROMAN CATHOLIC BIBLES IN ENGLISH

Cotton, Henry, *Rhemes and Douay*. Oxford: The University Press, 1855.

Jacobus, Melancthon Williams, Ed., *Roman Catholic and Protestant Bibles Compared*. The Gould Prize Essays. New York: Bible Teachers Training School, 1905.

BIBLES PUBLISHED IN AMERICA

O'Callaghan, E. B., *A List of Editions of the Holy Scriptures and Parts thereof, Printed in America Previous to 1860*. Albany, N. Y.; Munsell and Rowland, 1861.

Wright, John, *Early Bibles of America*. 3rd ed rev. New York: Thomas Whittaker, 1894.

Cotton, Henry, *Editions of the Bible or Parts thereof in English*. 2nd ed enlarged. Oxford: University Press, 1852. (This includes Bibles published everywhere).

Darlow and Moule, *Historical Catalogue of Printed Editions*. (This includes the various languages and also those in English published everywhere).

A. FIRST ENGLISH BIBLE PROBABLY THE BISHOPS.

Westcott, Brooke Foss, *A General View of the History of the English Bible.* 3rd ed rev. by A. W. Wright, pp. 95-102, 230-44.

Mombert, J. I., *English Versions of the Bible.* New and enlarged. pp. 265-93.

B. SECOND ENGLISH BIBLE PROBABLY THE GENEVA.

Westcott, Brooke Foss, *A General View of the History of the English Bible,* pp. 90-94; 212-30.

Mombert, J. I., *English Versions of the Bible.* pp. 239-65.

C. THIRD ENGLISH BIBLE PROBABLY THE KING JAMES VERSION

Scriverner, F. H. A., *The Authorized Edition of the English Bible,* etc.

Westcott, Brooke Foss, *A General View,* etc. pp. 107-21, 255-78.

Mombert, J. I. *English Versions* etc. pp. 338-442.

D. FOURTH ENGLISH BIBLE PROBABLY THE RHEIMS-DOUAI.

Westcott, Brooke Foss, *A General View,* etc. pp. 102-06, 245-55.

Mombert, J. I., *English Versions,* etc. pp. 293-338.

E. DUTCH, DANISH, SWEDISH AND FINNISH BIBLES

Norlie, Olaf Morgan, *The Translated Bible, 1534-1934.*

Darlow and Moule, *Historical Catalogue of Printed Editions.*

III. *EARLY BIBLES OR PARTS PUBLISHED IN AMERICA*

1. EFFORTS AT PUBLICATION DEFEATED

Wright, John, *Early Bibles of America,* 3rd ed pp. 51-4, 322-23.

2. EARLY EFFORTS AT REVISION

O'Callaghan, E. B., *A List of Editions,* etc.

For the Bay Psalm Book, see Long, William J., *American Literature.* Boston: Ginn and Co., 1913, pp. 44-6.

For Massachusetts Psalter, see Wright, *Early Bibles.* pp. 269-70.

For the Lord's Prayer by Mather, see Simms, *The Bible from the Beginning,* pp. 286-87.

For Psalterium Americanum, see Holland, John, *The Psalms of Britain.* London: R. Groombridge, 1843. pp. 140-45.

3. CLANDESTINE PUBLICATIONS

O'Callaghan, E. B., *A List of Editions* etc. pp. XIII-XVII.

Barker, Henry, *English Versions* etc. pp 250-53.

Wright, John, *Historic Bibles in America.* New York: T. Whittaker, 1905. pp. 71-2.

Myer, John Nichols, *Colonists' Bible a 'Bootleg' Book,* in New York Times, Sunday, November 7, 1926.

Nichols, C. L., *The Boston Edition of the Baskett Bible, a reprint from the Proceedings of the American Antiquarian Society, for April 1927.* Worcester: by the Society

Adams, Randolph G., *America's First Bibles,* in the Colophon, New Series. Summer 1935. No. 1. pp. 15-17.

IV. *SOME IMPORTANT BIBLES PUBLISHED IN THE EARLY REPUBLIC*

Wright, John, *Early Bibles,* etc.

Sachse, Julius F., *The German Sectarians of Pennsylvania.*

O'Callaghan, E. B., *A List of Editions,* etc.

V. *SOME NOTABLE PRIVATE TRANSLATIONS*

Simms, P. Marion, *The Bible from the Beginning.* pp. 239-78.

Goodspeed, Edgar J., *The Making of the English New Testament.* pp. 68-124.

Condit, Blackford, *History of the English Bible* 2nd ed pp. 389-428.

Mombert, J. I., *English Version of the Bible,* pp. 411-42.

Madison, John V.. *English Versions of the New Testament; a Bibliographical*

List. Reprint from Journal of Biblical Literature, Vol. XLIV, Parts III and IV, 1925.

VI. *THE FOUNDING AND WORK OF BIBLE SOCIETIES*

THE AMERICAN BIBLE SOCIETY

Dwight, Henry Otis, *The Centennial History of the American Bible Society.* New York: The Macmillan Co., 1916.

Wright, John, *Early Bibles,* etc pp. 259-68.

THE BIBLE FOR IMMIGRANTS

Bacon, Leonard Woolsey, *History of American Christianity.* pp 315-39

Turner, Frederick Jackson, *The Frontier in American History.* New York: H. Holt and Co., 1926.

Riegel, Robert Edgar, *America Moves West.* New York: Henry Holt and Co., 1930.

Paxson, Frederic Logan, *History of American Frontier, 1763-1893.* Boston: Houghton, Mifflin Company, 1924.

Ford, H. J., *The Scotch-Irish in America.*

Faust, Albert Bernhardt, *The German Element in the United States.*

VII. *THE BIBLE FOR AMERICAN INDIANS*

Jackson, Helen Hunt, *A Century of Dishonor.* Boston: Roberts Bros., 1885. (This is the classic indictment of our national policy in dealing with the Indians).

Huntington, Ellsworth, *The Red Man's Continent.* New Haven: Yale University Press, 1926.

Wright, John, *Early Bibles,* etc. pp. 269-303.

Moffett, Thomas C., *The Bible in the Life of the Indians of the United States.* New York: The American Bible Society, 1916.

For the Bible among Indians in Canada, see Wright, John,*Early Bibles,* etc. pp. 313-21.

VIII. *REPRESENTATIVE PROTESTANT TRANSLATIONS*

WHY THE BIBLE REQUIRES REVISION

Goodspeed, Edgar Johnson, *The Making of the English New Testament.* pp. 52-124.

Simms, P. Marion, *The Bible from the Beginning.* pp. 200-49.

Eadie, John, *The English Bible.* Vol. II, pp. 337-57, 365-480.

Mombert, J. I., *English Versions of the Bible.* pp. 460-521.

AMERICAN BIBLE SOCIETY REVISION

Darlow and Moule, *Historical Catalogue of Printed Editions* Vol. I. pp. 362-63.

Condit, Blackford, *History of the English Bible,* 2nd ed rev. pp. 420-23.

THE ANGLO-AMERICAN REVISION

The Anglo-American Bible Revision, by a Member of the American Revisions Committee. Philadelphia: American Sunday School Union, 1881.

Westcott, Brooke Foss, *Some Lessons of the Revised Version of the New Testament.* London: Hodder and Stoughton, 1897.

Roberts, Alexander, *Companion to the Revised Version of the New Testament.* New York: Cassell, Petter, Galpin and Co., 1881.

Kennedy, Benjamin Hall, *Ely Lectures on the Revised Version of the New Testament.* London: Bentley, 1882.

Price, Ira Maurice, *The Ancestry of the English Bible,* 4th ed pp. 283-98.

Mombert, J. I., *English Versions of the Bible.* pp. 442-521.

THE AMERICAN STANDARD BIBLE

Riddle, Matthew B., *The Story of the Revised New Testament, American Standard Edition.* Philadelphia: The Sunday School Times Co., 1908.

Simms, P. Marion, *The Bible from the Beginning.* pp. 200-38.

Robinson, George L., *Where Did We Get Our Bible?* pp. 176-84.

IX. *JEWISH TRANSLATIONS*

Daly, C. P., *The Settlement of the Jews in North America.* New York: P. Cowen, 1893.

Kayserling, Meyer, *Christopher Columbus and the Participation of the Jews in the Spanish and Portuguese Discoveries,* translated by Charles Gross. New York: Longmans, Green and Co., 1894.

Editors of Fortune, *The Jews in America.* New York: Fortune, 1936. (Finest thing in print, showing that the Jews are not a menace, and do not dominate our country).

Margolis, Max Leopold, *The Story of Bible Translation.* (Jewish treatment of the subject).

Simms, P. Marion, *The Bible from the Beginning.* pp. 254-56.

X. *TRANSLATIONS ECCENTRIC IN CHARACTER OR CLAIMS.*

Wright, John, *Early Bibles of America.* pp. 227-38.

Mombert, J. I., *English Versions of the Bible.* pp. 413-42.

Condit, Blackford, *History of the English Bible.* pp. 389-428.

Simms, P. Marion, *The Bible from the Beginning.* pp. 286-90.

XI. *SECTARIAN TRANSLATIONS*

Condit, Blackford, *History of the English Bible.* pp. 402-28.

Simms, P. Marion, *The Bible from the Beginning.* pp. 290-98.

Jewett, *Review of the New Testament of the Immersionists,* 1867.

MaGee, William, *Discourses and Dissertations on the Scriptural Doctrines of Atonement,* etc. New York: J. Eastburn, 1813. Appendix, pp. 195-500 contains a criticism of the Unitarian New Testament, London, 1808, Boston, 1809.

XII. *SOME NOTABLE DEVELOPMENTS AND SPECIAL EDITIONS.*

Bibles for the Blind, see Wright, John, *Early Bibles of America,* pp. 220-21.

Modern Reader's Bible, see Goodspeed, Edgar J., *The Making of the English New Testament.* pp. 121. Also, Simms, P. Marion, *The Bible from the Beginning.* pp. 267-69.

XIII. *MODERN SPEECH TRANSLATIONS*

Goodspeed, Edgar Johnson, *The Making of the English New Testament,* pp. 90-124.

Simms, P. Marion, *The Bible from the Beginning,* pp. 239-78.

Deissmann, G. Adolph, *Bible Studies: Contributions Chiefly from Papyri and Inscriptions to the History of the Language, the Literature and the Religion of Hellenistic Judaism and Primitive Christianity.* Edinburgh: T. and T. Clark, 1901.

Kenyon, Frederic G., *The Paleography of Greek Papyri.* Oxford: The Clarendon Press, 1899.

Milligan, George, *Selections from Greek Papyri.* Cambridge: University Press, 1910. Also, *New Testament Documents,* London: Macmillan and Co., 1913, and *Here and There Among the Papyri,* London: Hodder and Stoughton, 1922.

Deissmann, G. Adolph, *Light from the Ancient East.* New ed rev New York: George H. Doran Co., 1927.

Soden, Hermann von, *History of Early Christian Literature.* New York: G. P. Putnam's Sons, 1906.

XIV. *THE INFLUENCE OF THE BIBLE ON NATIONAL LIFE AND INSTITUTIONS COVERING THE SUBJECT IN GENERAL*

Dobschutz, Ernest von, *The Influence of the Bible on Civilization.* New York: Charles Scribner's Sons, 1914. (Very fine)

Dorchester, Daniel, *Christianity and the United States.* rev. ed New York: Hunt and Eaton, 1895. (A splendid account).

Thompson, Charles L., *The Religious Foundations of America.* New York: Fleming H. Revell Co., 1917. (Fine).

McClure, James Gore King, *The Supreme Book of Mankind.* New York: Charles Scribner's Sons, 1930 (Best thing in print).

An Outline of Christianity: the Story of Our Civilization. New York: Bethlehem Publishers, Inc., Dodd, Mead and Co., distributors, 1920. 5 vols. (The three last volumes cover the period of this book. Exceptionally fine).

Flynn, John Stephen, *The Influence of Puritanism on Political and Religious Thought of the English.* London: John Murray, 1920. (Very fine, showing that Puritanism remains a profound influence today.)

1. THE MAJOR INFLUENCES OF THE BIBLE HAVE BEEN BENEFICENT

    A. HOME AND FAMILY.

Calhoun, Arthur Wallace, *Social History of the American Family.* Cleveland: The Arthur H. Clark Co., 1917-19. 3 vols.

Goodsell, Willystine, *History of the Family as a Social and Educational Institution.* New York: The Macmillan Co., 1915. Chap. 10 discusses *"The Family in the American Colonies."*

Howard, George Elliott, *History of Matrimonial Institutions.* Chicago: University of Chicago Press, 1904. 3 vols.

Reed, Ruth, *The Modern Family.* New York: Alfred A. Knopf, 1929.

    B. THE CHURCH AND RELIGION

Baird, Robert, *Religion in America.* New York: Harper and Bros., 1856. (Old, but fine for religious conditions first forty years of the Republic).

For religious conditions of colonial era, see under Great Awakening, in Chap. I.

For Revival of 1800, see Bacon, Leonard Woolsey, *History of American Christianity.* pp. 230-45; for growth of the church since the Civil War, pp. 351-73. for Revival of 1857, pp. 342-45.

Bower, William C., Ed., *The Church at Work in the Modern World,* written in collaboration with Edward Scribner Ames and others. Chicago: University of Chicago Press, 1935.

Dargan, Edwin Charles, *Ecclesiology; a Study of the Churches.* 2nd and carefully revised ed. Louisville, Ky: Charles T. Dearing, 1905.

    GROWTH OF THE MOVEMENT FAVORABLE TO UNITY

Simms, P. Marion, *What Must the Church Do To Be Saved?* New York: Revell, 1913.

Bacon, Leonard Woolsey, *History of American Christianity.* pp. 398-420.

Ainslie, Peter, *The Message of the Disciples for the Union of the Church.* New York: Revell, 1913. Also, *If Not A United Church—What?* (Christian Unity Hand Book series, Vol. I. Lectures delivered at the Protestant Episcopal Theological Seminary in Virginia). New York: Revell, 1920.

Douglas, Harlan Paul., *Church Unity Movements in the United States.* New York: Institute of Social and Religious Research, 1934.

    THE SUNDAY SCHOOL

Trumbull, Henry Clay, *The Sunday School; its Origin, Mission, Methods and Auxiliaries.* (Lyman Beecher Lectures). Philadelphia: John D. Wattles and Co., 1896.

Brown, Marianna C., *Sunday School Movements in America.* New York: Revell, 1901.

Lankard, Frank Glen, *A History of the American Sunday School Curriculum.* New York: Abingdon Press, 1927. (The Abingdon religious education texts. College series).

THE CHRISTIAN ENDEAVOR

Shaw, William, *The Evolution of an Endeavorer.* Boston: Christian Endeavor World, 1924.

C. EDUCATION AND SCHOOLS

See under Schools and Colleges, in Chap. I.

Cubberly, Elwood Patterson, *Public Education in the United States.* Rev. ed enlarged, Boston and New York: Houghton, Mifflin Co., 1934.

Slosson, Edwin Emery, *The American Spirit in Education.* New Haven: Yale University Press, 1921.

Boone, R. G., *Education in the United States.* New York: D. Appleton and Co., 1889.

Thwing, Charles Franklin, *History of Higher Education in America.* New York: D. Appleton and Co., 1906.

D. THE STATE AND GOVERNMENT

Brewer, D. J., *The United States a Christian Nation.* Philadelphia: J. C. Winston Co., 1905. (Very fine).

McDonald, William, *Three Centuries of Democracy.* New York: Henry Holt and Co., 1923.

Cornelson, I. A., *The Relation of Religion to Civil Government in the United States of America.* New York: G. P. Putnam's Sons, 1895.

Hockett, Homer Carey, *Political and Social History of the United States, 1492-1828.* New York: The Macmillan Co., 1931.

Schlesinger, Arthur Meier, *Political and Social History of the United States, 1829-1925.* New York: The Macmillan Co., 1931. (Last two are companion volumes).

THE DECLARATION OF INDEPENDENCE

Becker, Carl Lotus, *The Declaration of Independence.* New York: P. Smith, 1933. (Fine).

Hazleton, John Hampden, *The Declaration of Independence: its History.* New York: Dodd, Mead and Co., 1906.

THE CONSTITUTION OF THE UNITED STATES

Farrand, Max, *The Framing of the Constitution of the United States.* New Haven: Yale University Press, 1934.

Bancroft, George, *History of the Formation of the Constitution of the United States of America.* New York: D. Appleton and Co., 1882. (Ponderous but valuable).

LIBERTY IN RELIGION

Cobb, S. H., *The Rise of Religious Liberty in America.* New York: The Macmillan Co., 1902.

Gates, Errett, *Religious Liberty in Massachusetts.* Chicago: University of Chicago Press, 1899.

Mecklin, John M., *The Story of American Dissent.* New York: Harcourt, Brace and Co., 1934. (Splendid).

The Johns Hopkins University has published a number of Studies in Historical and Political Science, devoted to this subject.

LIBERTY OF THE PRESS

For a contemporary account of the Zenger case, see Rutherford, Livingston, *John Peter Zenger; His Press: His Trial*. New York: Dodd, Mead and Co., 1904.

For a short account of the Zenger case, see Osgood, Herbert Levi, *American Colonies in the Eighteenth Century*. Vol. II, pp. 452-62.

Duniway, Clyde Augustus, *The Development of the Freedom of the Press in Massachusetts*. New York: Longmans, Green and Co., 1906. (Harvard Historical Studies XII. Fine history of freedom of the press.)

INTERNATIONAL RELATIONS

Jones, R. L., *History of the Foreign Policy of the United States*. New York: G. P. Putnam's Sons, 1933.

Barnes, Harry Elmer, *World Politics in Modern Civilization; the Contributions of Nationalism, Capitalism, Imperialism and Militarism to Human Culture and Anarchy*. New York: A. A. Knopf, 1930.

Page, Kirby, *War; its Causes, Consequences and Cure*. New York: George H. Doran Co., 1923.

Catt, Carrie Chapman and others, *Why Wars Must Cease*. New York: The Macmillan Co., 1935.

Habicht, Max, Ed., *Post War Treaties for the Pacific Settlement of International Disputes*. Cambridge: Harvard University Press, 1931.

Page, Kirby, *International Relations in the Light of the Religion of Jesus*. New York: Kirby Page, 1927.

THE LEAGUE OF NATIONS

League of Nations. Ten Years of World Cooperation. Foreword by Sir Eric Drummond. London: Secretariat of the League of Nations, 1930.

Morley, Felix, *The Society of Nations: its Organization and Constitutional Development*. Washington: The Brookings Institution, 1932.

Rappard, W. E., *The Geneva Experiment*. Oxford: University Press, 1931.

E. INDUSTRY AND LABOR.

GROWING INSISTENCE ON CHRISTIAN PRINCIPLES

Page, Kirby, *Christianity and Economic Problems*. New York: Association Press, 1924.

Tawney, Richard H., *Religion and the Rise of Capitalism*. New York: Harcourt, Brace and Co., 1926. Also, *The Acquisitive Society*, same pubs., 1928.

Chase, Stuart, *The Economy of Abundance*. New York: The Macmillan Co., 1934. (Splendid plea for a new economic order).

Frank, Glenn, *America's Hour of Decision*. New York: Whittlesey House, 1934.

Tugwell, R. G., *Battle for Democracy*. New York: Columbia University Press, 1935. (Fine plea for experimentation as only method of learning).

Laski, H. J., *Democracy in Crisis*. Chapel Hill: The University of North Carolina, 1935.

Plumb, G. E., and Roylance, W. G., *Industrial Democracy: a Plan for its Achievement*. New York: B. W. Huebsch, Inc., 1923.

Matthews, Shailer, *The Validity of American Ideals*. New York: The Abingdon Press, 1922.

Dalberg, A. O., *Jobs, Machines and Capitalism*. New York: The Macmillan Co., 1932. (For drastic shortening of working hours).

THE MODERN CHURCH ON SOCIAL AND INDUSTRIAL QUESTIONS

Ward, Harry Frederick, *The Social Creed of the Churches*. New York: Eaton and Mains, 1914. (Creed adopted by Federal Council of Churches, Chicago, 1912).

Shotwell, James Thompson, *The Religious Revolution of Today.* Boston and New York: Houghton, Mifflin Co., 1924.

Patton, Carl Safford, *Religion in the Thought of Today.* New York: The Macmillan Co., 1924.

Leighton, Joseph Alexander, *Religion in the Mind of Today.* New York: D. Appleton and Co., 1924.

Ward, Harry Frederick, *The New Social Order.* New York: The Macmillan Co., 1923.

Rauschenbusch, Walter, *Christianity and the Social Crisis.* New York: The Macmillan Co., 1907. Also, *Christianizing the Social Order,* same pubs., 1912.

    F. COMMUNITY AND ASSOCIATION

Hall, Fred S., *Social Work Year Book, 1929, 1933, 1935. A Description of Organized Activities in Social Work and Related Fields.* New York: Russell Sage Foundation, 1930-35. 3 vols.

President's Research Committee on Social Trends. Recent Social Trends in the United States: Report of the President's Committee . . . foreword by Herbert Hoover. New York: McGraw-Hill Book Co., Inc., 1933. 2 Vols.

    2. UNFORTUNATE INFLUENCES OF THE BIBLE. USED TO SUPPORT GLARING EVILS

For persecution of witches, see Witchcraft, in chapter I.

For support of war, see Abrams, Ray Hamilton, *Preachers Present Arms.* Philadelphia: Author, 1933. (Showing how completely ministers have been devoted to war).

For Biblical defense of slavery, see Priest, Josiah, *Bible Defense of Slavery,* etc. Louisville, Ky.: J. F. Brennan, 1851.

Baldwin, Samuel Davies, *Dominion . . . and the Divine Rights of Shem, Ham and Japheth.* Nashville, Tenn.: E. Stevenson and F. A. Owen, for the author, 1858.

Lea, Henry C., *An Historical Sketch of Sacerdotal Celibacy in the Christian Church.* 2nd ed. enlarged, Boston: Houghton, Mifflin Co., 1884. (Very fine).

    USED TO OPPOSE NORMAL PROGRESS

White, Andrew D., *History of the Warfare of Science with Theology in Christendom.* New York: D. Appleton and Co., 1910. 2 vols. (Finest thing on the subject in print).

    USED TO SUPPORT ERRATIC MOVEMENTS

Ferguson, Charles W., *The Confusion of Tongues.* Garden City, N. Y.: Doubleday, Doran, 1928. (Best discussion or erraticisms in print).

For fraud in Spiritualism, see Jewett, Pendie L., *Spiritualism and Charlatanism: or the Tricks of Media.* New York: S. W. Green, 1873. (Exposures by a committee).

    3. THE GOLDEN AGE OF THE BIBLE YET TO COME. GRAVE DANGER FACED BY AMERICA

Jones, E. Stanley, *Christ's Alternative to Communism.* New York: The Abingdon Press, 1935. (Splendid presentation).

Newfang, Oscar, *Capitalism and Communism: A Reconciliation.* New York: G. P. Putnam's Sons, 1932. (Very fine. The two must live together for some time at least. Plea for friendliness between them).

Soule, George, *The Coming American Revolution.* New York: The Macmillan Co., 1934. (Fine).

Rugg, Harold, *The Great Technology.* New York: John Day Co., 1933. (Splendid account of technical facilities developed in our day.)

Ward, Harry F., *Our Economic Morality: the Ethic of Jesus.* New York: The Macmillan Co., 1929. (Challenging statement of the real problem of modern Christianity).

Page, Kirby, *Incentives in Modern Life: Are the Motives of Jesus Practicable in Modern Business Life?* New York: George H. Doran Co., 1922. See also under Industry and Labor, in this chapter.

THE PERSON OF JESUS CHRIST

Pfleiderer, Otto, *The Early Christian Conception of Christ.* New York: G. P. Putnam's Sons, 1905.

Macintosh, H. R., *The Doctrine of the Person of Jesus Christ.* New York: Charles Scribner's Sons.

Brown, William Adams, *Modern Theology and the Preaching of the Gospel.* New York: Charles Scribner's Sons, 1914. (Chap. V discusses the Deity of Christ in the light of modern thought).

Tittle, Ernest Fremont, *Jesus after Nineteen Centuries.* New York: The Abingdon Press, 1932. (Makes clear that Jesus is the real living way for our generation).

Brown, William Adams, *Beliefs That Matter.* New York: Charles Scribner's Sons, 1929. Chaps. IV-VI, pp. 93-176. (Splendid treatment).

Sangster, W. E., *He is Able.* London: Hodder and Stoughton, 1936. (Fine for showing the power of Christ to transform).

INDEX

Aarhus, Rev, Rasmus Jensen, the first Lutheran pastor, 105.

Adler, Dr. Cyrus, 225; 265.

African slavery, a blot on American Christianity, 322; abolished by Biblical influence, 323.

Agricola, Mickael, his Finnish N. T., 109.

Aitken, Jane, published Thomson Bible, 140, 145.

Aitken, Robert, published first Bible in English openly, 125-7.

Alger, Israel, his pronouncing Bibles, 129.

Algonquin, Mass. dialect, Eliot's Bible in, 188, 190-2.

Allen, Rev. Ray, his Gospel of Mark, 284.

Allen, William, directed translation Rheims-Douai Bible, 99.

Allioli, Dr., ed Bible in German, 136.

Allison, Rev. Patrick, D. D., his petition to Congress, 126.

America, a Christian nation, 309; religious history begins with landing of Columbus, 309; Declaration of Independence Christian, 309-10; Constitution U. S. Christian, 310; state constitutions Christian, 311; Supreme Court says it is Christian, 311; Bible inspires progressive legislation, 312-13; dueling abolished, 313-14; religious liberty granted, 314-15; separation of church and state, 315-17; freedom of speech and press, 317; international relations increasingly Christian, 318; treatment of Cuba, Porto Rico, Philippines and China, 318-20; sentiment against war growing, 319-20; danger faced by America, 352-5.

American and Foreign Bible Society, 168, 182, 251.

American Bible Society, earlier societies, 161-2; organized 1816, 162-3; uses Bibles without note or comment, 163-4; service world-wide, 165; controversies over prayer in board meetings, 165-6; over use of the apocrypha, 166-7; apocrypha printed until 1827, 167; over sectarian translations, 167-8; over its revision of the Bible, 168, 209-11; providence aids in difficulty, 168-72; work among immigrants, 172-6; outstanding accomplishments, 176-80; depositories and foreign agencies, 180-1; how supported, 181-2; Bibles for the blind, 261-4; chief publishers of Bibles for Indians in the U. S., 187-99.

American Bible Union, 182-3, 251.

American charity, greatest in the world, 329-32, 335-37.

American expansion, 172-3.

American Relief Administration, 331-2.

American Standard Bible, 213-16; proposed revision, 218; 220, 226, 276.

American Sunday School Union, 140, 297.

Amusements, why necessary, 347.

Anderson, Rev. H. T., his N. T., 155; his "immersion" version N. T., 252.

Anderson, John, Jr., auctioneer, thought to have a Kneeland and Green Bible, 117-18.

Anglican church in America, 17-18.

Anglo-American revision of 1881-85, 211-12; unprecedented sale of N. T., 212-13; generous reception of the O. T., 213; bitterly attacked, 217; 219, 226, 276.

Apocrypha, a vital part of the Roman Catholic Bible, 62; its history, 63-5; some lost verses recovered, 123; trouble over, 166-7; printed in Protestant